AMERICA'S
THREE
REGIMES

AMERICA'S
THREE
REGIMES

A New Political History

MORTON KELLER

OXFORD
UNIVERSITY PRESS
2007

OXFORD

UNIVERSITY PRESS

Oxford University Press, Inc., publishes works that further
Oxford University's objective of excellence
in research, scholarship, and education.

Oxford   New York
Auckland   Cape Town   Dar es Salaam   Hong Kong   Karachi
Kuala Lumpur   Madrid   Melbourne   Mexico City   Nairobi
New Delhi   Shanghai   Taipei   Toronto

With offices in
Argentina   Austria   Brazil   Chile   Czech Republic   France   Greece
Guatemala   Hungary   Italy   Japan   Poland   Portugal   Singapore
South Korea   Switzerland   Thailand   Turkey   Ukraine   Vietnam

Copyright © 2007 by Morton Keller

Published by Oxford University Press, Inc.
198 Madison Avenue, New York, New York 10016
www.oup.com

Oxford is a registered trademark of Oxford University Press

Library of Congress Cataloging-in-Publication Data
Keller, Morton.
America's three regimes: a new political history / Morton Keller.
p. cm.   Includes bibliographical references and index.
ISBN 978-0-19-532502-7
1. United States—Politics and government.
2. Political culture—United States—History.
3. Social status—Political aspects—United States—History.
4. Republicanism—United States—History.
5. Political parties—United States—History.
6. Populism—United States—History.
7. Bureaucracy—United States—History.
8. Social change—United States—History.
9. United States—Social conditions.
I. Title.
E183.K48 2007   973—dc22   2007010982

Political buttons on front cover, title page, and part openers:
1. Metal coat button commemorating George Washington's inauguration,
ca. 1790. Courtesy of Kirk Mitchell, from the J. Harold Cobb Collection.
2. Button supporting any Democratic candidate in the 1904 presidential election.
Courtesy of Mark Warda, from 200 Years of Political Campaign Collectibles
(Clearwater, FL: Galt Press, 2005), 35. © 2005 Mark Warda.
3. Flasher button which alternates between the messages "Vote Democratic" and
"Vote Republican," from the late 20th century. Courtesy of Mark Warda,
from 200 Years of Political Campaign Collectibles
(Clearwater, FL: Galt Press, 2005), 126. © 2005 Mark Warda.

Design by Rachel Perkins

1 3 5 7 9 8 6 4 2
Printed in the United States of America
on acid-free paper

To Nelson Polsby,
whose generosity of spirit, largeness of soul,
and acuity of intellect will be evergreen

CONTENTS

ACKNOWLEDGMENTS

My thanks to colleagues (and also friends) who so generously read and sought to mend the text that I imposed on them: historians Patricia Bonomi, David Donald, Joanne Freeman, Stephen Graubard, Alonso Hamby, David Kennedy, James Patterson, Jack Rakove, Stephan Thernstrom, and Julian Zelizer; political scientists David Brady, Morris Fiorina, Shep Melnick, Sidney Milkis, Nelson Polsby, Kenneth Shepsle, Barry Weingast, and James Q. Wilson; and attorney Stanford Ross.

Berkeley's Institute of Governmental Studies provided hospitality. I owe more to the Hoover Institution than that estimable establishment can know. It offered ideal working conditions during a series of annual visits. And special thanks to the Hoover's Brady and Fiorina for encouraging a historian to trench on domains normally the province of political scientists.

AMERICA'S
THREE
REGIMES

INTRODUCTION

The American Polity
and Its Regimes

Progress, far from consisting in change, depends on retentiveness. When change is absolute there remains no being to improve and no direction is set for possible improvement: and when experience is not retained, as among savages, infancy is perpetual. Those who cannot remember the past are condemned to repeat it.

—George Santayana

I see gr-reat changes takin' place ivry day, but no change at all ivry fifty years.

—Mr. Dooley (Finley Peter Dunne)

THIS BOOK BEGAN as, and remains, an attempt to take a fresh look at the history of America's public life—politics, government, and law—from its colonial beginnings to the tumultuous present. But as the writing of the book progressed, the issues and atmospherics of the current public scene turned out to be an ever more intrusive presence. It is widely assumed that ours is a special time in American history: of a uniquely bitter politics and disillusioned electorate; an exceptionally dysfunctional president, Congress, and bureaucracy; a highly polarized Supreme Court. Titles of recent books on public affairs make the point: *Dark Ages America, Politics Lost, American Theocracy, The Twilight of Democracy, Protofascism in America, The Vast Left Wing Conspiracy.* Is this sense of special malaise accurate?

That question requires an answer grounded in history. True, the voice of history more often than not is unclear, ambiguous. But to disregard it when weighing the contemporary situation is to diminish our capacity to understand the time in which we live. Does the current situation bear any resemblance to the disarray of the 1850s and 1860s, when the collapse of the major parties led to the Civil War, a political and governmental failure of the first magnitude? Is the red state–blue state America so cherished by editorial Jeremiahs in fact a more polarized place than the America of the Great Depression? ("All right; we are two nations": John Dos Passos.) Are racism, sexism, hostility to gays, and the exclusion of the disabled and the mentally ill measurably different today from the American past? Is American foreign policy more aggressive, aggrandizing, imperialistic than ever before?

The subject of *America's Three Regimes* is the American *polity*: not only politics but law and government as well, from their earliest days to the present. The dictionary not too helpfully defines a polity as "a politically organized community." I take that to refer to those institutions that are most directly involved in defining and applying public power. These are politics (parties, elections, campaigns, voters), government (the presidency and Congress, the federal bureaucracy and public administration, state and local authority), and law (courts, judges, lawyers, and their cases).

Other American institutions—corporations, the media, advocacy groups, voluntary associations—are very much in the power-wielding business. And they are hardly absent from this book. But politics, government, and law are the battlegrounds where power is most visibly contested, where American public life is most fully lived.

This book examines the American polity not through the traditional framework of party systems but through the more expansive structure of *regimes*. A regime is "a manner, method, or system of rule or government," or more fulsomely "the set of institutions through which a nation makes its fundamental decisions over a sustained period, and the principles that guide those decisions." Montesquieu had something like that in mind when he detected a distinctive "spirit" in each regime. So did Madison when he spoke of "systems of policy." The most familiar usage is *ancien régime*, applied first in the 1790s to pre-revolutionary France and later extended to the other monarchies of early modern Europe.

The concept of a regime implies a *longue durée* view of history, commonly thought to be out of place in the quick-change, fast-paced American scene. Historians of the United States like to refer to "ages" (of Jackson, Roosevelt, and Reform; Gilded and Jazz) or "eras" (of Good

Feelings, Progressive) that last for no longer than a decade or so. But the regimes discussed in this book extend for a century and more. That allows plenty of time to see how American politics, government, and law worked out their complex, ever-evolving relationships with one another and with the larger society.

To speak of regimes underscores the fact that the sheer staying power of America's public institutions is as much a historical fact as the change for which our society is so widely celebrated. Americans like to think of themselves as a people eternally young. But the reality of our public life is very different. Our Constitution, only occasionally amended, is getting on to a quarter of a millennium. Our political parties are among the most venerable anywhere. Our legal system is of similar age and durability. We have a government that has gone through vast alterations in size, scope, and function, yet remains subject to the original constitutional precepts of the separation and balance of powers, federalism, and the Bill of Rights.

So a proper history of American public life must be as much about continuity, persistence, and evolution as about change, transformation, and revolution. To capture these qualities, I have divided the history of American public life into three long regimes:

Deferential-republican, running through the colonial period and the early Republic to the 1820s

Party-democratic, from the 1830s to the 1930s

Populist-bureaucratic, from the 1930s to the present

What conclusions emerge from this polity-regimes approach?

To speak of a deferential-republican regime is to suggest that the history of colonial America, the Revolution, and the early Republic had more unity than is usually assumed. Old World beliefs in social hierarchy and in what it took to establish a well-governed society set the terms of early colonial settlement. But New World realities immediately began to affect the way in which Americans conducted their politics, government, and law. From this perspective, the Revolution and the creation of the new nation were not only a reaction to the British imperial crisis of the late eighteenth century but also the culmination of a far longer and deeper process of historical change. A distinctive American polity gradually developed, playing off against inherited Old World ideas and institutions. When the time came first for revolution and then for state making, it occurred in what by then had become a familiar American mode: innovation dressed in the language and trappings of familiar ideas.

It is generally agreed that Americans did a fair job of nation-building (though not of slavery-ridding). What is not so widely recognized is how much practice they had in crafting new forms of politics, government, and law out of their inheritance of European ideas and institutions. Formal independence came with an eight-year-long revolution. But the new nation was also the product of nearly two centuries of colonial experience. Intimations of a distinctive American polity appeared in the earliest days of settlement. And substantial survivals of the Old World's deferential political culture persisted into the Early Republic.

Another lesson that emerges from this story is how much historical pressure it takes for a regime to change. A series of major events—the Revolution, independence, and the Confederation government, the drafting of the Constitution and the establishment of the new nation, the War of 1812, the economic and cultural forces released by independence and nationhood—were necessary conditions for the deferential-republican regime to give way to its party-democratic successor.

The party-democratic regime defined American public life for more than a century, from the 1830s to the 1930s. What explains that continuity, given the scale of the economic, social, and political change that swept over the nation during those years? The answer lies first in the ground rules imposed by the Constitution. Regularly recurring, winner-take-all elections meant that neither the factional, issue-by-issue politics of the colonial past nor the multiparty parliamentary politics of late-nineteenth- and early-twentieth-century Europe took hold in the United States. Instead, two large, interregional parties, diverse in class and ethnicity, emerged almost before the paint had dried on the newly crafted ship of state. Over time the parties changed in name and appeal, from Federalist to Whig to Republican, from Democratic-Republican to Democratic. But the very language of American politics, full of words drawn from everyday life, testified to the depth of the parties' social roots. Just how deep they were became evident as the system perpetuated itself in the face of major disruptions: secession and the Civil War, the strains of massive industrialization, immigration, and social change, the agrarian-Populist revolt, the Progressive movement.

A similar continuity prevailed in American government and law. True, those institutions were deeply flawed by class interest, racism, and gender discrimination. But the democratic ethos continued to draw strength from potent national traditions of localism, individualism, and liberty. The result was a stunted national state, which remained that way until well into the twentieth century. A small military, a spoils-ridden bureaucracy, and distributive rather than dirigiste land, tariff, and chartering policies kept the government's profile low and (save for slavery and territorial expansion) unmenacing. The American state was one not of bureaucrats and armies but of parties and courts. American law, too, remained what it came to be in the wake of the Revolution: a unique mix of innovation and preservation. As a result, the American polity avoided much of the class-defined, top-down character of its European counterparts. No wonder this party-led, democratic-in-spirit regime persisted for so long, and through so much.

It took profound forces of change to bring about the populist-bureaucratic regime in which we live today. The Great Depression and the New Deal of the 1930s, the Second World War and the Cold War, the post-1945 transformation of American social and economic life, and the cultural upheavals of the 1960s and after had a transformative power that echoes the half-century-long tumult of the late 1700s and early 1800s.

Since the 1930s, social and cultural issues that cut across traditional party lines, and those ever more influential power players the courts, the media, and advocacy groups, have done as much as the major parties to define American public life. Century-old patterns of ethnic, class, and regional voting and party identification have been turned upside down. Slackened party ties worked sea changes in the presidency and Congress. Government vastly expanded and came under the sway of bureaucracy and the courts on a previously unmatched scale. This regime has been maturing for three-quarters of a century and defines the public world in which we live today.

Each of America's long regimes wrestled with issues central to the character of its public life. *Freedom*—from England, of the self—was the major bone of contention in the deferential- republican regime. *Power*—as between the states and the nation, and by one person over another—played a comparable role in the party-democratic regime. *Rights*—of persons and groups—have had an equivalent place in the populist-bureaucratic regime of our own time.

By any reasonable historical accounting, the American polity has risen to these challenges. The republican regime successfully managed the break from British rule and the creation of a new, representative republic unlike any before, anywhere. The party regime created the world's most democratic polity, which defeated secession, ended slavery, and survived industrialization and immigration of unique rapidity and scale. The modern populist-bureaucratic regime created a welfare state (however limited), overcame the international threats of fascism and communism, and oversaw a large-scale expansion of individual and group rights at home.

Yet this celebratory tone hardly accords with the current state of American opinion. True, the reading public shows a stubborn taste for books that dwell on the achievements of great dead white males: Washington, Franklin, Adams, Hamilton, Lincoln, Theodore and Franklin Delano Roosevelt. But most academics, public intellectuals, and journalists tell darker tales: of the repression and exploitation of the poor by the well-off, of the darker-skinned by the lighter-skinned, of the female by the male, of the Third World by the United States. This less sanguine view of the American experience came to its maturity in the era of Vietnam, the civil rights movement, and the counterculture. It has not lessened in its intensity since. While the events of September 11, 2001, produced an outburst of social cohesion, that proved to be short-lived.

So to return to the beginning, where in fact do we stand today? Is the dark night of repressive government and irreconcilable cultural conflict our future lot? Or will our centuries-old public institutions adapt, as they so often have (but not always: consider slavery, the Civil War, racism, the Great Depression, errant foreign policy), to contemporary challenges?

The history of American public life that follows won't necessarily provide definitive answers as to where we are and where we're headed. But without knowing that history, our ability to think about those questions is measurably reduced. As William James reminded us, we live forward, but we understand backward.

PART ONE

THE DEFERENTIAL-REPUBLICAN REGIME

There are two big problems in writing history: Where to begin? Where to end? A medieval chronicler of the Burgundian court might (in fact one did) begin his tale with the expulsion from Eden. A historian writing a book like this one in the late nineteenth century might (some did) turn first to the *witenagemoten*—the tribal assemblies—of Anglo-Saxon England.

More modestly, I suggest that we start by imagining ourselves back into the mind-set of the colonists who came to America's shores in the early seventeenth century, and that of their successors who participated in the great founding drama of revolution, independence, and the creation of the United States. This is a story that stretches across almost two centuries. In the course of that time, American politics, government, and law evolved from age-old European traditions of aristocracy, monarchy, and deference to the innovative republicanism of the new American nation. The pace and character of that evolution were defined throughout by the tension between the pull of the European (in particular, English) background—remembered, imitated, imagined, improvised upon, rejected—and the ever-new, ever-changing realities of the American scene.

The constraints of pre-mechanical transportation and communication did much to shape the interplay between the New World and the Old. But it was also the case that settlers early and late—in particular, the large majority who came from the British Isles—carried with them a hefty baggage of political ideas and institutions. Early modern Europe, the backdrop against which the American progress from deference to republicanism played out, was hardly a placid, static place. The brutal conflict between the Protestant Reformation and the Catholic Counter-Reformation came to a climax in the Thirty Years' War of the early seventeenth century. Of special significance for the American colonies was the degree to which the conflict with Catholic Spain and France defined English public affairs. The recurring issue of royal succession—would England's monarch be Protestant or Catholic?—set the stage for major events from Henry VIII's creation of the Anglican Church in the 1530s to Spain's Great Armada of 1588 and, half a century later, the Puritan Revolution of the 1640s.

If religion took center stage through most of the seventeenth century, commerce and empire had a comparable place in the public life of the century that followed. A distinctive British state emerged after the Glorious Revolution of 1688, ending that island's long-festering religious and dynastic conflicts. At its core was a king-Parliament relationship based not on divine right but on a unique mix of hereditary monarchy confined by (limited) representative government. Under it there flourished a "fiscal-military state," in recurring war with France and facing the demands of a growing overseas empire. Other distinctive features of the English scene were a landed aristocracy and gentry with considerable local authority but firmly wedded to king and Parliament, and a common law whose primary purpose was to serve the interests of property and commerce.

America's first political regime, which stretched from the early seventeenth to the early nineteenth century, both derived from and reacted to this Old World backdrop. It inherited ways of thinking about power and authority that can be called deferential. And it developed a distinctively American form of governance that can be called republican.

Two questions are appropriate to ask about the history of this regime. How did the interplay between Old World ideas and interests and the settlers' homegrown evolution work out from the early 1600s to the early 1800s? Or to put it another way, how did the American polity evolve from its deferential, early modern, colonial origins into the United States of America?

OLD WAYS AND NEW

ALONG WITH THEIR families and their diseases, their views of religion and how to make a living, the early settlers in English America brought with them well-developed ideas of governance. John Winthrop, soon to be governor of the Massachusetts Bay colony, famously confided to his journal on the way to America: "God almighty in his most holy and wise providence has so disposed of the condition of mankind, as in all times, some must be rich some poor, some high and eminent in power and dignity; others mean and in subjection." Virginia's *Laws Divine, Morall and Martiall* of 1610 sought a polity based on biblical precepts and English common law. So did Massachusetts Bay's *Laws and Liberties* in 1648, which stipulated that the colony's laws and ordinances "be, as near as conveniently may, agreeable to the form of the laws and policy of England."

England had been in the colony-creating business since the sixteenth century, and the mainland American colonies could draw on a variety of forms. The joint stock company, in which investors and colonists secured a charter for their enterprise and shared its profits and risks, was one model. Used for pre-1600 ventures in Russia and Ireland, it was adopted by the early-seventeenth-century colonies of Virginia and Massachusetts Bay. Another, more common form was the proprietary colony, in which a favored individual or group was granted a royal charter. That was how Pennsylvania, Carolina, New Jersey, Maryland, and Georgia were founded. And then there were spin-offs from earlier colonies—Connecticut, Rhode Island, New Hampshire, North Carolina—that eventually got themselves legitimated by royal charters. New York, taken from the Dutch in 1664 and made a proprietary colony of the duke of York, became a royal colony after the duke morphed into James II in 1685.

This diversity of forms was matched by the variety of those who undertook the perilous business of colony making. Each side of the English Revolution had its outpost: Virginia was the abode of pro-Stuart Cavaliers, Massachusetts Bay of Cromwellian Puritans. New York's mix of first-citizen Dutch Calvinists and Anglican add-ons was different—but no more so than Pennsylvania, set up by the Quaker William Penn, or Maryland, established by the Catholic Calvert family.

These varieties of origin and religion were tempered by shared beliefs and experiences: by a common cultural currency. Founders and settlers alike sought to preserve as much as possible of their Old World heritage. This could sometimes take a bizarre turn. At the behest of the Carolina proprietors, philosopher John Locke came up with a scheme for a thoroughly retro social system, complete with such feudal trappings as caciques and landgraves, manor lords, and more officeholders than settlers. Even in the real colonial world, the patroonships (manors) of the Dutch settlers in New York had feudal tenants and quit-rents. Established churches were common, as were sumptuary laws pegging dress to social status. Most important of all, the adoption first of indentured servitude and then of slavery as solutions to the labor problem testified to the imprint of the European past on the colonial American present.

Even Penn's Quaker Pennsylvania remained deeply indebted to its English sources. It began in the 1680s with a scheme for large landholdings worked by unfree labor, similar to the initial plan for Virginia. Penn proposed in 1691 that the new settlement of Philadelphia be run by a small, self-perpetuating body of citizens, like Massachusetts Bay's Puritan saints. The town was supposed to follow the plan proposed (but never implemented) for London after its Great Fire of 1666: broad avenues and strategic squares, ideal for military control.

Many of the characteristic features of the Tudor state of the late sixteenth and early seventeenth centuries took root in the New World. These included a belief in the organic character of society, the importance of hierarchy and deference, a polity in which the church was presumed to be subordinate to civil authority, the thorough intermingling of law and politics, a balance of power between the executive and the legislature, and considerable autonomy in local government.

But over time, incontestable realities—of distance, land, labor, and loose control from the center—transformed this rich inheritance of ideas and institutions from the mother country. Three thousand miles of storm-tossed Atlantic and isolated settlements scattered along a thousand miles of coastline, the whole weakly linked by modes of transportation unchanged for centuries, put a premium on going it alone, on adapting to local conditions as they were, not as viewed through the prism of old-country institutions and beliefs. The result: a polity defined by the tension between the cultural and psychological need of its citizens to sustain their identity as colonizing Englishmen, on one hand, and the insistent pull of a new land that demanded new ways of thinking about, and doing, politics, government, and law, on the other.

The corrosive effect of remoteness from the Old World and the vastness of the New was evident in the earliest days of Plymouth and Massachusetts Bay. Plymouth Colony's leader, William Bradford, had to reassure his English backers that it was *not* true that women and children voted in town meetings. The first settlers of Massachusetts Bay brought with them the ideal of a cohesive, tightly knit religious community, "a city upon a hill." But the beckoning (if also frightening) wilderness quickly put an end to that. Two months after the Puritans' June 1630 landing, Winthrop complained of "some persons who never showed so much wickedness [that is, refusal to obey authority] in England as they have done here."

By September of that year, inhabitants of the initial Shawmut settlement (later Boston) had spun off a clutch of new towns (Watertown, Roxbury, Dorchester, Medford, Saugus, Charlestown), each with its own covenant (charter), church, militia—and attitude. In 1632 Watertown's citizens refused to pay taxes for a fort in Newtown (later Cambridge), on the ground that they were being taxed without adequate representation. Dissenter Roger Williams went a step further. In 1636 he founded a separate colony, Rhode Island, with a charter that made no reference to king, Parliament, or English law. (The growth of British imperial power made this impolitic, and the necessary obeisance was inked in later.)

This experience was not confined to disputatious New Englanders. Ethnically diverse New Yorkers gave both their initial Dutch and later English overlords a hard time. And soon after his colony got under way in the 1680s, William Penn complained to the settlers: "For the love of God, me and the poor country, be not so governmentish, so noisy and open in your dissatisfactions." As early as 1635, Virginia's settlers sent governor John Harvey back to England with the warning that if he returned he would be "pistoled or shot." Harvey soon returned to Virginia with the Crown's backing and shipped his opponents to the mother country for trial. But they so convincingly detailed Harvey's inadequacies that the charges were dismissed.

Remoteness and rambunctiousness made for an unsettled politics. Boston was given over to murky conflict between White Coats (involved in the town's Atlantic commerce) and Blue Coats (linked to interior agricultural and trading interests). In the course of the seventeenth century, Virginia's politics was defined by intergenerational clashes between a ruling elite of large planters and upstart youngsters driven by the urge to supplant their seniors.

This sort of thing was hardly unknown in England. But it was contained there by the dead hand of a finite stock of inherited land and a heavy inheritance of deferential law and custom. Things were different in America. Land was plentiful, and restraints on its disposal such as primogeniture and entail had little power. So when Americans later sought to find antecedents in the colonial past for their competitive, individualistic, democratic creed, there was plenty of experiential fodder lying around.

They were less inclined to look closely at the darker side of the colonial inheritance—in particular, the evolving relationships of white settlers with red Indians and black slaves. Yet the same conditions that spawned American freedom fed American racism.

European concepts of international relations defined the colonists' formal relations with Native Americans. Tribes were called "nations," agreements were called "treaties." But differences in culture and armaments, conjoined with the insatiable settler desire for labor (which the natives were socially disinclined to provide) and land (which, however lightly, they occupied), blocked any prospect of equality or assimilation.

The experience of Plymouth is revealing. Its settlers at first seemed ready to accept their Indian neighbors as participating members of the colony. Indian testimony was accepted in the Plymouth court, contracts between whites and Native Americans had legal standing, and Indians could bring charges of assault against whites. But from the mid-seventeenth century on, the Plymouth Indians' legal status eroded. Detailed regulations came to govern their drinking and other forms of social behavior: a paradigm for future white-Indian relations.

There was at first a tendency by Virginia's settlers to regard their African chattels as indentured servants—except that the time limit on their servitude was unclear or nonexistent. But the legal status of slavery as a life indenture that attached as well to their children had been established throughout the American colonies by the end of the seventeenth century.

This mix of widening freedom for whites and shrinking rights for Native Americans and African Americans was peculiar to the mainland American colonies. Those colonies' lower mortality and continuing white immigration made them full-scale settlements, burgeoning little commonwealths. In contrast, the West Indies plantations remained heavily reliant on massive infusions of slave labor, with a thin layer of white overseers and merchants.

Distinctive too was the colonists' special compound of anxiety and assertiveness. Bacon's Rebellion of 1676 in Virginia dramatically displayed that state of mind. The uprising resulted from the failure of William Berkeley, the colony's governor, to protect farmer-planters west of the Tidewater from Indian raids or to support their desire to acquire more land. Anti-tax sentiment also stirred the pot of discontent, as did the presence of thousands of indentured servants and a small but rapidly growing number of black slaves.

Nathaniel Bacon, the revolt's leader, and many of his core supporters were younger planters who lived on the cutting edge of settlement. Their conflict with the governor and his Tidewater clique was generational as well as economic. This theme would recur in the American future, as would their mode of protest: they held a convention, swore an oath of mutual loyalty, and formed themselves into an association.

The authorities' response to the rebellion was harsh, as befitted a new, insecure society. About a score of Bacon's followers were hanged. One member of the royal court thought it a bit much that Berkeley executed "more than ever suffered death for the horrid murder of that late glorious martyr of blessed memory," King Charles I. Charles II also found it excessive—not least because of its adverse effect on the Crown's tobacco revenue.

Leisler's Rebellion of 1689–91 in New York a decade later is sufficiently similar to suggest that something more than colony-by-colony contingency was at play. The restoration of the Anglo-Catholic Stuarts in 1688 and the consequent Glorious Revolution stirred unrest in a number of colonies. Boston dissidents turned against that colony's royal governor, Sir Edmund Andros, in April 1689. A month later New York's militia, supported by many of the colony's religious and ethnic dissenters, did the same against governor Francis Nicholson. The Crown responded by formally converting New York from a proprietary colony to a royal colony.

Jacob Leisler had come to Dutch New York in 1660 at the age of twenty and quickly became one of the colony's richest landholder-merchants. The leader of New York's post-1688 revolt, the strongly anti-Catholic Leisler set up his own, increasingly authoritarian regime. He appealed to a heterogeneous population, which included the Dutch majority, smarting under the shift to English rule; New York City artisans with grievances against the Anglicized merchant oligarchy; and Long Island farmers angry at the city's shipping and flour monopolies. Again, repression was violent: Leisler was hanged and then beheaded. And again, elite opinion on both sides of the Atlantic found this excessive.

Even in that quintessential repository of order and stability, the legal system, there were signs that a new, more volatile polity was taking shape within the carapace of received English forms. For the most part colonial American law echoed English common law (with a smattering of Dutch, Spanish, and Native American usages). Established legal processes offered stability and order to a society remote from old-country custom and precedent. But those recurrent American givens of distance (from English authority) and scarcity (of trained lawyers and judges, printed materials, and courts) encouraged innovation. John Winthrop succinctly framed the problem in 1646 when he admitted that while "a Commonwealth without laws is like a ship without rigging and steerage," allegiance to the mother country "binds us not to the laws of England any longer than while we live in England, for the laws of the Parliament of England reach no further, nor do the King's writs under the great seal go any further."

The problem of being at one and the same time dependent on and beyond English law vividly emerged in the Massachusetts town of Salem. The Glorious Revolution of 1688–89 raised worrisome questions as to the authority of the king's representatives. Adding to the anxiety was that killer settler-Indian conflict, King Philip's War of 1675–76, in which some twenty-five hundred New England whites died: in proportion, the largest casualty rate of any of America's wars.

It was in this superheated environment that several girls accused a number of old women (and a few old men) of being witches. Witchcraft was a familiar offense in seventeenth-century Europe, but by the 1690s it was on its way out in English jurisprudence. An educated elite looked with growing skepticism at both the legal procedure of witchcraft trials and the offense itself.

When the colony's new governor, William Phipps, arrived from the mother country in the late spring of 1692, he found Essex County's jails filled with suspected witches. The legislature was supposed to set up a new judicial system but was not scheduled to meet until the end of the year. And meanwhile there were all those prisoners...

The solution: a special court composed of prominent laymen, who were not trained lawyers and had no judicial experience. They relied on the precedents of English witchcraft law, which included such archaisms as "spectral evidence" (physical or behavioral signs of possession) and no attorney representing the accused. In an American first (but hardly a last), inexperienced judges turned to "experts"—ministers believed to be specialists on witches and witchcraft—to guide them. Those who confessed to witchcraft escaped execution. Those who did not were hanged (nineteen women) or crushed to death (one elderly man).

Public hysteria buoyed the work of the court but was quickly followed by a wave of remorse. Governor Phipps dismissed the judges. Those condemned who were still alive and the hundred or so accused awaiting trial were released. Prominent citizens heaped opprobrium on a proceeding that had turned into a public-order-threatening vigilantism. The trials came and went in less than a year.

On the face of things, nothing could have been more different than the 1734 trial of New York printer Peter Zenger. Here was not the dark, repressive ambience of Salem's witch hunt, but rather a case later celebrated as a milestone in the emergence of freedom of the press. Yet once again the special American mix of unprecedented distance, spatial and experiential, from English ways, combined with the need to maintain a sense of cultural identity with the motherland, had novel consequences.

In good eighteenth-century English political style, New York's royal governor, William Cosby, was embroiled in a factional struggle with the colony's chief justice, Lewis Morris. During the course of that conflict, Morris and his associates established the *New York Weekly Journal*, the colonies' first overtly political newspaper. It was printed in the shop of Peter Zenger, a recent German immigrant. The *Journal's* controlling voice was James Alexander, a lawyer-politician ally of the anti-Cosby Morris, who used the paper to attack the governor.

Cosby got his ally James Delancey, who had replaced Morris as chief justice, to convene a grand jury and charge it to indict Zenger for seditious libel. Delancey warned that if the jury found Zenger not guilty, "they would be perjured"—that is, subject to arrest and trial. As in Salem, the applicability of English law came into question. Since the time of the English Revolution in the early seventeenth century, political "outs" had defended their freedom to criticize political "ins." But by the early eighteenth century the charge of seditious libel—that is, vulnerability to prosecution for speech or writing that brought authority into disrepute, regardless of its truth—was gaining force in English law. The evolution of English libel law was quite different from that of law relating to witchcraft: not toward greater liberality but toward greater constraint. But as in Salem, American jurors ignored what was new and turned to what they thought was traditional English practice: this time in the cause not of repression but of freedom.

Chief Justice Delancey barred New York's leading lawyers from participating in the defense. In their stead came Andrew Hamilton of

Philadelphia, by repute the best lawyer in the colonies. (There already was an American bar sufficiently developed to *have* a "best lawyer.") Historian John Fiske observed that Hamilton conducted his case "according to the law of the future." But while that may have been its consequence, it was not the gist of Hamilton's argument. He conjured up a venerable common-law tradition that the jury might decide not only the *facts* of the case (were the words at issue published?) but also its *law* (were the published words libelous?). And he challenged Delancey's ruling that the libel could stand whether or not it was true. He argued that English citizens had a right to criticize their rulers, basing this on an invented history of the immemorial rights of Englishmen, carried over to America.

This was boldly innovative. It contributed to the growing American assumption that new procedural and intellectual wine might be poured into old bottles. As one of Zenger's supporters put it, "If it is not law, it is better than law, it ought to be law, and will always be law wherever justice prevails." After ten minutes' deliberation, the jury (dominated by opponents of the governor) acquitted Zenger. All adjourned to the Black Horse Tavern to celebrate this triumph of American liberty. All, that is, but Zenger, whose release from jail his champions forgot to secure.

The tension between Old World ways of governance and the indigenous ways of the colonists appeared to ease during most of the three-quarters of a century preceding the American Revolution. Britain's greater internal stability and the growth of its empire gave the American colonists the room they needed to embed their distinctive mode of public life. When the exigencies of imperial conflict changed the terms of the relationship with the mother country, the institutions, attitudes, and experience necessary to conduct an ultimately successful revolution were in place.

The union of England and Scotland in 1707, the crowning of George I in 1714, and the failure of rebellions against the new dynasty in 1715 and 1745 ended a century of British dynastic and religious conflict. In its place rose the distinctive politics of the Georgian age. Horace Walpole, the first recognizably modern prime minister, came into office in 1721, as did the first political parties—though they were far from the organized parties of the nineteenth century. Their shaky character is suggested by the derogatory origins, from peripheral areas, of their names: Whigs, derived from mid-seventeenth-century Scottish anti-monarchists, and Tories, from Irish supporters of the Stuart monarchy.

A "court" party, dominated by Whig oligarchs and committed to an aggressive naval and commercial policy and a strong central government, faced (and usually bested) a "country" party of Tories and rural gentry.

This was a narrowly class-bound, thoroughly deferential politics. The time span between parliamentary elections increased in 1716 from an anxiety-inducing two and a half years to a sedate seven. The number of voters in parliamentary elections and the number of contested seats went down. The whole was held together by a pervasive system of patronage, perquisites, and preferment.

The colonies profited substantially from these good times and easier ways. An extensive network of agents, mercantile and land companies, and religious and immigrant associations lobbied for American interests in London's halls of power. Their task: to secure favorable parliamentary legislation or Crown edicts and block unfavorable ones. Shared economic concerns (most notably the slave trade) and restrictive British imperial policy fostered the growth of a common colonial interest. The inhabitants began to be called "Americans," as distinct from "colonists" or "Englishmen."

Eighteenth-century American politics resembled the English country-court division in style and rhetoric. Royal governors, their councils, and the colonial assemblies (which resembled mini-Parliaments) fought over power and perks, land, trading rights, and other material matters. This congruence was reflected in the common vocabulary of colonial American and Georgian English politics: *interest, clique, junto, faction, hacks,* and *caucus* (the last initially American, quickly Anglo-American).

But surface similarities obscured underlying differences. Both law and lawlessness assumed a distinctive character in eighteenth-century America. Eighteenth-century English law was a bulwark of social order and tradition. By the time of William Blackstone's *Commentaries on the Laws of England* (1765—69), English common law had a social prestige comparable to that of the Church of England, the king, and parliament. Blackstone was widely read, and the forms of English common law widely followed, in the American colonies.

At the same time the colonists drifted away from the English conception of law as the receptacle of tradition and precedent. Well before the Revolution, American land, criminal, and family law had begun to evolve from instruments of preservation and constraint to instruments of adaptation and innovation. Land law focused on transfer and exchange more than (as in England) succession and maintenance. The punishment of criminals in English courts became more severe; in America it became less so. By midcentury only about a quarter of American criminal law rested on common-law principles, the rest on colonial legislative codes. And more so than in the mother country, courts and juries were integral parts of colonial American government.

Riots, a European fixture, took on a different character in America. If from the English perspective American law seemed more and more lawless, to Americans rioting came to seem more and more lawful. A classic medium of protest by society's voiceless became in America not so much a force for change as a way of preserving material goods and social order. When farmers in the Carolina backcountry organized to resist bandits and tax collectors, they called themselves "regulators." Here was the beginning of the American vigilante tradition: not European-style "primitive rebels" but yeoman citizens who found it necessary—as the Americanism had it—to "take the law into their own hands."

Disturbances in the seaport towns were frequent. But rarely were they bread riots or other classic European expressions of urban desperation. Rather, their targets included the increasing number of brothels in Boston (1734), the authorities' use of smallpox vaccine in a 1768 Norfolk epidemic, or sailors' protest against the Quaker elite's manipulation of the German vote in the 1742 Philadelphia election. These were lawful mobs: Boston rioters refused to act on Saturday or Sunday, the Lord's days.

Quotidian American politics was not just a carbon copy of English ways. Local officials (though usually from leading families) were more frequently elected than appointed in America, especially in New England and the middle colonies. The importance of local political roots could be seen in the early appearance of the custom that members of colonial assemblies live in the districts they represented, unlike the English practice of absentee MPs.

Instruments of self-governance abounded. Virginia's county courts and the local justices of the peace, New England towns and their magistrates and selectmen, and colonial assemblies everywhere were virtually autonomous governing bodies. Homeowners, shopkeepers, and wharf owners in the seaport towns took over public functions such as maintaining the streets and docks.

Comparable differences underlay the outward similarities of form in American and English elections. Especially in the South, there was much treating of voters to drinks on election day—"swilling the planters with bumbo"—just as in English towns. But there appears to have been little overt vote buying of the sort common in eighteenth-century English parliamentary elections. And substantial differences prevailed in voter eligibility and participation. Men with the right to vote ranged from less than 20 percent to 40 percent of the adult male British population. In most of the colonies, between 50 percent and 80 percent of non-indentured white males could (but not necessarily did) vote. Massachusetts governor Thomas Hutchinson complained of his colony that "anything with the appearance of a man" was eligible to cast a ballot. And John Adams reported that the taverns were "full of people drinking, . . . plotting with the landlord to get him, at the next town meeting and election, either for selectman or representative." A higher level of political participation existed in part because land-rich Americans more readily met property qualifications for voting. And by the mid-eighteenth century the American literacy level and the number of newspapers per capita outstripped the mother country.

While on its surface the American colonial polity resembled its British model, it was in fact headed in a very different direction. In the mother country, the king and his ministers became increasingly powerful: under the spurs of war and empire, something like a modern centralized state took form. The opposite was the case in America. These dynamic, self-sufficient colonies bred a rich politics of place, power, and preferment. Intergenerational conflict between newcomers (by birth or migration) and old-timers was a conspicuous fact of political life in a society relatively free of the legal and cultural devices that perpetuated established interest and position. Thus Peter Faneuil's hall, which he gave to Boston in 1742 to serve as a marketplace for the established mercantile families, became a cause of contention as newer merchants challenged the perks of older ones.

Colonial politics often involved family-dominated groups of substantial merchants, landowners, and speculators vying with the governors, and among themselves, over charters, patronage, and economic privileges. This disconnect from the concerns of most residents could lead to low (10–15 percent) turnouts at assembly elections and spotty representation. A third of Massachusetts's towns didn't bother to send members to the colony's General Court on the grounds that it was too distant, too costly, and not worth the trouble. Not surprisingly, the assemblies produced little legislation. Pennsylvania in 1765 enacted twelve laws, Connecticut eight, South Carolina nine. Bills often originated as petitions rather than as products of legislative draftsmanship.

Most royal governors, who came (and left) in profusion, were ill at ease with the intense, complex internal life of the colonies. In good imperial fashion, they usually sought both to govern effectively and enrich themselves through patronage, grants, and licenses. But this was not India or the Caribbean, where indigenous interests were weak. The governors proved to be no match for the scions of American planter and merchant families, rising young men—often lawyers—of ability and influence in rural communities and small towns, who turned naturally to their colony's assembly as a place to do necessary networking and get experience in politics and governance. The assemblies were where the members of the Revolutionary generation came to know one another and learned the techniques of challenging imperial authority, creating political alliances, and ultimately governing a factious people.

Consider the sad story of Sir Danvers Osborne. Recently widowed and seriously depressed, he became governor of New York in 1753. He set out to make his fortune in the accepted style of the empire. He expected the New York assembly to give him a salary, budget, and perks sufficient to support a grandiose lifestyle appropriate to his rank and station. But Osborne ran into a stone wall of resistance. "Then what am I come here for?" he plaintively asked one day. That night he hanged himself.

CHAPTER TWO

THE REPUBLICAN
REVOLUTION

ACOUNTERFACTUAL: THE WISE counsel of William Pitt and Edmund Burke prevails, and the American colonists' complaints over
British imperial policy win favor in the halls of Parliament. Consequently, restraints on the colonials' migration over the Appalachians are
lifted. Taxes and other impositions on a trade that is, after all, more than a
little beneficial to the mother country are reduced. The Americans are
given something more than virtual representation in Parliament.

The result: no American Revolution. Instead, there evolves a
commonwealth-like relationship between the mother country and an
American population predominantly of English origin, left alone in its
local and internal affairs, its loyalty sustained by the psychological succor
of empire citizenship, a steady flow of immigrants from the British Isles,
and the enchantment bestowed by distance. That relationship is only
strengthened by the French Revolution's descent into the Terror and
Napoleonic despotism.

If it can be argued, however fancifully, that the American Revolution
was not inevitable, then there is an obligation to explain how and why it
happened, and how and why it was followed by a quarter century of world-
class political and governmental innovation.

The American Revolution and its aftermath may be usefully compared
with the seventeenth-century English Puritan Revolution that preceded it
and the French Revolution that followed it. (As Mark Twain observed,
history does not repeat itself, but it rhymes.) Each of the three revolutions
began as an attack on royal power (Charles I, George III, Louis XVI), and

on the costs of war. Each evolved from protest to revolt through a legislative body (the Rump Parliament of 1649, the Continental Congress of 1774, the National Assembly of 1789). Each had to deal with defenders of the old regime (Cavaliers, Tories, monarchists) and with dissidents pushing for a deeper and sharper break from the past (English Levellers, American radical democrats, French Jacobins). Each underwent a generation of traumatic regime change (England 1642–1660, America 1775–1789, France 1789–1815). And in each revolution a military leader (Cromwell, Washington, Napoleon) headed the post-revolutionary state.

Here the game of similarity ends. The Old World revolutions were tumultuous—kings executed, old ways and beliefs sweepingly repudiated, republics proclaimed, new constitutions written, opponents fought, killed, exiled—but at the end of the day, monarchy and aristocracy were restored. The American Revolution was no tea party (though it did come after one). But it had no counterpart to the authoritarian iconoclasm of Cromwell's Puritan Commonwealth, or Robespierre and the Terror, or Napoleon's warfare state.

The English Revolution, coming after a century of Catholic-Protestant conflict, was profoundly religious in character. It completed the English Reformation. The Great Seal of the (brief) Puritan Commonwealth proclaimed: "In the First Year of Freedome, by God's Blessing Restored": more fulsome, and less abstract, than the American declaration "In God We Trust."

The rhetoric of the English Revolution had a prominent place in the historical imagination of the American revolutionaries. But this was a mixed legacy at best. True, the Instrument of Government of 1653—the English forerunner of the American Constitution—separated the executive from the legislature and provided for the election of members of Parliament (by voters with at least £200 worth of property, no small sum). But Parliament was under the control of a Council of State, and ultimately of the army and its head, Oliver Cromwell, who was not reluctant to eject pesky members when it suited him.

If repeated constitution-making practice made perfect, then France should have been in a class by itself. It churned out five charters of government between 1793 and 1802. From the vantage point of a prison cell (where he was soon to die), the philosopher Condorcet wrote that the first French constitution was superior to its American counterpart because it was purer, more accurate, more profound. A splenetic John Adams scrawled on his copy of Condorcet's article: "Pure! Accurate! Profound! Indeed!" In fact, the immediate legacy of revolutionary France was not liberty, equality, and fraternity but the ideological excesses of the Terror and the war-making authoritarianism of Napoleon.

The two European revolutions, for all the differences between the religious outlook of the seventeenth century and the (superficially) secular one of the eighteenth, had in common the prevalence of an absolutist mind-set. Cromwell rejected kingship but not the title of Lord Protector (or being called "your highness") and held court in Whitehall Palace and Hampton Court. When he died his son succeeded him. Napoleon crowned himself emperor, turned his numerous siblings into an instant royal family, and intended to turn over his crown to his son.

These details highlight the essential contrariety of the American Revolution. Rousseau's view that "no people could ever be anything but what the nature of its government made it" was at a polar remove from John Adams's belief that "[t]he government ought to be what the people make it." The 1789 French Declaration of the Rights of Man and of the Citizen—its compound title is revealing—may be compared with the American Declaration of Independence (1776) and Bill of Rights (1791). Some twenty-five hundred political pamphlets and sixty thousand *cahiers de doléance*—statements of grievances—preceded the French Declaration. The result was not an appeal to mankind on the basis of felt grievances, as in the American Declaration, but a manifesto for what Tocqueville called "the politics of the impossible, the theory of madness, the cult of blind audacity." It sought not to protect the individual from the state (as did the American Bill of Rights) but to assert the supremacy of the nation, as the embodiment of the people, over the individual. It contained no right to freedom of assembly, provision for jury trial, or right to counsel or judicial appeal, on the assumption that the prevalence of the general will made all of that irrelevant.

James Madison accepted the inevitability of factionalism in a free republic—"liberty is to faction what air is to fire"—and devoted himself to figuring out how to control it for peaceful purposes. The Jacobins sought not to check faction but to destroy it. (Saint Just: "Your interest demands that you forget your interest; the only salvation is through the public good." Robespierre: "[There are] only two parties, the party of good intentions and the party of evil ones.")

Americans of the time were well aware of the gulf that separated the two revolutionary nations. Alexander Hamilton told Lafayette: "I dread the reveries of your philosophic politicians." Gouverneur Morris, the primary drafter of the Constitution, concluded that the French "wandered in the Dark because they prefer Lightning to light."

The differences that distinguish the three great early modern revolutions from one another are summed up in their central figures: Cromwell, Napoleon, and Washington. On the surface the three had much in common. They had socially comparable family backgrounds: a marginal gentility sufficient enough to lead them to aspire to elite status, but tenuous enough to make them have to work for it. Their careers took off when revolutionary assemblies called them to service. And each rose to political eminence through performance in battle.

Cromwell, like Napoleon, had a consuming thirst for power, filtered through the pervasive religiosity of his time. It was said of him that "[h]e believed in his stars as much as Napoleon was to do." But his lust for power was rendered acceptable (not least to himself) by his belief that "[i]t matters not who is Commander in Chief, if God be so." His way of winning over his adversaries was hardly to appeal to reason: "I beseech you, by the bowels of Christ, see that you are mistaken." He believed that "[c]ivil liberty . . . ought to be subordinate to a more peculiar interest of God."

Napoleon's personality is more familiar—grimly familiar—today. He was in many respects the first modern dictator. "He seems," his brother Lucien said of him early on, "to have a strong leaning toward tyranny." To this Napoleon added a quintessentially Romantic temperament. He said in 1797, "At 29 I am tired of glory; it has lost its charm, and there is nothing left for me but complete egotism." He proceeded to stoke the fire of his self-regard by waging war for all but fourteen months of his fifteen years in power. He conducted brilliant campaigns, far more so than Washington. But he also abandoned his army when the going got rough in Egypt and Russia, in vivid contrast to Washington at Valley Forge.

One of the thin line of historians who speak well of Cromwell defends his hero by observing: "His were the qualities of George Washington, not of Napoleon Bonaparte; of the patriot, not the world conqueror." Not quite so. Cromwell's brutal performance in Ireland and his designs on Spain's holdings in the West Indies put him as close to Napoleon's ambitions as Washington's distaste for adventurism distanced him from the other two.

Despite their points of similarity, Napoleon had no particular affinity for Cromwell. Washington was another story. He kept a bust of the American on his desk, and when Washington died in 1799, he ordered the flags of the French army dressed in mourning crepe. Napoleon's memoirs, written during his St. Helena exile, included an apologia that revealed how entangled with the example of Washington was his self-regard:

If Washington had been a Frenchman at a time when France was crumbling inside and invaded from outside, I would have dared him to be himself; or, if he had persisted in being himself, he would merely have been a fool. . . . I could only be a crowned Washington. And I could become that only at a congress of kings, surrounded by sovereigns whom I had either persuaded or mastered. Then, and only then, could I have displayed Washington's moderation, disinterestedness, and wisdom. In all reasonableness, I could not attain this goal except by means of world dictatorship, I tried it. Can it be held against me?

It was his attitude toward power that finally set Washington apart from his European counterparts. Neither Cromwell nor Napoleon ever voluntarily relinquished it. Washington, whom Garry Wills called "a virtuoso of resignations," did so several times.

Washington, the father of his country, was himself childless, so contingency added to his restraint. (He once mused: "I have no child for whom I could wish to make a provision—no family to build in greatness upon my country's ruins.") But his Cincinnatus-like performance was in close accord with the prevailing spirit both of the Revolution and of the larger American polity out of which it emerged. Sam Adams warned: "[L]et us beware of continental and state great men." John Adams and Thomas Jefferson worried (unnecessarily) over the popular veneration of Washington and feared that he might have monarchical leanings.

Like so many of his generation, Washington saw the revolt against British rule and the creation of the new Republic freighted with a significance beyond his sense of self or even the American people. He told Lafayette in the spring of 1788, when the Constitution's ratification hung in the balance, "A few short weeks will determine the political fate of America for the present generation and probably produce no small influence on the happiness of society through a long succession of ages to come." In his first inaugural he proclaimed that "nothing less than the destiny of the republican model of government was at stake." This was hubris, but of a sort far removed from the religious fervor of Cromwell, the ideological fanaticism of Robespierre, or the untrammeled egoism of Napoleon.

No less remote from the European experience was the nation building to which the Americans, their revolution won and their Constitution written, now turned. Nineteenth-century Italian revolutionary Massimo d'Azeglio announced in the wake of his country's unification: "We have made Italy. Now we have to make Italians." The Americans' challenge was the reverse. They had made themselves. Now they had to make the United States of America.

The American Revolution was regime-changing in the most obvious sense. But it also legitimated native American ways of governance that had been building for generations. The American Republic that came out of it was what J. G. A. Pocock called a mix of "a new political society" and "a quasi-[r]epublican alternative to parliamentary monarchy." There was plenty of old wine in the bright new bottle of the United States of America.

As every schoolchild once knew, the revolutionary drama began with the imposition of a new British imperial policy in the wake of the Seven Years' War, which ended in 1763. The conclusion of what added up to a second Hundred Years' War with France forced Britain to face up to the massive cost of that enterprise. The military absorbed 60–70 percent of all government expenditure. With upward of 40 percent of that spending met by loans, there was a pressing need to raise new taxes to fund the national debt.

A powerful, confident new bureaucracy had led England through its eighteenth-century wars with France, Spain, and Holland for supremacy over the trading-and-colonies world. Now came the time for compensation. What was more proper than that the American colonies, major beneficiaries of the British triumph at arms, help bear the cost? So it seemed to Prime Minister George Grenville in England. Council of the Indies president José Gálvez of Spain sought to do the same with the Spanish West Indies. Foreign Minister Étienne de Choiseul of France turned in a similar way to the all-but-colony of Brittany.

The American colonists did not concur, and they had the attitude, experience, and resources to put muscle behind their opposition. True, their isolation from British politics and government kept them from exercising much influence in London. This was not unusual: colonists everywhere suffer from their remove from the imperial power center. What was special about the American case was the existence of a colonial society with forms of politics, government, and law that in effect added up to a new American polity *avant la lettre*.

The chasm separating colonial autonomy from imperial authority became more pronounced in the interplay of Britain's post-1763 policy and the American response. That response focused on the issue of the colonies' representation—or, more accurately, their lack of it—in Parliament and before the Crown. Americans schooled for generations in governing themselves found their absence from Parliament unacceptable. But the English authorities were quite at ease with the concept of virtual representation—which, after all, applied to the mass of disfranchised Britons as well as the colonies.

The new imperial policy struck unerringly at the most dynamic forces of American colonial life. The Stamp Act (1765) levied an impost on the business and legal documents and newspapers of an ever more sophisticated economy. The Declaratory Act (1766) equated America with downtrodden Ireland by affirming Parliament's authority to pass laws binding on Americans "in all cases whatsoever." The Sugar Act (1764) and Townshend Act (1767) put heavy new burdens on the booming American trade with the West Indies and Europe. The acts closing trans-Appalachian land to settlement by the colonists appeared to favor the interests of Indians and Canadian Catholic fur trappers: a surefire way to inflame American farmers, land speculators, planters, and merchants eyeing those toothsome acres. To add insult to injury, misguided policy required intrusive enforcement: demanding governors and councils, tax and impost collectors, and, as night follows day, troops—all of this imposed on colonies that for decades had been accustomed to march to their own drummer.

The American cultural and political infrastructure was up to the task of turning discontent into resistance. Lawyer-planter-merchant political elites, maturing in every colony for a century, swung into action. Committees of Correspondence shared information and mobilized opinion. Colonial printers flooded the towns and the countryside with Fast Day and Thanksgiving Day proclamations and sermons, oppositionist speeches in the colonial assemblies, and feisty broadsides and pamphlets. Colonists skilled in the business of claiming the rights of Englishmen insisted on no taxation without representation, no alienation of property without consent.

The American resistance took on a formal character with the Continental Congress of 1774. Planter-politicians Thomas Jefferson, Patrick Henry, George Mason, and George Washington and important lawyers such as John Adams took the lead in what became the revolutionary movement. (Full-time revolutionary Sam Adams was a rarity.) When the Liberty Boys rioted against British restrictions on trade, the organizing hand was their merchant and shipowner employers. A number of towns and counties drafted resolutions intended not to list their grievances—as, later, did the *cahiers* of the French Revolution—but to stiffen the backbone of Congress in resisting Britain's Coercive Acts.

The movement's leaders had substantial popular support. In June 1774 Philadelphia's protest organizers proposed that their chief resistance organization, the Committee of Nineteen, include seven "mechanics" and six members of German origins. Savannah's revolutionary committee was headed by a Jew and had a carpenter, a shoemaker, and a blacksmith among its members.

Opposition to the protest movement was almost as diverse as the coalition that supported it. Philadelphia Quaker merchants, western Massachusetts farmers, Baptists in New England, Anglicans in New York City, and small farmers in the Carolinas set themselves against the Revolution and independence. They did so either because they benefited from British policy, were protected by British authority, or were at odds with those elements in their colony who favored the patriot cause. The Revolutionary War was not only a struggle against the English and their Hessian mercenaries but (especially in the South) a brutal civil war as well. It was the longest American war until Vietnam, and about one in ten of the available male population fought in it.

Why, then, did the American Revolution not leave a heritage of bitterness and social division comparable to the English and French revolutions? For one thing, the American revolutionaries were more effective than their European counterparts in getting rid of their adversaries. There were about half a million Tories, and some eighty thousand of them were forced to leave the colonies—about six times the proportion of supporters of the French monarchy who fled after their cause was lost.

More important, most of what John Adams called "the people of parts and spirit" joined the rebellion. The supple Ben Franklin, a strong royalist until the eve of the Revolution, quickly became one of its doughtiest champions. Merchants (except the Philadelphia Quakers), the major Virginia planters, and the ablest lawyers and public figures were early and ardent supporters first of resistance to British policy and then of independence and the willingness to fight for it if necessary.

Why did men such as Franklin, who sought a place in the Empire, soldier-planter George Washington, ambitious for a spot in the British army, Massachusetts lawyer John Adams, on his way to a rich and rewarding career representing Boston merchants, young polymath Alexander Hamilton, by predisposition drawn to status, hierarchy, and rank, the mother's milk of Georgian England—why did these men join with such instinctive revolutionaries as Patrick Henry, Samuel Adams, and Tom Paine?

There is no single answer. John Adams, Jefferson, and Washington did not come to the patriot cause out of social or economic or political alienation. They belonged to solid families with generations of secure social standing. Instead, the imperial crisis became an open sesame to the public demonstration of what they already were: not colonials but Americans. Of the original fifty-five members of the Continental Congress, nine out of ten were native-born, most to the third or fourth generation. The only member of Congress not of American or British origins was a Swiss-born Presbyterian minister, and he opposed independence.

Unlike their French counterparts, the American revolutionaries did not get caught up in the business of destroying inherited institutions and reshaping human nature. What is most striking about the American actions stretching from the First Continental Congress of 1774 to the enactment of the Constitution and the creation of the United States—a quarter century of state making—was the practical, workaday manner (and matter) of their work.

Take, for example, the appointment of Washington as commander in chief, and compare it with the accession of Cromwell to military leadership in the revolutionary England of the early seventeenth century, or of Napoleon to a comparable position in revolutionary France. Washington's sensitivity to the dictates of Congress and the lack of any attempt on his part to use his military position to seize power contrast dramatically with the others. His appointment, aside from his manifest military appropriateness for the post—underlined by his appearance at Congress clad in the impressive uniform of a colonel of the Virginia militia—made eminent political sense. He was a southerner, and it was essential to secure the support of the South (in particular, Virginia) for a war that in its early stages was concentrated around Boston and then New York.

Another distinctive feature of this revolutionary effort, in marked contrast to its English predecessor and French successor, was the low level of religious (or anti-religious) orthodoxy. True, the heritage of evangelical enthusiasm fostered by the Great Awakening of the early eighteenth century colored the language and actions of the revolutionaries. John Adams observed that if moderate compromiser Harrison Gray Otis was the Revolution's Martin Luther, then firebrand Sam Adams was its John Calvin. The Continental Congress refused to meet on the Sabbath, and in 1777 it ordered twenty thousand Bibles to be distributed to the army. But these were not St. Johns in a hurry. Congress dutifully discoursed on its duty "to maintain, defend and preserve those civil and religious rights and liberties, for which many of our fathers fought and died": not a call to defend (or for that matter to assault) the ramparts of Orthodoxy. Frequent references to Old Testament Israel co-existed with no less frequent references to the pagan Roman republic.

In 1782, after six years and three committees, the Confederation Congress finally agreed on the design of a Great Seal of the United States. It spoke of a *novus ordo saeculorum*: a new order of the ages. But it was festooned with the pyramid-and-eye symbol of that quintessentially

European Enlightenment institution the Masons. And it displayed a proud eagle clutching olive branches in one talon and arrows in the other: a symbol straight from the reign of Holy Roman Emperor Charles V. Past, present, future: all was grist for the American revolutionary mill.

The same mix of radical thought and moderate-to-conservative action shaped the run-up to independence. Much rhetorical lip service was paid to the eighteenth-century English "radical" tradition of Whig pamphleteers John Trenchard and William Gordon and firebrand John Wilkes. But most members of the Continental Congress at first were reluctant to detach from Britain, or even to criticize the monarchy. They thought that their grievances could be addressed within the framework of the empire, and contented themselves with blaming anti-American elements in Parliament and corrupt ministers of the king. A majority favored a compromise settlement even after the battles of Lexington and Concord, the burning of seacoast towns, and the appearance of a British expeditionary force with a substantial number of Hessian mercenaries.

But British adamancy and an evolving American political culture moved Congress to the final break. British radical Tom Paine's pamphlet *Common Sense* (January 1776) put in words what more and more members believed. It flatly rejected "the so much boasted constitution of England," the monarchy, and hereditary rule, and called for a government based solely on popular choice: "We have it in our power to begin the world over again."

Now things moved swiftly. By July 1776 a committee had written, and after much amending Congress adopted, the Declaration of Independence. Thomas Jefferson was the prime draftsman, and later he sought to lock in the idea that it was the unique creation of his brain and pen. He predicted that the desk on which he wrote his draft would be "carried on the procession of our nation's birthday, as the relics of the saints are in those of the Church."

In fact, the Declaration (as Jefferson at times conceded) was the distilled essence of an emerging American political culture. Its drafting committee was multisectional: Jefferson of Virginia, John Adams of Massachusetts, John Dickinson of Pennsylvania. The document drew on the ideas and language of a century-long radical tradition: the English Declaration of Rights of 1689, the writings of John Locke, the deism of the Enlightenment. Its preamble was an eloquent declaration of independence. But the bulk of the document was a lawyers' brief (twenty-six of the fifty-six signers were attorneys) detailing the colonies' grievances against the king: "let facts be submitted to a candid world."

This was the tip of an iceberg of grievance welling up in the American colonies. About a hundred mini-declarations of independence appeared between April and July 1775, reflecting an old Anglo-American tradition of petitions and declarations. George Mason's preliminary version of the Virginia Declaration of Rights in 1774 had many of the most potent phrases of the Declaration's preamble. The fact that Congress heavily edited Jefferson's draft, eliminating about a quarter of the original text (including a condemnation of the slave trade and some of the more extravagant accusations of royal villainy) may have toned down the Declaration's revolutionary substance. But it certainly improved its political potency, and even its language, with changes such as "certain inalienable rights" for "inherent inalienable rights": a unique instance of successful document redrafting by committee.

When Ben Franklin naughtily reminded his fellow signers that if they didn't hang together they most assuredly would all hang separately, he was addressing not a group short on self-confidence but self-assured men of substance and standing, ready to formalize a state of independence that most of them thought was already a reality.

The extent to which the Revolution unleashed long-gathering forces of political innovation—forces that produced the first modern polity in the Western world—was evident as well in the new state constitutions written after July 1775. The colonial assemblies were cohesive and long-serving. They were ready to take the bit and run when the opportunity arose.

Every state except Rhode Island and Connecticut (who kept their colonial charters with references to the Crown expunged) wrote and enacted one or more new constitutions, thus forcefully launching the idea of a written constitution into the Western political world. Their substance was no less novel: bills of rights, a shared belief in popular representation, distrust of executive and judicial authority. Most governors would be chosen by their state legislatures and would have no power to originate legislation or to veto it, or to choose judges. And most state judiciaries had no power of judicial review.

In 1779 Massachusetts adopted a new procedure: a separate constitutional convention followed by town ratification. Its purpose was to more directly link constitution making to "the people." Local orneriness thrived. The town of Oakham's report on the results of its constitutional deliberation was: "Voted unanimously in the affirmative except for one person who is an old insignificant Tory and never ought to vote in any case."

But Pennsylvania was the only state that could be said to have toyed with radicalism. In part because Philadelphia's Quaker-Anglican elite opposed independence, a group of English radicals, including Tom Paine and David Rittenhouse, had outsized influence. The state constitution of 1776 eliminated the office of governor, retained Pennsylvania's unicameral colonial legislature (but created a Council of Censors to review legislative acts), removed property qualifications for voting, and strengthened office-holding restrictions on Catholics and Quakers. This had something of the tone and spirit of the French Revolution yet to come. Not coincidentally, it proved to be the least durable of the new state constitutions.

The Continental—from 1777, the Confederation—Congress had to tend to the demands of statecraft that came with independence. Its Articles of Confederation followed the familiar path of limited structural change and a pervading distrust of power. It was a blueprint for governance made necessary by independence and war, but little more than that. A Congress-led union of states with a central government that controlled the coinage, borrowing, an army and a navy, and foreign and Indian affairs stirred little or no controversy. The Articles specified that "[e]ach state retains its sovereignty, freedom, and independence." The states had veto power over changes in the document and retained control over commerce and taxation. There was no Confederation judiciary, and no member of Congress could serve more than three years in six.

It is not surprising that the Confederation Congress had no coherent factions or parties. Its major achievement was western land policy, embodied in the Northwest Ordinance of 1785, which excluded slavery and ensured both equality and a republican form of government as territories became states. Otherwise, with the war over, a lame and halting Congress attracted little public interest. Members' attendance dropped; Washington complained to Jefferson of its "inertitude." Robert Morris, the Confederation's superintendent of finance and the closest approximation of a strongman in the government, was replaced by a states-dominated Board of Treasury.

In its weakness, the Confederation reflected the mind-set of the generation that committed itself to and fought for independence. Washington, John Adams, Jefferson, and the others thought of themselves as Americans, but in a generic sense, as a people more than a nation. Adams called Congress "a diplomatic assembly" and spoke of Massachusetts as "my country." Jefferson and Washington had a similar view of Virginia. Distaste for fellow states rivaled distaste for England. A New York newspaper called Boston "the common sewer of America"; a Boston paper spoke of "the little, filthy, nasty, dirty colony of Rhode Island."

But the realities of the late-eighteenth-century Western world made a loose federation of colonies-turned-states unviable. The Confederation's vulnerability to international power politics and domestic strife heightened pressure to change the form of government. It became necessary to take another leap into the unknown: to create a new nation that was more than a confederation of states, and to do so on principles that reflected the political implications of the Revolution as well as the inherited political weight of the colonial past.

A pluralist/interest-group approach to politics, encased in the forms of republicanism, was the response. The federal Constitution was designed to temper the ill effects of those familiar realities interest and faction, not to deny that they existed. At the same time the drafters were aware that post-Revolutionary America needed an approach to governance that went beyond the assumptions of the colonial political past. "Influence," Washington warned in October 1786, "is no government."

As in the case of the Revolution, the Constitution did not emerge full-blown from anyone's brow; rather, it came from unfolding goals and possibilities. A scattering of representatives from the thirteen states gathered in Annapolis in September 1786, charged to remedy some of the more obvious defects of the Articles of Confederation. They found that they had neither the numbers nor the political capacity to do anything substantive, and disbanded with a call to the state legislatures to select a more potent group to gather in Philadelphia in the following year.

The most pressing issues of the time—state versus Confederation control over commerce and taxation, internal threats to social order—were not profound conflicts over ideology but divisions within the coalition that had won the Revolution. It is revealing that "commerce" was so widespread a concern. In the eighteenth century, that word referred to the general flow of trade and credit—close to what we mean today by "the market." Its enhancement was a shared concern of planters and merchants, market farmers and shippers: in short, those who opposed British imperial policy before the Revolution. British post-Revolutionary policy—closing the West Indies to American trade, flooding the states with British imports—reinvigorated that earlier alliance. New, Revolution-created interest groups—holders of Confederation bonds, privateers and army suppliers owed money by the government, army officers seeking back pay and pensions—also had a lively interest in a more effective central government. The backers of a new Constitution, the Federalists, were a coalition much like the Revolutionists of the 1770s: varied in their origins and interests, but bound together by a big idea.

No less revealing was the character of the Anti-Federalists, those who opposed the new Constitution. They were less enmeshed in the larger interstate and transatlantic economic and cultural relationships that engaged the Federalists. The Anti-Federalist merchant-shipowners of Rhode Island (no small segment in the state: it is estimated that nine out of ten Providence males owned at least part of a merchant vessel) were the exception that proved the rule. Rhode Island was the Tangiers of America, battening on the anarchic commercial and fiscal environment that so distressed its more substantial competitors in Boston and New York. The state sat out the federal convention and would be the last to ratify the Constitution. The Anti-Federalists (like the Populists a century later) have been called forward-looking critics of market capitalism. But differences of class, status, and wealth in late-eighteenth-century America only marginally shaped a polity that, for all its revolutionary rhetoric, still had a substantial inheritance of deferential traditions.

It is true that Shays's Rebellion in western Massachusetts, a violent protest against state taxes, strengthened the Federalists' belief that economic and social chaos loomed without a stronger central government. Governor James Bowdoin and his state militia confronted Captain Daniel Shays and his insurrectionary force of farmers (by no means poor—the very value of their land and crops made taxation paid in specie insupportable) for all the world like the British imperial authorities in the late 1760s and the early 1770s.

But this incipient revolt was quickly, almost bloodlessly squelched. The people of western Massachusetts in fact were complexly divided by religion and economic interest. Many Shaysites opposed the Revolution and independence. Now they challenged not the Commonwealth of Massachusetts but only one of its policies. Shays himself wound up with the Revolutionary War pension to which he was entitled. And in the 1790s the Shaysites supported the emerging Federalist party.

If there was one overriding impulse at play, it was the sense of participation in a profound historical event. Philadelphia physician and public figure Benjamin Rush observed in 1786 that the end of the Revolutionary War with England meant that "nothing but the first act of the great drama is closed. It remains yet to establish and perfect our new forms of government, and to prepare the principles, morals, and manners of our citizens, for those forms of government, after they are established and brought to perfection."

Fifty-five delegates came together in Philadelphia in May 1787 to write a new constitution, the same number as (and socially similar to) those who made up the First Continental Congress in September 1774. More than half were lawyers and/or college-educated. Almost 90 percent belonged to the Masons, whose deistic mix of rationality and piety, coupled with the status derived from secrecy and selectivity, strongly appealed to the founding generation.

Illustrious members of the cohort that sought and secured independence—most notably Franklin and Washington—were present. Washington presided over the convention. John Adams and Thomas Jefferson were abroad, representing the Confederation government in England and France. This may well have contributed substantially to the character—and success—of the Constitution. Jefferson was too attracted to Rousseauian perfectionism, Adams to the British model of parliamentary monarchy, for them to have contributed much to the workmanlike document that finally emerged. Instead, a younger generation, led by James Madison of Virginia, Alexander Hamilton and Gouverneur Morris of New York, and James Wilson of Pennsylvania, dominated the convention: men less encumbered by the precepts and assumptions of colonial and Revolutionary American public life.

That the end product would be a republic was taken for granted: no small thing, given the virtual nonexistence of that form of government in eighteenth-century Europe. So integrated into the American political psyche had the concept become that Madison declared without fear of contradiction that he and his fellow delegates "were now to decide the fate of republican government."

But the Constitution was not a sermon or a work of political theory. It was a *charter*—an assignment of power and authority—of a special sort: "a charter," said Madison, "of power granted by liberty, not a charter of liberty granted by power." Its preamble—"We the People of the United States, in Order to form a more perfect Union, establish Justice, insure domestic Tranquility, provide for the common defence, promote the general Welfare, and secure the Blessings of liberty to ourselves and our Posterity, do ordain and establish this Constitution for the United States of America"—sought to say what the new government was all about in as few words, and with as little rodomontade, as possible. What followed was a stripped-down set of rules designed to get a national government going.

The powers of Congress, the president, and the judiciary were briefly sketched out. (The Ninth and Tenth Amendments, added later, made it clear that everything else was reserved to the people and the states.) The essence of the Constitution lay in those Newtonian phrases "checks and balances" and "separation of powers." It was, said Charles Evans Hughes 150 years later, "the greatest instrument ever designed to prevent things from being done."

Rousseau once observed that the moment "a people allows itself to be represented it is no longer free: it no longer exists." The Constitution's divergence from this view was a matter of degree—180 of them. The French Declaration of the Rights of Man announced in 1789: "The source of all sovereignty resides in the nation; no group, no individual, may exercise authority not emanating directly therefrom." But in the course of the Philadelphia Convention, the word *nation* was struck from various drafts. Instead, the Republic was to be a "federal" one. *Foedus* was the Latin word for "treaty," suggesting that the Constitution was an accord among as-yet sovereign states. And indeed, the allotment of congressmen according to each state's population and the provision for two senators per state implied that legislators would act as emissaries of their commonwealths.

Yet for all its trailblazing republicanism, the convention was steeped in the ways of the deferential colonial political regime. Its deliberations were confidential, and no official record of the proceedings was distributed. (James Madison's notes, the most complete of the informal accounts kept by delegates, were not published until 1840.) Divisions among the delegates were sectional, economic, to a small degree ideological: much closer to the factionalism of colonial politics than to the party alignments to come. The Revolutionary past, not the imagined future, was the lodestone of the convention. As delegate Benjamin Rush put it: "[T]he same enthusiasm *now* pervades all classes in favor of *government* that activated us in favor of *liberty* in the years 1774 and 1775."

The most divisive issues were the character of the presidency, how to resolve potential conflicts between large and small states (in population) over taxation and representation, and how to count slaves—again, for purposes of taxation and representation. In each case the solution was thoroughly quotidian, with little reference to natural rights, the consent of the governed, and other big ideas. Roger Sherman of Connecticut, one of the Convention's movers and shakers, said that the argument was "not what rights naturally belong to man, but how they may be most effectually guarded in society."

The distrust of central authority so prominent in the Revolution and the Confederation government was a recurring theme in the deliberations of the Convention. But the danger of a weak central government was, after all, what had led to the Constitutional convention in the first place. So along with substantial regard for state autonomy, the Constitution gave significant (if vaguely defined) powers over taxation, commerce, and military and diplomatic affairs to the national government. And it created a new kind of head of state, the president of the United States.

The delegates spent much time on the constraints that should be imposed on that office. The chief executive's salary and duration got long and intense consideration. Above all, delegates worried over the mode of presidential selection: by the Senate, perhaps, or by some form of popular choice? The solution was an electoral college, made up of delegations from the states in proportion to their population, selected either by direct election or by the state legislature, the choice left to the states. The presidency as sketched out in the Constitution was an artful juggling of the need for a stronger national government, the fear of centralized power, and the desire to retain as much state autonomy as possible.

The same could be said of the Convention's two-house legislature, one reflecting each state's population and the other drawn equally from the commonwealths. This expeditiously settled the large state–small state dilemma: a slice-the-cake deal that historians would later (over-)dignify by calling it the Great Compromise.

The only issue that might have threatened the constitutional coalition was slavery: already a bone of contention for northerners such as Hamilton hostile to the institution and a source of guilt for Washington and other southerners. Madison thought that it would be "wrong to admit in the Constitution the idea that there could be property in men." So euphemism ("persons not taxed," "persons held to service") prevailed. Even Revolutionary hotblood Sam Adams kept his mouth shut on the issue. The common view was that slavery would fade away in the South, as it already was doing in the North. But the primary reason for leaving the institution alone was that nobody knew what to do about it without endangering the Union. The major concession to the widespread unease over slavery was the provision that the slave trade might be ended in twenty years' time if Congress chose to do so. What made this possible was Virginia's flourishing business of breeding and selling slaves to newer areas, and consequent readiness to see importation end.

The solution to the issue of whether or not slaves should be counted as persons (thus affecting a state's population, and hence its liability to taxation and claims to representation in Congress and the electoral college) was similarly cold-blooded: each slave would be considered three-fifths of a person. John Rutledge of South Carolina and Connecticut's Roger Sherman led in working this out. Connecticut shut its eyes to South Carolina's slavery and slave trade, while South Carolina accepted Connecticut's claim to western lands.

The drafters were as far from the religious fanaticism of the Puritan revolution as they were from the taste for despotism of the Terror and Napoleon. No religious test was required for office holding. As reverse-named Luther Martin put it, few members of the convention were "*so unfashionable* as to [think] that a *belief in the existence of a Deity* and of a *state of future rewards and punishments* would be some security for the good conduct of our leaders." Delegate Ben Franklin, aged and subject to bouts of religiosity, wondered: "How has it happened . . . that we have not hitherto once thought of humbly applying to the Father of Light to illuminate our understandings?" He proposed that a clergyman lead the convention delegates in prayer each morning. Washington did not lend his support, and Hamilton warned that such a step might "lead the public to believe that the embarrassments and dissensions within the Convention, had suggested this measure." There was no vote, and Franklin's proposal died. (Hamilton, informed by a Princeton minister-professor that "we are greatly grieved that the Constitution has no recognition of God or the Christian religion," is supposed to have replied to this naïf: "I declare, we forgot it!")

The same hard-nosed practicality prevailed when it came to ratifying the Constitution. The men who saw it through the convention were not about to let it run aground on the requirement set by the previous Annapolis Convention that all thirteen states would have to ratify. Instead, they baldly stipulated that only nine need do so.

The Constitution's supporters then turned to instruments of suasion honed during the years devoted to defining, rationalizing, and securing independence. The promise of a set of amendments—a Bill of Rights—specifically securing the civil liberties of the citizenry did much to mollify those fearful of a stronger central government. The *Federalist* of Hamilton, Madison, and Jay powerfully expounded the sophisticated, self-confident republicanism that Americans had been crafting for decades past. When more material political pressure was needed in the key ratification battles in Virginia and New York, the Constitution's supporters came up with that as well.

The Anti-Federalists, like the Tories before them, were numerous. The popular vote for members of the ratifying conventions—about 160,000, one twenty-fifth of the population—was close in several of the important states. The triumph of the Constitution came in part from the greater social sophistication of the Federalists. One study found that the pro- and anti-Constitution alignment in Pennsylvania could not be explained by differences of religion, native- versus foreign-born, class, education, city versus countryside, or region of the state. The strongest predictor was whether the voter had served in the Continental Army (which fought out of as well as within the state) or in the state militia (which fought in Pennsylvania alone). Those more traveled had a larger sense of the country and tended to support a stronger national government. It came down to a difference between cosmopolitans and locals.

There was another notable difference between the Federalist and Anti-Federalist leaders, and that was generational. Anti-Federalists Patrick Henry and Sam Adams were deeply involved in the movement for revolution and independence. Some opponents of the Constitution called themselves "Old Patriots of '75" or "Men of 1776." Declaration of Independence drafters Jefferson and Adams were lukewarm about the new charter of government, expressing strong reservations from opposite ends of the weak-government/strong-government spectrum.

The Constitution makers were generally younger men whose careers began with and after the Revolution, not before it—Hamilton and Madison most noticeably. They were more responsive to the needs of the new nation. They pulled along with them opportunists such as John Hancock of Massachusetts and Edmund Randolph of Virginia, who might have been expected to oppose the new Constitution. There were other unlikely sources of support. The Shaysites of western Massachusetts, against whom the Constitution was in part initiated, came to favor the implicit shift in taxation from land to commerce when the federal government assumed the debt of the states. And workers and artisans in the seaport towns—the supposed "radicals" of the Revolutionary era—welcomed a stronger government that might protect American trade from foreign competitors. The pro-Constitution vote in Philadelphia was 1,198 to 20.

As in the case of independence, and in fighting the Revolutionary War, a broad and diverse coalition had come together. But it was bound by the issue of the moment, not by any longer-range commitments or organization. This was, in short, the factional politics of colonial America transposed into the era of independence and revolution and now applied to Constitution making. The triumphant Federalist coalition, like the triumphant coalition for independence, expected to run the new national government as it had the Continental and Confederation Congresses.

But the ground rules of a new American government and the remorseless pressures of a rapidly changing American society would erode the underpinnings of both colonial deference and the Founders' republicanism.

CHAPTER THREE

FROM FACTIONS
TO PARTIES

A MERICAN PUBLIC LIFE from the 1770s to the 1820s was swept by changes of unprecedented scale and intensity. The colonial regime evolved from its Old World, deferential origins into the early Republic, and then into the beginnings of the party-democratic regime that would define public affairs for a century to come.

MAKING THE NEW REPUBLIC

Committing to and securing independence was the first stage of this process. Then followed the struggle to define the lineaments of the new nation, culminating in the Constitution. Next came the business of making the Republic a viable state. On February 4, 1789, the electoral college unanimously chose George Washington to be the nation's first chief executive. A month later the newly elected members of Congress began to meet in New York, and on April 30 Washington was inaugurated.

Many of those most directly engaged in the task of government making belonged to a political generation whose careers began with rather than culminated in the struggle for independence. By 1788, fourteen of the signers of the Declaration were dead, and "smart young men" such as Madison and Hamilton shared the spotlight with senior figures Washington, Jefferson, and Adams.

Newcomers and old-timers alike had a profound sense that what they were doing was novel and important. But they still were very much in thrall to the assumptions of the American political past. The state elections that chose Congress attracted only a fraction of eligible voters, as so often was the case in colonial, revolutionary, and Confederation times. And just as the faction supporting independence dominated the Continental and Confederation Congresses, so now the faction responsible for the federal Constitution dominated the new government of the United States. Twenty-six of the thirty-nine signers of the Constitution were in the government; fifty-eight of the sixty-nine members of the First Congress had supported ratification. The most conspicuous Anti-Federalists—Patrick Henry, George Mason, Sam Adams—were in state, not national, politics.

Nothing was self-evident in those early days. What, for instance, was the standing of the vice president? Was his the second-in-command position that incumbent John Adams thought it to be? Or was he, as unfriendly colleagues put it, "His Superfluous Excellency"? And how did the pecking order of other offices fall out? Was it better to be a senator than a congressman? (Madison didn't think so.) DeWitt Clinton left the Senate in 1802 to be mayor of New York City, and John Jay gave up the chief justiceship of the Supreme Court to run for governor of New York.

The chief concern was over the character and standing of that novel creation the presidency. With Washington the incumbent, a special aura attached to the office. But was the ambiguous analogy of an elected king appropriate for the chief executive of a republic? The First Congress devoted an inordinate amount of time to the question of how to address him. Some of the non-starters: "His Most Benign Highness," "His Elective Highness," "His Highness, the President of the United States of America and Protector of the Rights of the Same." The House of Representatives (and Washington himself) would have none of this and settled instead on "the president of the United States" and "Mr. President."

The question of his role remained. Was he to be a republican version of England's prime minister? Washington appeared to have something like that in mind when he went to Congress on August 22, 1789, to seek its support for an Indian treaty. Gadfly senator William Maclay moved to refer the request to committee. An affronted Washington declared: "This defeats every purpose of my coming here." He stalked out, and thereafter he (and his successors, until Woodrow Wilson) stayed away.

Influenced in part by his wartime experience as head of the army, Washington saw his department heads as his cabinet: in effect, his staff. (Napoleon never convened his ministers as a cabinet.) But an autocratic disdain for the legislature was not part of his makeup. During the Revolution he constantly testified before committees of the Continental

Congress and endured repeated investigations. The chevalier de Chas-tellux, a general in the French forces aiding the Americans during the Revolution, said of him in 1782: "This is the seventh year that he has commanded the army and he has obeyed congress: more need not be said." The ultimate expression of Washington's self-restraint was his re-fusal to serve more than two terms. (James Monroe was among many who had feared that "once he is elected, he may be elected forever.")

Washington and his successors up to Andrew Jackson in 1828 saw them-selves as "presidents above party": embodiments of a republican model of governance, in which leadership was supposed to rise above faction, in-terest, or party to civic-minded service to the people and the nation. Alex-ander Hamilton favored the selection of the president by direct election: not because he was having a democratic episode, but because he thought that less "cabal, intrigue, and corruption" would attend the process.

Congress, like the presidency, was subject to both received tradition and the innovative consequences of the Constitution. At first it closely resembled its immediate predecessor, the Confederation Congress. It too had an elite membership: some 40 percent of the House and half of the Senate were men of high social standing, and half had at least some col-lege education. The Senate, like the Continental Congress, did its business in closed sessions. (It had no visitors' gallery.) The House had no party or-ganization or standing committees, few procedural rules, a merely cere-monial Speaker, and floor rules that treated all members equally. Like the Confederation Congress, it relied on ad hoc committees to draft bills, some two hundred of them in the First Congress. As of 1800 it still had only four standing committees.

But Congress turned out to be a far more successful institution than its pre-Constitution predecessors. Its ability to settle on a permanent site for the nation's capital and to pass most of Alexander Hamilton's fiscal program stood in stark contrast to the failure of the Confederation Con-gress to deal with such issues. The difference apparently lay in the new ground rules governing Congress. Members voted as individuals, not as state delegations, so diverse interests found readier expression. A simple majority rather than a supermajority was sufficient to pass important legislation. And there was no serious constraint (save the still-undefined check of judicial review) on the writ of Congress.

When it came to lawmaking, the lines distinguishing the executive and the legislative branches had still to be drawn. In 1789 Washington suggested that Congress might want to propose amendments to the Con-stitution, thus clearing the way for what became the Bill of Rights. The drafter of his message: James Madison, expert on the Constitution, fellow

Virginian, close adviser to the president. A formal reply from Congress seemed to be called for, much as Parliament responded to messages from the king. So one was duly drafted and dispatched to the president. Its author: House Ways and Means chairman James Madison. Washington concluded that he in turn had to respond, and called (of course) on Madison to prepare the draft. Thus (self-)authorized, Madison went on to cull some two hundred constitutional amendments proposed in the state ratifying conventions into a list of nineteen and, finally, the first ten amendments: the Bill of Rights. Never again would the Constitution be so sweepingly, and so easily, amended.

The new government spent its first years in temporary quarters in New York and Philadelphia, following an established migratory tradition. (The Continental, Confederation, and federal Congresses met in seventeen buildings scattered over eight towns between 1774 and 1800.) But a permanent new nation needed a permanent new capital. That this would be called Washington was a foregone conclusion. That it would also be a new, planned city was an act of hubris commensurate with the high ambitions of the Founders. A third of the roll call votes in the First Congress were on the question of just where the capital should be. The decision to place it on the banks of the Potomac was the outcome of one of the earliest political deals in the new nation.

For the plan of the new capital, Congress turned not to a home-grown talent such as Jefferson but to Pierre Charles L'Enfant, a French engineer who had served in the Continental Army and stayed on after the Revolution. Drawing heavily on the spectacularly inappropriate model of Louis XIV's Versailles, he came up with a Baroque scheme, dominated by 160-foot-wide avenues suitable for the carriages of aristocrats and large-scale military displays.

Planned capitals on a grand scale were rare. Fourth-century Constantinople and Peter the Great's eighteenth-century St. Petersburg were the leading examples. Like its predecessors, Washington would be built in large part by unfree labor: black slaves. But Americans were skilled at giving new meaning to old precedents. The capital had no military defenses; rather, it was open to the nation that stretched equidistantly to the north and south. Its design was a physical representation of the Constitution. Congress was on the highest point, renamed Capitol Hill in a gesture to the Roman Republic and its Capitoline Hill. Pennsylvania Avenue (named after the middle state) linked the Capitol to the executive mansion. In the initial conception, the Supreme Court was symbolically located halfway between the legislative and executive sites.

The city was expected to become the nation's great center of the arts and learning: Washington wished to see a national university established there. He hoped too that it would be the major departure point for the flow of people and commerce westward over the Appalachians. To understate, things didn't work out that way. But the capital envisioned by the Founders nicely reflected the mix of American republicanism and old-regime *étatisme* so evident in the Republic's early days.

Aside from its (failed) Confederation experience, the new government had English and colonial models to draw upon. Hamilton sought to turn his Treasury secretaryship into a clone of the chancellor of the Exchequer. The House leadership appears to have shared his view. When Hamilton was appointed to the Treasury, it abolished the Committee on Ways and Means and relied on him for policy guidance. When he left office, the committee was restored.

Hamilton used his ties to President Washington to get army procurement shifted to Treasury from the War Department, which was weakly led by Henry Knox. He sought as well to make his department a powerful political instrument: not, at first, for party building, but to bolster his personal ambitions. It helped that Treasury had more than five hundred employees (the bulk of them customs collectors), compared to the twelve civilians in the War Department and a staff of six in Jefferson's Department of State.

About two thousand federal officeholders were appointed between 1789 and 1801. They staffed the customs houses, the postal service, internal revenue, and the federal courts. The first appointees were supporters of the Federalist faction or followers of individual leaders. Customs collectors, surveyors, and tax collectors favored Federalist merchants and other men of property. Federalist postmasters delayed, read, or lost the opposition's correspondence and saw to it that Federalist newspapers moved smoothly through the mails and Republican ones did not. By the time of the presidency of John Adams in the late 1790s, even judicial appointments (most consequentially, that of John Marshall to be chief justice of the Supreme Court) had a strongly partisan cast.

Congress provided a bare-bones federal court system in its Judiciary Act of 1789. But the judiciary as the third (and, said Hamilton, least dangerous) branch of government was not yet a significant player. The legislature determined the structure and responsibilities of the federal courts, and the scope of judicial review still was uncertain.

State courts, descendants of a hoary colonial system, were more important. And as in the past, the day-to-day activities of lesser courts and the work of a well-established legal profession defined the law of the new nation. In the cases he argued as a private attorney, Hamilton did much to make American commercial and maritime insurance law more responsive to new interests.

But while there was talk after the Revolution of scrapping English common law, that was easier said than done. Almost two centuries of legal existence under the English system could not readily be ignored, however strong the impulse to do so.

Legal historians speak of this period as one in which an earlier communitarian law of consensus and "ethical unity" took on a more structured, formal approach, in order to foster economic development (or, in the current jargon, "acquisitiveness"). That was a transatlantic development, occurring both in the England of Justice Mansfield and in the early Republic. But the American version of the process had distinctly republican qualities. Judge-made or jury-driven, American law became more individualistic and egalitarian, less trammeled by the past.

A revealing expression of the tension between the English common-law tradition and its emerging American alternative was the 1805 New York case of *Pierson v. Post*. Post was chasing a fox over "wild and uninhabited, unpossessed and waste land." But he was deprived of his hard-earned kill when Pierson suddenly appeared, killed the fox, and carried it off. Pierson broke no law. On the face of it, the case was a simple property dispute: whose fox was it?

Two New York appellate justices, Daniel D. Tompkins, later vice president and governor of New York, and Henry Brockholst Livingston, who went to the Supreme Court in 1806, took opposing positions. Tompkins reversed the lower court and gave custody of the fox to Pierson, the interceder. He did so on the ground that property in a wild animal was acquired only by possession: in this case, ten-tenths of the law. On what basis did he so conclude? American precedents were few. And English common law didn't help. That country did not have much "unpossessed" land. And cases of this sort usually involved a clash between a hunter and a landowner or were covered by statute. So Tompkins turned to venerable texts: Justinian's *Institutes*, the works of Bracton and Pufendorf. He concluded from them that mere pursuit did not bestow a legal right. Actual acquisition was what counted. Although there were deficiencies in the case to be made for Pierson's claim to the fox, it was best to rely on ancient authorities "for the sake of certainty, and preserving peace and order in society." If Post could secure a property right to the fox merely by pursuing it, this "would prove a fertile source of quarrels and litigation."

Livingston, dissenting, would have none of this. The whole issue "should have been submitted to the *arbitration* of sportsmen, without poring over Justinian." Since "men themselves change with the times, why should not laws also undergo an alteration?" And as for the basis on which new law was to be made, how about social policy? A fox is a "wild and noxious beast," committing "depredations on farmers and barn yards." It would be a "public benefit" to be rid of this pest. So beneficial, indeed, was the destruction of foxes that anyone who interfered with this good work was a wrongdoer. So if "the pursuer is within reach, or has a reasonable [a word that would come to be pervasive in American legal thought] prospect . . . of taking what he has thus discovered with an intention of converting to his own use," the prize should be his. Tompkins's was the voice of English law past, Livingston's of American law to come.

NEW WAYS OF POLITICS

New ways of conducting politics also were necessary. The Constitution's election rules forced leaders reared in the episodic public life of the colonial-Revolutionary past to propose coherent policies of broad appeal and create forms of political organization that transcended ephemeral factions.

The Constitution made no provision for political parties. That was evident in the selection of the president by the Electoral College and the Senate by the state legislatures. Nevertheless, with breathtaking speed the colonial-Revolutionary political culture of intermittent factionalism changed into something new: a politics of what have been called "cadre parties," standing between the deferential-factional politics of the past and the more democratic party culture to come.

The Federalists and the Republicans (aka the Jeffersonian or Democratic-Republicans) were from-the-top-down political organizations. On the national level they responded to the new electoral dictates of the Constitution. On the state and local levels they retained some of the old colonial-deferential ways of doing politics—but ways rapidly changing to reflect the more democratic, participatory urges of the citizenry.

The Founders were hostile to the idea of parties. Madison spoke of parties and factions interchangeably, and disparagingly. John Adams feared nothing so much "as a division of the Republic into two great parties, each arranged under its leader and converting measures in opposition to each other." Nevertheless, the Founders quickly moved to partisan identification, one that saw the opposition not as a contender to be lived with but as a repository of social evil to be removed. Discussing parties in the fall of 1791, Madison charged the Federalists with promoting the inequality of wealth. Hamilton sharply responded. Jefferson by March 1792 was speaking of "we" and "they," and in June complained to Madison that Hamilton dared to call "the republican party a *faction.*"

This change was due in good part to the Constitution. By prescribing winner-take-all presidential elections, it created a new political necessity: coalitions sufficiently large to ensure a majority of presidential electoral votes. The need to make that coalition more permanent than the issue-defined factions of the past was fostered by a fixed, frequent schedule of elections: a new House and a third of the Senate every two years, a presidential choice every four years.

Public policy making at first rested firmly in the hands of the leaders of the victorious pro-Constitution faction. Madison and Jefferson, Hamilton and of course Washington, the leaders of that group, were the most conspicuous figures in the early government. Secretary of the Treasury Hamilton set out to impose his views of proper public policy. His program of 1790–91 was the economic/fiscal counterpart of Madison's Bill of Rights, addressing major concerns that needed tending to if the new government was to succeed. He proposed that the federal government assume the states' remaining Revolutionary War debts and refinance its foreign and domestic obligations. To further strengthen the new nation's fiscal solidity, he wanted a national bank to handle its income and outgo, new excise taxes (especially on whiskey), and (something of an afterthought) subsidies to encourage manufacturing. The British model was obvious: a chancellor of the Exchequer–like secretary of the Treasury (Hamilton), backed by a monarch-like president (Washington), prescribing policy to a more or less complaisant legislature (Congress).

Madison's Bill of Rights had not been very controversial. Protecting citizens from government oppression was basic American doctrine. But Hamilton's economic program made for losers as well as winners. He believed that it was essential to bolster investor confidence in the new nation, even if bond speculators and states that had not paid off their war debts were major beneficiaries. This set off a wave of protest.

So far, so familiar: a faction united on one large issue (the federal Constitution) divides over the next one (Hamilton's fiscal program). Such had been the case with American critics of British imperial policy when protest turned to independence, and when the Revolutionary coalition split into Federalists and Anti-Federalists in the battle over the Constitution.

Hamilton's program was enacted through a down-to-earth political deal not unlike the quotidian compromises of the Constitutional convention. At a legendary dinner in 1790, Jefferson, Madison, and Hamilton agreed on a site for the new capital on the banks of the Potomac in return for Madison seeing to it that Hamilton's program won congressional approval.

The calculus of interests was complex. Madison's Virginia had paid off its war debts, and the federal assumption of other states' obligations would cost $5 million. But Madison and Jefferson were concerned enough about the well-being of the new republic, and a southern locale for the capital, to accept this. An intersectional agreement was made easier by the fact that the states with the largest remaining Revolutionary War debts (and thus the chief beneficiaries of assumption) were (northern) Massachusetts and (southern) South Carolina.

Washington and the other Virginians had high hopes for the Potomac site. They expected that with a proper canal system, the Chesapeake Bay area would become the gateway to the West. After all, population growth and westward migration had been more of a southern phenomenon than a northern one. In 1760 the populations of New York and North Carolina were about the same; by 1780, North Carolina had sixty thousand more people. And southerners in Congress may have supported Hamilton's program with the understanding that the North would not challenge slavery.

The bargain struck by Jefferson, Madison, and Hamilton smacked more of diplomacy by sectional envoys than haggling by party politicians. And their relationship to George Washington was not unlike that of contesting factions around a monarch. There was an echo here as well of the Tory-court/Whig-country party politics of England. Jefferson and Madison initially referred to themselves interchangeably as Whigs or Republicans, and Jefferson thought that Whigs and Tories were better names for the "two political Sects" than Republicans and Federalists.

But the differences between the two polities were more significant. English elections were far less frequent than those required by the Constitution and by the states, the voter base considerably more restricted, the system of representation more thoroughly deferential. And the United States, in contrast with Britain, was (and would remain) a weak state. Congress initially outnumbered the bureaucracy. The nation's first census, in 1790, was primarily to count the population for purposes of representation. The first British census, in 1800, was to determine the number of men available for its military. The United States went through only four years of war between 1783 and 1815, compared to twenty-five years for Britain. It is true that an American-like popular British patriotism took hold during the Napoleonic period. But its glue was the preservation of the monarchy, fear of Bonaparte, and anti-Catholicism: hardly major American concerns.

Only about half the members of the First Congress identified with the Washington-Hamilton administration or with Jefferson and Madison. The other half was nonaligned. Large issues and compelling ideology were necessary to foster the broad, sustained coalitions required by the Constitution's political ground rules. And clear-cut ideological differences (at least in rhetoric) did indeed quickly distinguish Republicans from Federalists. Madison's "A Candid State of Parties" (1792) spoke of two political groups sharply split over the distribution of power between the federal government and the states. Jefferson argued: "[W]ere parties here merely divided by a greediness for office, as in England, to take a part with either would be unworthy of a reasonable or moral man, but where the principle of difference is as substantial and strongly pronounced as between the republicans and the Monocrats [Federalists] of our country, I hold it as honorable to take a firm and decided part." Reacting in 1818 to John Marshall's pro-Federalist history of the 1790s, Jefferson insisted that the politics of that time "were contests of principle between the advocates of republican and those of kingly government."

Foreign policy was at the center of this rhetorical differentiation. From the time of the Renaissance, statecraft and diplomacy were subtle arts, the province of professional diplomats and the grand men of the realm, with little reference to popular sentiment or domestic politics. But the coalition building required by the Constitution put a premium on issues most likely to draw together, motivate, and sustain the loyalty of the largest possible number of supporters. Foreign affairs ideally served that purpose. Jefferson observed to James Monroe: "The [Franco-British] war has kindled and brought forward the two parties with an ardor which our own interests merely could never excite."

Of course, a weak new nation had to be concerned about its survival in the midst of the geopolitical and military storms set off by the French Revolution. But how one felt about that Revolution had domestic ideological resonance as well. It served as a sounding board for those attracted by the French Revolution's call for regime and social change, and for those more inclined to stability and order. At the same time the relative remoteness of the events in Europe made it easier for like-thinking Americans to come together on one side or the other across class, religious, or sectional lines. When votes, and not only "influence," were at stake, and not in occasional local elections but recurrently and nationally, a larger ideological context was needed. This the foreign affairs issues of the 1790s provided.

The utility of foreign policy as a political unifier was underscored by the leadership's determination to avoid the potentially far more explosive domestic issue of slavery. Foreign policy allowed alliances across sections; slavery had the opposite effect. It is not as though the issue was ignored. From early 1790, Quaker delegations submitted petitions to the House to end the slave trade. The reaction of many southern congressmen was violent, and Madison squelched discussion. Then the Pennsylvania Abolition Society petitioned for an end to slavery itself. The ensuing debate was fierce. But there was neither support for a biracial society nor doubt that the institution in time would fade away. Hence the inevitable decision to sidestep the issue.

For Jefferson and his supporters (and indeed most Americans), the outbreak of the French Revolution was a gratifying expression of flattery by imitation. When Tom Paine's pro-revolutionary pamphlet *The Rights of Man* appeared in 1791, Jefferson declared: "I have no doubt our citizens will rally a second time to the standard of *Common Sense* [Paine's contribution to American independence]." But Federalists came to regard the Revolution, especially after the beheading of Louis XVI and the advent of the Terror, as a descent into anarchy and violence. John Adams argued for the superiority of the English to the new French mode of government. Hamilton, who initially welcomed the Revolution, soon predicted that it would result in military dictatorship. Caustically he spoke of Jefferson's having "*a womanish attachment to France and a womanish resentment against Great Britain.*"

Much of this was political rodomontade. When the chips were down, Adams was loath to go to war with France or ally with England. And Jefferson and Madison's admiration for the French Revolution diminished when it devolved into the Terror and then the tyranny of Napoleon. Substantial slaveholding planters, they had no more taste for revolution from below than arrivistes John Adams and Alexander Hamilton had for rule by hereditary monarchy or aristocracy.

What happened instead—not for the last time—was that a major foreign policy issue became a useful way of expressing deep domestic differences over ideology, culture, and governance. The debate went on in a language of implication. To be pro-English, to decry the French Revolution as godless and anarchic, was (indirectly) to give voice to one's fears over the stability and soundness of the American experiment. To glorify the Revolution, to condemn its critics as pro-British "Monocrats," was to appeal to a different set of beliefs as to the meaning of the revolutionary past, the challenges of the nation-building present, and the prospects for the future.

Politicized foreign-policy making came to a head in the 1794–95 clash over the Jay Treaty. British interference with American trade in the Caribbean and Europe, residual disputes over Revolutionary War claims, and conflicting interests in the Old Northwest fed a potentially dangerous dispute between the United States and Great Britain. Washington sent Supreme Court chief justice John Jay to negotiate a settlement. He came back in 1795 with a treaty widely viewed as favoring seaboard merchants (a core Federalist constituency) rather than planters and western farmers.

Above and beyond economic interests, the fight over the Jay Treaty gave voice to the ideological difference between Federalists and Republicans. Jay and his treaty were vilified in Congress and on the streets as a capitulation to Britain. Outspoken Abigail Adams dismissed the treaty's critics as "mindless Jacobins and party creatures." The dispute led to the first Republican caucus in the House of Representatives and substantially sharpened voting along party lines. By one measure, party cohesion in the House went from 58 percent in 1790 to 93 percent after the Jay Treaty dispute.

In the mid-1790s Hamilton and Jefferson resigned from Washington's cabinet to return to their home states, where they immersed themselves in firming up their political bases. Washington never again spoke to Jefferson, and he broke with his onetime close confidant James Madison. Back in May 1791, Jefferson and Madison had gone on a "botanical expedition" to New York, in the course of which they appear to have discussed a political coalition with anti-Hamilton politicians Robert Livingston, George Clinton, and Aaron Burr. Now Burr visited Jefferson in Monticello to cement a New York–Virginia alliance.

Alliance building in the 1790s went on for the most part from the top down. It was in the hands of leaders steeped in deferential political ways, seeking to attract an electorate still small, marginally engaged, with what they took to be a rudimentary political consciousness. But the 1790s also were years in which both leaders and the electorate were exploring the political implications of their new Republic. The Federalists and the Jeffersonian Republicans, and the populace they wooed, occupied a middle ground between the factional, deferential politics of the colonial past and the more democratic party politics of the future.

As we have seen, the very plan of the new capital of Washington, a building in the 1790s, spoke of the still-strong influence of Old World models of governance. It was evident as well in the temporary capital of New York. Balls and soirées, salons run by politically engaged women of means, politics as theater: these political folkways of the Old World's old regime were (however clumsily) echoed in the New. George Washington was inaugurated in a symbolically chosen suit of domestic broadcloth ("homespun")—but with gilt buttons and diamond shoe buckles that told a different social story. Pennsylvania's iconoclastic senator William Maclay detected "European folly" in Jefferson's aphorisms.

The very legitimacy of the Republic came under challenge in these early days. In 1793 Edmond Charles Genêt—"Citizen Genêt"—came to America as an emissary of the Girondin-led French government. He proceeded to commission privateers and called for a Franco-American pact "to promote the extension of the Empire of Liberty." Inevitably Genêt's doings became a party issue. Republicans defended him and Federalists attacked him, and a popular demand rose for his recall. By that time the Jacobins were in power and wanted his head. Genêt escaped extradition and settled in America, marrying the daughter of New York Republican leader George Clinton: not the last *enragé* to elide into a *distingué* lifestyle.

Other ambitious, politically frustrated men—Revolutionary War soldiers George Rogers Clark of Vermont and James Wilkinson of Kentucky, Aaron Burr of New York (an "embryo-Caesar," thought Hamilton, which was how Jefferson, Madison, and Adams regarded *him*)—entered into shadowy conspiracies to detach parts of Louisiana or Florida from Spanish dominion, or parts of the trans-Appalachian West from American control. Federalists opposed to the War of 1812 later toyed with secession at the Hartford Convention.

The duel—an essential component of the fabric of honor and social gradation that defined the Old Regime—was part of the political culture of the republican regime. The paradigmatic encounter was the Burr-Hamilton duel of 1804. The two men had much in common: Burr could readily have subscribed to Hamilton's insight that "[e]very day proves to me more and more that this [American] world was not made for me." But for all its formalistic observance of the Code Duello, their encounter deviated from the Old World model. Duels in Europe were usually reserved for those of equal (and high) social standing. But while Burr was about as well-born as an American of the time could be—his grandfather was the distinguished theologian-philosopher Jonathan Edwards, his father was president of Princeton—Hamilton was an illegitimate immigrant from the West Indies. The interweaving of politics and honor that led to the duel may have been European in principle but was American in practice.

These artifacts of a past political culture co-existed with increasing signs that something new was taking form. The need to woo the largest possible body of supporters put pressure on old-regime ways. Hamilton used the Treasury to secure adherents very much in the style of Georgian England, but he also had to seek broader popular support at election time. Jefferson and congressional leaders such as Madison and Albert Gallatin of Pennsylvania assiduously cultivated sympathizers wherever they could find them.

Sectional sentiment was an important source of popular support. The makings were there: in the 1791 congressional vote on Hamilton's Bank of the United States, thirty-six of the thirty-nine in favor came from the North, nineteen of the twenty against came from the South. The division over the Constitution also fed into a developing party alignment. Most Anti-Federalists supported (and indeed helped to shape) Jeffersonian Republicanism. Most supporters of the Constitution became Federalists.

But the new order of things made it necessary to reach beyond state, sectional, and old-issue lines. The result made the factional politics of the past seem like simplicity itself. Republicans appealed to Scotch-Irish Presbyterians, Federalists to Quakers and Anglicans. Merchants in New-castle, Delaware, inclined to Republicanism in part because of their Presbyterian religious beliefs. Delaware planters inclined to Federalism in part because of their Episcopalianism, South Carolina planters in part because of their links to mercantile Charleston.

Subtle issues of timing and political situation could determine party identity. Patrick Henry and a few other Virginia Anti-Federalists supported the Federalist party because of their opposition to the regnant Virginia Republican dynasty of Jefferson, Madison, and Monroe. Up-and-coming young Virginian John Marshall also found in the Federalists a more promising political base than the dominant Jeffersonian Republicans, as well as a more sympathetic home for his nationalistic beliefs.

The need to mobilize a complex set of voters and keep them in line through a succession of elections spurred political innovation. Newspapers dedicated to the political view of their patrons were part of the eighteenth-century Anglo-American political world, and pamphlets and broadsides were important instruments in the struggles for independence and the Constitution. Now these devices were turned to the business of coalition building. John Fenno's *Gazette of the United States*, with financial help from Hamilton in the form of Treasury printing contracts, set out in 1789 "to endear the General Government to the people." Two years later Jefferson countered with Philip Freneau's *National Gazette*. These papers soon spoke for the burgeoning parties, not just for the leaders.

Political scandal sheets full of vitriolic comment were hardly unknown in Georgian England. But in America the goal was not so much to score points among political elites as to win over a larger world of political opinion. Benjamin Franklin Bache (the great man's grandson) and English émigré radical William Duane made their *American Aurora* a particularly virulent Republican organ. Its Federalist rival was William Cobbett's *Porcupine's Gazette,* its editor another English emigré, anti-French and, like Duane, finding in the new American politics a ready market for the rich English tradition of scurrilous journalism.

The Post Office Act of 1792 spurred (and was in part the product of) the rise of partisan politics. It subsidized low-cost news-paper delivery through the federal mail system, sped the expansion of that system to more localities, and protected the contents of the mails from surveillance by public officials. The hundred or so American newspapers in the early 1790s increased to about two hundred by 1800: more per capita than anywhere else in the world, almost all of them committed to one or the other of the political parties.

Parades, fêtes, songs, and dinners reinforced the parties as consequential institutions in the new Republic. Political clubs, gathering places for like-minded partisans, became important players in the ongoing Federalist-Republican contest. The most conspicuous were the thirty-five or so Democratic-Republican Clubs (modeled on France's Jacobin Clubs) that sprang up in seaboard towns during the mid-1790s, supporting the French Revolution and mobilizing voters. The Society of Tammany, a product of the patriotic fervor accompanying the Revolution, at first was not overtly partisan. But over the course of the 1790s it became part of the Jeffersonian Republican infrastructure.

A Federalist counterpart was the Society of the Cincinnati, from which Washington thought it politic to resign because of its membership requirement of longtime American ancestry. Washington Benevolent Societies perpetuated the cult of the Father of His Country, complete with elaborate celebrations of his birthday and renditions of "God Save Great Washington," an Americanized version of "God Save the King." Associations of this sort were far less prevalent in England, where they were discredited by their role in London's destructive anti-Catholic Gordon Riots of 1780.

The demands of the new politics nurtured a new breed: the professional politician. John Beckley, clerk of the House from 1787 to 1797, was a conspicuous example. His position as Jefferson's and Madison's man enabled him to act as a go-between, serving the Republican party leadership in key states. He helped bring New York, Pennsylvania, and

Virginia Republicans together, and later developed an ahead-of-its-time Pennsylvania Republican organization. That this was not yet quite the age of the classic American party pol is suggested by Beckley's background. He had gone to Eton and was a member of Phi Beta Kappa. His patronage payoff when Jefferson came to power in 1801: being named librarian of Congress.

Another recognizable American political type now emerged: the ideologue impatient with the compromises imposed by the culture of party politics. Virginians John Taylor and John Randolph advocated a pure states'-rights, small-government republicanism. In "A Definition of Parties" (1794), Taylor claimed that the Republicans deserved "rather the appellation of a 'band of patriots' than the epithet of 'a party.'" He and Randolph would be deeply disillusioned by the compromises that Jefferson and other party leaders found it necessary to make. George Logan, a Pennsylvania Quaker and "celebrated fanatic" who ardently supported the French Revolution, was another example. He went to France as a self-designated emissary to restore good relations between the two countries. The Logan Act of 1799, enacted to prevent such diplomatic entrepreneurship, is a monument of sorts to him.

The evolution of party politics was determined by the timetable of congressional and presidential elections and by the unfolding drama of the French Revolution, the rise of Napoleon, and the Franco-British contest for supremacy in Europe and the Atlantic world. Grand domestic and foreign policy issues gave the political battle ongoing social importance. Elections spurred the mobilization of supporters and were a recurring measure of failure and success.

Even the dreaded scourge of yellow fever was fodder for party identification. The Philadelphia epidemic of 1793 killed an estimated five thousand people and crippled the work of the government, then quartered there. Federalists labeled the epidemic a French import and called for quarantining Frenchmen resident in the city and banning trade with the French West Indies. Republicans held that it was of domestic origin, a consequence of the large cities that Jefferson so disliked. The parties differed over how to treat the disease. The Federalists plumped for the (ineffective) ingestion of bark and wine, while the Republicans (in particular, Dr. Benjamin Rush) favored (ineffective) heavy bleeding. Finally, a political compromise of sorts was reached: a mix of quarantine and sanitary reform.

Washington's Farewell Address of September 1796 warned his countrymen "in the most solemn manner against the baleful effects of the spirit of party." But while this was heartfelt, it also served Federalist needs in the upcoming 1796 presidential election. Federalist eminences Alexander Hamilton and John Jay drafted it, and Hamilton counseled Washington to delay publication until September for maximum political effect.

With Washington not in the running in 1796, the electoral vote splintered: primarily, but not yet overwhelmingly, on party lines. Vice President John Adams got seventy-one electoral votes. His chief opponent, Jefferson, got sixty-eight (none of them north of Pennsylvania), which made him Adams's vice president. Thomas Pinckney, Adams's running mate, received only fifty-nine votes, Jefferson's fellow Republican Aaron Burr only thirty. Anti-Federalist Sam Adams won twelve votes. Eight other contenders got one to eleven votes each. For all the newspaper pyrotechnics and party organizing in the campaign, voting generally was low. In Pennsylvania, where organized politicking was most advanced, only a quarter of qualified voters participated, substantially less than the average level for the state's gubernatorial contests.

While the parties' ability to attract voters grew slowly, their capacity to take on a widening range of issues was another story. Foreign policy, as we have seen, helped define the party creeds. So too did issues of social order and disorder. "Rebellions"—armed uprisings spurred by specific grievances—had been part of the American scene since the late seventeenth century. Now they fueled party conflict.

The Whiskey Rebellion of 1794 tested the new government as Shays's Rebellion had challenged the Confederation in 1786. More than seven thousand western Pennsylvania farmers engaged (with varying degrees of commitment) in armed resistance to a federal excise tax on whiskey, a major product of the region. Washington and Hamilton (who at times displayed Napoleonic aspirations) called on the states to supply a force of twelve thousand—larger than Washington's revolutionary army—to suppress the revolt.

This was a scenario uncomfortably similar to the one played out between tax-defying colonists and British enforcers in the years leading up to the Revolution. But now the threat of rebellion arose in a different political milieu. Local and state Republican leaders stirred up popular support for the whiskey rebels. The state government was reluctant to employ its militia, and Attorney General Edmund Randolph and others persuaded Washington to delay the use of force.

Only when federal negotiation failed and rumors spread that the rebels were dealing with the British did the government move. But political considerations dictated a moderate response after the revolt collapsed. All but two of the participants were acquitted, and President John Adams soon pardoned them. That did not prevent a lasting Jeffersonian Republicanism in western Pennsylvania from becoming part of the Whiskey Rebellion's legacy.

Another unsettling parallel with pre-Revolution British imperial policy was a clutch of new taxes to pay for the expansion of the armed forces. These included (of all unfortunate things) a stamp tax on documents, as well as a property tax based in part on the amount of window glass, a measure of wealth in those days. Prosperous Pennsylvania Dutch farmers were hard hit. The result was another armed resistance, Fries's Rebellion (1799), and a by-now-familiar sequence. Government troops crushed the rebels, and court proceedings led to some thirty indictments for treason. Although John Adams pardoned the leaders, Republican voting increased in the area.

The war between revolutionary France and England and her Continental allies dominated American political life in the late 1790s. The Federalists responded by passing the Alien and Sedition Acts in 1798, which sought to repress, not just counter, political opposition. The acts provided for the deportation of hostile aliens (but was never applied). They hit at anti-British (and hence pro-French) Irish immigrants flocking to America, vote fodder for the Republicans, by expanding the residency requirement for citizenship from five to fourteen years. And they gave (primarily Federalist) federal judges the power to fine and imprison critics of the government. These laws echoed English policy: a British Sedition Act had been passed in 1795, and in 1798 the Pitt government suspended the writ of habeas corpus and cracked down on radical political clubs.

President John Adams was reluctant to agree to the acts, and his intraparty rival Hamilton also criticized them: "We must not establish a tyranny." But many found it easy to equate criticism of the party in power with an attack on the government itself. Adams's wife, Abigail, hoped that the Alien Act might make it possible to remove the Swiss-born Albert Gallatin as leader of the Republicans in the House, and she encouraged her husband to sign the bills. Eighteen indictments were brought against Republican newspaper editors under the Sedition Act, and three of them were convicted. Congressman Matthew Lyon of Vermont briefly went to jail. But as in the case of the Whiskey Rebellion, there was a partisan backlash. Irish citizens in New York and Germans in Pennsylvania became more tightly bound to the Republicans.

The Jeffersonian Republican response to the Alien and Sedition Acts also revealed an unclear sense of the limits of the new political game.

The Kentucky and Virginia Resolutions of 1798, drafted respectively by Madison and Jefferson, raised the specter of unlimited state autonomy. Jefferson in particular was ready to claim the right of a state to nullify a federal law, and even the right of secession. But the Kentucky and Virginia legislatures, more responsive to the pressures for compromise inherent in a two-party system, drew back from a flat endorsement of the right of nullification.

The election of 1800, a dozen years after the creation of the Republic, came at a time when the nation's survival and character still were very much at issue. Jefferson, whose capacity for exaggeration was not the least of his talents, called the election "a revolution—as real a revolution in the principles of our government as that of 1776 was in form." During the campaign he said his party's goal was "to sink federalism into an abyss from which there shall be no resurrection of it." The Federalists saw their defeat in comparably dramatic terms: one spoke of "blood and ashes" descending over the land.

What Jefferson grandly called "the revolution of 1800" was in fact a way station in the transition from the deferential-republican regime of eighteenth-century America to the party-democratic regime of the nineteenth century. This was still an elite-run politics, replete with constraints on the popular will. Sectionally balanced tickets of notables faced each other: incumbent President John Adams of Massachusetts and Charles Cotesworth Pinckney of South Carolina for the Federalists, Thomas Jefferson of Virginia and Aaron Burr of New York for the Republicans. In eight states, including the major ones of Massachusetts, New York, and Pennsylvania, the legislatures still chose the presidential electors. In the five commonwealths with popular balloting, a little over a third of eligible voters participated: higher than the pro forma reelection of Washington in 1796, but not up to the turnout for state offices.

The selection of legislators, electors, and congressmen ran from October to December, often depending on local issues. When the smoke finally cleared, Jefferson and Burr had seventy-three electoral votes (fifty-three of them from the South and West) as against sixty-five for Adams (including all thirty-nine from New England), sixty-four for Pinckney, and a single throwaway for John Jay. The size of the southern electoral vote was bolstered by the rule that counted black slaves as three-fifths of a person: hardly a triumph of democracy.

Republican electors voted evenly for Jefferson and Burr, and the election went to the House, each state delegation having one vote. This gave the Federalists the decisive role in deciding which Republican—

Jefferson or Burr—would be president. What followed was a classic eighteenth-century minuet of polite disclaimers of ambition by the contestants, coupled with furious backstage maneuvering. Republican leaders in Virginia and Pennsylvania considered raising troops and marching on the capital to ensure Jefferson's assumption of office.

After thirty-five ballots, Jefferson won: in part because of his stature, manifestly greater than Burr's, and in part because he skillfully secured the decisive vote of Federalist James Bayard of Delaware. Hamilton strongly preferred Jefferson to Burr, his longtime enemy in New York politics: "Mr. Jefferson, though too revolutionary in his notions, is yet a lover of liberty and will be desirous of something like orderly government. Mr. Burr loves nothing but himself. . . . Jefferson in my view is less dangerous than Burr."

The dénouement showed how tenacious was the hold of the deferential-republican political culture. But it also revealed the need to adapt the Constitution to the new reality of party politics. The Twelfth Amendment of 1804 eliminated the danger of two candidates getting the same number of electoral votes for president by requiring separate balloting for president and vice president. It thus recognized the fact that candidates now ran not as independent notables but on party tickets.

Historically speaking, the significance of the election of 1800 lay in the fact that it turned out to be a peaceful transition of power from one party to another. The contrast with Napoleon's ongoing usurpation in post-revolutionary France, culminating in his (self-)coronation as emperor in 1804, could not have been greater. But it was hardly the ideological revolution that Jefferson proclaimed. Continuities of policy and practice were more evident than major change. Cozying up to Napoleon's France was not on Jefferson's dance card, and the Republicans were no less a cadre party than the Federalists.

Jefferson appears to have thought that once a major decision had been made—as in the case of independence, or the Constitution, or the election of 1800—party contention was no longer an option. The Federalists were destined for the political oblivion to which the Tories and Anti-Federalists had been relegated. As he put it, "The Republicans are the *nation*." Yet he famously announced in his inaugural: "We are all Republicans; we are all Federalists." Republican politicos around the country wanted to know just what he meant by that when it came to the distribution of patronage. Jefferson hurriedly explained that Republicans were entitled to their "just share" reflecting their strength in the country at large—a share that he estimated at two-thirds to three-quarters of the electorate.

He made much of his intention to dismantle the federal bureaucracy erected by the Federalists, and instituted a register of federal employees so that the public would know their number and names. But the 127 top offices when he became president in 1801 had been reduced to the not dramatically lower figure of 123 by the time he left in 1809. The repeal of the 1801 Federal Judiciary Act opened the door to the appointment of a number of Republican judges, United States attorneys, and internal revenue and custom officials. The Federalist power structure was badly weakened, that of the Republicans largely strengthened. This was not surprising, given the pressure for jobs: some ten thousand applicants for about three hundred positions.

The Republicans lifted succession in a deferential politics to a high art with their quarter- century-long Virginia dynasty. Jefferson (1801–9) was followed by James Madison (1809–17) and James Monroe (1817–25). They tried to crush the political opposition (as did the Federalists before them). Government deposits were shifted from the Federalist-dominated Bank of the United States to Republican-dominated state banks. The Alien and Sedition Acts were quickly repealed, but the administration brought seditious-libel proceedings against Federalist newspapers in New York and elsewhere. And it tried unsuccessfully to impeach Supreme Court justice Samuel Chase for his overenthusiastic enforcement of the Alien and Sedition Acts. If that had succeeded, Chief Justice John Marshall would have been the next target.

Nor was Jefferson loath to exercise executive power vigorously when he thought it necessary. The prospect of purchasing the Louisiana Territory from France arose in 1804. He indulged in predictable agonizing over the constitutionality of the purchase, but finally—predictably—decided that neither a constitutional amendment nor the prior approval of Congress was necessary. He sent Lewis and Clark to explore the new territory to the Pacific, and regarded the removal of blacks and Indians to the territories in the West as the most desirable way to deal with American race relations.

Jefferson's response to American expansion westward trumped his Atlanticist past. In his inaugural he spoke sweepingly of "a chosen country, with room for our descendants to the hundredth and thousandth generation . . . it is impossible not to look forward to distant times, when our rapid multiplication will expand itself beyond those limits and cover the whole northern, if not the southern continent with a people speaking the same language, governed in similar forms and by similar laws." He told Madison in 1809: "[W]e should have such an empire for liberty as [the world] has never surveyed since the creation."

While there was always a substantial gulf between the idealistic republican language of the Founders and their political practices, no one raised that disjunction to so high a level as did Jefferson. His most eloquent defense of freedom of the press came when he was not in office, his sharpest condemnation ("It is a melancholy truth, that a suppression of the press could not more completely deprive the nation of its benefits, than is done by abandoned prostitution to falsehood. Nothing can now be believed which is seen in a newspaper") when he was in office. Not until Woodrow Wilson—of whom French premier Clemenceau said that he talked like Jesus Christ and acted like Lloyd George—would American politics see his like.

Small-government Republican rhetoric and strong-government behavior continued after Jefferson left office. Secretary of the Treasury Albert Gallatin prominently opposed Hamilton's dirigiste economic policies. But in 1810 he proposed a Hamiltonian ten-year plan that included a transportation network of canals and highways, to be built by the federal government, and subsidies for manufacturers. The Republican Congress allowed the Federalist-dominated Bank of the United States to lapse when its charter expired in 1811—and then in 1816 created a Republican-dominated Second Bank. For good measure it endorsed federal support of internal improvements and tariff protection for new industries.

These inconsistencies alienated more ideologically committed Republicans. Virginians John Randolph and John Taylor regarded Jefferson and his successors as traitors to the cause of pure Republicanism. Randolph and a small band of like-thinking Republicans called themselves the Tertium Quids (third somethings): revealing in its very eighteenth-century Latin label and in its sense of alienation from the emerging two-party political culture.

The War of 1812 was a significant benchmark in the development of that culture. As attacks on American shipping by England and France grew, Jefferson responded with an embargo on imports from those countries and on American exports everywhere. He equated opposition to the embargo with treason, and used the army and navy to enforce it. This had predictably disastrous economic results, especially in Federalist New England. But it responded to a growing strand of American opinion that defined itself in terms of a self-sufficient, westward-looking future rather than its relations with the Old World.

Jefferson's successor Madison followed a similar path. He backed American settlers who took control of West Florida from Spain in 1810. And he went along with the sentiment that the impressment of American seamen and the seizure of American ships, especially by England, were "trampling on rights which no independent nation can relinquish."

In June 1812, Madison asked for a declaration of war against England. Congress complied—and came close to declaring war on France as well. The rationale for war was British assaults on American's Atlantic shipping. But congressmen from the areas most directly affected—New England, New York, New Jersey—voted against the war declaration. Once again, a new force in American politics relied on familiar language to justify fresh aspirations.

That new force was a generation of younger politicos, as distinctive and cohesive in their views as the founding generation they were beginning to displace. Born in the late 1770s and 1780s, they came into public life as inheritors rather than creators of the American Republic. Seventy new members—almost half the House—entered with the Twelfth Congress in 1810. Conspicuous among the new breed were westerners Henry Clay and Richard Johnson of Kentucky and Felix Grundy of Tennessee, South Carolina planter spokesmen John C. Calhoun and William Lowndes, and Peter Porter from western New York.

Contemptuously labeled "War Hawks" by old-style Republican John Randolph, they took control of the House (Clay became Speaker on his first day in Congress) and called for war with England. Theirs was a new American nationalism, defined more by the defense of national honor ("war or submission") and the attractions of expansion ("on to Canada!") than by the Atlanticist interests of the planters and merchants who had dominated American politics before then. Calhoun declared that the war marked "the commencement of a new era in our politics" and would "prove . . . to the world, that we have not only inherited that liberty which our Fathers gave us, but also the will and power to maintain it."

The war went badly: a failed invasion of Canada, the British occupation and burning of Washington, victory at New Orleans only after a peace treaty had been signed. Nevertheless, it gave a powerful boost to a bumptious, democratic American nationalism. In one formulation, the eighteenth-century republican ideal of civic virtue morphed into unchecked self-interest, the sturdy yeoman into the self-made man. The war produced in Andrew Jackson a popular hero who embodied these traits and the coming democratic-party regime, much as Washington did the deferential-republican regime now drawing to an end.

Why did the Federalists fail to adapt to a changing American political world? After all, the Jeffersonians also were an elite-run party. And the Federalists matched their opponents in party organization and campaign technique. Election turnouts of eligible white males reached impressive levels in the early 1800s, products of a vigorous two-party politics: 70 percent in Pennsylvania in 1808, 68 percent in Massachusetts in 1812, 81 percent in New Hampshire in 1814.

The Federalists had a well-developed network of country, town, ward, and school district committees. Like the Republicans, they used office-holder caucuses to choose candidates and employed committees of correspondence, newspapers, celebrations, parades, and symbols to rally the faithful. New York Federalist Philip Schuyler wrote to William Cooper (novelist James Fenimore Cooper's father) of Cooper's upstate New York campaign in 1792: "Reports say, that you was very civil to the young and handsome of the [female] sex, that you flattered the old and ugly, and even embraced the toothless and decrepit, in order to obtain votes—when will you write a treatise on electioneering?" A Republican stalwart told Jefferson of how the Federalists handled a key legislative election in Charleston: "Hundreds more voted than paid taxes—the lame, crippled, diseased and blind were either led, lifted or brought in carriages to the poll." The Federalist Washington Benevolent Societies matched anything the Republicans had. Five thousand people crowded into Washington Hall, built by the Philadelphia branch, at its 1816 dedication: the largest indoor crowd in America to that time.

But the core ideology of the Federalists—mercantile, Atlantic-oriented, still in thrall to deferential colonial and British political beliefs—crippled their ability to compete successfully in the rapidly changing American world of the early nineteenth century. They were less able than their Republican opponents to appeal to new immigrants or to the growing proportion of Americans who lived in or turned their faces toward the West. Too many of their leaders were like Oliver Wolcott, who headed the Connecticut Federalists: "That he never stooped to court the suffrage of any man is a beauty not a blemish of his character. He blushed at the thought of being a man of the people." The Federalist *New York Daily Advertiser* asked how Republican Aaron Burr could "stoop so low as to visit every corner in search of voters" during the 1800 campaign.

A potential political harvest for the party arose when the Old Northwest, heavily peopled by emigrants from Federalist New England, began to be organized into states. But the Federalists, closely tied to eastern mercantile interests, did not support the rush to statehood. By the early 1800s, western New York and Ohio were turning Republican. Federalist opposition to the War of 1812 was the final blow. Every vote for war in the House and Senate was Republican. Every Federalist (by now down to forty), along with twenty-two of the more traditional Republicans, voted against. This decisively ended the party's ability to oppose the Republicans on anything like equal terms.

But Republican leaders Jefferson, Madison, and Monroe were no less steeped in the political culture of the eighteenth century. By the 1820s the Republican party of the Virginia Dynasty was almost as outmoded as the Federalists. The Era of Good Feelings, after the War of 1812, in fact saw the demise of Jeffersonian Republicanism as well as the Federalists.

It was in keeping with the theatrical nature of American politics in an age of independence, revolution, Constitution making, and creating a new republic that the end of the deferential-republican regime should be marked by an event of high symbolic content. That was the near-simultaneous passing of eighty-three-year-old Thomas Jefferson and ninety-one-year-old John Adams on July 4, 1826, the fiftieth anniversary of independence. They had resumed contact (through correspondence) after an eight-year alienation, a product of the politics of the early Republic. At the end they had a shared sense of remove from a political culture that was changing at bewildering speed from the world in which they had come of age.

PART TWO

THE PARTY-DEMOCRATIC REGIME: THE DEMOCRATIC POLITY

The torrents of change that swept over America from the 1770s to the 1830s created a new regime, party-dominated in form, democratic in culture. This regime persisted in "deeply embedded permanence" for a century, in the face of the Civil War, the rise of the world's largest industrial economy, and profound transformations of American society and culture. The most significant fact about American public life from the 1830s to the 1930s was the continuity, in form and content, of its party politics, its government, and its legal system.

The Democrats and Whigs of the 1830s and the 1840s had more in common with each other than they had with the Jeffersonian Republicans and Federalists from which they claimed descent. No less pronounced was the degree to which American government and law in the new regime differed from its predecessors. The all-but-simultaneous appearance of a more democratic politics, a more diverse and inclusive public policy, and a more responsive and innovative legal system supports the view that what happened in the early nineteenth century was not merely a shift from a Federalist-Jeffersonian party system to a Jacksonian-Whig one but something more profound: a regime change in American public life.

It is appropriate to ask just how democratic this new regime was. After all, "universal suffrage" excluded women, Native Americans, and almost all African Americans. Elites were overrepresented in officeholding and policy making. Third parties and other forms of dissent made it clear that the hegemony of the two major parties was constantly contested.

But these modify rather than deny the proposition that American public life was party-dominated in practice and democratic in spirit. National parties were the inevitable consequence of the Constitution's electoral ground rules. But their evolution into mass democratic institutions reflected the values and mores of a new American society. The parties were (generally) effective outlets for the fears and desires of an ever more heterogeneous culture. They (generally) tempered, at the same time as they gave voice to, the divisive tendencies of American individualism, localism, sectionalism, economic interests, and ethno-cultural diversity. And they effectively served the interests of politicians seeking to maximize their place in the political system.

For all its utility, the party-democratic regime faltered on three major counts. The first was that massive failure of politics and governance, the Civil War. The second was its inability to deal equitably with the problem of race. The third was the inadequacy of its response to the regulatory and social welfare challenges posed by industrialization.

The new polity had its origins in the context of the international crises that dominated public life from the 1760s to 1815. Then other large concerns—the growth of the American economy, the development of the American West—took center stage. The turn away from relations with the Old World to the American future at home—from the Atlantic and the East to an internal American "empire" (a term used by, among others, Washington, Hamilton, Jefferson, and Madison)—would have profound policy consequences.

The growth of market capitalism (in fact an evolutionary process with deep roots in the colonial past) was a conspicuous factor in American public life after 1815. Some of the most consequential technological innovations to that time—the cotton gin, the steamboat, the railroad, the telegraph, the reaper, the sewing machine—came with a rush, heightening the impact of an expanding American agriculture, industry, and commerce. So too did new forms of economic organization—corporations, factories, plantations—and new or expanded forms of labor: factory hands in place of artisans, slaves instead of indentured servants.

But there was no simple cause-and-effect relationship between this economic transformation and the evolution of the polity. To ascribe Jacksonian democracy and southern pro-slavery politics to a market-capitalism-driven polity is more than a reach: it is a stretch. Nineteenth-century American politics, government, and law emerged from far more than changing economic realities. They dealt with a range of social concerns as diverse as American life itself. And they reflected the need of politicians, civil servants, and lawyers to adapt to a changing polity as much as to the wants of interest groups.

Major economic interests—slavery, land and agriculture, commerce and industry—of course sought, and secured, political representation. But so too did sectional, religious, ethnocultural, and even family-based interests, values, and beliefs. Intertwined with geopolitical and material change was a sweeping transformation of society and culture: in particular, the rise of a popular American nationalism. Albert Gallatin optimistically observed after 1815: "The people have now more general objects of attachment with which their pride and political opinions are connected. They are more American; they feel and act more like a nation."

This new American nationalism had European counterparts. Popular identification with the nation rose as well in England, fed by loyalty to the monarchy, anti-Catholicism, and hostility to Napoleonic France. Spurred by the Revolution and Napoleon's empire, the French also experienced a rise in their sense of a national self. Similar stirrings could be seen in the Low Countries and in what would come to be Germany and Italy.

But in sharp contrast to the United States, post-1815 European states perpetuated the monarchical and aristocratic forms of the old regime. The failure of the abortive revolutions of 1830 and 1848 blocked the spread of democracy on the Continent. No major European country was a republic until France in 1871. Vienna workingmen demonstrated in the 1890s for voting rights that in America were half a century old.

The Whigs and Tories of Victorian England were the closest European counterparts to nineteenth-century American parties. But the novels of Disraeli and Trollope, and the realities of the age of Wellington and Canning, Melbourne and Peel, Palmerston and Russell, and Disraeli and Gladstone, make it clear that Britain's political culture remained steeped in the deferential-aristocratic politics of the eighteenth century.

English parties were loose, frequently shifting alliances of family groups and subsidized retainers. Commoners were a small minority in British cabinets. An unsalaried Parliament was dominated by Whig and Tory aristocrats and kept to a schedule of convening during the London social season and adjourning in December for fox hunting and estate visiting. It included rotten boroughs with few (and in a small number of cases no) voters, county seats at the disposal of local squires, and a severely limited electorate. That electorate slowly expanded through a series of reform acts over the course of the century. But it remained far below the American norm. The agenda of the Chartist movement of 1839–40 consisted of demands—male suffrage, a secret ballot, no property qualifications for voting, equalized electoral districts, salaries and an end to property qualifications for MPs, annual meetings of Parliament—almost all of which were already in place in the United States. British historian Michael Bentley concludes: "At no time during the period discussed in this book [1815–1914] did Britain experience democracy."

American popular nationalism rested not on the concept of a historic *volk* of the sort that fueled its European counterparts but on a political ideal: of free (white male) people in a republic. The early and mid-nineteenth century saw the emergence of what came to be internationally recognized as an American character type: brazen, assertive, and individualistic, defined by the vibrant present and not by an imagined past. The eighteenth-century embodiment of America as Columbia, trailing clouds of reference to classical mythology and other Old World prototypes, gave way to Uncle Sam: male, bumptious, classless, incontestably home-grown, incontrovertibly democratic. American nationalism rested on a rampant, competitive individualism that displaced the values of harmony, balance, and order of the republican era. Not surprisingly, the result was a new public culture.

CHAPTER FOUR

THE CULTURE
OF DEMOCRATIC
PARTY POLITICS

F OR ALL THE early Republic's commitment to representative government, voting and officeholding did not substantially change from the colonial pattern until the 1820s. The Constitution prescribed a republican form of government, not a democratic one. Property, religious, tax, age, gender, and racial restrictions abounded. The president was chosen by an electoral college, not voters, and in most states until the late 1820s, electors were selected by the legislature. Congressmen were the only directly elected federal officeholders.

Survivals of a more deferential political era abounded. In New York, the Council of Appointment designated mayors and other local officials. In some states the legislature chose the governor. Tennessee's new constitution in 1796 (written with the help of Andrew Jackson) provided that the state assembly appoint justices of the peace—key local officials—for life. The JPs in turn appointed county officers. In Virginia, deferential political ways lived on. Planter John Campbell wrote to his son David in 1811: "I have heard with much pain that you have not recovered your health yet. Would a session in the legislature be of benefit to you."

It is not surprising that after 1815, when four decades of revolution, nation making, and war finally came to an end, popular interest in affairs of state sharply dropped. The Era of Good Feelings, the label commonly attached to the post-1815 decade, might more accurately be called the Era of No Feelings. The presidential election of 1820 brought out 568 Baltimore voters (of a population of 63,000). Richmond (population 12,000) produced 17 votes; 9 percent of New Jersey's eligibles trickled to the polls. Turnouts of 2 or 3 percent of potential voters for state and local elections were common in Virginia, Maryland, and Massachusetts. Two-thirds of Virginia's congressional seats in the early 1820s were uncontested.

But a winner-take-all electoral system and an increasingly democratic popular culture raised the stakes for wider political participation. Jeffersonian Republicans tried to ease the way of immigrants to the ballot even before they completed the rite of naturalization. To halt the steady erosion of popular support, New York's Federalists sought the removal of voting restrictions on free blacks (many of them the servants of Federalist families). Constitution-revising conventions in New York (1821) and Virginia (1829) removed most of the remaining constraints on free white adult suffrage and officeholding.

Along with broadened suffrage came an increase in the range and number of public offices. Sheriffs, coroners, district attorneys, city recorders, county clerks, militia officers, road surveyors, inspectors, public notaries, tax assessors, fence watchers, and election officials were part of the rapidly growing workforce of the American polity. Some of these offices dated back to the previous deferential political regime. But now prerogative gave way to patronage: allegiance to a party, as much as to a person, became the most important means of access to office.

By the 1850s, all state senators and almost every governor were directly elected. Mississippi, not ordinarily thought of in modern times as at the cutting edge of American democracy, in its 1832 constitution was the first to provide for an elected judiciary. By 1828 voters directly chose presidential electors in every state but South Carolina.

Presidential candidates initially were chosen by party caucuses of congressmen, state and local candidates by state legislators. Party conventions began to spread after 1800, on the township, ward, county, district, and state levels. The first formal state nominating convention was held in Pennsylvania in 1817. And in 1831 the Anti-Masonic party held the first nominating convention for a presidential candidate. Public affairs once thought fit only for elites entered into the realm of popular politics.

Among them were the creation of new townships, counties, and states and the relocation of county seats and state capitals. These were almost always in the geographical center of the county or the state: an act of democratic symbolism as well as a response to population growth.

Hand in hand with this structural transformation went a no less profound change in political culture. In the deferential-republican regime, ambitious young men such as Alexander Hamilton, John Adams, and George Washington adopted the social and cultural trappings of elites. Now the reverse was more often true: an egalitarian *nostalgie de la boue* became a prerequisite for political success. Daniel Webster felt it necessary to proclaim his "special feeling for log cabins and their inhabitants. I was not myself born in one, but my older brothers and sisters were.... If ever I am ashamed of it may my name ... be blotted forever from the memory of mankind."

A claim to humble origins was in fact no reach for most successful politicians. Andrew Jackson and John C. Calhoun had unimpeachably hardscrabble childhoods. Martin Van Buren's supposed taste for a luxurious style of life, certainly not inherited, got him into political trouble. The Whigs often were labeled the party of the well-born. But leading members Horace Greeley (whose family was so impoverished it migrated *to* Vermont seeking economic opportunity) and prototypical poor boy Abraham Lincoln hardly fit the template.

Especially revealing was the change in American political language. As was appropriate to a democratic politics, oratory and verbal discourse replaced the proclamations and newspaper essays, signed with anonymous classical names such as Publius, of the former regime as the favored mode of political communication.

The public men of the early Republic continued to use the hermetic language of eighteenth century Anglo-American deferential politics— *junto, faction, clique, cabal, interest*—even as they cultivated the language of republicanism: *liberty, independence, representative, Republic, federal, union*. The rise of a more varied and flexible, self-consciously American political language was an important part of the quest for national self-identity that underlay the new party-democratic regime. Federalist Noah Webster's *American Dictionary of the English Language* sought to confine American English within a proper, rule-bound form. Unfortunately for its author's hopes, it appeared in 1828, the year Andrew Jackson was elected president. Jefferson more perceptively favored the priority of "usage" over "grammar." He foresaw what was coming: "The new circumstances under which we are placed call for new words, new phrases, and for the transfer of old words and new objects." Madison agreed:

"New ideas, such as presented by our novel and unique political system, must be expressed either by new words, or by old words with new definitions."

Tocqueville observed that the literary style of a democracy was "vehement and bold." This was conspicuously so in the case of political language. A vocabulary drawn from everyday life, very different from the elitist, insider terminology of the deferential politics of the eighteenth century, rose in pace with the new party culture. Its sources were the farm, the racetrack, gambling. William C. Fowler, an Amherst College professor of rhetoric, listing in 1850 what he called "low expressions" in American English, found them to be "chiefly political."

But this was *OK* (an invented Americanism: initially political, soon universal) in a democratic regime. While English parliamentary candidates *stood* for office, American candidates *ran*—and *bluffed, bolted, backed and filled, stumped for votes, dodged the issue, took a walk.* Their campaigns were tempestuous affairs, replete with *booms, landslides, avalanches, prairie fires, tidal waves, stampedes,* and *clean sweeps.* Their political world was filled with the material imagery of agrarian life. They *barnstormed* on *platforms* composed of *planks;* they were *dyed-in-the-wool* party men. Candidates were *dark horses* when they didn't have the *inside track* as a *front-runner.* They had a *running mate* or could serve as a *stalking horse* for a *favorite son.* Once in office they enacted *pork barrel* legislation, as often as not the product of *log-rolling.* They were *lame ducks* when they lost reelection. *Fence-mending* was a political as well as agricultural duty. A *bellwether* was both the bell-toting lead sheep of a flock and a representative voting district.

The new democratic politics was not an uplifting spectacle, as artist George Caleb Bingham's Hogarthian election scenes make clear. Quarrels between public men evolved from tightly circumscribed affairs of honor, such as the Hamilton-Burr duel, to no-holds-barred brawls (a different sort of "satisfaction," indeed), as in the drawn-out street fight between Andrew Jackson and Thomas Hart Benton and his brother Jesse in 1813, or Preston Brooks's violent assault on Charles Sumner in the Senate in 1857.

The political culture of the democratic regime produced as well a sea change in the social character of corruption. The Founders identified corruption with the patronage and perquisites of the ancien régime. Now charges of the abuse of power took on a very different class meaning. The spoils system—a term first applied to the Jackson administration's appointments policy—identified a new style of political corruption: not aristocratic perquisites, but widely distributed payoffs in a democratic polity. The previous republican reliance on virtuous leaders now gave way to reliance on the wisdom of "the people."

Many well-educated, socially superior Americans found this new political culture distasteful. And indeed it faithfully reflected less admirable aspects of American life: a communal political identity that eschewed class but not the exclusion of blacks, Indians, and women; a popular politics given to hyperbole and demagoguery; a predisposition to conflict over consensus. But most of the population found it stimulating, entertaining, a compelling form of social expression. Election parades, barbecues, and meetings enlivened day-to-day routine. Nicknames (Old Hickory, Old Tippecanoe, Old Rough and Ready) humanized political leaders. Town and county place names (Franklin, Washington, Jefferson, Madison, Jackson, Independence, Hope, Freedom, Harmony) embedded popular public men and political ideals in the nation's social memory.

When he came visiting in the early 1830s, Alexis de Tocqueville encountered a political system run by a new breed of professional politicians. Previous party builders of the republican regime such as John Beckley or Aaron Burr had a national political orientation. But from the 1820s on a different sort of political professional appeared, with deep local roots. Two prime examples were Democrat Martin Van Buren and Whig Thurlow Weed, both, appropriately, from New York, where the new economic and social forces of post-1815 American life had their fullest sway.

Van Buren was born in a village near Albany, where his tavern-keeper father was active in local politics (which went with the business). The son turned to politics as a career not because of the pull of grand national issues but because it was a trade ready at hand, and clearly a growth enterprise. He rose through the ranks of the regnant Jeffersonian Republicans in his county, holding positions such as fence viewer (important in securing the goodwill of farmers) and surrogate (the officer who dealt with wills and estates). Relying on democratic rhetoric, Van Buren and his associates wrested control of the state party from DeWitt Clinton and the established Jeffersonians.

In some respects the Albany Regency, Van Buren's state machine, resembled earlier Republican political organizations such as Thomas Ritchie's Richmond Junto in Virginia and Burr's New York operation. (John Quincy Adams noted Van Buren's resemblance to Burr in character, manner, and appearance.) But Van Buren's political style was adapted to the demands of a democratic political culture. Frequent elections with a rapidly growing electorate increased the need to be on the qui vive when it came to organization and ideology. That meant seeing to it that patronage served the party's needs and ending artifacts of a more deferential past such as an independent judiciary.

Van Buren put together a previously unmatched base of local supporters: masters and examiners, lower and circuit court judges, justices of the peace. His chief lieutenants William Marcy and Silas Wright ran things in the state after he levitated to national politics as senator, vice president, and president. Van Buren was the first state boss to turn national party fixer. That he should be Jackson's successor as president announced, as much as did Jackson's presidency, that a new political regime had come into being.

Van Buren defined himself more by his political skill and party identity than by his ideological commitments. He once gave a speech on the tariff, and after he was done a listener turned to his neighbor: "Mr. Knower! That was a very able speech!" "Yes, very able." "Mr. Knower! On which side of the Tariff question was it?" "That is the very point I was thinking about when you first spoke to me." As revealing was Van Buren's supposed comment after a defeat in Congress: "Yes, they have beaten us by a few votes, after a hard battle. But if they had taken the other side . . . we should have had them!"

Van Buren was quite aware that his was a new kind of politics. His *Inquiry into the Origins and Course of Political Parties in the United States* (written in the 1840s, published in 1867) argued that parties and party politics were not the threat to the nation's liberty that the Founders feared, but rather an essential instrument of democratic government in a free Republic. Unmentioned, but implicit, was the utility of mass parties for the politicians themselves. The parties turned out to be superb instruments for gathering the funds and recruiting the workers that the new democratic politics required.

Van Buren's Whig counterpart Thurlow Weed, also an upstate New Yorker, came from even humbler origins. His entrée into politics was not the local tavern but another major high road to popular politics: journalism. He began as a printer's apprentice, and in 1829 entered on a thirty-year career as editor of the *Albany Evening Journal*. A master of the style and techniques of the new mass politics, Weed built and ruled New York's Whig party in the 1830s and 1840s, much as Van Buren did with the Democrats in the 1820s. Like Van Buren, he became an important player (though not an officeholder) in national party politics.

Another new artifact of the party-democratic regime was the single-issue third party. The Anti-Masons of the late 1820s were the first of the breed. This movement began in upstate New York as a reaction to the supposed murder of William Morgan, a lapsed Mason, by members of the order fearful that he would divulge its ceremonial secrets. But larger themes lay below the surface.

Masonry enabled socially ambitious Americans to satisfy their need for quasi-religious affiliation and ceremony in an ostensibly secular form. Washington, Franklin, Jackson, and by the 1820s a probable majority of New York's officeholders were members. In response, Anti-Masonry spoke to the widespread fear that American society was losing its republican purity and that a secretive Masonic elite was exhibit A in this descent. Similar concerns had nourished the anti-Federalists' reaction to the Constitution, but they never became a distinct political party: a measure of the change in political culture.

Anti-Masonry appealed to a popular mind-set similar to the one that fueled anti-Catholic sentiment in England at the time, and later in the United States. In large part it was an urban phenomenon, flourishing in new towns such as Rochester. Its jeremiads against privilege and elitism appealed to people who were a part of, and simultaneously full of anxiety over, rapid economic and social change.

Party-bereft former Federalists, and National Republicans such as Thaddeus Stevens in Pennsylvania and Thurlow Weed and William Henry Seward in New York, jumped aboard this new political vehicle. The Anti-Masonic party brought fresh ideas and techniques into American politics. In 1828 it called for a constitutional amendment prohibiting members of secret societies from holding public office or serving on juries. And it was the first party to hold a national convention (in Baltimore, in September 1831), where it chose former attorney general William Wirt as its presidential candidate. (Not an ideal selection: Wirt, like so many prominent Americans, had been a Mason.) The major parties quickly and more successfully adopted the national convention device, well suited as it was to a political regime in which power rested on a coalition of state-based party organizations.

As the opposition to Jackson jelled into the Whig party in the early 1830s, the Anti-Masons met the customary fate of third parties: they disappeared. Most of the party's adherents became Whigs. A broadly inclusive national party was the only viable instrument in the new regime.

"Politics," said an observer, "appear to swallow every other interest, and the whole surface of the earth seems covered with politicians as Egypt once swarmed with locusts." This echoed Tocqueville's aperçu: "To take a hand in the regulation of society and to discuss it is [the American's] biggest concern and, so to speak, the only pleasure an American knows."

It has been argued that, except when issues were compelling and sharply drawn, sustained interest in politics was confined to those who practiced it professionally. The degree of organized effort thought necessary to attract voters suggests that there is something to this. But compared to other societies of the time (or to America today), it is apparent that the party regime did successfully engage its white male constituency and define the terms of public controversy.

PARTY WARS

The most conspicuous feature of the new regime was the emergence of the Jacksonian Democrats and the Whigs as the world's first mass-based political parties. Just as the Constitution made no provision for the rise of parties, so did politics after the War of 1812 offer little forewarning of what was to come. James Monroe's two presidential terms from 1817 to 1825, the Era of Good Feelings (the label was conjured up by a Boston paper when the Virginian president visited New England in 1817), reinforced the belief that old party passions were spent. Monroe himself declared: "[T]he existence of parties is not necessary to free government." Only one electoral vote was cast against his second term in 1820.

A new generation of politicians—Monroe's presidential successor John Quincy Adams, Henry Clay of Kentucky, Daniel Webster of Massachusetts, John C. Calhoun of South Carolina—claimed a common Republican party identity. They agreed on major aspects of foreign and domestic policy: the Monroe Doctrine, a national bank, a protective tariff, internal improvements. With spectacular lack of prevision, Calhoun declared: "I belong to no section or particular interest."

The post–War of 1812 accord was summed up in Henry Clay's American System. (Jefferson also used that term.) In the tradition of eighteenth-century dirigisme, Clay called for a government program of roads, canals, and tariffs tying southern cotton, western grain and cattle, and eastern manufacturing into an integrated, self-sufficient whole. In a sense the Monroe Doctrine and the American System added up to a second declaration of American independence from Europe. The only significant protestors—rather like the Tories and the Anti-Federalists—were a diminishing band of old-style Federalists and old-style Virginia Republicans led by John Randolph, John Taylor, Spencer Roane, and *Richmond Enquirer* editor Thomas Ritchie, alienated from mainstream American politics since Jefferson's time.

But this hiatus in partisanship was brief and skin-deep. Virginia, first in the number of congressmen in 1800, slid to third behind New York and Pennsylvania by 1820, and the Virginia dynasty lost its taste for an American "empire for liberty." Madison backtracked from his post-war activism to veto an internal improvements bill in his last day in office, and Monroe agreed that there was in fact no constitutional authority for it. Nor was there much popular enthusiasm, in a highly individualistic and self-seeking culture, for John Quincy Adams's from-the-top-down call for "liberty by design."

And it was clear that the Constitution's electoral rules abhorred a non-party vacuum. The elections of 1824 and 1828 laid the groundwork for the party politics of the party-democratic regime, as those of 1792 and 1796 had for the proto-parties of the republican era.

From 1788 to 1824, presidential selection was steeped in the deferential political world of the eighteenth century. Every chief executive from John Adams to John Quincy Adams was either vice president or secretary of state before his elevation. And all could claim membership in a dynasty: of Founders (Washington, Adams, Jefferson, Madison, Monroe), of Virginians (Washington, Jefferson, Madison, Monroe), of family (Adams and son John Quincy Adams).

The disappearance of the Federalists and a changing American political culture ended these Buggins's-turn practices in 1824. Instead of the Republican congressional caucus certifying who was next in line, the diverse interests of an expanding America made themselves heard. A rump caucus of Republican congressmen chose Virginia-born Georgia politician William H. Crawford as an appropriate successor to the Virginia Dynasty. But Andrew Jackson of Tennessee, incumbent President Adams of New England, and Henry Clay of Kentucky boycotted the caucus and ran separate candidacies.

Most states still chose their electors through their legislatures. Adams won a slight plurality of a deeply divided electoral vote, even though Jackson got 40 percent more popular votes. For the second time since 1800, a presidential election went to the House. Clay threw his votes to Adams and in consequence became secretary of state: a widely condemned "corrupt bargain."

The political future lay not in factional warfare but in the rapid reemergence of two-party politics—and of a dominant political figure, Andrew Jackson of Tennessee: war hero, Indian fighter, first non-gentry president, a figure sharply at odds with the American political past. Adams ran again in 1828 as the candidate of a newly crafted party, the

National Republicans, in a last-gasp attempt to resurrect the party politics of the early Republic. Jackson won by a decisive popular margin: 56 percent to 44 percent. The 1.2 million votes cast—50 percent of those eligible voted, about the same proportion as today—was three times the size of the 1824 total, the largest percentage increase in American political history.

In only two states, Delaware and South Carolina, did legislators still choose the presidential electors. Selection by the electorate added to the value of party organization as the most efficient way to gather a greatly expanded harvest of votes. Though Jackson had a strongly led campaign headquarters in Washington, local organizations were crucial to his success in Ohio, Kentucky, New York, and Pennsylvania. Correspondence and township committees numbering in the hundreds were common. Increased public interest also led directly to the first election polling (of sorts). At a variety of assemblies—endorsement rallies, militia musters, grand juries, Fourth of July celebrations—participants were asked whom they favored. For all its randomness, this opinion gathering reasonably prefigured the result.

Regime change indeed! We are far from the world of the Revolution, the Constitution, and the early Republic. Yet Jackson and his Democratic and Whig successors often identified with the republican past. Emotional ties to the Revolution and the early Republic were strengthened by the fiftieth anniversary of independence in 1826, Lafayette's triumphant return to the country, and the heavily freighted symbolism of Thomas Jefferson and John Adams passing away on July 4 of that year. Lafayette paid his respects both to the surviving Founders and to the next generation of leaders: Jackson, Webster, Clay. His tour was a reminder of how much had happened (the table at his New York banquet was graced with a seventy-five-foot model of the Erie Canal) in how brief a time (all of the nation's former presidents except Washington were still alive when Lafayette arrived).

Jackson laid claim to the Cincinnatus persona that had served Washington so well: "I had retired from the bustle of public life to my farm, there to repair an enfeebled constitution, worn out in the service of my country." He remodeled the Hermitage, his Tennessee home, so that it resembled Mount Vernon, and when he left office he toyed with the idea of a farewell address. He claimed that his political ideas were "imbibed in no small degree, in the times, and from the sages of the revolution," and pledged himself to a program of "reform retrenchment and economy" designed to restore the nation to its virtuous past.

Jefferson endorsed him in 1826, and like his Virginia predecessors, Jackson's core support was in the South: 92 percent of his 1828 electoral vote came from slave states. When the Jacksonian Democratic party took form, Martin Van Buren struck up an alliance with Thomas Ritchie and the Virginia Dynasty that echoed the New York–Virginia alliance of the 1790s. Van Buren told Ritchie: "The country has once flourished under a party thus constituted & may again."

But these were old trappings for a new politics, not unlike the American revolutionaries' justifying themselves with the rhetoric of the English radical Whigs. Jackson in fact oversaw a sea change in American political culture. His predecessors subscribed to a deferential-republican political style, defined by honor, service, (public) virtue, and personal self-restraint. Jackson's jagged personality, the product of his hardscrabble youth, continued into adulthood. Jefferson told Daniel Webster that Jackson's tendency to "choke with rage" made him an ineffective senator. He married a woman who was not quite legally divorced. He was regarded as a new kind of public man: western, unconfined, free from identification with the deferential-republican political culture of the past. He was the first American president to be the object of an assassination attempt; his response was to club his deranged English attacker.

Jackson comfortably defeated Henry Clay, the first candidate of the new Whig party, in 1832. Four years later his chosen successor, Van Buren, faced three candidates running under the still-jelling Whig label. The result revealed how evenly the two parties had come to divide the electorate: Van Buren got 764,198 popular votes, his Whig opponents 736,147.

It was in the election of 1840 that the new political culture fully emerged. Just as it took the better part of a decade for the Jeffersonian Republicans to win power in 1800, so did the Whigs in the course of the 1830s adapt to, and finally succeed at, the politics of the new party-democratic regime. In 1840 as in 1800, real issues—the Panic of 1837 and ensuing hard times, which made Whig economic policy more appealing—fed the transfer of political power. But the most striking aspect of the 1840 election was the large influx of new voters, second only to 1828. The proportion of eligible males voting rose from 57.2 percent to 80.2 percent. The Whigs had mastered the new style of party-democratic politics.

Indian fighter and popular general from the West Andrew Jackson (Old Hickory) now was replicated by Indian fighter and popular general from the West William Henry Harrison (Old Tippecanoe, nicknamed after the site of his most famous victory). Like Jackson, Harrison ran as a man of the people. A log cabin was the prime symbol of his candidacy. Though he came from a substantial Virginia planter family and had considerable wealth, he did indeed spend some time in a humble dwelling— encased within the mansion he later built around it. A flood of songs, symbols, parades, and favors for voters (including glass log cabins filled with the product of Pittsburgh's E. C. Booz distillery, thus adding *booze* to the American language) gave a visible gloss to the new politics.

The Whigs differed subtly from the Democrats in their party culture. Issues and individual candidates mattered more than party organization and loyalty—a consequence, perhaps, of their later origins. Whig turnouts in off-year elections were usually lower than those of the Democrats. But these were differences of degree, not kind. Thurlow Weed masterminded the Whigs' 1840 triumph as Van Buren did Jackson's 1828 victory. Whig congressmen used their franking (free mail) privilege to flood constituents with campaign material. Ambitious young Whig Abraham Lincoln told his Illinois fellow partisans: "Organize the whole state, so that every Whig can be brought to the polls . . . divide the country into small districts and appoint in each a sub-committee . . . and make a perfect list of voters and ascertain with certainty for whom they will vote . . . and on election day see that every Whig is brought to the polls." After it was over, a Democratic magazine admitted: "We have taught them to conquer us!"

Party and personal appeal displaced policy. Harrison's campaign was not burdened by a platform, and in his inaugural speech he all but exempted himself from the demands of presidential leadership: "It is preposterous to suppose . . . that the President, placed at the capital, at the center of the country, could better understand the wants and wishes of the people than their own immediate representatives." Given this view of his role, it was not inappropriate that Old Tippecanoe should be the first president to die in office, a month after his inauguration.

It is reasonable to make the counterfactual argument that this should have been a time of diminishing popular interest in politics. The great causes of the past—revolution, nation making, national self-preservation in the Napoleonic era—were gone. In their place was the quotidian business of a society of questing go-getters and material and physical expansion. Then how did the Democratic and Whig parties maintain their appeal as the nation's dominant political voices?

Observing the parties in the early 1830s, Tocqueville detected a sharp division between them: "The deeper we penetrate into the inmost thought of these parties, the more we perceive that the object of the one is to limit and that of the other to extend the authority of the people." But by

1840 the Whigs were as fully committed as their opposition to a politics of mass appeal and democratic sentiments. It was of the essence of the party-democratic regime that party differences were not fundamental and irreconcilable (as were the Patriot/Tory and Federalist/Anti-Federalist divisions of the past). Democrats and Whigs shared a common ground of beliefs sufficient to avoid deeply divisive issues such as slavery and to allow the peaceful acceptance of turnover in party control.

Like their Federalist and Republican predecessors, the new parties relied on complex sets of cultural and policy positions, keyed to core constituencies defined by location, religion, ethnicity, economic interest, and family tradition. The Democrats appealed to subsistence farmers, immigrants, Catholics (up to 90 percent of the Catholic vote in the large cities was Democratic), and anomalies such as Dutch and German farmers in New York and Pennsylvania who were well enough off to be Whigs but were repelled by what they saw as that party's threat to their religious and social values. The Whigs were strongest among evangelicals, the commercial classes, and the more prosperous agricultural counties (though not in profoundly Republican Virginia).

Jacksonian democracy has been described as many things, including an attempt to resurrect pristine Jeffersonian Republicanism, the voice of a surging new American market capitalism and cultural and economic nationalism, and a populist protest against the market economy. The party's ideological fuzziness in fact goes far to explain its political success.

The Jeffersonian Republican stress on limited government had an important place in Jacksonian Democratic rhetoric. Jackson declared: "My political creed was formed in the old republican school." (Both he and Van Buren had Anti-Federalist fathers.) "The world is governed too much," announced the Jacksonian *Washington Globe* in the 1830s, a sentiment echoed by the *Democratic Review* in the 1840s: "The best government is that which governs least."

The party sought also to identify itself with a more radically egalitarian creed. In 1840 it formally adopted the name Democratic, instead of calling itself Republican in homage to Jefferson. Jacksonian class-warfare rhetoric appeals to historians in search of historical validation for a liberal-left tradition in American politics. "Never," sighs Charles Sellers, "has the majority seemed so close to actually ruling."

But Jacksonian anti-capitalism was encased in an agrarian-yeoman ideal far indeed from a social democratic state. Further muddying the ideological waters was the widespread readiness of the Democrats to temper their populist rhetoric with a healthy respect for enterprise and moneymaking. And as was the case with Jefferson when he was faced with the prospect of acquiring Louisiana, small-government principles readily co-existed with expansionist ambition. The *Democratic Review* held that it was the "manifest destiny" of the United States to absorb Texas, California, and much else besides: the Jefferson-Madison "empire for liberty" updated. When Jackson faced Calhoun's states'-rights nullification *défi* in the early 1830s, he fell back on a nationalism that the Federalists would have applauded: "Without union our independence and liberty would never have been achieved, without union they can never be maintained."

The Whigs distinguished themselves from the Democrats on a number of economic and social issues, as state legislative roll call votes made clear. They more readily supported the expansion of bank credit, government subsidies for internal improvements, protective tariffs, and the distribution of the proceeds of land sales to the states. These policies appealed to most voters and help explain the party's political successes. But the Whigs were hardly dirigiste. As one of them—Abraham Lincoln—put it: "The legitimate object of government is to do for a community of people, whatever they need to have done, but can not do, *at all*, or can not, *so well do*, for themselves—in their separate, and individual capacities."

Jackson's presidency evoked Whig hostility to the dangers of autocratic executive power that arguably gave them as strong a claim as the Jacksonians to a Jeffersonian Republican heritage. Anti-corruption, like republicanism, was a weapon in the armamentaria of both parties. Jacksonians found American liberty threatened by vested private interests and the Bank of the United States. The Whigs found the same threat in the Jacksonians' spoils system and their authoritarian leader.

Jackson's war on the Bank induced former National Republicans and conservative Democrats to join the new Whig party. Master organizer Thurlow Weed wanted it to be called the Republican party. But the name Whig, given wide currency in an April 1834 speech by Clay seeking "to rescue public liberty" from the threat of King Andrew, sent a strong message with its imputation of hostility to government absolutism. (The Democrats in turn spoke of the "Wig" party as "a cover for bald [F]ederalism.") So neither new party adopted the name of the Republican political tradition to which both subscribed—further testimony to the fact that a new political regime had come into being.

Democrats sought national purification through the reform of banks, corporations, and the currency. Whigs sought to do the same through social issues such as education, temperance, abolition, and humanitarian reform. The Whigs' greater responsiveness to temperance and anti-Catholicism helped them break the Jacksonian hold on the Old Northwest states of Illinois and Michigan. Whig editor Horace Greeley held that his party appealed to "Working Men who stick to their business, and go on Sunday to church rather than the grog-shops."

While Whig supporters often were more prosperous and enterprising than their Jacksonian counterparts, this was a tendency, not a bright line of division. The distinction between Jacksonian Democratic egalitarianism and Whig individualism was only tangentially a distinction of class. Both parties subscribed (in slightly variant ways) to a liberal capitalist consensus: the Whigs through equal opportunity, social mobility, and the harmony of classes, the Jacksonians through a range of appeals that reached from agrarians drawn to a static society to on-the-make westerners and urban go-getters. The true dissenters—home-grown (and more often foreign-born) radicals, the remnants of the old-style Republicans, the new southern states'-rights dissenters led by Calhoun—were conspicuous for their marginality.

The political dynamic of the party-democratic regime required the parties to be sensitively responsive to changes in the public mood. The still-fragile framework of American nationalism and the social implications of regime change from a deferential party culture to a democratic one colored the political agenda. For all his commitment to Jeffersonian ideals, Jackson's first term was dominated by new issues that called for un-Jeffersonian positions. One was his growing split with Vice President Calhoun over the 1828 tariff, and the subsequent threat by Calhoun and South Carolina to seek its nullification by state fiat. Another was the division in his administration over the social standing of Peggy Eaton, the morally challenged wife of the secretary of war.

Jackson's 1832 reelection campaign and his second term, which shifted from resonant political and cultural to materially attractive economic themes, testified to his party's increasing cohesiveness and self-assurance. His removal of federal deposits from the Bank of the United States and his subsequent veto of a congressional attempt to recharter the Bank were ideological statements as well as assertions of the power of the presidency. Jackson defined the Bank issue as a social conflict: a showdown between "the rich and powerful" and "the farmers, mechanics, and laborers." He withdrew federal deposits from the Bank, he said, "to preserve the morals of the people, the freedom of the press, and the purity of the elective franchise."

Whigs called the war on the Bank of the United States an example of Democratic hostility to development and of Jacksonian autocracy, "rapidly tending," said Henry Clay, "towards a total change of the pure and republican character of the government, and the concentration of all power in the hands of one man." The Bank war hastened the coalescence of Jackson's opposition into the Whig party, much as the Jay Treaty had done for the Jeffersonian Republicans in the 1790s. Foreign affairs were no longer contentious, so it is not surprising that a domestic issue resonant with economic and social implications played a similar role.

The dominant politicians of the era (Jackson and Van Buren aside) were John C. Calhoun of South Carolina, Henry Clay of Kentucky, and Daniel Webster of Massachusetts. These three regional giants made the Senate their forum. They spent decades seeking to balance their regional identities with the national alliances they hoped would take them to the presidency. The result was an endless dance of position shifting on issues (in the course of which Calhoun morphed from a full-blown nationalist to a states'-rights nullifier and Webster from a supporter of the Federalists' separatist Hartford Convention in 1815 to a Unionist Whig) and of political alliances made and broken, worthy of a Renaissance city-state.

The adaptive power of the new political regime was evident in the election of 1844. Clay, the ablest and most popular Whig leader, finally got his heart's desire, the party's presidential nomination. But he faced the first dark horse candidate. James K. Polk, a less-than-conspicuous Tennessee politician, was chosen by the Democrats because he was not mired in the economic issues that contributed to the Whig victory of 1840 but rather was identified with the widely popular annexation of Texas and westward expansion. The response of Clay's Whigs (though less so Clay himself) was to compensate for their anti-annexation position with appeals to anti-Catholic nativism. The two candidates corralled 92 percent of the popular vote, and Polk narrowly won: a triumph of the new party-democratic political culture.

But Clay lost the decisive electoral votes of New York because of the anti-slavery Liberty party's candidate, James G. Birney. A very similar scenario played out in 1848. Zachary Taylor, the Whigs' second superannuated general-candidate, defeated the Democrat Lewis Cass, another one of the undistinguished regulars so frequently nominated by the professional politicians who ran the party. This time the Free Soil party candidacy of Martin Van Buren, who like Theodore Roosevelt three-quarters of a century later bolted from his party in quest of a return to the presidency, made the difference. The close balance between the major parties was a tribute to their capacity to speak to popular desires. But it increased the ability of splinter parties to have an outsized impact on the electoral outcome. The new party-dominated political culture had rapidly assumed the character that (with the exception of the Civil War era) it would sustain for a century to come.

CHAPTER FIVE

GOVERNING
A DEMOCRATIC POLITY

T HE PARTY-DEMOCRATIC REGIME not only created a new politics but transformed government and law. The republican approach to governing in the early Republic assumed that elite rulers would disinterestedly serve the public interest. In the new regime, "the democratic ideal of popular self-rule was translated into a reality of party government through the medium of yet a third concept—that of the rule of the majority."

GOVERNANCE

What this meant in practice was a party-run spoils system, where partisanship trumped expertise. Among the consequences: a grand widening of subjects considered fit for political consumption, and the unalloyed spoliation of Native Americans and African Americans. Minority rights had little room in a majoritarian heaven. It is not surprising that the Bill of Rights went into a century-long slumber as a significant subject of American constitutional law.

The new regime brought large changes of attitude and practice in the major instruments of government. President Andrew Jackson differed from his predecessors as much in his approach to the presidency as in his public persona. He dropped Washington's cabinet-as-general-staff approach and instead relied heavily on a group of informal advisers called his

Kitchen Cabinet. (The very name suggests a style distant indeed from the more formal hierarchical model of the deferential-republican regime.) The cabinet itself showed the erosive effects of the rise of a vibrant, unstable party politics. There were three secretaries of state, four secretaries of the Treasury, two secretaries of the navy, and two attorney generals in a single twelve-month period during Jackson's second term.

Jackson was a forceful president. He faced down Calhoun over South Carolina nullification, got rid of the First Bank of the United States, and oversaw the removal of the Creeks and other Indians from their ancestral lands. The implication here was that the chief executive in the party-democratic regime would have great power. But Jackson's successors (until Lincoln) were an undistinguished, generally inept lot. The constitutional primacy of the legislature as well as popular hostility to centralized government meant that Congress and the states, not the president and the federal bureaucracy, were the major shapers of public policy.

But Congress itself had much institutional maturing to do. An attempt to double its members' salaries (to $1,500) in 1816 led to fearsome slaughter in the ensuing election. Two-thirds of the House (including the entire Ohio delegation) and half of the senators up for reelection were swept away, and the survivors hurriedly repealed their "salary grab." A number of states required their senators to vote as the legislature instructed them to do.

Congress had no seniority system and little in the way of staff. Turnover was high, in part because the city of Washington was hardly a lodestone of livability, in part because most American public affairs were conducted elsewhere, in the states and localities. The average congressman lived out his Hobbesian legislative life—nasty and short—in party- or section-affiliated boardinghouses. Between 1800 and 1830, two-thirds of congressmen served two terms or less, two-thirds of senators lasted for one term or less. More than half of the 242 members of the Twenty-fourth Congress (1835–37) were not around in the Twenty-fifth.

In a far-flung, decentralized country, most congressmen were more intimately tied to their home districts, through an extensive postal system and a constant flow of petitions from their constituents, than to the political life of Washington. Political reputations depended largely on oratory, widely circulated in newspapers. Members devoted most of their time to dealing with patronage requests. The contrast with Britain's Parliament, where members had only token ties to their districts, could not have been greater.

Still, Congress was at the apex of the constitutional system. And as the gathering place of the parties' leaders, it confronted the nation's most contentious issues. The Senate was dominated between 1825 and 1850 by the oratory, deal making, and convoluted (and unsuccessful) presidential politicking of the Great Triumvirate of Webster, Clay, and Calhoun. They personified the interplay of party, section, and politics that defined, and eventually crippled, national policy making during the pre–Civil War decades.

Congress quickly evolved from its Parliament-inspired origins into a body appropriate to a party-dominated democracy. Supreme Court justice Joseph Story observed: "The House of Representatives has absorbed all the popular feeling and all the effective power of the country." New procedural rules expedited business and served the interests of the party majority. The same purposes were served by standing committees designed to bring some continuity and party discipline to the business of Congress, by Speakers closely attuned to the dictates of their parties, and by investigations (usually driven by partisan politics).

By European measures of public power—an imperial capital, a large, entrenched bureaucracy and military, economic and social guidance by the central state—American government was a puny thing. Washington was not the grand metropolis envisaged by L'Enfant but a scraggly, fever-ridden town, the Capitol unfinished and the Supreme Court tucked into its basement. When the new Treasury building was built in 1832, it sat plum on the line of L'Enfant's scheme for a grand avenue linking the Capitol and the White House, an aspiration lost to memory. Gouverneur Morris, the chief drafter of the Constitution, sourly observed: "We want nothing here but houses, cellars, kitchens, well-informed men, amiable women, and other little trifles of this kind to make our city perfect." The most impressive physical presence of the government was to be found elsewhere, in structures that met state and local needs: customs houses and post offices in the large cities, lighthouses and forts (one of them where the Civil War began) along the coast.

The formal apparatus of the American state was fragile. But in matters peculiar to the American situation—the disposal of public lands, organizing the territories and creating new states, Indian affairs, the postal service, tariff policy—its responsibilities were large. The Post Office, Treasury, and War Departments were more complex and extensive than any private business of the time.

The civil service of the early Republic in theory was free from the evils of monarchical-aristocratic England. Pure republican standards of appropriate education and disinterested, uncorrupt service to the people were supposed to be what counted. Bureaucratic structure mattered less.

Before the 1830s only two reorganizations took place: of accounting procedures in the Treasury and the Department of the Navy.

This changed under Jackson. Almost every department was reorganized at least once: not for greater efficiency, the Jacksonians said, but to restore the original republican ideal of purity, endangered over time by the inroads of corruption. Under the rhetoric lurked the earthier reality of the party regime. Van Buren's associate William L. Marcy famously declared in an 1832 congressional debate: "To the victor belong the spoils of the enemy." The "spoils system" of jobs for the faithful was rationalized by the democratic belief that almost any citizen could handle almost any government job, and that in consequence it was necessary to rely more on the rules and regulations defining the work than on the character and respectability of the persons engaged to do it.

Governance was democratized and subject to party rule. Jackson promised that "[r]otation in office will perpetuate our liberty" by eliminating "official aristocracy." During his first eighteen months as president, about a tenth of the roughly ten thousand federal employees were discharged, including some 40 percent of the six hundred or so in Washington. An appalled critic concluded: "The government, formerly served by the *elite* of the nation, is now served, to a very considerable extent, by its refuse." The change in fact was subtle: Jackson appointed more onetime Federalists than his Republican predecessors combined. He staffed his government with more appointees from the booming Southwest, his section, and with more lawyers than in the past (though in those pre-accreditation days, that had relatively little social significance).

Scandals on a new scale, involving democratic rather than aristocratic corruption, followed in the wake of this turnover. The most dramatic: New York City collector of customs Samuel Swartwout, who absconded overseas with about $1 million, more than 5 percent of the government's annual budget. There was fiddling in mail delivery contracts and Land Office transactions. Amos Kendall, a member of Jackson's Kitchen Cabinet who became postmaster general, and land commissioner Ethan Brown strengthened the inspection system in their bailiwicks, thereby validating the ironic truth than whenever an attempt is made to democratize government, the result is likely to be an extension of federal power: "spoils bred bureaucracy." The Post Office was the government agency that had the most direct and continuous contact with the people. For years, every state delegation had a seat on the House Committee on Post Offices and Post Roads. The result: between 1792 and 1828, 2,476 new postal routes were established, and only 181 were discontinued. With the advent of the party-democratic regime, the postal service became an even more important instrument of state. By 1831 the mail system employed over three-quarters of the federal civilian workforce. The nation's 8,700 postmasters outnumbered the 6,332-man army. There were seventy-four post offices for every 100,000 Americans, compared to seventeen in Great Britain and four in France. The system distributed 39 million copies of newspapers in 1840, and journals named *Post, Express,* or *Mail* multiplied.

This growth had substantial political consequences. The large-scale distribution of and exchanges among the overwhelmingly partisan newspapers of the nation facilitated the rise of the national parties. And it added to the political importance of papers and their editors. Jacksonian politicos Amos Kendall and Duff Green saw to it that post office jobs in the cities were a source of patronage (and, through kickbacks, of party funds) and that postmasterships everywhere were in the hands of loyal party workers. When the Whigs took over the presidency in 1841, the turnover in postal jobs far surpassed anything seen before.

Postal policy as well as personnel came under the sway of politics. Sunday mail delivery faced growing criticism from Presbyterians and Congregationalists. More significant was the assault on the delivery of abolitionist literature in the South. Postmaster General Kendall and President Martin Van Buren joined southern spokesmen in supporting a clampdown. Far from serving as a template for the active state, the postal service became a prime instance of the subordination of state building to party politics in the new regime.

A MORE COMMON LAW

By its very nature, law should have been the sector of the polity most resistant to regime change. But the legal system at large, and not just the Supreme Court, followed the election returns. In style, structure, and substance, American law marched in lockstep with politics and government.

English legal ways were deeply embedded in the training of the numerous lawyers (Jefferson, Hamilton, and John Adams among them) who led the early Republic. The authority most often quoted in the debates of the early sessions of Congress was the English jurist Blackstone, though of course for American purposes. But the pressure on American law to develop in pace with the other governing institutions of the new nation was irresistible. There was talk of rejecting English common law as unrepublican. Legislative acts, on the other hand, had special worth because they "speak of the public voice." And the courts of the new republic tended to defer to the will of the national and state legislatures. A codification movement in the 1840s went a step further. One of its rationales was that if the law could be reduced to a few, readily comprehensible rules, it would be within the reach of all. Every man his own lawyer: a democratic regime indeed!

American jurisprudence also underwent a sea change. That transformation is evident in the work of Supreme Court chief justice John Marshall, his Jacksonian successor Roger B. Taney, and Massachusetts chief justice Lemuel Shaw, arguably the most influential jurists of the early nineteenth century.

Marshall was chief justice of the Supreme Court for thirty-four years, from 1801 to 1835. He defined the Court's place in the American constitutional system and laid down major guidelines for the respective powers of the federal government and the states. His was the judicial legacy of the early Republic: a staunch Federalist concern that national prerogatives be protected from encroachment by the states, a strong belief that the nation's future prospect depended on safeguarding vested economic interests. Inevitably that legacy came under strain when it clashed with the political and economic culture of the new regime.

In *Marbury v. Madison* (1803), Marshall worked out a political way of resolving an essentially political problem: the Court's relationship to Congress and the presidency. His was an institutional adaptation comparable in long-term significance to the peaceful succession in power from John Adams to Thomas Jefferson after the election of 1800. The issue in *Marbury* was whether or not a last-minute appointee of outgoing President Adams could be denied his position by the incoming Jefferson administration. Marshall rejected the Federalist Marbury's claim, thus pleasing the Jeffersonians. But he did so on the ground that the provision of the 1789 Judiciary Act under which Marbury sought the reinstatement of his office was unconstitutional. There was little Jeffersonian Republican criticism of *Marbury*. But the fact that no other congressional law was voided until the *Dred Scott* decision in 1857 suggests that an interventionist Court had little place in the party-democratic regime.

A number of Marshall's most important decisions dealt with the constitutional status of chartered enterprises. In *Fletcher v. Peck* (1810), *Dartmouth College v. Woodward* (1819), and *McCulloch v. Maryland* (1819), he used the contract clause of the Constitution to shield a land company, a colonial college, and the Bank of the United States from hostile state policies. These decisions had in common the dirigiste eighteenth-century belief that it was proper public policy to safeguard vested interests, as well as the assumption that the Court had the right—indeed, the duty—to make policy pronouncements as long as they were encased in the protective cocoon of constitutional interpretation.

As time went on, Marshall responded to the changing face of the American economy. In *Gibbons v. Ogden* (1824) he again relied on the Constitution—in this case, its commerce clause—to resolve a question of economic development. But now he favored new rather than old enterprise: a consortium that challenged the steamboat monopoly in the waters around New York held by Robert Fulton and his associates. But for all his judicial skill, much of Marshall's jurisprudence fell on fallow ground. Expansive applications of the Constitution's contract and commerce clauses to economic issues did not take hold until the late nineteenth century.

When Marshall left the Court in 1835, he was followed by Roger B. Taney, who embodied the party-democratic regime as much as Marshall did the deferential-republican one: "as thorough going a party judge as ever got on a court of justice," thought Daniel Webster. Taney's *Charles River Bridge v. Warren* (1837) decision reflected the expansive, *sauve-qui-peut* spirit of the time. It supported the public need for a new Boston-Charlestown bridge over the charter privileges of an older competitor. Taney rejected the view that the courts' chief responsibility was to protect vested interests: "While the rights of private property are sacredly guarded, we must not forget that the community also have rights." In one of the first Court dissents, old-time Jeffersonian Republican Joseph Story took issue: "I stand upon the old law . . . in resisting any such encroachments upon the rights and liberties of the citizens."

New ways of legal thinking cropped up as well in the state courts and civil law. State judges, like their political counterparts, became important public figures: in part because so much economic and social policy was made and enforced on the state level, in part because they were so interwoven with the political fabric. Between 1845 and 1855, judges came to be popularly elected for limited terms in fifteen of the twenty-nine states, and judicial appointments were deeply enmeshed in party politics in the others.

The most important state judge of the time was Lemuel Shaw, who wrote some twenty-two hundred decisions in the course of his thirty years (from 1830 to 1860) as chief justice of the Massachusetts Supreme Judicial Court. Shaw dealt with every major economic and social issue of antebellum America. A Federalist turned Whig, he did as much as anyone to adapt American law to new conditions.

Among Shaw's most notable cases were *Commonwealth v. Hunt, Farwell v. Boston & Worcester Railroad* (both decided in 1842), and *Roberts v.*

Boston (1849). His *Hunt* decision rejected the prevailing judicial practice, rooted in English common law, of using the law of criminal conspiracy to judge the actions of labor unions. Instead, Shaw viewed worker-employer relationships as in essence a contract between parties of equal legal standing. The same emphasis on contract underlay his *Farwell* decision. Shaw introduced the fellow-servant rule into American law: if an employee's injury was due to the negligence not of his employer—the other party to his labor contract—but of a co-worker, then the employer escaped liability. *Hunt* and *Farwell* replaced the old common-law master-servant paradigm, which focused on the lesser party's obligations and the higher party's responsibility, with a contractual model of equal parties freely entering into voluntary relationships: a legal rendering of the underlying social assumptions of the democratic regime.

Deference to the legislature was as much a part of legal thought as of political thinking in these decades. In *Roberts*, which involved the constitutionality of Boston's segregated schools, Shaw came down strongly on the side of the duly elected school committee and its power to distinguish between blacks and whites (or men and women, or adults and children), so long as it did not base this on unreasonable grounds—and in Shaw's view it did not. The other side of that legal coin emerged in 1855, when the court raised no objection to a new state law that forbade racial distinctions in the admission of children to the public schools. In this as in so many other matters, the legislature ruled.

The work of Shaw and other influential judges such as John B. Gibson of Pennsylvania, who endorsed legislative supremacy and judicial restraint when it came to economic policy, was echoed in state decisions nationwide. A growing infrastructure of annual printed state judicial reports (by 1820, eleven of the thirteen original states had them), treatises, and digests increased the circulation of legal positions and ideas, much as the *Congressional Globe* did the debates and decisions of the national legislature. In this sense the most influential state judges played a role complementary to that of party leaders Van Buren, Clay, Webster, and Calhoun, who negotiated the back-and-forth interchange of political doctrines and issue stands between their state and regional locales and the national political arena.

Just as politics took an increasingly prominent place in American life, so did the law. There was an exponential increase in lawsuits and lawyers (or perhaps, in terms of cause and effect, lawyers and lawsuits). Tocqueville concluded that lawyers were the most privileged of the country's citizens, the closest equivalent to an American aristocracy. But while lawyers were prominent among the political elite, the freedom to become one was broad indeed. Aside from a usually pro forma examination, all the aspiring attorney needed was the ability to attract clients. What legal scholar Roscoe Pound called "the strange notion of an inherent national right of the citizen to practice law" took hold. By one estimate there was one lawyer for every thousand people by 1850, far more than in any other country.

American law expanded in subject matter as well as size. Corporations, banks, insurance companies, merchants, and small businessmen generated heavy business in property and contract law. Railroads, factories, and machines were prolific sources of negligence and liability lawsuits, enough to produce a new subsection of law: torts. And social relationships stretching from marriage to slavery (not that great a stretch, given the legal standing of wives) added substantially to the litigation menu.

Public law also grew exponentially. As towns expanded, so did the need to deal with crime, fires, and other urban problems. The concept of a "well-regulated society" based on a democratically justified police power to provide for health, safety, welfare, and morality came into legal being. In *Commonwealth v. Alger* (1851), Shaw provided the landmark judicial definition of the states' police power: "the power vested in the legislature by the constitution, to make ... all manner of wholesome and reasonable laws ... as they shall judge to be for the good and welfare of the commonwealth." The police power proved to be a major justification for judicial endorsement of state regulation.

Echoing the perception of parties as spurs to a vibrant and expanding democracy, law came to be what legal historian James Willard Hurst called an "instrumentalist," "way-clearing" force for the "release of energy," assisting rather than impeding economic and social change. Like party politics, American law was less inclined to stand on precedent and the protection of vested interests, more inclined to turn judging and rule making into innovative instruments.

Was the transformation of American law in fact an application of democracy? Or is it best seen as the handmaiden of the new market capitalism of the early nineteenth century? It is true that the bulk of American law, like American politics and government, dealt with economic issues. But to isolate law from the democratic impulse of the time is to ignore its larger social character.

The continued easing of land transfer through simplified registration of land titles and deeds served not only land companies and speculators but also the substantial number of Americans busily buying and selling farms and other real estate. The rise of tort law provided a device, long before the appearance of workmen's compensation and other instruments of the modern welfare state, to cushion some of the shock of a machine civilization. The same might be said of contract law. The assumption that a contract was the product of the will of independent parties made it a widely accessible legal instrument. The American innovation of common-law marriage assumed that marriage, like work and other social arrangements, was a contract entered into freely by equal parties. Similarly, the inclination to let juries determine criminals' intent, capacity, and punishment made criminal law, like contract law, less fixed, less elitist, less oppressive. Taken together, these innovations added up to a regime change in law comparable in spirit and substance to what was happening in politics and government. True, this was limited legal democracy. But so too was political participation: limited, yes, but also democratic.

THE ECONOMIC AGENDA OF A DEMOCRATIC POLITY

The prevailing view is that in the Hamiltonian-Jeffersonian conflict over the character of the American state, Jefferson's less-is-more view prevailed. And indeed, at the beginning of the nineteenth century, states incurred little or no debt, lived with minuscule budgets, passed precious little legislation. One session of the Connecticut legislature in the 1790s devoted itself primarily to imposing a tax on dogs. The next session was given over to discussing whether or not to remove that levy. Local government was no different. The primary issue in the Massachusetts town of Brewster in 1807–8: "the anti-federalists want to enclose the burying grounds, but the federalists are for continuing free access to the hogs."

The rise of a mass-based party system and the widespread belief that nothing was beyond the reach of a free people opened the door to an unprecedented expansion of public policy. The relationship of government to economic development and social issues took on an unexpected character, shaped more by the dynamic of party politics than by the dictates of eighteenth-century economic mercantilism or social deference.

Tariff and land policy came to be defined by particular economic interests, not broad national concerns. Compare, for example, Madison's nationalist tariff-for-revenue act of 1789 with the fiercely specific conflicts over tariff making from 1816 to 1828. Or contrast the Northwest Ordinance of 1785 and the early Land Acts from 1796 to 1820—attempts to develop the West in an orderly manner—with the intense regional and local politics that swirled around land distribution schemes (preemption, graduation, distribution, homesteading) in later decades.

The national outlook of the American System faded away. The states took the lead in chartering, subsidizing, and regulating roads, canals, railroads, banks, and industry. Somnolent legislatures morphed into frenetically active ones. Between 1819 and 1846 the New York legislature alone passed some sixteen hundred laws dealing with turnpikes, insurance companies, railroads, banks, bridge companies, and manufacturing.

The party system was a much more accessible battlefield than the more deferential political regime of the past. The tail of party politics wagged the public policy dog. Economic policy, traditionally defined as the protection of vested interests, came to be shaped by the demands of a wider electorate and a more diverse economy. Pressure grew for politics (and government and law) to remove privileges, monopolies, and regulations, to open opportunity to new groups, to be broadly distributive rather than narrowly preferential.

One result was the transformation of the corporate charter from a charily granted instrument of privilege to a widely available tool of enterprise. So-called free incorporation laws extended the advantages of the corporate charter to a much broader social range of entrepreneurs.

A similar development occurred in banking. Hamilton's economic program relied on federal policy to establish the fiscal security necessary to attract foreign investment. The Bank of the United States, modeled on the Bank of England, was its capstone. But party politics colored both the Jeffersonian Republicans' decision not to renew the bank's charter in 1811 and the creation of a second bank (initially controlled by Jeffersonians) in 1816. When Jackson killed the bank in 1832, he justified his action with democratic rhetoric (in both the general and party senses of the word). At the same time many Jacksonians had personal and political stakes in state banks, the new repositories for federal deposits.

Under free banking laws, state-chartered banks multiplied to meet the voracious credit and currency demands of a rapidly growing economy: from 29 in 1800 to more than 300 in 1820, 901 in 1840, and 1,562 in 1860. This expansion generated an intense state and local banking politics dealing with the grant of charters, regulation, government deposits, and loans. Banking policy, once the quintessential elite-insider concern, became part of the common currency of popular politics.

Monetary matters followed a similar path. There was no federal gold or silver coinage from 1815 to the early 1830s. Instead, unregulated small-denomination paper money—*shinplasters*, a term reflecting the popular view of their real worth—was issued by state banks (including *wildcat banks*, fly-by-night operations located in the backwoods, where wildcats roamed and currency redemption was difficult) as well as by towns and bridge companies: in short, any entity with enough standing to get away with it. About fourteen hundred counterfeited or altered note series appeared during this period. A currency-hungry society was ready to accept risks. But slack supervision had heavy social costs and hence provided more raw meat for political controversy.

"Internal improvements" had a conspicuous place in the national agenda well before the coming of the party regime. The cheaper and faster movement of goods and people was as necessary as access to capital and as popular as land acquisition. Washington and other Founding Fathers were drawn to sweeping internal improvements plans. Jefferson's secretary of the Treasury, Albert Gallatin, proposed an ambitious canal-turnpike program in 1808. Secretary of war John C. Calhoun famously declared in 1816: "Let us bind the Republic together with a perfect system of roads and canals. Let us conquer space." The centerpiece of Henry Clay's American System was a national transportation program.

But these schemes did not survive the change from a republican regime to a democratic one. Jackson's Maysville Road veto of 1829 was a death sentence for federal internal improvements plans. Instead, annual appropriations bills, in which Congress doled out funds for projects (lighthouses, river and harbor improvements) tied to the local political needs of congressmen became the norm. Canal and railroad development passed into the hands of states, localities, and private entrepreneurs. The assumption was that the size and importance of these projects made them vulnerable to corruption if the national government was in charge. (Not that state and private developers turned out to be slouches on that count.) This was pork barrel policy in its purest form, as non-programmatic as could be.

The intensely party-driven, increasingly sectional politics of the new regime weakened federal authority and stymied national plans. The advantages of central policy were lost. But so too were the disadvantages of remoteness, rigidity, and misjudgment that come when central planning — "seeing like a state" — is the norm.

The policy benefits — and costs — of the old and the new approaches to internal improvements are evident in a comparison of New York's Erie Canal (1816–24) with Pennsylvania's Main Line Canal of the late 1820s and early 1830s. The Erie Canal was the great engineering achievement of the age. But this was no triumph of democratic politics. New York in 1816 was arguably the *least* democratic of American states save for South Carolina. Through his control of New York's Council of Appointment, Governor DeWitt Clinton sat at the apex of a hierarchical government structure. He and his associates were free to approach the problem of building a canal linking New York City and the Great Lakes in an efficient, cost-effective manner. That is why they chose a lock canal to Lake Erie rather than the easier but less economically promising alternative of a water-level canal to Lake Ontario. They secured the best engineering advice and ample financing, and the canal was completed rapidly and within budget, though at a heavy cost in lives to the Irish immigrant workers who built it.

Pennsylvania's Main Line canal no less strikingly displayed the policy pitfalls of the democratic regime. The state, and Philadelphia in particular, had to respond to the challenge of the Erie Canal. While New York had a head start in attracting the flow of goods between the upper Midwest and the coast, Pennsylvania could tap a cutting-edge new technology: the railroad. But geography, demography, and politics negated that potential advantage.

The Appalachians posed a substantial obstacle to Philadelphia's access to the Ohio River and the West. Pennsylvania's widely dispersed population had relatively little to gain from that access. And the state had a more vibrantly democratic politics than New York. All of this worked against a single, efficient mode of transportation to the West. Instead, local political pressures led to a slowly growing web of canals that fed almost every county in the eastern part of the state, and then a spectacularly cumbersome system of portage over the mountains: a clumsy, expensive response finished just in time to be outmoded by the railroad.

Private enterprise and a democratic polity had their virtues. Railroad building was the most dynamic enterprise during the pre–Civil War decades. Mileage went from 73 in 1830 to 30,636 in 1860. There were a few state- and locality-built railroads, but the overwhelming majority of the lines were constructed and run by private companies. Politics, government, and law conjoined to smooth the way of this massive takeoff. Their contributions ranged from charters and rights of way to massive subsidies (in bonds, loans, land). Needless to say, this generated a railroad politics, and a railroad law, more extensive than any previous interplay between the economy and the polity. It was appropriate that Lincoln should make his way both as a Whig politician and as a railroad lawyer.

Widespread popular hostility to privilege and monopoly opened the door to railroads, which were easily chartered and lightly regulated. This paid off in rapid and energetic economic growth. But it came at a high cost in corruption, jerry-built lines, and bond defaults (public as well as private, overseas as well as at home). It was during these pre–Civil War decades that the distinctive American mix of a dynamic but unsteady economy and a democratic but often ineffective state emerged, never to disappear.

THE SOCIAL AGENDA OF A DEMOCRATIC POLITY

Social policy in the party-democratic regime closely resembled its economic counterpart. Social issues flooded into the political mainstream of the party regime: a release of social energy comparable to the release of economic energy. Here too an ever broader agenda, engaging an ever wider portion of the populace, imposed an ever greater strain on the polity's ability to cope.

Two new groups of reformers appeared in the 1820s. One consisted of elites marginalized by social and political change. Ex-Tory Quakers and politically declining Federalists were early advocates of the abolition of slavery. Pioneers for better treatment of the blind, the insane, and prisoners also tended to come from old Federalist families. Here was the beginning of the American tradition of elite reform stoked by alienation from the political-social mainstream.

A broad evangelical impulse that sought purification not only of the soul but of the social body soon overshadowed the genteel social reformers. The first significant political expression of this new force was the Anti-Masonic movement of the late 1820s. Anti-Masonry's rapid evolution into a political party was part of a large-scale morals revolution that transformed American social policy much as the market revolution did economic policy. The political implications of this social politics proved to be even more profound than its economic counterpart. It set the polity on the course that culminated in the Civil War.

Like other important historical forces of the time—liberalism and nationalism, the commercial, transportation, and industrial revolutions—the new agenda of social reform was not limited to America. The Enlightenment, evangelical Protestantism, and nineteenth-century bourgeois anxiety over threats to social order fed support for prison reform, opposition to slavery, and the temperance movement in Europe—most notably in Britain—as well.

But they did so in a very different social and political ambience. Nineteenth-century European social reform (to say nothing of radicalism) challenged the existing, traditional order of society. The American reform impulse rested on the belief that the social evils it addressed were in themselves evidence of change: of threats to, or falloffs from, an existing set of American ideals. And because American politics now had a broad democratic base, social issues entered into public life on a scale unmatched elsewhere. Causes with a traditionally marginal or tangential relationship to mainstream politics and government, such as prison and asylum reform, education, temperance and prohibition, nativism, and ultimately opposition to slavery, came to occupy prominent places in the American public agenda.

A common explanation of the rise of social reform is that it was fed by the stresses of the market economy. The reduction of artisans to hired labor fueled labor radicalism; the influx of new, often Catholic immigrants spurred nativism. Elites sought greater social control by regulating drink and fostered mass education as a way of imposing their bourgeois values on a fractious people. Even opposition to slavery can be wedged into this interpretation with some tugging and hauling; as historian Charles Sellers puts it, "[L]iberalism was so endemic in this bourgeois slaveocracy that even its polemical vanguard could not help feigning philanthropy."

But the social politics of pre–Civil War America rarely assumed the language or character of class conflict. Religious, ethnic, and sectional identity were far stronger predictors of social attitudes. The great common denominator in the panorama of reform was a new, widely shared view of what politics and government might be called upon to do.

The model of social goals pursued through political action, first crafted by the Anti-Masonic party, was repeated in the Workingmen's and Anti-Monopoly parties that sprang up (and quickly faded away) in eastern cities during the 1830s. It is difficult to set them in a modern tradition of radical (to say nothing of Marxist) protest. Their belief was that "the world is governed too much." Like the Anti-Masons, they dwelt on hostility to privilege ("monopoly" in place of "Masonry"). But what they wanted was the removal of constraints on opportunity: charters, regulation, inspection, licensing. New York's Workingmen's party included shopkeepers and even the mayor. The Jacksonian Democrats absorbed them, as the Whigs absorbed the Anti-Masons. But like their predecessors and successors, they imposed constant pressure on the major parties to take heed of extra-party expressions of discontent.

The consumption of alcohol was very heavy in seventeenth- and eighteenth-century America. But Americans' drinking habits were a non-issue during that period. Colonial legislation sought to regulate the quality rather than the quantity of liquor sold. American alcoholic intake may well have been declining by the early nineteenth century, but now it became a consequential political issue.

The inclination to regard drink as a social evil was strengthened by evangelical Protestants' belief in the morality of self-control and by the behavioral concerns of an expanding middle class. These people regarded drink as a threat not only to individual salvation but also to the nation's moral and material progress. The Sons of Temperance (with more than two hundred thousand members) and the Washingtonian Societies, with parades featuring children bearing anti-drink banners, campaigned for the cause in American cities. Like the party politics it closely resembled, the temperance movement schooled large numbers of Americans in the art of organized mass advocacy.

Inevitably the campaign against liquor became political, and inevitably its goals became more ambitious. Voluntary temperance yielded to enforced prohibition. Public policy replaced private choice, as reformation of others (such as Irish and German immigrants) became more important than reformation of the self. In England, where a more limited, deferential politics held sway, the crusade against drink did not become a major political issue.

Nativism and anti-Catholicism, long present in American life, became substantial causes in pre–Civil War America. They were closely interwoven with the anti-drink and anti-slavery movements as ways of preserving American freedom. They got political legs from the 1830s on, primarily in response to rising Irish immigration, but also because all was grist to the mill of a more democratic party politics. One nativist group called itself the New York Protection Association: like Anti-Masons and prohibitionists, nativists wanted to safeguard the purity of the Republic.

In a by now familiar pattern, nativism quickly became political. Nativist parties, often overlapping with their Workingmen's counterparts, sprang up in a number of cities. Their primary goal was legislation to prohibit voting by non-citizens and to extend the number of years required for citizenship—the Federalist Aliens Acts of the 1790s updated to the democratic state politics of the 1840s. Local nativist parties won a number of elections in 1844 and moved on to a national convention in 1845.

Women's rights had only a marginal place in public life. A party regime was not a friendly venue for a cause so at odds with prevailing social beliefs. Even so, the reform spirit of the time was an incentive to pioneers such as the women who gathered at Seneca Falls, New York, in 1848 to call for gender emancipation in language that hewed closely to the Declaration of Independence. And as the American public policy agenda came to include morals- and values-drenched issues such as drink, education, and slavery, the fact that women were so closely identified with the guardianship of social virtue gave them a new claim to (non-voting) participation in public affairs.

The dictates of coalition building inclined the major national parties to be wary of divisive causes such as prohibition and nativism, and most of all abolitionism. The very success of the English anti-slavery movement underlined how difficult it would be to resolve the issue in America. The two countries shared a common ground of elite discomfort with slavery at the turn of the nineteenth century. Parliament abolished the slave trade in 1807; Congress did so in 1808, after the lapse of the Constitution's twenty-year ban. The London Anti-Slavery Society (organized in 1823) and the American Anti-Slavery Society (begun a decade later) had similar evangelical reform sources. But Parliament ended slavery in the British Empire in 1833 with relatively little political conflict. That nation's political ruling class, reinforced by strong Anglican and dissenter disapproval of slavery, readily overrode West Indian planters and domestic interests with a stake in plantation profits. Abolition in the British Empire was as much the achievement of an elitist political culture as was New York's Erie Canal.

So happy a resolution was not possible in pre–Civil War America, for reasons much like those that led to the failure of Pennsylvania's Main Line Canal. The scale and importance of slavery in the South—a region centrally engaged in the political life of post-1815 America—gave its "peculiar institution" an entirely different place on the public agenda. Instead of abolitionism being a feel-good cause whose resolution incurred little political cost, it loomed as the great, unmanageably divisive issue in American public life.

Almost all mainstream political leaders, from Founders Jefferson, Madison, and Adams to Clay, Webster, Jackson, and Van Buren, sought to avoid or tamp down the slavery issue as a threat to the nation or to their parties. In response, neither ardent critics nor passionate defenders of slavery had much use for the trimming or equivocation that was the mothers' milk of party politics. Abolitionist Samuel May Jr. thought that "[p]arty organization, drill, and machinery are worthless." Alabama secessionist pioneer William Yancey declared: "If this foul spell of party which binds and divides and distracts the South can be broken, hail to him who shall break it."

But once the party-democratic regime opened the door to a new politics of economic interest and social reform, nothing could prevent the most sensitive of all American issues from finding a place within it. On November 13, 1839, in Warsaw, New York, in the midst of the state's heavily evangelical "burnt-over district," where Anti-Masonry, temperance, and prohibition had flourished, a group of abolitionists established the Liberty party, the first political organization dedicated to the end of slavery.

CHAPTER SIX

CRISIS

B Y THE MID-1840S it seemed that Americans had come closer than any nation in history to an affirmative answer to the question of whether a people can govern themselves. A boisterously self-confident popular nationalism flourished. A burgeoning economy and international identification of America with freedom and opportunity drew a swelling flood of immigrants from the British Isles, Germany, and Scandinavia. Widespread primary education and literacy, innovative religious and secular forms of association, a broadly accessible legal system, and a party politics of unmatched popular appeal fostered cloying self-congratulation at home and attracted considerable attention (liberals admiring, conservatives alarmed) abroad.

But from the 1840s to the 1860s, the United States slid into one of the most catastrophic political failures of the nineteenth century. Eleven of the Union's thirty-four states seceded to form a new nation. A civil war of unprecedented scale and human loss raged for four years. And while secession and slavery were brought to an end, racism and discrimination continued to flourish.

This experience was especially painful to contemplate when set against other countries' responses to nationalism and slavery. The rending of the American Union coincided with the midcentury easing of class and religious tensions in Victorian England and the unification of Germany and Italy. Britain ended slavery in the West Indies in 1833, as did Brazil in the 1870s. Even benighted Russia peacefully freed its serfs in 1862.

The how and why of the Civil War is a seminal problem in American history. Torrents of ink have been spilled arguing that it was essentially a clash between two economic systems, agrarian and industrial; or a conflict between two cultures, the feudalism-like slaveocracy of the South and the free men–free land–free labor culture of the North; or the result of short-sighted statesmanship and incompetent politics.

It now seems fairly well settled that there was no profound economic clash between the North and the South over land, markets, or capital. Southern cotton was a staple complementary to, not competitive with, northern and western wheat and corn. Bankers, merchants, and manufacturers in the North and Midwest lent and sold to the South on a substantial scale. Southern planters (especially the bigger ones) had comparably close relationships with northern middlemen in the cotton trade and looked to the North for credit and supplies (including cloth and foodstuffs for their slave labor).

Nor is it clear that the sectional schism rose from a profound cultural gulf. North and South together, after all, devised, fought, and won the American Revolution and created the Republic that followed it. And while they differed over slavery, the regions had similar attitudes on race. Mainstream thought, both high-toned and popular, took black inferiority as a given. Many hostile to slavery (such as Henry Clay and Abraham Lincoln) favored the colonization of blacks overseas, slave or free. Nor were the regions sharply divided by religion or ethnicity.

What, then, overrode these common denominators of interest, ideology, and culture? The proper place to look is in the words and actions of the generation that lived through the tragedy. And what most strikes the observer is the degree to which that generation defined and debated issues in political and constitutional terms. Understandably we view the Civil War today primarily through the lens of slavery and race. But contemporaries experienced it in the context of the political system in which they lived. The greatest failure of the party-democratic regime ineluctably emerged from that regime's character and structure.

Oracle-like, we can examine the entrails of the American polity during the 1840s and 1850s for portents of what would happen in the 1860s. What first commands attention is the decay—in political theorist Moisei Ostrogorsky's phrase, the "weakened spring"—of the major instruments of government: the presidency, Congress, state and municipal authority, the courts, the parties.

Something profound in the American psyche was at work here: a tension between the popular distaste for status, privilege, expertise, and control, on one hand, and the belief that these constraints were necessary to preserve social order, on the other. It was as if Americans were exploring the outer limits of a polity based on that evocative Americanism, the self-made man. Tocqueville took note of the consequence for the American state. "[N]othing strikes a European traveler in the United States," he observed, "more than the absence of what we would call government or administration. One knows that there are written laws there and sees them put into execution every day; everything is in motion around you, but the emotive force [by this he meant authority in the traditional sense] is nowhere apparent. The hand directing the social machine constantly slips from notice."

A case in point: A visiting committee of congressmen took a look at the United States Military Academy at West Point, since 1815 the country's primary source of engineers. It recommended that the cadets be nominated by militia companies, not congressmen and other grandees. And it proposed that the curriculum be stripped down so that the cadets would not have "their ardor quenched by the cold process of mathematical demonstration, nor the minute investigation of scientific studies." A deconstructionist demon was loose in the antebellum American psyche, eroding what Lincoln called "the mystic bonds of Union."

PRESIDENT AND CONGRESS

A *tour d'horizon* of the weakened springs of government properly begins with the presidency. Andrew Jackson, a two-term president (as were four of his six predecessors), restored something of the luster of the office lost under Madison, Monroe, and John Quincy Adams. But this turned out to be a false dawn. He was followed by a series of undistinguished one-termers, stretching from Martin van Buren in 1836 to James Buchanan in 1856. Two of them, Whigs William Henry Harrison in 1841 and Zachary Taylor in 1850, died in office: personal fragility echoing institutional frailty. Taylor's feeling for the power of his office was not keen: "I wish . . . [Vice President Millard] Fillmore would take all of the business [of government] into his own hands."

John Tyler, who finished out Harrison's term in the early 1840s, was the first incumbent president not to run for reelection. His immediate successor, James K. Polk, was the first dark horse president, little known before his nomination ("Who is James K. Polk?" was a saying of the time), the compromise choice of an 1844 Democratic convention deadlocked by its newly installed two-thirds voting rule. Polk was the first president to commit himself to only one term.

Next in this thinning gray line was Democrat Franklin Pierce in 1852 (nominated after forty-nine ballots). According to a Whig jibe, he was "the hero of many a well-fought bottle": so far had the Washington-Jackson-Harrison-Taylor warrior tradition decayed. The sequence of Taylor's successors Millard Fillmore (1850–53), Pierce (1853–57), and James Buchanan (1857–1861)—perennial high fliers on every worst-presidents list—concludes the case for the decline of the office.

The presidency eroded in part because of the rise of state party machines and bosses, whose ceaseless bargaining at the national nominating conventions made it likely that the eventual candidate would be most pols' second choice at best. Nor was a political system resting on weak local government and facing no great external threat or internal challenge a breeding ground for strong chief executives. Congress in effect recognized that fact by denying the president funds for administrative assistants, or even a private secretary, until 1857. Before then, the chief executive relied on relatives (Zachary Taylor and his son-in-law took care of Taylor's correspondence) and presumably on the kindness of strangers.

Congress, by constitutional decree the first branch of government, matched the presidency in its diminishing capacity to govern. At first the party-democratic regime produced a golden age of senatorial giants—Clay of Kentucky, Webster of Massachusetts, Calhoun of South Carolina: powerful orators, commanding political intellects, influential if often fickle spokesmen for their states, their regions, and (they hoped) the nation. None made it to the presidency they so ardently desired. All ended their days obsessed by a sense of failure: a tribute of sorts to a political regime designed to evade the country's major issues.

As the years passed, Congress, like the presidency, turned out to be less and less able to cope with the pressures of a culture in which individual (or regional, state, and local) interests prevailed. Between 1830 and 1860 the average congressman served for only four years. The senatorial average was a bit over five, less than a full term. The growing sectional split further weakened the capacity of Congress to function as an effective legislative body. The selection of a new Speaker for the Thirty-first Congress in December 1849 took three weeks and sixty-three ballots; there were thirty candidates. Congress in the 1850s was a "cave of the winds," in which conflict over sectionalism, the territories, and slavery was ever more frequent, resolution ever more difficult.

Members came armed, and with increasing frequency they assaulted one another. During the debate over the Compromise of 1850, South Carolina's Henry Foote drew a pistol on Missouri's Thomas Hart Benton and then was disarmed by New York's Daniel Dickinson: a novel form of intersectional dialogue. In 1856 Congressman Preston Brooks of South Carolina viciously attacked Charles Sumner of Massachusetts on the Senate floor. When Lincoln was inaugurated in front of the half-finished Capitol dome in March 1861, he needed only to look behind him to be reminded of how tentative and incomplete was the Republic he swore to uphold.

The gridlock of the 1850s began with the failure of Henry Clay, the great congressional figure of previous decades, to secure his version of what became the Compromise of 1850. Clay sought a single, "omnibus" measure (he took the term from the new horsecars appearing on city streets) designed to resolve—as definitively as the Missouri Compromise had thirty years before—sectional conflict over the territories and slavery. It ranged from the admission of California as a free state and countenancing slavery but not the slave trade in the District of Columbia to a tightened fugitive slave law and the denial of congressional authority to regulate the interstate slave trade. Clay relied on his highly personal approach to congressional leadership to put his bill across. But a fragmented Congress was in no condition to respond.

The debate over Clay's act included the swan songs of the Great Triumvirate. Calhoun (he was too weak to speak, and his words were read by a colleague) condemned it as a plot to transform the "federal republic" into "a great national consolidated democracy" ruled by the North. Webster in response pled (for over three hours) "for the preservation of the Union." Calhoun and his southern followers were not moved. Nor was Senator William H. Seward of New York, who dismissed legislative compromise as "radically wrong and essentially vicious" and called instead for adherence to "a higher law" that refused to countenance slavery. The rising young Democrat Stephen Douglas of Illinois, more attuned to the way in which sectional commitments were eroding other forms of political identity, broke up the act into separate bills and won sufficient support, issue by issue and congressman by congressman, to come up with the measures known as the Compromise of 1850.

But this was a short-lived victory in the face of the gathering forces of disunion. By 1854, only four years later, the settler flow into the area acquired in the Louisiana Purchase made it necessary to organize the Kansas and Nebraska Territories. Douglas sought to build on his 1850 success by applying the principle of popular sovereignty in his Kansas-Nebraska Act of 1854, which left the question of slavery or no slavery to the settlers. Popular sovereignty was a paradigmatic product of the time. It rested on the belief in majoritarian democracy that dominated American public life. And it replaced the Missouri Compromise with what in effect was the declaration of a weakened Congress's inability to deal with slavery in the territories. The extent of that inability was made clear by the Kansas-Nebraska Act's explosive political consequences.

GOVERNMENT AND LAW

As the presidency declined and Congress degenerated, federal, state, and local government—highly politicized, more than a little corrupt—became another casualty of the culture of the party-democratic regime. The ideal of a disinterested, elite civil service found no purchase in a polity given over to popular representation, an egalitarian ethos, and party politics. Only one head of a cabinet department came from the bureaucracy between 1829 and 1861. Of the seventy-six cabinet members who served during that period, twenty-four held office for less than a year, and another twenty-one for less than two.

By common consent, economic and social policy was best left to the states and localities, where (in theory) the writ of the people ran strongest. But here too confidence in government declined. The splurge of state support for canals and then railroads collapsed in a welter of default and corruption. Between 1840 and 1855, nineteen state constitutions in the North and West were amended to limit government debt and to constrain or forbid state lending for railroads or other internal improvements.

The New York constitution of 1846—"the People's Constitution"— took the democratic spirit of the time to its logical conclusion. It called for the election of the state's canal commissioners, inspectors of state prisons, and the state engineer (his only qualification was that he be "a practical engineer"). Gone was any legislative power over, or state subsidies for, economic development, special bank and other charters, and most forms of regulation, including "all offices for the weighing, gauging, measuring, culling or inspecting of any merchandise, produce, manufacturer, or commodity whatever."

As with the presidency and Congress, suspicion of government and a share-the-wealth approach to public office led to rapid and widespread turnover in state positions. Governors generally served one- or two-year terms. In late-eighteenth-century New York, a relatively modest 30 to 50 percent of legislators in a typical session were first-termers, and a quarter of them served four terms or more. By the middle of the nineteenth century first-termers were 70–80 percent of the whole, and only 5 percent served more than four terms. All of *three* Democratic members of New York's 1845 session had prior legislative experience.

America's cities were slow to adopt the instruments of modern urban government. Their legal status as municipal corporations gave them a place in the government pecking order that the Constitution had not provided. But this meant that, like private corporations, they were instruments of the states that chartered them—and thus of legislatures dominated by farmer and small-town interests.

The growing demand for municipal services was met in good part by charities (hospitals, asylums, relief for the poor) and private water, horse-car, and fire companies. Instead of general property taxes, towns relied on special assessments for public improvements. Everywhere one looked, the prevailing view of the relationship between citizen and state was as stripped-down and one-to-one as possible.

Urban politics underwent the same democratization that occurred on the national and state levels. During the deferential-republican regime, wealthy men and their interests ran the urban political show. A prime example: Josiah Quincy, whose career capaciously included four terms as a Federalist congressman, sixteen years as president of Harvard, and in between a fruitful three terms (from 1823 to 1828) as Boston's second mayor after the city gave up town meetings and became a municipal corporation. Quincy pioneered in rudimentary city planning and urban removal, and he improved basic services: garbage removal, firefighting, public safety. His was a display of civic responsibility that echoed on a local scale the large visions of Henry Clay's American System and John Quincy Adams's National Republicanism.

But with the coming of the party-democratic regime, elite urban governance gave way to the dictates of the new party politics. Ward, district, and city politicos displaced the rich and well-born. The original Tammany Society of the 1790s was a merchant-dominated fraternal order typical of the republican regime. But from the 1830s on, Tammany Hall, the society's clubhouse, became a synonym for the general committee of the Democratic Party of New York County, the archetypal urban political machine of the party regime. Fernando Wood, the most prominent pre–Civil War Tammany mayor, was corrupt, immersed in patronage politics, in all respects the antithesis of Josiah Quincy, and a fit contemporary of the weak presidents and ineffective congressmen so conspicuous in the years before the Civil War.

From midcentury on, the words most frequently applied to American urban politics were *machine* and *boss*. Neither was complimentary. The linkage of "the machine" with urban politics was in place by the 1850s, related, it is thought, to the volunteer fire engine companies that were the building blocks of organizations such as Tammany. Hughie McLaughlin, the "boss laborer" in charge of hiring at the Brooklyn Navy Yard in the 1850s, parlayed his job-giving role into the leadership of the Brooklyn Democratic organization. His title appears to have moved into politics along with his function.

Between 1825 and 1850, 72 percent of New York's mayors and over 90 percent of Philadelphia's were merchants or lawyers. These worthies continued to chair municipal meetings and committees. But by the 1850s they made up only 5 percent of a tally of more than a thousand New York City officials. Instead, ill-educated, socially underprivileged professional politicians came to dominate urban government as they did state and national governments in the democratic regime. And hand in hand came that distinctively American phenomenon the genteel urban reformer: a business or professional man seeking to contain the political clout of the immigrant poor, reduce taxes, and most of all challenge the hegemony of the boss and the machine.

American law, like government, had a potential for social discord that blossomed in midcentury. The darker side of the new legal mind-set appeared in the courts' response to the constitutional issues raised by slavery. For all the cultural nationalism of the time, no commensurate legal or constitutional concept of national citizenship had yet emerged. The Bill of Rights for the most part protected individuals from state laws, thereby implying that it was on the state and local levels, not the national level, that one's identity as a citizen lay. So too did social identity (white or black or Indian, free or slave, man or woman), and membership in civil associations such as parties, churches, towns, or villages.

It is not surprising, then, that the courts' confrontation with slavery focused on the relationship between the states and the federal government rather than on the issues of citizenship or civil rights. When he reviewed the enforcement of the fugitive slave law in *Commonwealth v. Aves* (1836), Massachusetts chief justice Lemuel Shaw (no defender of slavery) took what in the context of the time was a moderate position. He held that a state could declare that slaves in its boundaries were property but could not impose that standard elsewhere. Supreme Court justice Joseph Story in *Prigg v. Pennsylvania* (1842) tried another, related tack. He struck down as unconstitutional a Pennsylvania personal liberty law protecting fugitive slaves. And he held that the national government was the only body responsible for enforcing the federal fugitive slave law. This had two consequences: state officials refused to cooperate with slave-seeking slaveholders, and the Compromise of 1850 created a body of federal marshals and commissioners charged to apprehend fugitive slaves.

The bottom line was that the fugitive slave issue deepened intersectional animosity out of all proportion to the small numbers involved.

But this was as nothing compared to the reaction to Chief Justice Taney's decision in *Dred Scott v. Sanford* (1857), which Lincoln aptly called "an astonisher in legal history." That intensely political decision gave voice to the widespread belief in the racial inferiority of blacks, slave or free, and the southern view that the federal government had no right to interfere with slavery as an institution anywhere: neither in the new territories nor in any state.

It did so by declaring that the Missouri Compromise—since 1819 a bulwark of the political effort to tamp down the issue of slavery in the territories—was unconstitutional. This was the first Supreme Court rejection of a congressional statute since *Marbury v. Madison* in 1803. Taney argued that neither Congress nor any state could interfere with the property rights of slaveholders. The implication: not only the Missouri Compromise but also the Compromise of 1850 and the Kansas-Nebraska Act of 1854—indeed, any law that required or even permitted the exclusion of slavery anywhere in the United States—was unconstitutional. Slavery was a national institution. And African Americans, slave or free, had "no rights that any white man was bound to accept."

Taney tried to equate his slavery policy with Jackson's attack on the Bank of the United States as an assertion of popular rights. But this was a nightmarish application of Jacksonian principles. It appeared to echo Calhoun's chilling view that "[s]lavery is indispensable to a republican government," and it implied that slavery was not just an institution peculiar to the South but a legally protected national labor system. Lincoln said of Stephen Douglas's popular sovereignty principle: "When he invites any people, willing to have slavery, to establish it, he is blowing out the moral lights around us."

PARTIES AND POLITICS

What was to keep this autarkic, issue-racked American polity from spinning out of control? The answer, obvious to all thoughtful observers since the 1820s, was the major political parties. If these too were swept away, then little was left to restrain the forces that threatened to pull the Union apart.

The American state may have been a lame and halting thing. But that could not be said of the parties in the 1830s and 1840s. Party identification—"the partisan imperative"—seemed to intensify as access to the ballot grew. Democrats and Whigs were closely competitive, broadly attractive, innovative, and energetic national parties: fit instruments for a democratic society. Between 1836 and 1852 they rotated the presidency: Van Buren (D), Harrison (W), Polk (D), Taylor (W), Pierce (D). Neither was a sectional party: until the 1850s, there were slightly more southern Whig than southern Democratic congressmen.

But from the late 1840s on, this equilibrium came apart. Within a decade the Whigs disappeared. And most Democratic leaders adopted a southern-oriented, pro-slavery position, thereby alienating a substantial portion of their northern constituents. As the major parties fractured, powerful third parties rose, focused on the potent, divisive issues of nativism and abolition. Abraham Lincoln was elected president in 1860 as the candidate of the new Republican party, the South responded with secession, and the nation descended into civil war. Hardly a triumph of the democratic—or party—ideal.

The evitability or inevitability of this story has its attractions as a topic. But a final resolution seems unlikely. Let us focus instead on why the arts of political compromise could not deal with states' rights, slavery, and the territories.

One danger sign: the growing belief that party-dominated government was corrupt. Washington banker William W. Corcoran, who "lent" money to Webster, Calhoun, and Stephen Douglas, flourished in the new political culture. So did Sam Ward, "king of the lobby" (the word *lobby* taking on an increasingly disreputable meaning). Revelations of vote fraud in the large cities became commonplace.

The first congressional investigation of government corruption, conducted by the Covode Committee in 1859, found ample ground for indignation. The source of this broom sweeping was not a burst of civic high-mindedness but the desire of a newly Republican-led House to attack the Democratic Buchanan administration. The old Jacksonian ideal of government by the people had become another warning sign—along with slavery (or opposition to it), Catholicism and immigrants (or anti-Catholicism and nativism), drunkenness (or prohibition), and states'-rights secessionism (or federal supremacy)—that the grand American experiment was failing.

The major parties appeared to be losing their broadly inclusive character. The egalitarian language of the Jacksonian Democrats took on a sharper, narrower tone. America was defined less as a harbinger of freedom to the downtrodden peoples of the world and more as a nation with a "manifest destiny" to dominate the hemisphere, as Democratic newspaper editor John L. O'Sullivan put it in 1835. Stephen Douglas of Illinois, the leading Democratic senator of the 1850s, wanted to "make the area of liberty as broad as the continent itself," though modestly he "did not wish to go beyond the great ocean—beyond those boundaries which the God of nature had marked out." Ardent Jacksonian John Wentworth of Illinois looked forward to the day when the Speaker of the House would recognize not only "the gentleman from Texas" but also "the gentleman from Oregon, the gentleman from Nova Scotia, the gentleman from Canada, the gentleman from Cuba, the gentleman from Mexico, aye, even the gentleman from Patagonia."

Along with spread-eagleism, the post-Jacksonian Democrats defined themselves more and more as the party of white supremacy: now, and for a long time to come, a means of maintaining party concord between the swelling Irish Catholic immigrants of the North and the white Baptists and Methodists of the South. White supremacy replaced the common man as the keynote of post-Jacksonian democracy. The party warned of a "conspiracy" of abolitionists, nativists, and Whig manufacturers. Anti-slavery Democrats began to leave the party, many going to the Free Soilers of 1848 (whose presidential candidate was born-again slavery opponent Martin Van Buren) or to the Whigs.

Manifest destiny and white supremacy did not keep the Democrats from weak-government, states'-rights rhetoric designed to appeal to both government-fearing Catholic immigrants and secessionist-minded southerners. The result: a Democratic program that left slavery, drink, and most social and economic regulation alone while calling for forceful government action against abolitionists and fugitive slaves. But the popular appeal of this message eroded in the North as increasing numbers of voters came to believe that a conspiratorial "slave power" threatened their way of life.

The Whigs did not match the grassroots support, strongly held ideas, or party organization of the Democrats. Their strength lay in their economic policy stands and attractive leadership: Senate titans Clay and Webster, military heroes and presidential candidates William Henry Harrison (1840), Zachary Taylor (1848), and Winfield Scott (1852).

This made for a thinner party culture. Taylor was ready to accept either party's nomination and campaigned in 1848 with no platform. Scott too preferred not to have a party platform in the 1852 campaign and tried to appeal to both sections. (He was soundly beaten by the even more pallid Democrat Franklin Pierce in an election with a smaller turnout than any since 1836.) The deaths of Taylor in July 1850 and of Clay in June and Webster in October 1852 were serious losses to a party so invested in its leaders. Looking back in 1879, a Mississippi newspaper-man concluded: "The Whig party died of too much respectability and not enough people."

The first serious sign of the Whigs' vulnerability appeared in their opposition to the Mexican War of 1846–48 (though not as dramatically as the War of 1812 hurt the Federalists). They were weakened too by their slow response—again, like the Federalists—to a changing economy: in this case the shift from commercial ties between northern merchants and manufacturers and southern planters to the new relationship between the East and the burgeoning Midwest. Nor did the old Whig commit-ment to internal improvements have the same appeal after British capital and private railroad building replaced government projects.

Most of all, the Whigs were more deeply divided than the Democrats over the territories and expansion, slavery and abolition, immigrants and Catholics. This made them highly vulnerable to the special-purpose politics that exploded in the 1850s, the logical extension of the do-your-own-thing ethos of America's democratic culture.

Few or no regulations constrained entry into the political system. It was as easy to form a party and run for office as to decide that you were a doctor or a lawyer or a teacher. The parties printed and distributed their own ballots, which were cast in public (thus making it harder for a voter to split his ballot). Most of all, the party-democratic regime fostered, and flourished within, a political culture that encouraged the inclusion of a broad range of social and economic issues.

It is not surprising that the popular concerns of greatest intensity—immigration and Catholicism, temperance and prohibition, slavery and the territories—found a voice in new political organizations that weak-ened the tempering force of two-party politics. As never before (or since) in American history, the 1850s were marked by an explosion of state and local third parties and by the rise of substantial national third parties, the Know-Nothings and the Republicans.

The anti-Catholic, nativist Know-Nothings of the 1850s, like the Anti-Masons of the 1820s, first appeared in New York as a social group focused on a supposed threat to the Republic. Again like the Anti-Masons, they rapidly spread and soon turned into a political party. Ostensibly the American Party (called Know-Nothings because its members were sup-posed to say "I know nothing" when asked about their organization) was a political response to the inflow of three million immigrants, most of them Irish and German (and Catholic), between 1845 and 1854—

a number equal to 15 percent of the 1845 population, the largest proportion of newcomers in the history of the United States.

The political rise of the Know-Nothings was meteoric. In 1854 they almost totally swept Massachusetts's offices and elected forty-three congressmen. Former president Millard Fillmore ran as the Whig-American party candidate in 1856 and won 21 percent of the popular vote. The party's anti-immigrant, anti-Catholic program had interregional appeal (though with differing political consequences). In the North and Midwest, Know-Nothingism adopted a distinctly Whiggish, anti-slavery tone. It focused on the Irish as supporters of slavery and on the Irish and Germans as Catholics and opponents of temperance or prohibition.

The party's lure in the border states was different. Nativism was a way of diverting a divided public's attention from the all-consuming conflict over slavery in the territories. Know-Nothingism also had considerable attraction in parts of the South—Georgia, Alabama, Mississippi—where immigrants were scarce but anti-Catholic sentiment and fear of immigrants as carriers of anti-slavery attitudes were easily stirred. The Know-Nothings also had some appeal to that substantial (if unmeasurable) minority who regarded both major parties with distaste and found an outlet in third-party politics.

If they had had only the Know-Nothings to contend with, the Whigs might have been able to absorb them, as they did the Anti-Masons in the early 1830s. Like the Anti-Masons, the Know-Nothings lacked consistency (they recruited Catholic workingmen and European immigrants to oppose the Chinese in California) and a larger sense of social purpose. Their only legislative proposal was a bill imposing a twenty-one-year naturalization period for immigrants; it was so contrary to the American inclusionary tradition (to say nothing of the country's labor needs) that it got nowhere. The same tensions that fueled the Know-Nothings ultimately tore the movement apart, as its northern and southern wings were absorbed into a politics where slavery and the Union mattered more than the threats of immigrants and Rome.

A more attractive new party, the Republicans, appeared on the political scene in the mid-1850s. They rapidly replaced the Whigs in the two-party politics that the ground rules of the Constitution required, and have retained that position ever since.

The Republican party was a product of the explosion of northern resentment over the Kansas-Nebraska Act, spiced by concurrent high feeling over immigrants, drink, and Catholicism. Congress passed the

Kansas-Nebraska Act in May 1854. On July 6, ten thousand people met in Jackson, Michigan, to form a new party, and adopted the name Republican (as did a similar group in Wisconsin). Other alliances called themselves Anti-Nebraska, Anti-Administration, Fusion, Independent, and People's parties. But Republican was the label that stuck. It did so because no other title (except perhaps Democratic, but that was already spoken for) so evocatively echoed the American political past. The names of the Republicans' anti-slavery predecessors, the Liberty and Free Soil parties, had less historical resonance.

In the fall 1854 elections the Democrats lost an estimated 350,000 votes to coalitions opposed to the Kansas-Nebraska Act. Only seven of the forty-two northern congressmen who supported the act were returned to office. By now the free land–free labor–free men theme, which had had only limited appeal when it appeared in the 1840s, attracted a wide following. The growing fear that the South wanted to make slavery a national institution, and the seeming readiness of the Democratic party to cooperate, tipped many of what Lincoln called "the plain old Democracy" toward the Republicans. The same conspiratorial purposes attributed to Masonry, the Bank of the United States, and the Catholic Church now attached to the "slave power." The Republican party's substantial nativist strand attracted not only Know-Nothings but also many native-born Protestant Democrats. And as the Whigs came unglued, a rolling tide (from west to east) of its followers joined the new party.

This mix kept the Republicans from falling into the classic third-party trap of too constricted an appeal. The party survived precisely because it transcended narrow class, ideological, and (excluding the South) sectional lines. It fashioned a broad, powerful message that sharply contrasted with the corruption of Jacksonian Democratic ideology, the xenophobic narrowness of the Know-Nothings, and the ideological senescence of the Whigs. Opposition to slavery (though not immediate abolition, as many abolitionists bitterly noted) was at the core of the Republican emergence. But it did not stand alone. A former Free Soiler said that he was for "freedom, temperance and Protestantism, against slavery, rum, and Romanism."

The Republicans appear to have attracted the most dynamic ideological, economic, and social elements of the North and the West. The party's stress on tariff protection won it important support from manufacturers (and workers). Its free land–free labor ideology attracted farmers responsive to the theme that the territories must not be turned over to slavery.

The party's builders were politics-hardened professionals, products of the rich experience in issue defining and vote getting afforded by the party-democratic regime. The strands of ideology and experience that gave the new party its tensile strength are summed up in the rise of Abraham Lincoln, as iconic a figure of the new regime as George Washington was of the one that preceded it.

Lincoln was borne aloft by the most powerful social, economic, and political currents of his time. His humble frontier origins and upbringing and his rise to circuit-riding lawyer, successful railroad attorney, and important political player in Illinois Whig politics more than met the popular political requirement that he be a self-made man. His extraordinary way with words was no less crucial in a political culture that expected its leaders to communicate effectively with the electorate. He found in the 1850s an agenda that gave full vent to his speculative and generalizing genius and catapulted him into national politics. (Iconoclastic historian David Waldstreicher dismisses Lincoln as "another onetime frontier brawler, Indian fighter, and party hack" who "found in war a way to ennoble the party battle, unify Americans, and relive the Revolution." That *can't* be right.)

Lincoln's breakthrough moment was the Illinois senatorial election of 1858. For the first time a state party convention—with fifteen hundred delegates attending—chose its senatorial candidate. Numerous county conventions seconded Lincoln's nomination. Another first: the major issue in the campaign was whom the new Illinois legislature would select as United States senator, testimony to the importance of the slavery-in-the-territories issue and to the fact that the incumbent was Stephen Douglas, chairman of the key Committee on Territories.

Challenger Lincoln proposed no less than fifty debates. Incumbent Douglas naturally objected, and they compromised on a not insignificant seven. Crowds of ten thousand or more gathered to hear (or try to hear) the candidates. A court reporter took the first stenographic record of a political debate. Extensive newspaper coverage and distribution (Douglas used his franking privilege to send out 345,000 copies) secured national attention. The Democrats retained enough seats in the Illinois legislature to return Douglas to the Senate. But the election gave Lincoln a national reputation and a strong claim to the Republican presidential nomination in 1860.

The election of 1860 is on everyone's list of the most important in American history. Most historians and political scientists see it (along with

1828, 1896, and 1932) as a transforming election, marking the passage from one party system (Jacksonian Democratic and Whig) to another (the Civil War system).

But it is not clear that the Civil War marked so sharp a break in party culture. Nor did Lincoln's victory signal a tectonic shift in the electorate. His vote total, less than 40 percent, was the lowest for a winner in American political history, and the voter turnout of 82 percent of eligibles was the second highest. The combined popular vote of northern Democrat Stephen Douglas and southern Democrat John C. Breckinridge exceeded Lincoln's.

Despite the steady attrition in the South's relative position in Congress and the electoral college during the 1850s, the polity responded sensitively to that section's interests. President-elect Lincoln, who was not on the ballot in ten southern states, tried mightily to mollify southerners. He spoke of putting slavery "where the public mind shall rest in the belief that it is in the course of ultimate extinction," hardly a clarion call for abolition. In early 1861 two-thirds of the House approved, and Lincoln had "no objection" to, an amendment forbidding any future alteration of the Constitution that enabled Congress to interfere with the "domestic institutions" of any state, "including that of persons held to labor or service by the laws of said state."

Democratic presidents Franklin Pierce and James Buchanan were sympathetic to the South and slavery. And the Democrats controlled the House (except for 1855–57) and the Senate from 1849 to 1859. Southern Whigs and allied northern "Cotton Whigs," border staters thirsting for compromise, and Taney's *Dred Scott* decision were additional evidence against the idea that southern slavery faced an imminent (or even prospective) threat to its existence.

The slavery-in-the-territories controversy, so central to the politics of the 1850s, turned out to be no real issue at all. Kansas was down to two slaves by 1860, Nebraska had fifteen, Utah twenty-nine, and New Mexico twenty-four, almost all the house servants of government officials. Nor was the flow of fugitive slaves northward, so conspicuous a source of southern anxiety, a major problem. Despite highly publicized instances of fleeing slaves caught or evading capture, there were only 803 fugitives in 1860, one-fiftieth of 1 percent of the slave population.

Many leading southerners were reluctant to leave the Union and had a lot to lose by doing so. Nevertheless, the belief that it was an acceptable, necessary step to sustain slavery led eleven southern states to secede in the wake of Lincoln's election (though in only three of them was secession ratified by the voters). At the same time the dominant view in the North was that the Union must be maintained at all costs and (for an increasing number) that slavery must be brought to an end.

How was it that two such opposed mind-sets had come into being? Why was the northern response not, in the formulation of Horace Greeley's *New York Tribune*, to "let the erring sisters depart in peace" but rather to resist secession with force? And why did the two sides pursue their respective courses with a tenacity that produced the bloodiest war of the nineteenth century?

Large historical explanations are not hard to come by. Demography inexorably consigned the South to deepening minority status in the Union, with all that meant for congressional and electoral power. None of the five states admitted from 1848 to 1861 had slavery. Although the cotton culture prospered, the growth of northern agriculture and manufacturing threatened to create an economic gap between the sections. And while racist denigration of African Americans was a national phenomenon, it was compounded in the South by a complex mix of guilt and defensiveness that came from being enmeshed in an institution rejected by the rest of the Western world.

There is a still more profound explanation for the South's turn to secession. The most distinctive feature of American society was, arguably, its (white) people's freedom to develop their own social, cultural, and economic institutions. No central authority defined or regulated their churches, schools, social customs, economic enterprises, or political parties. When that freedom to choose faced threats internal or external, the recurrent American response was to strike out on a new course: of settlement (westward migration), of institution making (religion, language, mores, parties), of government (the Revolution and the Constitution).

Alone among the nation's major institutions, slavery's legitimacy depended on an increasingly uncertain polity. It took no great leap of the social imagination for most white southerners to conclude that to form one's own nation in the face of necessity was an eminently American thing to do. From this perspective, secession was a logical conclusion to decades of decline in government authority and growth in individual freedom of choice. This was not so much a challenge to the culture of the democratic regime as an application of it—the product, in the formulation of David Donald, the foremost historian of the period, of "an excess of democracy."

No less intricate and deeply rooted were the sources of the North's reaction to secession. Most white southerners, for their own good reasons, saw secession as a defensible application of American experience. Mainstream northern public opinion came to the opposite conclusion.

Only ardent abolitionists and those who were pro-South—outliers on the bell curve of northern attitudes—were ready to see the Union break up. Most held to the view that the United States of America had a near-sacred social meaning: "the last best hope of mankind," in Lincoln's words. Secession was an unacceptable challenge to their identity as Americans. To allow it was a confession of social and cultural, even psychological, defeat. Lincoln asked in his first inaugural address: "Is there in all republics this inherent and fatal weakness? Must a government, of necessity, be too strong for the liberties of its own people, or too weak to maintain its own existence?" For him, and for most northerners, there could be only one answer: no. Any other would be a confession that the American experiment had failed. This belief was as deeply held in the North as was the belief in the South that being an American included the right, if necessary, to create your own nation.

CIVIL WAR, UNCIVIL PEACE

The Civil War not only is the grand national epic but also was long seen as the great divide between the agrarian-artisanal early Republic and urban-industrial modern America. It was in the course of the war that the country first flexed its newly grown ideological and economic muscles. It proved itself able not only to preserve itself as a nation and to rid itself of its most indefensible social institution but to produce in Lincoln a political figure of world stature and to demonstrate a military and state capacity that (if it so chose) could have made it a world power.

Nationalism, liberalism, industrialism, bourgeois society, the powerful state: all of the hallmarks of the modernizing nineteenth-century Western world came to a realization of sorts in the United States during the 1860s. Small wonder that Karl Marx, casting about in the 1870s for a likely headquarters for his First International, at one point chose New York on the assumption that the leading bourgeois nation was the logical—indeed, the (Marxian) scientifically predestined—setting for socialist revolution. Nor is it surprising (though it is certainly a historical distortion) that in discussing the rise of the all-devouring modern state, literary critic Edmund Wilson put Lincoln alongside Bismarck and Lenin in the first rank of ruthless consolidators.

But was the political culture of the pre-war regime swept away by the winds of civil war? Was the heritage of the war a new political culture, a new form of government, a new body of law? Was New York senator

Daniel Dickinson right to predict that *"political parties,* in the old sense of the term, are to exist *no more in this country"*?

Certainly the wartime experience did much to support expectations of regime change. The scope of the northern war effort breathtakingly expanded over the course of the conflict. The initial assumption was that a weak central government lacked the resources to fight effectively and that a decentralized, voluntaristic society would take up the slack. Localities, states, individual politicians, and groups of citizens (butchers, blacksmiths, men named Smith) organized their own regiments. State governors Oliver Morton of Indiana, John Andrew of Massachusetts, and Andrew Curtin of Pennsylvania independently contracted for weapons, matériel, and loans at home and abroad. Congress asserted itself as an autonomous branch of government with its Joint Committee on the Conduct of the War.

Independent organizations defined and pursued their own wartime agendas, including the anti-war, pro-Confederate Copperheads (the nickname given to members of the Knights of the Golden Circle, a group of southern sympathizers in the North) and the pro-Republican Union League Clubs. The United States Sanitary Commission, run by elite reformers, took on the responsibility of tending to the Union wounded—and a lot more besides. Its head, Massachusetts clergyman Henry W. Bellows, proposed that he and his fellows form "a sort of volunteer Congress and debate, consider and agree upon some wise course for the preservation of the country—to shape a policy for the government." Lincoln with subtle irony called the commission his "fifth wheel."

But decentralized voluntarism was no more able to win a mid-nineteenth-century war than a late-eighteenth-century revolution. One order of business was to sculpt the executive branch, the bureaucracy, Congress, the Republican party, and the army into institutions capable of victory. Lincoln was as central to this effort as he was in defining the nation's war aims of preserving the Union and abolishing slavery.

The war shattered the stasis afflicting pre-war American government. The southerners' departure from Congress, a Supreme Court enlarged to give Lincoln new appointments, and the wartime need for strong national authority opened the door to an outburst of state building unmatched since the time of the country's founding. Intellectuals and political theorists, before the war given over to the celebration of individualism and a weak, decentralized state, now advocated a "Great Republic." Even Ralph Waldo Emerson, the philosopher of American individualism, did his bit as a member of the public visiting committee for West Point.

Under Lincoln the presidency took on the kind of power that Americans had worried about since the nation's beginning. When he came into office twelve hundred of the top fifteen hundred federal officeholders left or were fired, a turnover far greater than any before then. Congress was not in session when Fort Sumter was attacked, and Lincoln turned to the rarely used device of a presidential proclamation to pronounce a state of hostilities and authorize an expanded army. (The Supreme Court accepted this assumption of authority by a 5–4 vote.) He used the same instrument to suspend the writ of habeas corpus, and with his Emancipation Proclamation to end slavery in the Confederate states.

Unprecedented too was the wartime suppression of dissent. Pro-Confederate Clement Vallandigham of Ohio was jailed and exiled. About fifteen thousand other citizens were arrested under orders from the secretaries of state and war. More than three hundred newspapers were suspended for varying lengths of time.

The sheer scale of the financial, human, material, and organizational demands of the Union war effort overwhelmed state, local, and private resources. The federal budget was $66 million in 1861, $1.3 billion in 1865: a tenfold increase even after taking inflation into account. Salmon P. Chase's Treasury Department was obliged to engage in fiscal and monetary policies on a scale and of a complexity far beyond anything faced (or imagined) before. Edwin M. Stanton's Department of War became a monster federal agency, responsible for doling out huge contracts and clothing, feeding, training, and deploying millions of men. It produced the first recognizably modern big-government bureaucrats: Quartermaster General Montgomery Meigs and up-and-coming young railroad man Andrew Carnegie, in charge of the United States Railroad Company, the government-run railroad that supplied the Union armies.

Congress contributed to the quickening pace of wartime government. (Lincoln in 1863 ordered work on the Capitol's unfinished dome to continue: "When the people see the dome rising it will be a sign that we intend the Union to go on.") A legislative torrent unmatched since the Republic's first, formative days poured out of the Republican-dominated legislature. It included the Pacific Railroad Act and the incorporation of the Union Pacific Railroad (the first nationally chartered corporation since the Second Bank of the United States), the groundbreaking Homestead Act and Morrill Land Grant College Act, the Morrill protective tariff, and the National Banking Act (which made the first provision for federal paper currency, or "greenbacks"). These added up to what has been called "a blueprint for modern America." Indeed, war seemed, in the aphorism of the early-twentieth-century social critic Randolph Bourne, to be the health of the state.

Party politics put heavy pressure on Lincoln's wartime presidency. But in the last analysis it strengthened more than harmed the Union war effort and the authority of the federal government. As a plurality president, Lincoln had to appeal to pro-war Democrats. This had costs, among them the appointment and retention of inept Democratic general George McClellan and an initial emphasis on the war as a struggle for the Union rather than against slavery. In the 1864 election Lincoln renamed the Republicans the Union Republican Party and chose War Democrat Andrew Johnson as his running mate. The result (enhanced by the absence of the South) was a 55–45 percent popular vote victory over Democratic candidate McClellan: the largest margin, and the first two-term presidency, since Andrew Jackson.

A vocal Radical Republican wing of the party, centered in Congress, pushed for (and legitimated) Lincoln's moves toward emancipation and, through Generals Grant and Sherman, for war à outrance that finally crushed the Confederacy. Party politics helped Lincoln sustain a sufficiently broad base of support during the war's difficult early years, and ultimately to define its purpose in terms that justified its staggering human costs.

The beliefs that slavery lay at the core of secession and that human freedom was the ultimate justification for the preservation of the Union made the end of that institution a war aim comparable to keeping the nation together. By 1865 more than 120,000 members of the million-man Union army were black, each a potent argument that the abolition of slavery was a necessary goal. Lincoln's Emancipation Proclamation of 1863, and finally the Thirteenth Amendment (1865) abolishing slavery, were arguably the most important actions of the federal government in the nineteenth century.

What made all this possible was not only the unfolding logic of the war but also the ability of a democratic polity to respond when sufficiently challenged. The Civil War has been called a people's war. The individual expressiveness that so hobbled the party-democratic regime in ordinary times now showed a striking capacity to respond to the nation's gravest crisis.

That capability was stoked by the attractive power of the war's great emotive causes, preserving the Union and expanding human freedom. The narrative line of an unending flow of bloody battles (five to six thousand separate engagements) and a gradually unfolding victory was brought home to the nation by a large body of war correspondents, who fed telegraph-reported stories to an extensive infrastructure of newspapers and magazines. Influential opinion shapers such as Thomas Nast's powerful drawings and political cartoons in *Harper's Weekly* reinforced support for Lincoln, abolition, and the war effort. An expanded mail delivery system kept the troops in close contact with their families and neighbors, making the war a widely, and intensely, shared experience.

The source of the Confederacy's failure and the North's success lay ultimately in the sectional disparity of men, matériel, and money. But just as the Union victory depended on its political and administrative ability to mobilize its resources, so was the South's defeat in good part the product of an ultimately crippling deficit in politics and government. During the war's early years, the South's martial élan and the advantages of fighting a defensive war served it well. But ultimately the Confederacy was borne under by its inability to convince either its Union enemy or the nations of Europe, or perhaps its own people, that in fact it was a new nation.

One difficulty was that much of the Confederacy's ideology and structure echoed the Union it claimed to have left. The new nation sought a legitimacy based on the American Revolution, the Declaration of Independence, and the Constitution. Washington and Jefferson were its patron saints. (A proposal that the new country be called the Republic of Washington narrowly lost in the Confederate congress.) Alexander H. Stephens, who became the Confederacy's vice president, said that the purpose behind the Confederate constitution "was to sustain, uphold and perpetuate the fundamental principles of the Constitution of the United States."

But these claims were undermined by the centrality of its commitment to slavery. As Stephens put it, the "cornerstone" of the Confederacy was "the great truth that the negro is not the equal of the white man; that slavery—subordination to the superior race—is his natural and normal condition." The *Charleston Mercury* tried to echo the Founders when it declared of the drafting of the Confederate constitution: "It now remains to be seen whether, with slave institutions, the master race can establish and perpetuate free government." But a mid-nineteenth-century nation whose prime purpose was the perpetuation of human slavery faced insurmountable moral problems.

Ambiguities and inconsistencies suffused the government of the Confederacy. Its constitution pledged to establish a "permanent federal" government based on the states rather than the people. Yet that document was the supreme law of the land—and had no provision for secession from the Confederacy. Its president was limited to one six-year term: more than enough, as things turned out. The Confederate congress was tightly constrained by state loyalties, as befitted a body of states'-rights secessionists. Its constitution provided for a supreme court, but the state-driven Confederacy never created one. Of necessity, state courts relied on the precedents of the pre-war federal judiciary.

This experiment in states' rights and limited government was forced by the exigencies of war to enact conscription and (unlike the North) forbid substitutes, flood the country with depreciated Confederate currency, impress goods from the citizenry, and suspend the writ of habeas corpus. Even its core commitment to slavery finally had to be compromised. While the property right of slavery was guaranteed, the importation of slaves from overseas was forbidden. And toward the end of the war attempts were made to enlist black troops, with emancipation as the lure.

The Confederacy was a government increasingly authoritarian in its methods, increasingly impotent in its authority. During its brief life there were fourteen appointees to its six cabinet posts (including six secretaries of war). It had no capacity to deal with the inclination of states such as Georgia and North Carolina to keep their troops and supplies to themselves. Robert E. Lee may have been the most able of the Civil War's generals, but there was no centralized Confederate military machine comparable to the Union army of Grant and Sherman. At the end of 1864, 196,000 Confederate troops were on duty—and 200,000 were absent without leave.

Political parties were another American public institution that the Confederacy failed to adopt. There is some dispute over whether the Confederacy was weakened or strengthened by this lack. But a strong case can be made that party-run elections might have softened interstate and factional differences. A study of roll-call voting in the Confederate and Union congresses shows considerably more predictability in the latter: a measure of the unifying effect of party.

The emotional impact of the titanic struggle to preserve the nation's body by securing the Union, and its soul by ending slavery, came to a melodramatic climax fit for the Romantic Age. Lee surrendered at Appomattox on April 9, 1865, Palm Sunday. That conjunction invoked a great religious outpouring of calls for reconciliation, in the spirit of Lincoln's second inaugural address the month before: "With malice toward none; with charity for all."

Five days later, on Good Friday, Lincoln was shot, and died the next morning. On the following day, Easter Sunday—Black Easter—enormous

crowds poured into the nation's churches, and the tone of public sentiment abruptly changed to a passionate desire for punishment and revenge.
"Not often in human history," observed historian John Lothrop Motley,
"has a great nation been subjected to such a sudden conflict of passions."

This Wagnerian climax to the great national drama of the Civil War
might reasonably have been expected to put the final stamp on a sea
change in the American polity. Now, surely, was the time for regime
change as profound and consequential as the one that followed the Revolution and the creation of the Republic. The consequences of the wartime effort seemed clear enough: a powerful, centralized American state,
a broad conception of American citizenship transcending the barrier of
race. Post-war intellectuals sensed that they lived in a time of special
promise, when political ideals and spiritual values had a unique chance
to shape the public agenda. George W. Curtis, editor of the influential
magazine *Harper's Weekly*, declaimed: "[W]e are mad if the blood of the
war has not anointed our eyes to see that all reconstruction is vain that
leaves any question too brittle to handle." Historian and chemist John
W. Draper turned his gaze "from the hideous contemplation of a dis-
organization of the Republic, each state, and county, and town setting up
for itself, . . . to a future I see in prospect—an imperial race organizing its
intellect, concentrating it, and voluntarily submitting to be controlled by
its reason."

Much in post-war public policy echoed these expectations. At its core
were the constitutional amendments and legislative acts that set the terms
of the Confederate states' reentry into the Union and defined the status
of black Americans. The three amendments adopted between 1865 and
1869—compared to none during the preceding sixty-one years and the
ensuing forty-three—embedded new concepts of citizenship and race in
the Constitution. The Thirteenth Amendment's abolition of slavery led
logically to the creation of a national citizenry entitled to due process and
equal protection under the Fourteenth Amendment, and finally, in the
Fifteenth Amendment, to a flat-out commitment to race-blind suffrage.

The Civil Rights Act of 1866, the Reconstruction Act of 1867, and the
Enforcement Acts of 1870 and 1871 put legislative meat on these constitutional bones. The South was divided into military districts, and substantial detachments of federal troops were posted to oversee southern
political reintegration and secure the citizenship rights of the freedmen.

That was not all. Lesser but related actions included the Freedmen's
Bureau of 1866 to foster education and land ownership for the ex-slaves,
Congress-chartered Howard University, created in 1867 primarily to train

black lawyers, and the broad-scale removal of racially discriminatory provisions in federal statutes. Black political participation—voting and officeholding—was at the core of this effort, as it had been for white males at the inception of the party-democratic regime forty years before.

Other groups shared in this post-war expansion of the democratic ethos. Pre-war policy toward Native Americans had two goals: seize Indian lands and remove the tribes to the trans-Mississippi West. President Ulysses Grant's Peace Policy of 1869, in which religious denominations were to take over the Indian agencies on the reservations, and the Dawes Act of 1884, designed to induce Indians to become yeoman farmers, had a different social purpose: social and cultural integration. Ely Parker, a Seneca who was a member of Grant's wartime staff, became commissioner of Indian affairs, an appointment inconceivable in pre-war America.

Women's rights—most particularly the right to vote—had lurked for decades on the fringes of public consciousness. Now it claimed a place by the side of black suffrage. A number of Republican senators gave lip service to women's suffrage legislation, and the party's 1872 and 1876 platforms spoke vaguely of "respectful consideration" of the "honest demands of this class of citizens for additional rights, privileges, and immunities." But aside from women getting the right to practice law before federal courts, concrete gains were limited to the states. "School suffrage"—voting and running for school boards—appeared in a number of communities. And women won the right to vote in elections in the female-starved Wyoming and Utah territories in 1870, the first sizeable political units anywhere to do this.

If a more inclusive view of citizenship was one apparent outcome of the war, another was a strengthened sense of the reach of government. A Japanese visitor to Washington said in 1871: "It is . . . claimed by the best thinkers that the American Government was never more powerful and influential for good than it is at the present time." A British observer had the impression that "the central departments of the Government are upon a much more complete footing, with larger and more various establishments, than anything of the kind that we have. All these centralized departments are the creation of the last few years."

Non-military federal expenditure in 1869 reached a higher proportion of the national income (4.6 percent) than it would for the rest of the century. The government's infrastructure proliferated. It included new Cabinet departments (Agriculture in 1862, Justice in 1870) and a flock of new agencies: the National Academy of Sciences (1863), the office of the commissioner of immigration (1864), the Bureau of Statistics and the

Bureau of Education (1866), the United States Weather Bureau in 1870, the office of the commissioner of fish and fisheries in 1871. In what Henry Adams later called "almost its first modern act of legislation," Congress in 1867 funded a geological and topographical exploration of the territory that lay between the Rockies and the Sierras. And in an impressive instance of non-military muscle flexing, Congress provided land grants and subsidies for the completion of the first transcontinental railway in 1869, an event welcomed as "a new chapter in American nationality, in American progress and in American power."

Washington itself underwent a new birth not only of freedom (the city became a testing ground for black civil rights) but of civic improvement. Congress made it a federal territory in 1871, which enabled the capital city to have home rule through a territorial government. The Board of Public Works and its strongman Alexander R. Shepherd oversaw a rebuilding of the city's infrastructure reminiscent of (though hardly comparable to) Baron Haussmann's rebuilding of Paris. The Republican Congress readily allocated the necessary funds. As Thomas C. Platt of New York put it, "[W]e are here to make this capital city exemplify the civilization of our country." And so it did: not only with grand structures such as the State, War, and Navy Building (for a time the world's largest office building) and the Library of Congress (then the world's largest library) but also with a healthy dose of corrupt contract letting under Boss Shepherd.

A comparable if less conspicuous growth in government activity went on in the states and cities. "The work of the politics of the war" led to "great organic changes" in state constitutions reflecting the acceptance of black citizenship and more active government. A number of them reduced or removed restrictions on black voting and other civil rights. There was a surge of state regulation of education, welfare, public health, economic development, and working conditions, in stark contrast with pre-war laissez-faire—a prelude to the Progressive legislative outburst at the turn of the twentieth century. States began to create railroad, health, and charities commissions. State and city taxation and indebtedness swelled in response to the need to improve the infrastructure in pace with population growth, and because the idea of active government itself had new currency.

The transformation of government went hand in hand with a major challenge to the established forms of party politics. Lincoln's wartime expedient of a Union Republican party that reached out to War Democrats did not long survive the 1864 election. His assassination in April

1865 put ex-Democrat Andrew Johnson in the presidency—at precisely the time when the Republicans, from their state, congressional, and governmental power bases, set out to translate the war's goals into legislation. Johnson sought to consolidate his anomalous position in the 1866 congressional election by resorting to a Democratic version of Lincoln's 1864 Union Republicans: a National Union party made up of Democrats and Republicans ready to accept the defeat of the Confederacy and the end of slavery but not much else. In a dramatic demonstration of the ideological intensity generated by the war, Johnson's hostility to the congressional Republicans' reconstruction plans led to the first attempted impeachment of a president. That this happened was testimony to the degree to which the war unleashed powerful new political forces.

It is often said that out of the Civil War and Reconstruction there emerged a new party system, following the Federalist-Jeffersonian Republican one of the Founders and the Jacksonian-Whig system of the pre-war decades. It has been argued too that a strong American national state—a "Yankee Leviathan," as one label has it—was a product of the war, and that a "second constitutional regime," based on the Fourteenth Amendment, came into being.

But the political, governmental, and legal experience of the United States in the late nineteenth and early twentieth centuries does not support this view. From the larger perspective of a party-democratic regime stretching from the 1830s to the 1930s, the changes wrought on the American polity by the Civil War appear ephemeral and superficial. Radical Reconstruction turned out to be not the beginning of a new age in American race relations but a false dawn of civil equality, soon overwritten by resurgent popular, political, and legal racism. The active state of the war quickly fell prey to the powerful countercurrents of localism and laissez-faire that dominated nineteenth-century American public life. The new constitutional regime foretold by the Fourteenth Amendment did not come into being until well into the twentieth century.

The Civil War and Reconstruction were not a time of regime change but rather an interlude after which the culture of the pre-war party-democratic regime—two-party politics, a weak national state, a politically responsive legal system—rapidly reasserted itself. The late-nineteenth- and early-twentieth-century American polity stunningly demonstrated the ability of older American views of politics, government, and law to persist in the face of massive economic, social, and cultural change.

What was different was that before the Civil War, the primary challenge facing the regime was the place of government power in a democratic culture. After the war, that regime had to deal with the challenges posed not by the meaning of democracy but by the character and consequences of the economic and social change wrought by American industrialization.

PART THREE

THE PARTY-DEMOCRATIC REGIME: THE INDUSTRIAL POLITY

For all the intimations of regime change during the Civil War–Reconstruction era, it soon became apparent that quite another scenario was playing out. There was not, after all, to be a second American Revolution. The American polity was no more fundamentally altered by the end of the Confederacy and the restoration of the Union than American racism was by the end of slavery. As historian Joel Silbey put it, "Martin Van Buren's template remained in place."

The most significant feature of late-nineteenth- and early-twentieth-century American public life was the persistence of existing ways of going about politics, law, and governance. This was the case even in the face of the massive new challenges raised by the age of industrialism. The American polity by 1930 was far closer to that of the preceding century than to the regime that emerged in the three-quarters of the century to come. It would take the Great Depression, the Second World War, the Cold War, and the post-war transformation of American life to bring about regime change comparable to that of the late eighteenth and early nineteenth centuries.

In one sense the persistence of the democratic-party regime was a triumph. It weathered massive economic, social, and cultural tensions without coming apart as it did in the 1850s. But in other respects, *success* is not the appropriate word. For all the ability of the political system to absorb and integrate newcomers from outside and migrants within, it fell short (how short became evident in the Great Depression of the 1930s) in regulating the new industrial economy, in providing social welfare responsive to the needs of most of its people, and in responding to the demands of ethnic and racial diversity.

CHAPTER SEVEN

THE AGE OF
THE POLITICOS

I N THE WAKE of the Civil War and Reconstruction, the major parties
resumed their sway over American political life. This is not to say that
nothing had changed. There was a dramatic inversion of major party
dominance. The seven decades of American political life from 1861 to
1932 were a near mirror image of the six decades from 1801 to 1859.

	1801–1859	1861–1932
Presidency (terms)		
Democratic-Republican/Democratic	12	4
Federalist/Whig/Republican	3	14
House (majorities)		
Democratic-Republican/Democratic	25	12
Federalist/Whig/Republican	5	23
Senate (majorities)		
Democratic-Republican/Democratic	26	4
Federalist/Whig/Republican	4	31

The second significant change was in the tone of the polity. Simply
put, American politics, government, and law became more highly organized, a development common to other major institutions of industrial society: business, agriculture, labor, education, the professions. The

democratic polity of the early nineteenth century evolved into the industrial polity, in which the problems of governance raised by an industrial age replaced the problems of governance posed by the conflict between state and federal power.

This change in political culture can be seen in the contrasting views of the major foreign observers of pre– and post–Civil War American public life. Alexis de Tocqueville's *Democracy in America,* written in the 1830s, viewed the nation's politics through the prism of the democratic idea. James Bryce's *The American Commonwealth* half a century later took on the task "of portraying the whole political system of the country in its practice as well as its theory." In contrast with Tocqueville's "treatise . . . upon democracy," he offered what he called a more inductive, objective study of the political system: "its framework and constitutional machinery, the methods by which it is worked, the forces which move it and direct its course." Bryce equated the "machinery" of the parties with the "machinery" of government: "Parties have been organized far more elaborately in the United States than anywhere else in the world, and have passed more completely under the control of a professional class. The party organizations in fact form a second body of political machinery, existing side by side with that of the legally constituted government, and scarcely less complicated."

Late-nineteenth-century America and Europe had a common need to confront the consequences of industrialism. Substantial political parties, a partisan popular press, pressure to expand access to the ballot—American traits all—had a conspicuous place in Britain, French, and German public life as well. But European politics made its way in a world dominated by monarchies and aristocracies, established churches, and bureaucratic and military elites. And international power politics meant that diplomacy and foreign relations, war and the threat of war, were far more important than in America.

British party politics continued to be the closest counterpart to the United States. Benjamin Disraeli's Conservatives sought to unite the gentry and the masses with appeals to patriotism and prosperity that resembled the American Republican creed. British Liberals, like American Democrats, drew on their country's Celtic and agrarian fringes. Gladstone echoed Jeffersonian-Jacksonian rhetoric when he spoke of "the masses against the classes" and "the nation against selfish interests."

But even after the British Reform Acts of 1868 and 1884, some 40 percent of Britain's adult males—including lodgers, tenants, domestic servants, soldiers, and sailors—were voteless, and remained so until 1918. (The comparable American figure for the non-enfranchised in 1880 was about 14 percent.) Although Parliament had a growing number of commercial-industrial members, its aristocratic-gentry component continued to dominate. The tone and composition of that body remained leagues away from the American Congress, whose most characteristic figure was a self-made small-town lawyer turned professional politician.

Local ties, party loyalty, and ethno-cultural identity mattered far more in the American political scene than in its British counterpart, which remained in thrall to a deferential model of representation. Over the course of his sixty-two years in Parliament, William Gladstone switched from the Tories to the Liberal party and never set down political roots in a constituency. In the election of 1880 he successfully stood for parliamentary seats in both the Scottish Midlothian district (with 3,620 voters) and the English city of Leeds (with an electorate of 50,000). He chose to represent Midlothian and passed his Leeds seat on to his son Herbert: hardly an exercise in democracy. (Addressing mass meetings made Gladstone's Midlothian campaign a landmark in British political history. The idea came from Liberal grandee Lord Rosebery, who had observed a Democratic convention in New York.)

The Civil War contributed greatly to the change in American political culture from the age of Tocqueville to the age of Bryce. A generation of politicians was schooled in the arts—and the organizational demands—of military conflict. Novelist Brand Whitlock, observing a political parade of the time—"the smell of saltpeter, the snorts of horses, the shouts of men, the red and white ripple of the flags that went careering by in smoke and flame"—found in it "some strange suggestion of the war our political contests typify, in spirit and symbol at least." An Indiana politician said of the 1888 Republican convention: "The excitement, the mental and physical strains, the conflicting emotions in the hope of victory and the fear of defeat, in such a convention as that was, are surpassed only by a prolonged battle in actual warfare, as I have been told by officers of the Civil War who later engaged in convention struggles."

The language of American politics was enriched before the war by images drawn from the farm and the racetrack. Now it drew on the metaphor of politics as war. A pastiche assembled by historian Richard Jensen: "From the *opening gun* of the *campaign* the *standard bearer*, along with other *war-horses fielded* by the party, *rallied* the *rank and file* around the party *standard*. . . . Precinct *captains aligned* their *phalanxes shoulder-to-shoulder* to *mobilize* votes" (emphasis added).

As the memory of the war faded, a vocabulary that reflected the darker side of the new political culture—manipulation and corruption—came to the fore. The *party faithful* were (of course) *good soldiers, rock-ribbed regulars*. But they were also *hacks, henchmen, hangers-on, cronies, ward heelers.* The pressure to get out the vote led to a flock of illegal practices: *floaters, repeaters, ballot box stuffing, the cemetery vote.* Party politics was an expensive business, fueled by *boodle, graft, loot, ripper legislation, slush funds,* and *rakeoffs.* And now the *boss* and the *machine* became more pervasive, more ominous.

The Civil War and Reconstruction spawned terms of political opprobrium reflecting the ideological intensity of the time: *Radical Republican, Copperhead, carpetbagger, Scalawag.* But then party factionalism (*Stalwarts* and *Half-Breeds* among Republicans, *Redeemers* and *Bourbons* among southern Democrats) and the denigration of anti-party reformers (*mugwumps, goo-goos, do-gooders, man-milliners*) became more common verbal currency: the language of a politics defined more by party identity than ideology.

The shift in political culture from the Civil War–Reconstruction politics of ideas to the late-nineteenth-century politics of organization is reflected in the art of Thomas Nast, the preeminent political cartoonist of the time. During the 1860s and early 1870s, Nast's cartoons dwelt on core Republican beliefs: preserving the Union, ending slavery, protecting the civil rights of the freedmen, opposing the power of the Catholic Church, exposing the corruption of the Tweed machine. But in the mid- and late 1870s he made a very different contribution to American political iconography: the Republican elephant and the Democratic donkey, beasts without substantive ideological identity (except perhaps that the elephant was massive and lumbering, the donkey scrawny and neutered).

There was other visual testimony to the predominance of organization politics. Hulking new state capitals rose in New York, Pennsylvania, and Indiana (the last overseen by a board of commissioners made up of the two major parties). So did equally over-the-top city halls in Philadelphia and San Francisco. Between 1869 and 1871, Tammany boss Tweed's New York Court House swallowed over $13 million (more than four times as much as the Houses of Parliament, built between 1840 and 1888) and never was completed. Like the swollen ranks of public employees that filled them, these megaliths were testaments not to the rise of an active, autonomous state but to political parties that battened on the prospects of graft in the buildings' cost and politicos who reveled in the reflected glory of the buildings' ostentation.

National conventions provided another occasion for organizational muscle flexing. These were hugely attended affairs: eighteen thousand were at the 1880 Republican gathering in Chicago. Party leaders made their mark through convention oratory, eternal in duration by modern taste and of doubtful intelligibility to vast audiences without the benefit of amplification. But these spectacles entertained and energized the party faithful. And behind the show, the bosses did their necessary business of selecting candidates and cementing their relations with each other.

Elections, the cornerstone of the party-democratic regime, were frequent, far more so than today. An Iowa politician complained, "We work through one campaign, take a bath and start in on the next." Much was at stake: "So many offices depend upon the result of elections that electioneering is made a business, and politics are reduced to a trade," said one observer. And as an industrializing society became more complex, so did the business of politics. A candidate for the Michigan supreme court offered up a doleful litany of the interest groups with which he had to deal:

> I had not thought of the Homeopaths, but the other Elements of discord I have had brought too closely to be overlooked. The Railroad vote on a single issue would amount to nothing; but when the Democrats hang together—as they will—it makes a large defection.... The Prohibition movement in this light is important.... The colored vote...will be against me.... There is a special grievance arising out of the Tax title question which will not appear openly.... It is impossible to know just what wires are working.

This was the world of the politicos, the professional politicians whom foreign observers Bryce and Max Weber regarded as a new class. Britons, Bryce noted, speak of "politicians" in a generic sense, Americans of "the politicians" as a social group. "What characterizes them as compared with the corresponding class in Europe," he concluded, "is that their whole time is more frequently given to political work, that most of them draw an income from politics and the rest hope to do so, that they come largely from the poorer and less cultivated than from the higher ranks of society, and that... many are proficients in the arts of popular oratory, of electioneering, and of party management." The politicos of the Gilded Age were half feudal chieftains, half sophisticated organizers of men and money. They differed from their pre-war counterparts in the scale of their operations and the degree to which an organizational model—an industrial one—superseded the more democratic, voluntaristic party culture of the past.

New York Republican leader Roscoe Conkling said in an 1876 campaign speech: "We are told that the Republican party is a machine. Yes. A government is a machine; the common-school system of the State of New York is a machine; a political party is a machine. Every organization which binds men together for a common cause is a machine." His New York Democratic rival Samuel J. Tilden used a more organic metaphor, describing a party as "a living being, having all the organs of eyes, ears, and feelings." In practice he was as fully committed to the organized, systematic conduct of politics. They echoed but also elaborated on the party-building work of their predecessors Thurlow Weed and Martin Van Buren.

The disputed election of 1876, which in many respects resembled the moment of contested truth in 2000, is a measure of how far we are today from the political culture of the late nineteenth century. Then as in 2000, a Democratic popular majority was trumped by a post-election decision that gave the determining electoral votes (including those of Florida) to the Republican candidate. But while the later crisis was ended by judicial fiat in early 2001, the settlement of 1877 came out of the culture of organizational politics.

It was the work of an intensely partisan electoral commission, which (after some slick maneuvering) had a one-vote Republican majority. The commission decided every contested vote in favor of the Republican Hayes, enough to give him the presidency. A threatened filibuster (and, indeed, more violent opposition) was averted by northern Democrats, and especially by Speaker Samuel J. Randall, who was swayed by Republican assurances that patronage in Louisiana, hitherto controlled by a Radical Republican regime, would be abandoned to the Democrats. President Hayes fulfilled a pledge to put a southern Democrat, David M. Key, in charge of the Post Office, and Key gave a third of his region's postal appointments to his party fellows.

ELECTIONS AND PARTIES

Elections were the market, votes the product of the politicos' world. Poet James Russell Lowell called them "majority manufacturers." They were indeed successful entrepreneurs, fit contemporaries of Andrew Carnegie and John D. Rockefeller. They produced the highest turnouts in American political history: a mean of 78.5 percent of eligible voters (including the South) from 1876 to 1896. It is estimated that in the latter year over 95 percent of eligibles in the Midwest voted. State and local turnouts ranged from 60 to 80 percent, unmatched since.

Elections were frequent and ballots were long: the pre-war practice of subjecting almost all public offices to the vote persisted. Like so much else, this served the interests of the parties and the men who ran them. So too did the party-dominated local, state, and national conventions at which candidates were chosen. (Only 5–10 percent of candidates were selected by primaries in the 1880s.) Social critic John Jay Chapman observed in 1890 that "our system of party government has been developed . . . to keep control in the hands of professionals by multiplying technicalities and increasing the complexity of the rules of the game."

This roiling, combative, highly organized political culture produced a close national balance. Scientist Simon Newcomb observed in 1880: "[O]ne of the curious phenomena of the present time is the tendency to a balance between the two parties—a tendency which seems to be rather on the increase." Henry Adams agreed: "[T]hough no real principle divides us, ... some queer mechanical balance holds the two parties even." He concluded that "in democratic politics, parties tend to an equilibrium." And so they did, creating an island of electoral equipoise between the more one-sided politics of the 1860s, the 1890s, and early 1900s.

Presidential Election	Percentage of Difference Between Winner and Runner-up
1860	10.4
1864	10.3
1868	5.0
1872	11.9
1876	2.7
1880	0.1
1884	0.2
1888	0.9
1892	3.4
1896	4.4
1900	6.0
1904	18.8
1908	8.7

People continued to be excluded from the ballot on grounds of sex, age, race (by law in the case of Chinese Americans and Native Americans, by force for increasing numbers of African Americans), the lack of a fixed or legal residence, and incarceration in prison or an asylum. But voting after the Civil War was open to more Americans than ever before, a sign of the pressure to maximize turnout. Even black voting in the South persisted after white southerners regained control. One (suspiciously high) estimate is that during the 1880s about 60 percent of eligible blacks voted, compared to about 70 percent of eligible southern whites. But the black—and, less so, the white—trend was downward as the South became a one-party region. Between 1876 and 1892, Deep South voting was halved. Otherwise, obstacles to white male voting were minimal. During the 1870s aliens in more than twenty states could vote if they had taken out their first papers for naturalization.

Identifying, motivating, and turning out the party faithful was not politics on the cheap. The competitive pressure in closely contested states and districts required the large-scale mobilization of vote gatherers, poll watchers, and the like. More than a fifth of northern voters are thought to have played an active—and often paid—role in these recurring public dramas.

At first the most productive form of fund-raising was through office-holder and contractor kickbacks. Republican federal employees were "asked" in 1878 to give 1 percent of their salaries to the Republican Congressional Campaign Committee. Business contributions were increasingly important. Banker Jay Cooke gave $1,000 to the Pennsylvania Republican campaign in 1864, $30,000 in 1872. By the end of the century, significant contributions came to the Republicans from large national corporations.

The Democrats too had commercial and banking supporters. But their most substantial extractions were through their city machines. Estimates of the money collected by New York's Tweed Ring in the 1870s range from $45 million to $200 million. The leaders of the ring handsomely rewarded themselves, but the take also paid for a costly politics. As Tweed grandly if imprecisely explained, "[T]he money . . . was distributed around in every way, to everybody, and paid for everything, and was scattered throughout the community."

How extensive was election fraud in the late nineteenth century? Critics then and since point to widespread vote buying and falsified counts. The accusations in part reflect inter-party mudslinging and reformers' distaste for the character of late-nineteenth-century politics as much as uniquely high levels of dishonesty. Both the incentive to fraud and the inclination to detect it were concentrated in a few closely contested states. It appears that outright fabrication or miscounting of votes was not common in those places: the active presence of the two parties militated against it.

There does seem to have been large-scale vote buying. The inhabitants of many small towns considered it a reliable income source. An estimated one out of three New Jersey voters took money for their votes. This was nothing new. Since colonial times, the citizenry expected some inducement—liquor, food, ultimately cash—for doing their civic duty. For farmers and workers living close to the bone, a vote was a fungible commodity, not to be given away. Humorist Finley Peter Dunne's Mr. Dooley observed of turn-of-the-century Chicago that many of its citizens had two pleasures in life, working and voting, both of which they did at the rate of a dollar and a half a day.

When a court reporter in 1867 sought a sentence to test the keyboard of that new invention the typewriter, he came up with "Now is the time for all good men to come to the aid of their party." The major parties combined impressive organizational prowess with an ideological and emotional appeal that spoke powerfully to Americans, both natives and newcomers: enough to absorb third-party challenges, in sharp contrast to the pre–Civil War years.

Year of Election	Third-Party Votes %	Number of Third Parties
1856	22.0	2
1860	30.9	2
1864	—	—
1868	—	—
1872	0.5	2
1876	1.1	3
1880	3.5	3
1884	3.2	2
1888	3.5	5
1892	11.0	3
1896	2.3	4
1900	2.9	5

The Michigan supreme court declared in 1885 that "parties, however powerful and unavoidable they may be, and however inseparable from popular government, are not and cannot be recognized as having a legal authority as such." But that very lack of legal standing meant almost no state regulation, thus allowing party leaders to conduct primaries and conventions as they saw fit. The major parties controlled every stage of the electoral process. Almost all newspapers, the major source of political information, were partisan. The parties printed and distributed their own ballots and then made sure that they were cast. "Big Tim" Sullivan of Tammany Hall was said to have his ballots perfumed so that they could be tracked at the ballot box by scent as well as by size, shape, and color.

Most of all, the parties relied on large-scale, detailed organization. At its turn-of-the-century apogee the Pennsylvania Republican machine, "the strongest and most enduring state-wide party organization that has yet appeared in America," supposedly had lists of more than 800,000 voters, classified as habitual, reliable, doubtful, wavering, accustomed to "fumble in the booth," et cetera. Indiana's Republican campaign director sent money and instructions to his 10,000 district leaders in 1888 to organize the more than 250,000 Republican voters into "blocks of five." Ticket splitting was minimal: party-produced ballots hardly lent themselves to that. Indiana's 520,000 voters in 1888 gave GOP candidate Benjamin Harrison about 2,000 more votes than the Democrat Grover Cleveland. In that same election Harrison got 1,676 more votes than the Republican gubernatorial candidate; Cleveland got 10 more than the Democrat running for governor.

Bryce thought that "neither party has any principles, any distinctive tenets. Both have traditions. Both claim to have tendencies." And it is true that most politicians, who all too vividly recalled the consequences of a deeply ideological politics, tended to shy away from the explosive issues of race, religion, and class. Republican John Sherman of Ohio observed in 1873: "Questions based upon temperance, religion, morality . . . ought not to be the basis of politics." When Tammany boss Richard Croker was asked to declare himself on gold versus silver as a basis for the currency, he responded: "What's the use discussing what's the best kind of money? I'm in favor of all kinds of money—the more the better."

But in fact the parties relied on ideas as well as organization, themes attractive enough to secure persistent, closely balanced blocs of voters. In a country of joiners, they were able to forge what historian Paul Kleppner called "not aggregations of individuals professing the same political doctrines but coalitions of social groups sharing similar ethnocultural values." For seventy years, from the early 1860s to the early 1930s, the Republicans were America's normal majority party. Core Republican strength lay in the cultural-demographic band stretching from New England and the Northeast to the Midwest and the Pacific. The Republicans on one level were the party of industrial and then finance capitalism, of business and then big business. They also were the preferred party of middle- and working-class Protestant Americans. The party appealed to those who subscribed to pietistic and evangelical Protestant sects: a more reliable predictor of Republicanism than class, rural-urban, or immigrant-native distinctions.

What initially held these disparate elements together was the shared but gradually fading memory of the Civil War. The party properly claimed credit for the two great accomplishments of the age: the preservation of the Union and the end of slavery. Summoning up that past—"waving the bloody shirt"—went hand in hand with the evocation of the "Grand Old Party," the GOP: a label that appeared around 1880, when the Republicans were all of twenty-five years old.

What it was to be a Republican was inseparable from what it was not to be a Democrat—the party (said a Republican) of "the old slave owner and slave driver, the saloon keeper, the ballot box stuffer, the Ku Klux Klan, the criminal class of the great cities, the men who cannot read or write." *Harper's Weekly* editor George W. Curtis rhetorically asked: "Which party depends upon the ignorance and prejudice of the voters? Which is strongest in the slums of great cities, and in rural parts of the Union where there are fewest schools?" This echoed the common Whig perception of the pre–Civil War Democrats.

As time bleached the bloody shirt, other grounds for Republican party bonding became more important. The great ideological challenge facing the post-Reconstruction GOP was to refashion its core appeal to the exigencies of the industrial age, to speak to people for whom the Union was a given and slavery a memory. Its response was to be the party of Protestantism and prosperity: "of the men who do the work of piety and charity in our churches" and disapproved of slavery, drink, and Catholicism, of "the men who administer our school systems, the men who own and till their own farms, the men who perform the skilled labor in the shops."

The protective tariff was the keystone of the Republican policy arch. The language of the party's national platforms evolved from the pro forma declaration that "the duties levied for the purpose of revenue should so discriminate as to favor American labor" (1880) to the flat-out "We are uncompromisingly in favor of the American system of protection" (1888).

"Protection" spoke to important strands of public opinion: obviously to manufacturers and some agricultural interests, but also to industrial workers endangered by competition from cheap labor abroad, and (in its social connotation) to those fearful of the social dangers posed by drink, polygamy, and the beliefs and behavior of non-Protestants. The term also implied a proactive state. That is why so many turn-of-the-century Progressives, and so much of Progressivism, had Republican roots.

Ideological adaptation went hand in hand with a change in the character of party leadership. The political generation identified with the great causes of the Union and opposition to slavery—Lincoln himself, Lyman Trumbull of Illinois, William Henry Seward of New York, Charles Sumner of Massachusetts, Thaddeus Stevens of Pennsylvania—was followed by politicos who defined themselves more by their commitment to the party as a self-perpetuating organization than as a carrier of grand ideas. Indiana Republican pioneer George W. Julian complained in 1878 that the new party leaders "were not only in favor of perpetuating the organization, but they treated it as an institution."

During the 1870s the GOP was rent by a donnybrook between "Stalwarts" and "Half-Breeds": a clash that on the surface seemed to have all of the meaning—or lack of meaning—of the conflicts between the Byzantine Greens and Whites or the Appalachian Hatfields and McCoys. Nevertheless, this obscure factional struggle dominated American politics for a season and was the context for the assassination of a president.

The Stalwarts—among them Simon Cameron of Pennsylvania, Zachariah Chandler of Michigan, John Logan of Illinois, Roscoe Conkling and Chester Arthur of New York, and Oliver Morton of Indiana—were somewhat older than their opponents. They were the leaders of the organizational Republicanism that succeeded the more ideological party of the Civil War–Reconstruction years. They supported a third term for Ulysses Grant. They called themselves the Old Guard, the staunch (indeed, stalwart) watchdogs of the Grand Old Party.

The Half-Breeds, who included James G. Blaine of Maine, George Frisbie Hoar of Massachusetts, and John Sherman and James A. Garfield of Ohio, were more recent party leaders, readier to abandon the cause of black suffrage in the South and turn to new issues rather than dwell on past principles. The Half-Breeds' rise to party power culminated in the nomination of Garfield as the 1880 GOP candidate.

On July 2, 1881 (six weeks after an anarchist assassinated Czar Alexander II), the mentally unbalanced Charles Guiteau shot Garfield, declaring: "I am a Stalwart, and now [Vice President Chester] Arthur is President." The proximate cause was that Guiteau had failed to obtain an appointment from the new administration. Like John Wilkes Booth's assassination of Lincoln, Guiteau's act illuminates the political culture of its time. Booth's madness fed on the ideological cause of the Confederacy, Guiteau's on the shift from a politics of ideology to a politics of organization.

The Democrats had more difficulty redefining themselves in late-nineteenth-century America. Their wartime identification with disunion and slavery secured their dominance in the post-war white South. But it threatened their competitiveness elsewhere. The party controlled *no* northern state in 1865 and less than a third of Congress in 1866. Some thought the Democrats were bound to fade away, like the Federalists and the Whigs.

But the party retained the support of the growing body of Irish Catholic voters and of poorer white farmers in the lower Midwest, many of southern origins: a zone of demographic settlement comparable to the Republican sweep across New England and the North. The core problem facing the Democratic party was to sustain its appeal to its odd coupling of native-born southern Protestant farmers and Catholic urban immigrants.

It did so with a party ideology that was liturgical, libertarian, and populist. As before the war, the party attracted those who belonged to particular religious sects: Catholics, obviously, but also the more liturgical or ritualistic branches of the major Protestant congregations, as distinct from the pietistic-evangelical sects to whom the Republicans appealed.

The party had a libertarian appeal to those who wanted less government, a theme with Jeffersonian roots. New York Democrat Clarkson Potter distinguished the Republicans from his party: "One for having the government power do much, the other for having them do little; one for having the exercise of government centralized, the other for having it localized." Another Democratic spokesman attacked "paternal control, with its tariffs and monopolies, and sumptuary laws, and government oversight, which leaves the citizen no individual action or judgment."

The Democrats' pre-war identification with white supremacy persisted: in the South, of course, but in the North as well. Now that theme was subsumed within a more general appeal to states' rights and limited government: retrenchment and reform, as the catchphrase had it. White southerners found in this a rationale for resisting Radical Reconstruction and then eliminating black suffrage, with the concurrence of their northern Democratic allies. Irish and German voters in northern cities responded to a message that equated the active state with prohibition, Protestant Bible reading in the schools, and other distasteful forms of social control.

Finally, Democrats appealed to poorer farmers and workers with a populist rhetoric of opposition to corporations, wealth, and privilege. In doing so they sustained an attractive continuity with their Jeffersonian-Jacksonian past, much as the Republicans, with their mantra of prosperity and piety, built on their identity as the party of the Union and opposition to slavery.

A Democratic party usually shut out from federal patronage found organization building more difficult than message massaging. August Belmont, the Rothschilds' American representative, was the unlikely (and ineffective) caretaker chairman of the Democratic National Committee from 1860 to 1872. The real post-war reconstruction of the party went on at the state and local levels. Samuel J. Randall of Pennsylvania and Samuel J. Tilden of New York built effective state organizations. Tilden believed that "the Divine Being has impressed upon everything order, method and law," and he corresponded regularly with two or three friends in each of his state's hundreds of election districts. During the 1876–77 electoral dispute, when his claim to the presidency—and it was a good one—was at stake, he maintained an Olympian (or neurotic) calm. When the issue finally was resolved against him, he rested easy "with the consciousness that I shall receive from posterity the credit of having been elected to the highest position in the gift of the people without any of the cares and responsibilities of office." The end of the purposeful, ideological politics of the Civil War period could not have been more complete.

The most notable post-war Democratic organization was William Marcy Tweed's Tammany Hall. The spectacular revelations that revealed "in how many ways, and under what a variety of names and pretexts, immature and greedy men steal from that fruitful and ill-fenced orchard, the city treasury," obscured the fact that more than stealing was involved. The Tweed Ring's substantial aid to the Catholic Church and parochial schools and its large-scale distribution of food and fuel to the poor, coupled with massive get-out-the-vote machinery, made for a reliable Democratic vote-producing machine. Tweed associate Peter Sweeny observed: "To do what we did in bringing out our vote, getting it registered and then polled, required constant and very great as well as expensive labor." Tammany's power, he concluded, derived from "the completeness of its organization and the thoroughness of its discipline . . . The organization works with the precision of a well-regulated machine."

Although Tweed himself was Protestant, the identification of Irish Catholic politicos with Democratic urban machines became a cultural stereotype of late-nineteenth- and early-twentieth-century American politics. The clannishness, barroom bonding, and mastery of the arts of organization and manipulation that flourished in Ireland under the harsh regimen of English rule traveled well to the teeming cities of America. Rufus Shapley's political novel *Solid for Mulhooly* (1881) told the story of Michael Mulhooly's rise to control of "a political machine as complicated, as ingenious, as perfect as the works of a watch." The "very plain talks on very practical politics" of Tammany man George Washington Plunkitt were published (presumably with some literary license) by journalist William L. Riordan in 1905. They painted a picture of the machine as the provider of necessary services (jobs, help in disasters) to constituents in return for votes and access to what Plunkitt called "honest graft."

Plunkitt's was literally a parochial world. Protestant-Republican Philadelphia, he said, was "ruled almost entirely by Americans." (In the same spirit two Irish congressmen crossed paths one day on the steps of the Capitol. "Anything going on inside, Jawn?" asked one. "No, nothing but some damned American business.") This perspective helped Irish politicos reach out to urban immigrant voters even less attuned to the American mainstream.

The Democratic party led a shadow life in the post–Civil War South, masquerading under names such as Conservative, Constitutional Union, and Conservative Union. But the southern experiment in Radical Reconstruction state government, based largely on blacks and the remnants of the pre-war Whigs, quickly wilted before a resurgent white Democratic party. Terrorism and murder played a conspicuous part in that restoration. (The word *bulldoze* now took on a political connotation, referring to the custom of using a bullwhip to keep blacks from the polls.) By 1874 Democrats dominated almost all southern legislatures and congressional delegations.

Some of the "Redeemers" (as southern Democrats identified themselves) toyed with the idea of appealing to black voters in the South. Wade Hampton of South Carolina said after he became governor in 1876, "I regard myself as having been elected by the colored people." But that possibility withered in the face of pervasive racism and the rise in the 1880s of a more conservative Democratic leadership, a counterpart of the Republican Half-Breeds.

A "Bourbon" Democratic style of party leadership emerged during the 1880s in both the North and the South. The name implied a political attitude that forgot nothing and learned nothing, a traditionalist strain that made the Democrats in historian Henry Adams's mind "the last remnants of the eighteenth century; . . . the sole remaining protestants against a bankers' Olympus."

Bourbon Democrats had close ties to business and commercial interests, were relatively indifferent to the issues of the Civil War and Reconstruction, and espoused an ideology of free trade, hard money, limited government, and personal (white) freedom. Grover Cleveland, the preeminent Bourbon Democrat, was the only president of his party between

James Buchanan in 1857 and Woodrow Wilson in 1913. But Democratic presidential candidate Tilden won a popular (if not electoral) majority of the vote in 1876, only a decade after the Civil War: testimony to the power and effectiveness of the Democrats' post-war recovery. As in the case of the Republicans, a potent mix of ideology and organization ensured the continuity of the party-democratic regime.

CHAPTER EIGHT

A STATE OF PARTIES
AND COURTS

I NDUSTRIALISM AND ITS social consequences might reasonably have been expected to foster the creation of an American version of a regulatory-welfare state. Instead, industrial America was governed by what has been called "a state of courts and parties," defined by court-defined rules and party-defined interests. It might better be called a state of parties and courts, for politicians had the commanding voice in late-nineteenth-century American government.

PRESIDENT AND CONGRESS

The nineteenth-century American presidency consisted of a mountain of greatness (Lincoln) bounded on either side by lowlands of mediocrity. Here as elsewhere, the Civil War worked no sea change. Ulysses Grant was a forceful general, but as president he pledged to be "a purely administrative officer," and he deferred to Congress and his friends, with unfortunate consequences for his reputation. His Republican successors Rutherford B. Hayes, James A. Garfield, Chester Arthur, and Benjamin Harrison were, thought novelist Thomas Wolfe, "lost Americans" with indistinguishable "gravely vacant and bewhiskered faces." Bryce devoted a chapter of his *American Commonwealth* to the question of "why great men are not chosen president." He concluded that the power of party bosses and the requirements of mass politics were not likely to lead to the selection of the best and the brightest.

Once in power, presidents spent more time on party patronage than public policy. Not that the office was geared up for large things: Grant made do with a staff of three, and Cleveland answered the White House doorbell and handled the household accounts. Presidents exercised limited control over major departments such as Agriculture, Interior, and Treasury. Those agencies had long-established relationships with their most important constituents and with Congress, to which they submitted their budgets directly until the 1920s. Their oversight of customs, taxes, farmers, veterans' pensions, land grants, and the Indian Office made them important outlets in the distribution of the benefits and patronage that were the mother's milk of the party regime.

Not the presidency but that great gathering place of party chieftains, the Congress, was the prime mover in government. When Woodrow Wilson examined the American state in 1884, he called his book *Congressional Government*.

The power of Congress rested in part on its members' ability to serve their constituents through pension and other private bills. That was the chief source of the growth of its legislative agenda, from an average of seventeen hundred proposed acts per session before the Civil War to between ten thousand and twenty thousand in the 1880s. Private (in particular, pension) bills came to overshadow public acts: a constituency service not unlike those provided by city and state party bosses, and a prime example of party government. Congress was also the channel through which more substantial interests sought benefits from the federal government. Congressmen offered services in the form of pension bills or tariff schedules, and received votes, campaign contributions, or at times more direct compensation in return.

But, as before the Civil War, institutional stability was an elusive thing. The Senate and the House were as likely as not to be in the hands of different parties. New members made up between 30 and 60 percent of Congress, and the average congressman's length of service was five years. "What ultimately may seem most remarkable about early Gilded Age Congressional Government," says historian Margaret Thompson, "is that it managed to function at all."

To make Congress serve larger party interests required considerable tightening up of its ways of doing business. Much has been made of the extent to which Congress became a more "institutionalized" place during the late nineteenth century. From 1874 on, all members of the House were elected on the same November day. Before this, the election season stretched over as much as eighteen months: a strong disincentive to party unity.

That unity depended on more than shared ideology. The House came to be run by powerful committees—Ways and Means, Rules—and by the Speaker. This brought bill making more fully within the control of the party elders. Seniority played a similar role. It became the norm in the selection of committee chairs, key congressional players. In the Forty-seventh Congress (1881–83), only two of thirty-nine chairmanships were seniority-based. Twenty years later, in the Fifty-seventh Congress of 1901–3, forty-nine of fifty-seven were so chosen. House filibusters came to an end, replaced by an enforced time limit on speeches. The profound congressional need for bloviation was met by turning the *Congressional Record*, a public document that replaced the privately printed *Congressional Globe* in 1873, from a repository of what was said on the floor of the House to a compendium of what congressmen wished they had said, and the responses—"[laughter]," "[applause]"—they thought their words should have evoked.

Strong Speakers—Democrat John G. Carlisle in the 1880s, Republicans Thomas B. Reed in the 1890s and Joseph G. Cannon in the early twentieth century—treated the House not as a club or a deliberative body but as an instrument of party policy. The Rules Committee (with the control that its title implied) was the dominant congressional unit by the century's end. Procedural changes that strengthened the hand of the leadership and contained the minority were the work of party men for party purposes.

The Senate was more resistant to change than the House. It was also a more powerful body, not so much because the upper chamber was where the major issues of the time were resolved as because that was where most of the state and national party bosses hung their hats. The great figures of the late-nineteenth-century Senate were not spellbinding orators, regional spokesmen, and presidential aspirants of the cut of Clay, Webster, or Calhoun. Rather, they were men whose power base lay in their influence in state party machines, their capacity to sway their colleagues in committee dealings, and their skill in serving substantial economic interests. Such were William Allison of Iowa, longtime chair of Appropriations, and Nelson Aldrich of Rhode Island, who presided over Finance.

BUREAUCRACY

The federal government of post–Civil War America resembled its minimalist pre-war predecessor more than it did the late-nineteenth-century European states, with their large armies, balance-of-power diplomacy, imperialist ambitions, aristocratic civil services, and state railroad, liquor, tobacco, and lottery monopolies. The Civil War tax structure was dismantled. And the military quickly reverted to its pre-war status: a decaying navy, a stripped-down army devoted primarily to Indian warfare. Lack of funding, a strong tradition of local law enforcement, corruption, and party politics reduced the Department of Justice to near impotence. A nationalized greenback currency was the only notable surviving wartime innovation.

About a quarter of the federal statutes on the books in 1880 had to do with the public domain and land settlement. Almost all of those thousands of laws served particular interests. No significant bureaucracy crafted or oversaw the development of the territories. Subsidies spurred westward expansion and the building of the transcontinental railroads; protective tariffs fostered the growth of industrial and agricultural production. For better or worse (probably for better), state-directed agricultural and industrial development was all but nonexistent.

A scattering of new bureaus in the Department of Agriculture, the Bureau of Labor (1884), and the Civil Service Commission (1883) and Interstate Commerce Commission (1887) were the most notable additions to the federal bureaucracy in the late nineteenth century: modest indeed when set against the scale of national economic growth. Complaints about the inefficiency of the Pension, Land, and Post Offices reflected the disconnect between static government and a growing society. They led to the first large-scale congressional inquiries into the workings of the bureaucracy, the Cockrell Committee of 1887–89 and the Dockery Committee of 1893. These bodies confined themselves to generic proposals for more efficiency and better bookkeeping. This was no prelude to the rise of an administrative state but a reminder that governance in the party-democratic regime was quintessentially political and partisan.

Federal employment and expenditure did grow substantially during the late nineteenth century. The number of government workers increased by more than 400 percent, from 51,000 in 1871 to 240,000 in 1901. Federal spending rose by 180 percent, at a time when the nation's population increase was 84 percent. A sign, perhaps, of a burgeoning, autonomous national state? Not really. The expansion was intimately tied to party considerations. This was party-dominated government at work.

Employment in the postal service went from 37,000 in 1871 to 136,000 in 1901. In part this was a response to the nation's growing economic and social needs. But it also was a way of perpetuating the Post Office as a repository of government-subsidized agents of the party in power. That is why some forty thousand postmasters were replaced when Democrat Grover Cleveland became president in 1885.

The Customs Office was an important meeting place for the nation's political and economic business. Tariff duties, as before, were a major source of federal revenue: 56 percent of the total in 1880, 41 percent in 1900. How they were collected was important to major commercial and business interests. Friendly (or hostile) customs enforcement and salary kickbacks from the customs houses' ample staffs made them important sources of party (and politicians') income.

The third leg of the party-serving federal bureaucracy was the pensions system. Payments to Civil War veterans absorbed 20 percent of the budget in 1880, 34 percent in 1890, 27 percent in 1900. The Pension Office, with 6,200 employees, occupied the world's largest government office building in the 1890s. Private pension bills made up 40 percent of House and 55 percent of Senate legislation in the mid-1880s. At their peak, veterans' pensions aided an estimated 60 percent of elderly male dependents in the North: on its face a widely-based welfare program. But only Union veterans were recipients. And the system was run by a tightly interlocked group of Republican politicos and the Grand Army of the Republic, the chief spokesman for veterans and a wholly owned subsidiary of the GOP.

In principle, the goal of civil service reform was to create an American state run by apolitical bureaucrats. In practice, the civil service was as much a part of the party regime as the postal, customs, and pension systems. When Republican supremacy began to get shaky in the mid-1870s, Ben Butler's rule that civil service reform was "always popular with the 'outs' and never with the 'ins' unless with those who have strong expectation of soon going out" kicked in. The Pendleton Act of 1883, spurred by Garfield's assassination, initiated an American civil service system. By 1900 more than a third of government employees were covered by its rules. But unlike the politically detached civil service that emerged from Britain's Trevelyan-Northcote Report of 1853, the American system had almost everything to do with politics. When one party gave way to the other (as happened in 1885, 1889, 1893, and 1897), civil service protection was a convenient way for the outgoing administration to embed incumbent placeholders.

The prevailing image of government in late-nineteenth-century America is of a "Great Barbecue," a carnival of corruption. The surge of scandal has been linked to the slackened morality of post–Civil War American political life and to a burgeoning industrial capitalism that contaminated the political system. But it had more complex causes and consequences. The major corruption scandals of the time involved activities—Crédit Mobilier and the Pacific Railroad, the Whiskey Ring and excise taxes, the Star Routes scandal and the postal service—that taxed the limited capacity of American government. Bribery and kickbacks were a way of getting things done, in a manner that both relied on and strengthened the parties. Most of the showcase corruption revelations occurred in the 1870s, when the post-war party culture was taking form. In this sense they were part of the cost of the new organizational politics.

The political culture also put a premium on exaggerating the scale and extent of corruption. Partisans, independent journalists and newspapers seeking to influence public affairs, and reformers and intellectuals displaced from power and influence by the politico-run parties had a common interest in portraying American politics as deeply corrupt. Stronger party organizations in fact may have reduced extractions by individual political freebooters. "The weakness of party organization is the opportunity of corruption," concluded a contemporary observer. Less dangerous, more efficient ways of raising political money took over: salary kickbacks from government workers and, increasingly, corporate contributions.

STATES AND CITIES

To some degree state government resembled its federal counterpart. State activism too fell off after the Civil War era. Taxation was localized and limited, debt declined, spending stagnated. "[L]egislatures," according to one observer, "have ceased to create or concentrate public sentiment; they have become clearing houses for the adjustment of claims." Bryce concluded that "[t]he spirit of localism . . . completely rules them." Many states had sixty-day legislative sessions every other year, and the turnover of members from one session to another was about 75 percent. State lawmaking, like its federal counterpart, was more a matter of specific responses to specific interests than confrontations over large issues of public policy.

State governors and administrative departments were in no position to offer a more dynamic model. Chief executives, usually creatures of their party, tended not to control their states' budgets (such as these were). Many of them lacked veto power, their staffs were minute, and department heads often were separately elected.

State constitutional revision, a common pre–Civil War pastime, went on unabated in the late nineteenth century, but to no great effect (except, at the century's end, black disenfranchisement in the South). The tendency was to crimp state legislative power. There was, said an observer in 1897, a "passionate desire... to control and limit public government." The prevailing sentiment was that government's "essential principles are settled, the general scheme is complete." All that remained was "the refinement of civilization"—which for most politicians meant the perpetuation of the party regime.

The tension between that regime and the demands of an industrial society was most keenly felt in the cities. Class and ethnic conflict, and the discord between efficiency and democracy, had special immediacy there. James Bryce concluded in the 1880s that American cities were the great failure of American democracy. A generation later, muckraker Lincoln Steffens found pervasive corruption in the nation's city halls. Critics held that inefficiently delivered public services, festering slums, and police venality and incompetence added up to a broken system of urban governance. They agreed that the parties were to blame. Bosses and machines were responsible for a rising tide of corruption, of special service to special interests.

Urban political power resided in local party machines. But cities were also chartered municipal corporations, "creature[s] of the state, made for specific purposes, to exercise, within a limited sphere, the powers of the state." This opened the door to close state oversight. "The position of the city," said one expert, "has been changed from that of an organization for the satisfaction of local needs to that of a well-organized agent of state government." As a result, "the history of American city government since 1870 came to be largely involved in a struggle for emancipation from central control."

There is a shadow-play quality to the disquisitions on "home rule" and the respective powers of mayors, aldermen, city councils, and independent boards that so engaged late-nineteenth-century reformers. When they called for home rule against state legislatures, they often found themselves in awkward alliance with city machines. But on the question of who should rule at home, the conflict between politicos and reformers was unremitting, with the reformers usually outgunned.

Most municipal reformers assumed that the propertied and the educated should dominate urban affairs. They subscribed to the view that "a city is a corporation; ... as a city it has nothing whatever to do with general political interests; ... party political names and duties are utterly out of place there.... Under our theory that a city is a political body, a crowd of illiterate peasants freshly raked in from Irish bogs, or Bohemian mines, or Italian robber nests, may exercise virtual control." Machine politicians usually responded with far greater sensitivity to the cities' heavily immigrant voters. "Think what New York is and what the people of New York are," declared Tammany boss Richard Croker. "One half, more than one half, are of foreign birth.... They do not speak our language, they do not know our laws, they are the raw material with which we have to build up the State. How are you to do it on mugwump [genteel reformer] methods?... There is not a mugwump in the city who would shake hands with them."

THE LAW'S DOMAIN

The late-nineteenth-century American legal system assumed a character that resembled the political parties. Like them, it had strong continuities with its pre–Civil War past. But it was more highly organized and more deeply engaged in governing an industrial society.

The judicial system was the only branch of government that integrated federal, state, and local layers of authority and thus could respond to issues in a relatively coherent way. Judges were firmly embedded in the party regime—they were elected by voters or appointed by officeholders—which allowed them to engage more readily in the policymaking and administrative activities of the American state. They were helped too by the fact that most politicians were more interested in personal and institutional self-preservation than public policy making.

Legal historians make much of the rise of a "formalist" style of judicial reasoning in the late nineteenth century: more rule- and precedent-laden, more rigid than the "instrumentalism" of the innovative pre–Civil War decades. This was the style of an increasingly professional culture of lawyers and judges, out to assert their authority. Late-nineteenth-century courts were more ready than their predecessors to resolve conflicts between levels of government, between individuals, between states and corporations. And they did so with the same taste for legal innovation so evident in their pre–Civil War predecessors.

The most notable constitutional issue of the late nineteenth century was the degree to which the states and the federal government could tax and regulate corporations. That issue was defined primarily through thrust and parry between the legislative and the judicial branches. Most historians conclude that the result of this matchup was courts 1, legislatures 0.

Judges defined acceptable regulation and taxation through an ongoing interpretation of two doctrines: the police power of the states to protect the public's health, safety, morals, and welfare, and the check to that power implicit in the due process requirement of the Fourteenth Amendment. Hundreds of court decisions balanced these rules against each other. The result was massive judicial oversight of the states' ability to tax and regulate an industrial economy.

However formalistic the courts' reliance on rules and precedents may have appeared, in fact it was a stunning instance of judicial creativity. That is evident in the story of the most influential constitutional treatise (and best-selling law book) of the time, Michigan supreme court justice Thomas M. Cooley's *Constitutional Limitations Which Rest upon the Legislative Power of the States* (1868). It appeared at the height of the legislative activism of the post-war years. Cooley thought it the duty of the judiciary to intervene when legislation threatened the "personal, civil, and political" rights of the individual. And he found in the concept of substantive due process (hitherto part of the arsenal of advocates of black civil rights) a useful check on the states' police power.

Cooley well served those who wished to reverse the government activism of the Civil War–Reconstruction era or who opposed state taxation and corporate regulation. *Constitutional Limitations* derived its authority from its façade of pure legalism. Hundreds of judicial decisions cited the book. These were duly listed in subsequent editions, thus adding to its authoritative (and substantive) heft.

In a similar way, the legal concept of the municipal corporation opened the door to substantial judicial involvement in urban affairs. John F. Dillon's *The Law of Municipal Corporations* appeared in 1872 and went through five editions (ballooning to five volumes) by 1911. Like Cooley's *Constitutional Limitations*, it was both a monument of and a spur to judicial oversight of government.

Morrison R. Waite, the Supreme Court's chief justice from 1874 to 1888, was a strong, unabashed Republican partisan. He was also committed to making the Court *primus inter pares* among the three branches of government. He once said of a couple of senators that they were "innocent fools. . . . do they yet know that they only formulate a mass of stuff printed as the Statutes of the U.S. but that nine fellows, sitting in black gowns made the '*Laws*' of the U.S."

The Court struck down only two congressional acts between 1789 and 1864 but voided twenty-two between 1864 and 1898. It limited the rate-making authority of the Interstate Commerce Commission and the trust-busting authority of the Sherman Antitrust Act, found a federal income tax law unconstitutional, and sustained a federal injunction against striking railroad workers: "related aspects of a massive judicial entry into the socioeconomic scene, . . . a conservative-oriented revolution."

The view that corporations as legal "persons" were entitled to the Fourteenth Amendment's safeguards only gradually emerged. The Supreme Court in fact was slow to use that amendment to protect *anyone's* rights, not least those of the freedmen who were its intended beneficiaries. Then the Court's use of Fourteenth Amendment due process took off, in pace with the emergence of large corporations. Between 1887 and 1910 the Court handed down 558 Fourteenth Amendment decisions, almost all of them dealing with economic regulation, not civil rights. But the net result was far from a wholesale assault on the regulatory power of the states. Of 243 pre-1901 decisions, 93 percent upheld the state law at issue, as did 76 percent of the 315 from 1901 to 1910. The Court sustained state laws by comparable margins in cases based on the contract and commerce clauses.

It was true that "the notion seems to be thoroughly fixed in the minds of some judges that there are certain natural rights of property which are beyond the control of the legislatures." But Justices Stephen Field and David Brewer fretted over the rise of corporate power and generally accepted state regulation of corporations under the police power. While John F. Dillon was second to none in his solicitude for private property, he insisted "with equal eagerness upon the proposition that property is under many important duties toward the State and society, which the owners generally fail to appreciate."

The work of the courts should be seen in the context of the political culture of which they were a part. True, they struck down more laws than their predecessors. But then there was more legislation to be reviewed. Both branches of government were responding to the demands imposed on them by a rapidly changing society. As was the case before the Civil War, judicial interpretation had close links to the political system with which it was intertwined.

Over the course of the second half of the nineteenth century, a number of socially significant activities moved from the legislatures to the courts, including divorce, adoption, name changes, and the supervision of elections. Most notably, civil law litigation expanded. The courts became an important place of resort for individuals and corporations who sought redress either from the state or from each other. A flood of cases engulfed state and federal trial courts. The Supreme Court's docket went from 240 cases a term in the 1860s to 1,124 in the late 1880s.

The rise of an urban-industrial society stoked an explosive growth in the range and number of legal issues. The greater mobility made possible by the railroad age fed crimes such as bigamy and swindling. Technology and its products had a similarly expansive effect on crimes against property. More than half of the one hundred thousand criminal arrests in Chicago in 1912 were for violations that had no legal existence a quarter of a century before.

The established view in American law that most relationships consisted of individuals voluntarily entering into contract-like understandings continued to determine the courts' responses to worker-employer, husband-wife, buyer-seller, and manufacturer-consumer litigation. But burgeoning accident cases, the inevitable by-product of an industrializing society, strained the traditional view that liability and compensation depended on clear evidence that the defendant had been negligent. The dangers inherent in factories, railroads, and cities required a broader view of fault. State legislatures' capacity (or inclination) to deal with industrial accidents was low indeed, so the courts filled the gap. Wisconsin's supreme court passed on about forty-five thousand such cases between 1875 and 1905. A swarm of lawyers were ready to represent plaintiffs on a contingency fee basis, and jury decisions favored the injured party by a ten-to-one margin. The payments upheld on appeal have been described as a kind of compensation insurance, of the sort later embodied in workmen's compensation. They may also have served as a primitive form of safety regulation, in that the costs of accidents spurred firms to be more attentive to accident prevention. The effectiveness of this form of compensation is at best questionable. But clearly the courts assumed a quasi-administrative role in governing an industrial society.

PUBLIC POLICY

It served the interests of most politicians to avoid conflict on a number of divisive matters: labor versus capital, the civil rights of blacks and women, religion (Protestant versus Catholic in particular), prohibition. The currency issue, with its ample baggage of class and sectional conflict, hovered on the margin of party politics until the 1890s. Instead, the parties' agendas focused on the distribution of politically useful benefits. Pension and other private bills and the endless business of tariff scheduling made up the bulk of what Congress did: constituent-defined public policy indeed.

But economic change created a new agenda. As the railroad network grew, legislative policy shifted from incentives to build (land grants, bonds, subsidies) to how to manage a mature system. Generally ineffective state railroad commissions and regulatory Granger laws cropped up after the Civil War. The post-war Court, still sympathetic to an active state, upheld the Granger laws in *Munn v. Illinois* (1877). But here as elsewhere, state building did not last. The Court's *Wabash* (1886) and *St. Paul* (1890) decisions struck down state railroad rate regulation on the grounds that it interfered with interstate commerce and that its reasonableness was a judicial matter and not a legislative one.

Growing farmer-merchant pressure for regulation led Congress—its policy-making prerogatives challenged by the Court—to intervene. The Interstate Commerce Act of 1887 set up the first federal regulatory agency, the Interstate Commerce Commission (ICC). The ICC served the political need of congressmen to respond to pressure from merchants, farmers, and some railroads; almost all members of Congress supported it. The commission had a vaguely defined power to penalize rate discrimination. But this hardly heralded the birth of the modern administrative state. The ICC saw itself rather as "a new court," charged "to lay the foundations of a new body of American law." That meant that the judicial system remained the final arbiter in rate controversies.

The rise of large corporations recharged old Jacksonian antimonopoly sentiment. As in the case of railroad regulation, the states moved first. They regulated "foreign" (out-of-state) corporations and passed antitrust laws aimed at corporate consolidation across state lines. These were inadequate, and an all-but-unanimous Congress responded with a federal law, the Sherman Antitrust Act of 1890. Once again the regulatory response rested on a judicial model rather than an administrative one. The Department of Justice was charged to bring legal action against "every contract, combination in the form of trust or otherwise, or conspiracy, in restraint of trade or commerce."

The ICC and the Sherman Antitrust Act came around the high noon of late-nineteenth-century Republican power, when for the second time since the early 1870s the GOP won the presidency and both houses of Congress. One-party dominance produced a significant body of legislation besides the Interstate Commerce Act and the Sherman Antitrust Act, the first that could be called a program since the Civil War:

- The Omnibus Bill of 1889 made possible the admission of four reliably Republican western states (North and South Dakota, Montana, and Washington), thereby adding eight senators and a scattering of congressmen and electoral votes to the GOP total. The creation of new states, which before the Civil War had been a sectional issue, now was subject to the dictates of party politics.

- The Dependent Pension Act of 1890 largely expanded the number of veterans and their dependents eligible for coverage of Civil War pensions: an intensely Republican party-related mode of social welfare.
- The Sherman Silver Purchase Act of 1890 was a sop to the rising western-agrarian demand that more silver be bought to supplement gold as a bullion backing of the currency.
- The McKinley Tariff of 1890, the pièce de résistance on this menu, substantially raised tariff rates and thus enshrined the protectionism that had become the signature policy plank of the GOP.

The Republican program also included an Enforcement Bill: on its face, one last attempt to use federal power to protect black voting in the South. The fact that this was the only item on the agenda that failed to pass is a measure of the collapse of the cause of race-blind citizenship.

Here in sum was the Republican response to a changing society: token gestures to issues past (black suffrage in the South) and present (the power of railroads and big business, the currency needs of farmers), strengthening party interests through larger Civil War veterans' pensions and new Republican states, and the centerpiece McKinley Tariff, which responded to important business and labor interests as well as the party's ideological core. This was a blueprint not for a modern state but for the preservation of Republican political hegemony.

Most economic and social policy making went on at the state and local levels: just what the Founders ordered. The states, not the federal government, were the first to react to the economic and social consequences of industrialism. Courts gave them considerable leeway under the police power to protect the health, safety, welfare, and morals of their citizens. State boards of taxation, railroads, charities, and health began to appear. An occasional legislative commission looked at working and housing conditions. When the states did seek to impose regulations, they focused on objects and activities of broad and direct public concern: medicine, liquor, foodstuffs, commodity futures, life insurance policies. Not surprisingly in a polity committed to distribution rather than regulation, the allocation of scarce goods (through occupational licensing or access to land, water, and mineral rights) continued to be a major concern of state and local lawmaking.

Two other issues increased in importance: the definition of social status and the control of personal behavior. While the Civil War and Reconstruction ended slavery, and in theory enacted race-blind citizenship, late-nineteenth-century practice turned out to be something else again. A civics text in 1873 assured its readers that "it is not the *pedigree* but the *thoughts* of the man that make him an American." By 1887 this was not so self-evident, and revision was necessary: "in deference to the present uncertainty, the Lecture in former issues of this work on the 'Universal brotherhood of man,' has been omitted from the present edition. For the design of this work limits it to the exposition only of those ideas which are universally accepted."

Civic and social status was the business of states and localities (subject, ultimately, to review by the courts). Majority white sentiment against black equality in the South and against Asian citizenship in the West met with only token resistance from a diminishing band of equal-rights advocates. The Supreme Court's *Civil Rights Cases* decision of 1884 eviscerated the civil rights acts of the Reconstruction era. And in *Plessy v. Ferguson* (1896) the Court gave segregation a standing in American law and public policy comparable to what *Dred Scott* had sought to give to slavery almost forty years before: striking testimony to the continuity of nineteenth-century racial policy.

Lip service was paid to the assimilation of Native Americans. But the appeal of Indian land to white occupiers outweighed that ideal. The Dawes Severalty Act of 1887 was the federal government's major statement on Indian policy. Its ostensible aim was to enable Indians to obtain homesteads and thus take on "the habits of civilized life." In practice its effect was to speed up the absorption of reservation lands by settlers and corporations. The Supreme Court concluded in *Elk v. Wilkins* (1884)— in the same year as its *Civil Rights Cases* decision—that Indians were not citizens within the meaning of the Fourteenth Amendment. Justice John Marshall Harlan, a lonely advocate of race-blind citizenship, accused his colleagues of holding that "there is still in this country a despised and rejected class of citizens, with no nationality whatever."

Asians fared little better. California's 1879 constitution excluded resident Chinese from suffrage. State laws empowered municipalities to exclude them and banned "aliens incapable of becoming electors" from getting occupational or even fishing licenses. The Supreme Court in 1887 refused to accord resident Chinese the (slim) safeguards of the postwar civil rights acts. Congress passed successive Exclusion Acts in 1882, 1892, and 1902 that effectively ended Chinese immigration.

Women escaped the racial onus that attached to blacks, Indians, and Asians. But prevailing social attitudes saw to it that the polity was not much more responsive to their claims on equal citizenship. The Supreme Court in 1894 held that a state's refusal to allow a female attorney to practice law did not violate her constitutional rights. Opposition to women's suffrage remained strong. Advocates conducted 480 campaigns and 17 state referenda (almost all in the West) between 1870 and 1910 to get the issue on the ballot. But only two women-deprived western states, Colorado (1893) and Idaho (1896), adopted female suffrage.

The tide of immigrants from southern and eastern Europe was another source of political concern. But the historical sanctity and economic utility of immigration, and the migrants' rapid absorption into the political culture of the North, impeded restriction. Exclusion was limited to particular classes of immigrants: contract labor (opposed by unions), paupers, the diseased, anarchists, women imported for immoral purposes.

Pressure grew as well on legislatures and the courts to intercede in previously sacrosanct realms of private life: relations between parents and children and between husbands and wives. This was not easy work for a polity disinclined to involve itself in personal relationships. But the police power of the states provided legal cover. And the way was smoothed by the fact that much of the intercession consisted of the familiar government task of allocating property rights.

By the end of the century every state said that child support was a moral obligation, and most said that it did not depend on the child's service to its parents. This was a distinctively American development. At the same time illegitimacy and adoption, up to now casually treated, came to be more closely regulated on the ground that both moral propriety and property rights were at stake.

Pre–Civil War American courts recognized common-law marriage, reflecting the prevailing belief in free individual choice. Now marriage came to be regarded as a contractual relationship that, like its economic equivalents, required rules and oversight. Courts and legislatures tried to balance traditional social standards and individual freedom. It was widely believed that women had an "inherent incapacity, as a rule, to deal judiciously with their own property, or to act with even ordinary wisdom in the making of contracts." But by the end of the century married women had broad legal power to contract, lend and borrow, keep or transfer their own property, and escape attachment for their husbands' debts.

The same conflict of attitudes applied to divorce, which before the Civil War seemed on the way to becoming accepted social practice. In

Connecticut one in ten marriages were dissolved. Indiana law allowed seven grounds for separation, including "any other cause for which the court shall deem it proper that a divorce shall be granted." Marriage, thought one commentator, had become "a contract easily made and easily ended." Then a strong countercurrent set in: testimony to the social uneasiness that grew in pace with American economic and social change. By 1887 the statutory grounds for divorce had declined from a peak of more than four hundred to fewer than twenty.

The hand of government was most conspicuous in education and the regulation of social mores: not coincidentally, realms in which party politics had a prominent place. Education in the South, never high on the regional agenda, was further hurt by white voters' disinclination to pay for (or even to countenance) the education of blacks. The lines were differently drawn in northern and western immigrant cities. Democratic machines were ready to make schooling available to their immigrant constituents. But rural- and Republican-dominated state legislatures had little desire to see state aid go to urban schools.

The courts held that education was a state responsibility: "school districts are but agents of the commonwealth." But in practice, education was locally funded, and local interests set school policy. A ubiquitous political issue was whether or not to consolidate local school systems into more centralized and efficient districts. Consolidation was slow and difficult, constantly checked by a localism as strong among rural Republicans as among Democrats.

The most conspicuous flash point in school politics, as before the Civil War, was Protestant-Catholic conflict over state aid to religious schools and over reading the Protestant King James version of the Bible in the public schools. In the late 1870s some Republican politicians turned to anti-Catholicism to replace the declining causes of the Civil War–Reconstruction era. President Grant warned that the next great struggle in America would pit "patriotism and intelligence on the one side, and superstition, ambition, and ignorance on the other." He called for a constitutional amendment prohibiting public aid to church-related schools. Congressman James G. Blaine sponsored an amendment to that purpose, and Presidents Hayes and Garfield warned against Catholic influence in the schools. This got nowhere: education was too much a local matter for federal intervention. But by the turn of the century twenty-three states forbade public grants to religious schools.

The weak American state, the close balance between the parties, and a public culture in which individual freedom and limited government were highly valued kept sectarian conflict out of national (though by no means out of state and local) politics. One exception: Mormon polygamy, which punched all sorts of buttons. Federal and state laws forbade the practice, and the Supreme Court agreed that "acts inimical to the peace, good order and morals of society" could not be countenanced.

That applied as well to more general regulation of behavior. The resurgence of Sunday blue laws after a long post-colonial absence ostensibly ensured workingmen a day of rest. The courts upheld them as a valid application of the states' police power to protect the health and morals of their citizens. But the conspicuous support of religious organizations made it clear that a Protestant liquor-and-entertainment-free Sunday was what advocates had in mind.

Growing concern over morality and public health came hand in hand with industrialism, immigration, and larger cities. The result was a burgeoning politics of social control over gambling, tobacco, drugs, and (as before the Civil War) alcohol. Legalized gambling, in state lotteries and on racetracks, was common before the Civil War. Now, like divorce, it fell into disfavor as a practice "tending to corrupt the public morals." Almost all states had anti-lottery laws by 1890, and Congress (upheld by the Supreme Court) forbade lotteries the use of the mails. State anti-cigarette statutes appeared in pace with the growth of that industry, adding up to a fairly widespread (and thoroughly ineffective) body of state laws by the early 1900s. Drug regulation also began to spread. Much of it was the work of the American Pharmaceutical Association, a body more anxious to shield its members from the competition of freelance patent medicine vendors than to protect the public from narcotics addiction.

Alcohol was another story. Prohibition became the most powerful cause of native-born Americans responding to social change. Senator Henry Blair of New Hampshire, a Radical Republican who favored federal aid to public but not parochial schools, introduced the first national prohibition amendment in 1876. Its wording closely resembled the Constitution's prohibition of the slave trade. Blair expansively predicted that "[u]pon discussion of this issue the Irishman and the German will in due time demonstrate that they are Americans." But here as elsewhere, there was not yet the political will for so strong an assertion of government authority. Only Kansas, North Dakota, and Maine had prohibition laws by 1903.

The polity managed to avoid or tamp down issues with the lethal potential of slavery and secession. But it retained its capacity to give voice to many of the wants and fears of an industrializing America. How well it responded was another matter; one that became more prominent as the century neared its end.

The post–Civil War party regime well served the interests of most politicians and seemed to satisfy the preferences of most voters. But a growing number of dissenters took exception to the dominant political culture. An unspoken subtext to these challenges was whether the grievances bred by industrial and agrarian distress would have disruptive political consequences in any way comparable to the regional slavery clash of the 1850s. When several major strands of dissent came together in the 1890s, there was indeed some resemblance to the pre–Civil War decade of the 1850s. But this time the dénouement was very different.

The most conspicuous critics of major party politics after the Civil War were journalists, writers, and intellectuals, small in number but large in influence. The anti-slavery movement and then the Civil War and Reconstruction gave them a sense of the potential for power that resided in words and ideas. But then the rise of a more quotidian party politics elbowed them off the stage on which politics was played and into the wings from which it was observed. Theirs was a classic case of displacement. Poet James Russell Lowell wrote a melancholy "Ode to the Fourth of July, 1876," giving voice to that disaffection:

> Is this the country that we dreamed in youth
> Where wisdom and not numbers would have weight,
> . . .
> Where shame should cease to dominate
> In household, church, and state?
> Is this Atlantis?

Political fiction echoed Lowell's disillusionment. Mark Twain and journalist Charles Dudley Warner published *The Gilded Age: A Tale of To-Day* (1873), "a novel of reaction and despair" that gave the era its most enduring label. They contrasted the corrupt alliance of politics and entrepreneurship with the idealism of the anti-slavery and pro-Union causes. The innocent-turned-spoilsman congressman of John W. De Forest's *Honest John Vane* (1875) is counseled by an older colleague: "Don't go into the war memories and the nigger worshipping; all those sentimental dodges are played out. . . . Special legislation—or, as some people prefer to call it, finance—is the sum and substance of congressional business in our day." Henry Adams's *Democracy* (1880) dwelt on the theme of a gross, corrupt politics, and beyond that the failure of democracy itself. He later told his brother Brooks: "I bade politics good-bye when I published *Democracy*."

Dashed ambitions fed that venerable instrument of political disaffection, the third party. The Liberal Republican movement of 1872 was the creation of editors, journalists, and political reformers distressed by the replacement of a politics of ideas by a politics of organization. The party's 1872 Cincinnati convention was the work of a "Quadrilateral" of newspaper editors. A contemporary observer concluded that it was "less a theory of politics than a theory of journalism which constituted the motive power" of Liberal Republicanism. Appropriately enough, the party's presidential candidate was *New York Tribune* editor Horace Greeley.

The Democrats co-opted Greeley as their candidate, and the Liberal Republicans did not long survive his decisive defeat. Their base was too narrow: "The whole movement had the questionable aspect of proceeding downward from the leaders, instead of upward from the masses." What remained was a tradition of distaste for politicos by intellectuals, journalists, professionals, and civic-minded businessmen that would figure in American politics for generations to come.

The genteel reformers' dislike of professional politicians was fully reciprocated. Party regulars dismissed them as goo-goos (good government people) and mugwumps (reformers divorced from the major parties). New York Republican senator Roscoe Conkling famously observed: "When Dr. Johnson defined patriotism as the last refuge of a scoundrel, he was unaware of the infinite possibilities of the word reform."

The do-gooders' major issues were civil service and ballot reform, old causes to which they attached new meaning. In the early days of the party regime, reform of the civil service meant taking government offices out of the hands of elites and giving them to the party faithful, thus widening the people's access to the bureaucracy. Ballot reform meant expanding white male voting. Now reform meant to limit, rather than expand, access to government jobs and the ballot.

A non-partisan, merit-based civil service held out the prospect of efficiency, expertise, and economy. One advocate equated it with the public health movement, which "aims to do for the physical health of the people something quite analogous to what reform in the civil service aims to do for their political health." New-style ballot reformers also thought that to restrict access to the ballot was to purify it.

But the late-nineteenth-century party regime bent these causes to its own purposes. Civil service became an incumbency-maintenance program, locking in placeholders when party turnover threatened. Southern Democrats turned stiffer voting requirements into a way of eliminating black and poor white voters. When northern business and professional men sought to do the same with immigrants in the large cities, they faced generally successful opposition from the political machines.

A second strand of dissent consisted of a flock of minor parties nibbling away at the major parties' hegemony. Their collective record was meager: not above 3.5 percent of the vote total until the 1890s. The most successful was the Greenback-Labor party. It peaked in 1878, when its dual theme of currency inflation and opposition to monopoly attracted farmers and workers burned by falling crop prices and failed strikes. In the congressional election of that year the party collected more than a million votes and elected fifteen congressmen.

But the Greenbackers could not transcend the ethno-cultural alignments that defined the major parties, and were prey to co-optation. Every successful 1878 Greenback congressional candidate ran on a coalition ticket with the Democrats. In 1880 the Boulder County, Colorado, Greenbackers condemned the corruption of the major parties, declined "to place a ticket in the field for this contest, and . . . advise[d] the members of the party to hold themselves aloof and take no part whatever in the election": not exactly the high road to political success.

The post–Civil War party regime faced—and faced down—its first major challenge in the 1890s. Between 1888 and 1892 the Democrats made unprecedented inroads in the classically Republican midwestern states of Iowa, Wisconsin, and Illinois. As a result of the 1890 election, their House membership grew from 159 to 235, as against only 88 Republicans: the largest party majority since the Civil War. And the Democrats won state offices in the Republican strongholds of Pennsylvania and Massachusetts as well as Wisconsin and Illinois.

This dramatic revival of Democratic strength continued in the 1892 presidential election, when Grover Cleveland returned to office after his 1888 electoral (but not popular) vote defeat by Benjamin Harrison. Cleveland's plurality of four hundred thousand votes in 1892 was the largest since Grant's demolition of Greeley in 1872. The close balance between the parties of the 1880s had suddenly shattered, with wide-ranging consequences, as when victorious Democrats indulged in large-scale gerrymandering of congressional districts, Republican-controlled courts resisted, and electoral chaos ensued.

Prohibition and English-only school laws—causes with a pronounced anti-Catholic and anti-immigrant tone—had destabilizing consequences in the Midwest. Prohibitionists took over the Iowa Republican party in 1891, and it paid a stiff political price in German and other immigrant-ethnic defections. Senator John Spooner said of the GOP's 1890 Wisconsin defeat: "The [English-language] school law did it—a silly, sentimental and damned useless abstraction."

The Democrats benefited from the rising inflow of immigrants. And they won the support of old-stock middle-class voters put off by the machine politics and big-business leanings of the GOP state and national party organizations. Most notably, a rising agrarian revolt in the Plains drew away traditional Republican voters. A major third party, the first since the Know-Nothings of the 1850s, suddenly emerged. The Populists won a million popular votes and twenty-two electoral votes in 1892, the strongest showing by a third party since 1860. In 1894 they increased their popular vote total to a million and a half and took eleven congressional seats.

In good organizational politics style, the GOP quickly responded. It downplayed prohibition in Iowa and Ohio, and half the Republican state legislators joined the Democrats to repeal Wisconsin's English-only law in 1891. And a volatile economy led to a dramatic political backswing. As the party of greater social and cultural freedom, the Democrats benefited from the ethno-cultural wars of the early 1890s. As the party of prosperity, the Republicans profited from the Panic of 1893 and the ensuing depression. The House, 61.2 percent Democratic in 1892, was 29.4 percent Democratic after the 1894 election, the largest shift since the beginning of the Civil War.

The presidential contest of 1896 had all the attributes of a realigning election: high turnout, new campaign styles and party ideologies, substantial alterations in voter behavior. The takeover of the Bourbon-Cleveland Democrats by William Jennings Bryan and the cause of silver as a currency base constituted the biggest change in a major party since pre–Civil War days. But in the taxonomy of this book, the election stands as a monument to continuity, not change. It became a case study in the capacity of the major parties to maintain their dominance in American political life.

There is a striking symmetry in the form (though certainly not in the substance) of the parties' responses to the challenge of 1896. By nominating Bryan and adopting a platform that co-opted the Populist cause of free silver, the Democrats defined themselves as the party of reform more fully than at any time since Jackson and Van Buren. Bryan was a lawyer who came from an old Jacksonian Democratic family and represented Nebraska's most urban congressional district. He made his mark as an eloquent free-trade critic of the McKinley Tariff of 1890. He took on agrarian grievances and the free-silver panacea while remaining solidly within the Democratic party fold. In 1896 he became the first Democratic presidential candidate since 1860 who was not from the Northeast.

Bryan brought to his party an evangelical reformism that previously was part of Republican party culture. Historian Richard Hofstadter called him "the Democrat as Revivalist," which before then would have been oxymoronic.

The other emblematic Democratic figure in 1896 was John Peter Altgeld, the German-born governor of Illinois and éminence grise of the Bryan campaign. Altgeld was the first Democratic governor of Illinois since 1852. He came from neither the Bourbon conservatives nor the Irish-dominated machine politics that played such a large role in the late-nineteenth-century Democratic party. He pardoned the surviving Haymarket anarchists, in prison for their role in a bomb explosion that killed some policemen; opposed Grover Cleveland's dispatch of troops to break the Chicago railroad strike of 1893; and had a strong interest in prison reform. He was a precursor of twentieth-century Democratic urban liberalism.

The Bryan-Altgeld alliance had its tensions. Bryan had little feel for labor or urban issues, while Altgeld had little interest in free silver. But party self-interest dictated a new response to the economic challenge of the 1890s. Building on his evocative "Cross of Gold" speech at the party convention, Bryan made free silver a crusade with the populist appeal of Jackson's war against the Bank of the United States.

Bryan steered clear of the Populist party. And by adopting much of its message, he consigned it to third-party limbo. He transformed presidential campaigning with six months of cross-country sweeps totaling more than eighteen thousand miles, and he gave more than six hundred speeches to an estimated five million people. At one meeting, the lights were arranged to cast a halo over his head. Crowds often surged forward to touch his clothes.

The Republican party reacted with comparable energy to the unsettling political environment of the 1890s. Mark Hanna and William McKinley were the GOP's counterparts to Altgeld and Bryan, though in background and beliefs they were as different as their party cultures. Hanna headed a Cleveland family firm with substantial shipping, iron ore, and streetcar interests. He introduced the Republican party to the organizational and financial potential of big business, as Altgeld introduced the Democrats to the potential of urban liberalism. Hanna made the 1896 GOP campaign a precursor of twentieth-century politics with a massive program of "education" through thousands of speakers and an estimated two hundred million pamphlets. This was, said McKinley, "a year for press and pen." The art of modern public opinion formation now joined the established party standbys of ideology and organization.

McKinley engaged in as rich a mix of traditional and new politics as his opponent Bryan. He was a Civil War hero and longtime congressman, representing an Ohio district well stocked with farmers, miners, and factory workers: a base from which he emerged as the great GOP spokesman for the protective tariff. He had good relations with Catholics and labor, and steered clear of the divisive ethno-cultural issues that had so harmed the GOP earlier in the decade.

Altgeld reluctantly bent to the mood of the moment by accepting free silver as the chief campaign issue. So did Hanna, who would rather have dwelt on the tariff. He oversaw a campaign in which a gold-backed currency emerged as the embodiment of public morality and economic solidity, while silver was portrayed as an inflationary threat to workingmen's wages, businessmen's contracts, and middle-class savings.

Using his broad connections in the business community and the fear engendered by Bryan, Hanna tapped corporate money on a scale not seen before. Unlike Bryan, McKinley did not venture out to meet the voters. Instead, Hanna's money and cooperative railroads arranged to bring the voters to meet McKinley. He received an estimated three-quarters of a million visitors at his Canton, Ohio, home.

This innovative election had unsettling effects on both parties. Gold Democrats (including Grover Cleveland) backed McKinley, silver Republicans (including several western senators) endorsed Bryan. Traditionally Democratic cities were drawn more to McKinley's message of prosperity than to Bryan's agrarian radicalism. The Democrats lost New York for the first time since 1848. Bryan's evangelical campaign style, not surprisingly, alienated Irish Catholics and new immigrants. Nor did the older farm areas of the Northeast and the Midwest, given over to truck and dairy farming, respond to a message aimed primarily at Plains wheat and southern cotton growers. The result was the largest Republican presidential victory since Grant's in 1872. No state north of the Mason-Dixon line and east of the Mississippi went for Bryan.

But for all that was new about the election of 1896, its bottom line was the continued hegemony of the major parties: survival through adaptation. The Republicans solidified their strength in their ancestral home, the Northeast and the Midwest. The Democrats retained their southern base, only temporarily alienated their urban Irish support, and sowed the seeds of a new agrarian-urban liberalism that would serve them well in the twentieth century. The party-democratic regime successfully confronted the crisis of the 1890s. But in the early years of the new century it faced an even greater challenge to its domination of American public life.

CHAPTER NINE

THE PROGRESSIVE
INTERLUDE

T HE PROGRESSIVE MOVEMENT of the early twentieth century fed on political discontents accumulating since the Civil War. But Progressivism itself was something new under the American political sun. It challenged the ethno-cultural and regional divisions so central to the nineteenth-century party culture. And it came up with new public policy: new in the way it was formulated, in its substance, and in its consequences.

The story of Progressivism is usually told with an eye to the American political future. Here, it is argued, is the true seedbed of the New Deal, of the administrative state, of progressive jurisprudence. But when looked at from the perspective of the nineteenth-century party-democratic regime, a different narrative line emerges.

Certainly it is the case that many of the political and policy initiatives that we associate with modern American public life—the active presidency, congressional reform, new administrative agencies and regulatory policies, a proactive foreign policy and overseas conflict—appear in the Progressive years of the early twentieth century. But so too does a sharp reaction against those developments in the 1920s. The American polity of 1930 was far closer to the polity of 1900 than to that of 1960. Progressivism, like the agrarian revolt of the 1890s, became a showcase for the party regime's impressive powers of absorption, adaptation, and persistence.

WAR AND IMPERIALISM

There are occasions when, with crystalline clarity, a large national event reveals the changing dynamic of the political culture. Such was the Spanish-American War of 1898 and the ensuing debate over the acquisition of overseas territories.

Foreign affairs were at the epicenter of public life in the early Republic. But for the rest of the nineteenth century, westward expansion, slavery and secession, agrarian discontent, and the concerns of an industrial society defined the public agenda. Then at century's end the issues of overseas war and territories suddenly took center stage. Neither the war nor the empire that came out of it was of any great moment. But they were revealing outlets for the expression of national aspirations and anxieties, in ways that foreshadowed the domestic Progressive interlude to come.

The war with Spain was a unifying cause. Almost no one, not even Christian socialists, opposed it. *Cuba libre*, sensationalized by the mass-circulation press of Joseph Pulitzer and William Randolph Hearst, appealed to urban immigrants. By identifying with American ideals of freedom and self-determination, they affirmed their connection with the new motherland. (This despite—or in part because of—the Catholicism of many immigrants and the barely concealed anti-Catholicism of the press assault on Spanish rule.) The cause appealed as well to southern ex-Confederates, who saw in war with Spain a way of burying the divisive past. (This despite the fact that the folks to be liberated were far from spotlessly white.) And it struck a chord too in the Populist-agrarian revolt heartland of the West, as a way to put aside the hard times and political defeat of the decade's earlier years. (This despite the fact that the people at stake offered little in the way of a market for American staples.)

But the post-war acquisition of American colonies was something else again. It is true that geopolitical strategists concerned about naval bases and coaling stations, as well as ambitious businessmen dazzled (or blinded) by the prospect of access to overseas markets and raw materials, had a self-interested stake in an American empire. But as was the case a century earlier with the American response to the French Revolution, the debate over imperialism had more to do with domestic beliefs about America's past and future.

Advocates of imperialism—old-family easterners Theodore Roosevelt and Henry Cabot Lodge, reform-minded midwesterners Albert Beveridge and (for a time) Robert La Follette—were ambitious young politicians attracted by the goal of a benevolent American empire. Most of them would later warm to the idea of turning to government for domestic economic and social reform.

The leading anti-imperialists were ideological odd fellows: steelmaster Andrew Carnegie, labor leader Samuel Gompers, agrarian spokesman Bryan, Republican grandee and House Speaker Thomas B. Reed, former Democratic president Grover Cleveland, conservative social Darwinist William Graham Sumner, mugwump E. L. Godkin, socialist Henry Demarest Lloyd. Most were no less racist than their imperialist opponents: they regarded the lesser breeds in Puerto Rico and the Philippines not as a challenge to be taken up but as a burden to be avoided. What bound them together was age (they tended to be in the evening of their careers) and a shared sense that (as Cleveland put it) "the fatal un-American idea of imperialism" was "a new and startling phase in our national character." They were, Theodore Roosevelt said, "men of a bygone age having to deal with the facts of the present."

THE PROGRESSIVE IMPULSE

The politically pathbreaking character of the Spanish-American War and the debate over imperialism episode carried over into domestic turn-of-the-century American politics and government. Change was in the air, at home as well as overseas. The presidency and Congress shook off some of their late-nineteenth-century institutional torpor. A wave of legislative and administrative reform swept over national, state, and local government. Four amendments between 1913 and 1920 were the first substantial tinkering with the Constitution since the Civil War–Reconstruction era. Women, African Americans, and Native Americans began, however tentatively, to find a new voice in public life. The states turned into busy laboratories, regulating working and housing conditions and policing social behavior. The cities produced a new breed of activist mayors and substantially expanded public services. This was the agenda of a polity confronting the new American industrial order on a scale not seen before.

Party machines stood next to the trusts as the most conspicuous objects in the Progressive bestiary. During the 1890s the "Australian ballot"—government-issued, often without party designations, secretly cast—came into general use, in the hope that it would reduce the power of party bosses. Another popular nostrum, direct primaries to select state and national candidates, multiplied after 1900. Many Progressives believed that the political process would be purified if "ignorant" voters—

immigrants in the North, blacks and poor whites in the South—were removed from the electorate. Poll taxes, literacy tests, and stricter registration made it more difficult to vote. By the same token, women's suffrage appealed because it was thought to add substantially to the native-born, middle-class vote.

Arguably the most consequential change in electoral politics during the Progressive era was the rise of non-voting, from 29 percent of eligible voters in 1896 to a high of 58 percent in 1904. The decline in turnout was due only in part to tightened registration and voting restrictions. The major parties were finding it more difficult to rely on their traditional appeals to region, ethnicity, and historical memory. Demographic and cultural change—the coming of age of the new immigrants and their children, the spread of a new popular culture—eroded the fabric of strong party identification.

The Progressive challenge to the traditional political culture included new ways of defining public policy. For most of the nineteenth century, the parties controlled the issue agenda. Now extra-party voices— journalists and intellectuals, social critics, lawyers, social scientists, advocacy groups—seized the initiative.

Newspapers and magazines fat with ads, printed on fast presses and distributed on fast trains, reached a mass readership. Publishers, editors, and journalists were not beholden to the parties (though they were often in thrall to their own political ambitions). Hearst's *New York Journal* observed in 1898: "Under republican government, newspapers form and express public opinion. They suggest and control legislation. They declare wars. They punish criminals, especially the powerful.... The newspapers control the nation because THEY REPRESENT THE PEOPLE."

The new journalism came up with a distinctive mix of sensationalism and reform: muckraking, in Theodore Roosevelt's derisive term. It addressed a new American public, trans-class and multi-ethnic. A magazine composed of selections from the nation's press with the suggestive title of *Public Opinion* had appeared in the 1880s. Among the leading muckraking magazines of the Progressive period were the evocatively named *Cosmopolitan* and *Everybody's* (which claimed an unprecedented six hundred thousand subscribers in 1903). Their attacks on corruption in politics and business overrode the regional and ethno-cultural appeal of the major parties.

Historian Richard Hofstadter called the multiple strands of discontent that fed Progressivism "the complaint of the unorganized against the consequences of organization." But another large, no less authentic part of Progressivism was what British novelist and social critic H. G. Wells labeled "the revolt of the competent," presumably against the consequences of social and economic *dis*organization. Many businessmen, labor leaders, professionals, intellectuals, and journalists, whose politics ranged from socialist to social imperialist, believed that the problems of an industrial society called for rational, planned, active-government solutions. American Progressivism embraced a rich diversity of issues, interests, ideas, inputs, and expectations. Indeed, that was the distinguishing feature of early-twentieth-century American public life. And it explains why interpretations of the character and meaning of Progressivism are so varied.

The Progressive interlude was not peculiar to the United States. Most notably in Britain, a New Liberalism with more than occasional similarities came into prominence at the same time as American Progressivism, reflecting similar strands of social, economic, and political discontent. But a still-elitist English political culture and a strong tradition of dirigisme rather than party-political direction of public policy made for a continuing divergence between American and British (to say nothing of Continental European) public life.

The core of Progressivism was a thrust for institutional change, parried by the established political culture. This scenario, which stretched from 1900 to 1930, played out in city and state government, the presidency, Congress, the courts, public policy, and the course of national politics.

In its narrative arc, Progressivism echoed the Civil War–Reconstruction sequence. Like the initial northern response to secession as a threat to the Union, the Progressive impulse sought to preserve an older America from the transforming power of big business and big politics. But over time the Progressive impulse expanded to include new realms of political, economic, social, and finally foreign policy: a dynamic much like that of the late Civil War and the Radical Reconstruction years. Then in the wake of World War I, as in the wake of Reconstruction, there was a reaction, a rollback. During the 1920s, as in the 1870s, the party regime regained control of American public life.

CITY AND STATE

After a 1905 visit, H. G. Wells described American government as "marooned, twisted up into knots, bound with safeguards, and altogether impotently stranded." A central Progressive objective was to change this: to make government a more supple and effective tool of reform. That impulse first appeared in middle-sized midwestern American cities. The hard times of the 1890s hit those towns hard, and their political machines were not so deeply entrenched as in the larger, older cities of the East. New political voices and ideas were more readily heard there.

Pride of place goes to Detroit's Hazen Pingree, a self-made go-getter from Maine who became one of the largest shoe manufacturers in the Midwest. The city's Republican organization induced Pingree to run for mayor in 1889 because he could pay his own way in what seemed like a hopeless campaign. He won, primarily because the growing Polish-German immigrant portion of Detroit's population was alienated from the Irish-dominated Democratic machine. A Protestant Yankee was enough of an outsider to be acceptable.

Pingree brought not bureaucratic efficiency but small-town ideals of honesty and economy to government. He summoned the members of Detroit's Board of Education to a public meeting at a downtown theater and dramatically announced: "There are quite a number of members of this board who are going to jail tonight." The police, waiting in the wings, then came onstage and led the miscreants off. When the city's newspapers tried to ignore him, he communicated with the voters by means of a large bulletin board outside City Hall. He responded to the depression of the 1890s with his Pingree Potato Patch Plan, in which vacant city lots were turned over to the poor to grow vegetables.

Tom Johnson, mayor of Cleveland from 1901 to 1907, also was a successful businessman—but in streetcars and steel, not shoes. And while he too placed great weight on citizen participation, his model was not a New England town meeting but a gathering of stockholders voting on company policy. He went a step beyond Pingree in public policy as well, plumping for public ownership and operation of streetcars and other utilities.

As the Progressive commitment to more efficient, corruption-free government took hold, smaller cities experimented with new forms such as non-elected city commissions and city managers. A handful of them could even claim mayors who called themselves socialists, though their collectivist impulse did not go much beyond public utilities: "gas and water socialism."

New York City offers a revealing fix on the evolution of urban Progressivism and how and why it ran out of steam. In 1913 the home of Tammany elected as its mayor thirty-four-year-old John Purroy Mitchel, a graduate not of the school of hard knocks but of Columbia College and New York University's law school. Mitchel ran on a Fusion ticket, a device by which the city's "better element" now and then revolted against Tammany rule. He thought New York's problems could be handled "only by men of business judgment and constructive ability, unhampered by party ties." Seeking "government by 'up-lifters,'" he put experts into key city posts, and dismissed as inefficient hospitals and orphanages run by the Catholic Church. He tried to adopt the Gary, Indiana, system of education, in which immigrant children were channeled into the industrial and vocational skills required by a new economy.

Mitchel's advanced urban progressivism had disastrous political consequences. The Church, teachers, the police, and Tammany rebelled against government by experts. Immigrant parents protested the consignment of their children to proletarian status. There was, one critic said, "[t]oo much [upper-class] Fifth Avenue, not enough [working-class] First Avenue." Tammany hack John Hylan swept into office in 1917 with an ethno-cultural appeal to the city's immigrants and their children.

Most city machines effectively adjusted to the new demands of urban politics. Boston's Irish pols were responsive to Progressive urban reform. New York's Tammany ward bosses reached out to the flood of Jewish and Italian immigrants. (That was not always easy. One of them complained that although when he visited his neighborhood's synagogues he respectfully removed his hat, for some reason this did not sit well with the congregation.) Tammany boss Charles Murphy endorsed popular Progressive causes such as factory safety laws and municipal ownership of the subways. When publisher William Randolph Hearst sought to make his way in New York City politics by preaching a brand of urban populism, Tammany co-opted him by making him its (unsuccessful) candidate for governor.

City machines and bosses retained their supremacy over urban politics, but at a cost. Many of them responded with a heightened ethnic tribalism to the pressure for 100 percent Americanism during and after World War I. Catholic Democrat James Michael Curley in Boston and Protestant Republican William Hale Thompson in Chicago played essentially the same game in the 1920s, appealing to their polyglot constituencies by demonizing an Other (Protestant Brahmins in Curley's case, Perfidious Albion for Thompson). This brand of politics often went hand in hand with untrammeled corruption: in Tammany's New York and Thompson's Chicago, and in Boss Crump's Memphis, Boss Cox's Cincinnati, and the Vare brothers' Philadelphia. New York mayor Jimmy Walker was an emblematic figure. He combined old-fashioned Tammany machine political morality with full-throated participation in the hedonistic urban culture of the 1920s.

By the turn of the century, the states had joined the cities as showcases of the failure of American government. With a Gallic passion for classification, a 1905 French map ranked six American states as free from corruption, thirteen as partially corrupt, and twenty-five as utterly corrupt.

The tensions of the 1890s produced a new breed of reform-minded state governors, as it did city mayors. John Peter Altgeld of Illinois was the first, in 1893. Hazen Pingree went from mayor of Detroit to governor of Michigan. Theodore Roosevelt, fresh from the Spanish-American War, put in a brief but invigorating two years as New York's chief executive before going on to national office in 1901.

The iconic figure in this first generation of Progressive governors was Robert La Follette of Wisconsin. Before he moved to the Senate in 1905, he compiled a record that added up to a what's-what of state Progressivism: railroad and public utilities commissions, state banking regulation, conservation and water power franchise laws, civil service and lobbying legislation, the first direct primary.

After La Follette went to Washington, his associates turned to a more advanced Progressivism. A state efficiency commission and the first state income tax in 1911, stricter factory regulation, restrictions on child labor, and a greater receptivity to prohibition added up to the Wisconsin equivalent of John Purroy Mitchel's mayoral performance in New York City.

And the political consequences were similar. Business interests chafing under new taxes and regulations were a predictable source of opposition. But many farmers rebelled against the new stress on urban and industrial labor problems. Immigrants (Catholics in particular) opposed child labor regulation, women's suffrage, and prohibition. Building-trades unions and Social Democrats disliked, respectively, new regulation of occupations and the Progressive stress on efficiency and expertise. The same social and cultural pluralism that helped to create the politics of Progressivism nourished a varied and consequential opposition to it.

Southern states came up with their own, chilling variant of the new politics: what historian C. Vann Woodward called "Progressivism—for whites only." The southern demagogue, a distinctive political type combining a populist rhetoric of hostility to "the interests" and a fierce commitment to white supremacy, dominated early-twentieth-century southern politics. Tom Watson of Georgia, James K. Vardaman and Theodore Bilbo of Mississippi, and Jeff Davis of Arkansas were representative figures, analogues of the Curleys and Thompsons in northern cities.

During the 1920s the states, like the cities, settled down to a style of governance that retained some of the attributes of Progressivism. Governors gained more power, more attention was paid to administration. But with a few exceptions, such as governors Al Smith in New York and Gifford Pinchot in Pennsylvania, economic and social reform took a backseat. Instead, state policy responded to the physical demands of modern life: new highways, schools, hospitals, prisons. This required ever higher levels of spending and taxation, all quite congenial to the patronage-and-machine politics of the party regime.

THE PRESIDENCY, CONGRESS, AND THE COURTS

A new era in the presidency appeared to open when forty-three-year-old Theodore Roosevelt took office in 1901 (the youngest president until that time) after William McKinley was murdered. Once again an assassin's dementia illuminated the political culture of the time. Leon Czolgosz's claim to be an anarchist and his view of McKinley as plutocracy's servant spoke of the tensions of an industrial society as much as Booth's pro-southern fanaticism embodied the passions of the Civil War era and Guiteau's presentation of himself as a disappointed office seeker reflected the organizational politics of the late nineteenth century.

TR's persona was as singular as his youthfulness. Well-born, Harvard-educated, a historian, a man of action, and a preternaturally vivid personality (no predecessor was widely known by his initials), he differed dramatically from his Gilded Age predecessors. TR initiated more anti-trust actions by the Department of Justice, oversaw the passage of railroad and pure foods regulatory acts, and paid conspicuously greater attention to conservation than his predecessors. He imposed himself with equal force on foreign affairs, initiating the building of the Panama Canal and the peace treaty that ended the Russo-Japanese War. Most of all he imprinted his personality on the media (and thus on politics) as no predecessor had done.

TR's immediate successor, William Howard Taft, more of a lawyer-administrator than a politician, ran for no substantial office before he became president. From personality to policy to politics, his was a pallid second act after TR's star turn. Still, Taft in his way was a Progressive president, surpassing TR in antitrust suits and subscribing to an administrative more than political model of the presidency.

Woodrow Wilson's pre-presidential political career was almost as thin as Taft's: a two-year term as governor of New Jersey. An academic career capped by the presidency of Princeton University would have seemed to be a definitive disqualification for high public office in the party-democratic regime. But in the political environment of the Progressive years, it smoothed Wilson's way to the White House. Like TR before him, his presidency was defined by strong presidential leadership on major issues, domestic and international. His chief domestic achievements, the Federal Reserve, the Federal Trade Commission, the Clayton Antitrust Act, and the Federal Farm Loan Act, may be regarded as a Democratic version of TR's Progressivism. His leadership of America's entry into World War I was the capstone to the (temporary) transformation of the presidency from Gilded Age inanition to Progressive assertion.

But nowhere was the resilience of the pre-Progressive political culture more evident than in the post-1920 presidency. Warren Harding, Calvin Coolidge, and Herbert Hoover governed far more in the self-effacing style of their pre-1900 predecessors than of the Progressive presidents.

There was more to Harding's presidency than party regularity and intellectual vacuity. He opposed the government's wartime censorship and criticized the New York Assembly when in 1919 it expelled five members for being socialists. While president he pardoned socialist leader Eugene Debs, whom the Wilson administration had jailed for seditious wartime utterances. He embodied both the superficiality and the live-and-let-live style of the political culture of the party regime. "Harding," said TR's acid-tongued daughter Alice, "was not a bad man; he was just a slob."

Harding died in office, and Vice President Calvin Coolidge's justice-of-the-peace father swore him in by the light of an oil lamp in his barebones Vermont cabin: a primal old-American mise-en-scène, avidly recounted by the mass media to millions of Americans in the Year of Our Ford 1923. Silent Cal in fact was an Amherst College graduate who turned his hand to poetry and translated Dante's *Inferno*; he had been a competent, mildly Progressive governor of Massachusetts. But as president he turned old-American Yankee taciturnity into a minor art form, assiduously praised big business, small government, and low taxes, and looked askance at the new immigration, thus becoming the truest voice of the GOP in the 1920s.

Coolidge's successor Herbert Hoover, though steeped in a Progressive background of sophisticated executive management, maintained the 1920s GOP presidential style of embodying the values and outlook of pre-industrial American society. Everything about these presidencies—from the corruption of the Harding years to the old-America personae and pro-business, weak-government records of Coolidge and Hoover—testified to the durability of the political culture of the party regime.

Congress too was affected by the winds of Progressive change. And like other sectors of the polity, it reverted to type when those winds subsided.

Tension grew after 1900 between the major parties' desire to retain control over the legislative process and Progressives looking to function outside the party box. Joseph Cannon, a Republican who became Speaker of the House in 1903, sought to control (and limit) legislative business in the interest of his party, as his powerful predecessor Thomas B. Reed had done in the 1890s. At first he was successful. He reduced the number of private acts and resolutions passed by Congress from 6,249 in 1905–7 to 235 in 1907–9. But Cannon had to cope with the policy-making proclivities of congressmen touched by the Progressive impulse as well as with traditional partisan politics. In 1910 a coalition of Democrats and midwestern Republican insurgents stripped him of his power to control appointments to Rules and other standing committees and limited his capacity to impede the legislative process.

Four years later the Seventeenth Amendment ended the selection of senators by state legislatures and vested it in the electorate: another institutional upheaval. Like the revolt against Cannon, the direct election of senators was an attempt to lessen the control of party bosses. Opinion differs over whether the amendment was the work of the parties themselves, responding to public pressure, or of intra-party conflict (eastern conservative versus midwestern Progressive Republicans, southern versus northern Democrats). Its most visible immediate effect was to increase the number of first-termers, from thirteen of ninety in 1905 to about half of ninety-six in 1914.

But in the long run the House and the Senate remained in thrall to the parties. Congress as an institution did not stray far from the party-defined rules and customs of the past. Cannon's failure to respond to the constituency needs of his fellow Republicans appears to have been at least as destructive to his authority as were policy differences. In 1907 longtime House parliamentarian Asher C. Hinds published a five-volume work, *Precedents of the House of Representatives*, which codified some 7,346 procedural technicalities. In so complex an institution, party leadership might be challenged, but it could not be avoided.

The decidedly un-Progressive entrenchment of the seniority system in Congress continued to grow. And the regional and urban-rural sorting out of party allegiances made for more safe seats, hence longer incumbencies. First-term members in the late nineteenth century (1871–99) averaged 42.6 percent. From 1901 to 1933 that figure was almost halved, to 22.9 percent. The Fifty-seventh Congress, elected in 1900, was the first in which more than two-thirds of the House consisted of returning members, and the average term of service was more than three years. Greater longevity and the seniority rule for committee chairmanships fit like fingers in a glove. By the early 1900s, it was the all-but-inviolable norm in the House. Southern Democrats benefited most.

This is not to say that the Progressive interlude left no traces. Longer tenures of office and the triumph of seniority increased the potential for members' autonomy. Party leaders were less able to punish the disloyalty of Progressive-tradition mavericks such as George W. Norris of Nebraska. And the Progressive inheritance of extra-party pressure groups persisted. The 1920s saw the rise of Congressional *blocs* representing farmers and veterans and of influential interest-group lobbyists such as Wayne Wheeler of the Anti-Saloon League and Gary Silver of the American Farm Bureau Federation.

Perhaps because of the Progressive threat to party government, partisanship appears to have been relatively muted in the early-twentieth-century Congress. Contested elections, traditionally decided in favor of the majority candidate, sharply declined in number and were judged more frequently on the merits of the case. During the 1920s GOP Speaker Nicholas Longworth had close relations with Texas Democrat John Nance Garner (who succeeded him as Speaker in 1931), sharing illegal liquor and easygoing conviviality in "Board of Education" meetings, where they worked out procedural and other House matters.

While inter-party comity grew, party control of the workings of Congress remained deeply embedded. Steering committees that set party agendas and shaped legislation were in place by the time of World War I. So were Senate party whips. The Senate's leaders enhanced their management by unanimous consent agreements, the upper house's equivalent of the House rules limiting debate and amendments. The press began to speak of majority and minority leaders. Roll call votes breaking along strict (over 90 percent) party lines increased between 1881 and 1923.

All in all, Congress in the 1920s ran very much as it had in the late nineteenth century. John Tilson, the Republicans' floor leader, observed at the end of one session in the mid-1920s: "It will probably be said with truth that the most important work I have done during the session has been in the direction of preventing the passage of bad or unnecessary laws." That statement that would have been unexceptionable in the 1880s.

The legal system, like Congress, responded to the challenge of Progressivism but remained true to its traditional precepts. Legal scholar Roscoe Pound questioned the sanctity of contracts and due process, setting off much talk of a new Progressive jurisprudence. More substantive was the ferment in criminal and family law. Sentencing, punishment, and prison conditions came under considerable scrutiny. There were some attempts at reform, which generally meant liberalization and uniformity. The same could be said of the law of marriage and divorce and the legal standing of women. The Chicago Municipal Court pioneered in the application of social science and social work in an urban setting. But these forays were tentative and marginal. Substantial change in American criminal and family law, as in the law of contracts and torts, would have to wait for the post–World War II years and the rise of a new regime.

Progressive attorney Louis D. Brandeis set out on a new legal path with his fact-laden *Muller v. Oregon* (1908) brief, which induced the Supreme Court to uphold a state law limiting women's working hours. But this decision owed as much to Victorian gender sentimentality as to changing social values. In *Lochner v. New York* (1905), male bakers were the workers whose hours were to be regulated, and the majority struck down the law.

The Supreme Court in the 1920s followed the rest of the polity in adhering to older ways. Holmes and Brandeis struck a new note with their free-speech opinions, but usually in the minor key of dissents. Chief Justice Taft presided over a Court that was more ready to apply the Sherman Act prohibition of conspiracies in restraint of trade to labor unions than to large corporations. And twice it turned down a national child labor law on constitutional grounds. The main lines of constitutional law, as of common law, remained entrenched in the presumptions of nineteenth-century American jurisprudence.

POLICY

Herbert Croly, the editor and public intellectual whose *The Promise of American Life* (1909) could lay claim to be the gospel of Progressivism, declared that "[o]verthrow of the two-party system" was "indispensable to successful progressive democracy." And indeed the most prominent issues of the period—antitrust and railroad regulation, conservation, prohibition, World War I, immigration restriction, women's suffrage—played out with comparatively little regard for party lines, in sharp contrast to the pre-1900 past.

What to do about large corporations was the major economic issue of the Progressive years. Big business came with a rush: the years from 1895 to 1904 saw the creation of 157 holding companies with a combined capitalization of over $4 billion, embracing a seventh of the nation's manufacturing capacity. Newspapers and magazines intensively explored the dangers of this new economic presence.

The antitrust crusade was shaped more by economists, lawyers, judges, and competing business interests than by party leaders. Republican politician Robert La Follette and Democratic attorney Brandeis made opposition to bigness a bipartisan matter. Regulation of the trusts, rather than their dissolution, stemmed from Supreme Court decisions: *Northern Securities* (1904, in which newly appointed Justice Oliver Wendell Holmes's decision infuriated President Theodore Roosevelt, who had appointed him) and the "rule of reason" set down in the Court's 1911 *Standard Oil* and *American Tobacco* decisions.

New regulatory agencies further diluted politicians' capacity to define the scope of business regulation. The Federal Trade Commission, formed in 1914, was charged to control business practices through consent decrees and cease-and-desist orders. It took hard work by Wilson and Democratic House leader Oscar W. Underwood to secure their party's acceptance of so dirigiste an agency. Ultimately the House unanimously approved the creation of the FTC, and only five senators voted against it.

But this no more signified the rise of an administrative state than did the Interstate Commerce Commission a generation before. The Justice Department of the 1920s almost never met a big business it didn't like: it blocked only one of thirteen hundred corporate consolidations between 1919 and 1928. Nor did the FTC significantly regulate business practices or fraudulent advertising. Judicial decisions, said one commissioner, "completely devitalized" the FTC, "reduced it to terms of a futile gesture." The power of corporate-business interests, clashes between the branches of government, and above all the sheer complexity of the modern economy made aggressive regulation by an administrative state all but impossible.

Nowhere was this incapacity more evident than in the realm of railroad rate regulation. The conflict among railroads, farmers, and merchants that led to the ICC evolved into a far more complex regulatory *ronde* of railroads, farmers, manufacturers and other shippers, passengers, unions, politicians, judges, regulators, and the "public interest." The conflicting demands of efficiency and order, of democratic control and public accountability, of lower rates and corporate profits, plus the roiling impact of the new technology of the motor vehicle hobbled the capacity of government to regulate this key sector of the American economy.

The courts remained the final arbiters of ICC rate decisions, reversing well over half of those that came before them for review. Congress responded with the anti-rebate Elkins Act of 1903 and the Hepburn Act of 1906, which strengthened the ICC's rate-setting powers. The complexity of rate setting and the delays of review by the courts led to the Mann-Elkins Act of 1910, which set up a Commerce Court whose sole task was to pass on ICC decisions.

But this Progressive version of the administrative state quickly ran aground on the shoals of America's political culture. During its brief life the Commerce Court frequently overrode the ICC. In turn the Supreme Court reversed four of the five Commerce Court decisions that came before it, and Congress in 1913 closed down this ill-fated experiment. In the same year it passed a Valuation Act requiring the ICC to determine the worth of the railroads' property, its reproduction cost, and the value of the roads' franchises and goodwill, in order to provide a more rational economic basis for rate setting.

Meanwhile, mismanagement by the railroads, the competition of motor transportation, and the ICC's resistance to rate increases eroded the quality of the rail system. Despite a spike in profits during World War I, the explosion of automobiles, trucks, and buses deepened the economic trough into which the roads were falling. The ICC continued to treat railroads as a regulated public utility, closely monitoring rates. But congressionally mandated valuation got more and more bizarre. By the mid-1920s, 260,000 miles of track had been evaluated, ties counted, bridges and terminals inspected, the age and condition of masonry determined, elaborate depreciation tables prepared. This massive exercise in futility cost close to $100 million. And then the Great Depression knocked the railroads, and any rational basis for rate setting, into a cocked hat.

Trusts and railroads were old issues. New technology—telephones, electricity, motor vehicles, movies, radio—raised a host of fresh problems. The Progressives came up with a variety of answers. But these were hardly regime-transforming. What is most striking about the Progressive response to modern times was the degree to which it rested on existing, often quite venerable regulatory instruments.

Did the uninterrupted flow of service provided by public utility corporations (telephones, streetcars and subways, gas and electricity) and by radio broadcasting require new forms of supervision? Apparently not. State public utilities commissions and the Federal Radio Commission were modeled on state railroad commissions and the ICC. These agencies relied on their power to grant certificates of public convenience and necessity: in short, licenses, a pre-modern form of trade and craft regulation that had fallen into disfavor during the laissez-faire years of the early and mid-nineteenth century.

Did the onrush of the motor vehicle pose new threats to property and public safety? States and courts responded to this unsettling new instrument with familiar regulatory devices: licensing and registration, rules of the road, the traditional negligence and liability standards of tort law.

Did movies and radio programs endanger public morality? State film censorship boards popped up, relying on the state's police power to protect morals. But the free-speech model of the print media proved to be a more powerful precedent. The movie studios soon assumed responsibility for the purity of their product, as did radio stations and networks.

Did tumbling prices after World War I threaten tobacco, cotton, and fruit farmers? One answer was massive cooperatives: not the communal sort envisioned by utopians and Populists, but thoroughly commercial, cartelized combines, legitimized by Congress and the courts, empowered to set production quotas on a scale that the biggest of big businesses dared not attempt.

Did burgeoning cities need to exercise some control over the location of private homes, apartment houses, businesses, and factories? Established nuisance law and the venerable police power of the states provided a legal basis for the rapid spread of zoning, both for use and, increasingly, for aesthetic purposes.

If this was a regulatory revolution, it was a very limited one. The existing political, legal, and governmental regime was scarcely altered by it. Not a new administrative state but the old state of parties and courts continued to hold sway. The rapid spread of "capture"—control by the interests regulated, and by the political parties—was common to public utility commissions, motor vehicle supervision, broadcast licensing, and zoning.

Public health and the environment inevitably became substantial concerns in a modern urban-industrial society. The Pure Food and Drug Act of 1905 was the first federal attempt to regulate a realm previously left to (and generally ignored by) the states. The conservation of land and resources also for the first time claimed a significant place as a public issue. Theodore Roosevelt thought his conservation policy was his greatest presidential achievement.

But these policy realms required complex systems of oversight and regulation, well beyond the capacity (or the will) of the party regime. Conflict between advocates of conservation for aesthetics and conservation for use was as conspicuous as the more Manichean confrontation between preservers and despoilers of the land. Behind the cause of pure food and drugs, so attractive to urban consumers, lurked the desire of large producers to use regulation as a weapon against lesser competitors. Again, a familiar scenario of industry capture of the regulatory apparatus emerged. Food and drugs, and land and natural resources, were too deeply entangled in webs of producer, middleman, and consumer interest to be effectively regulated by a weak state.

For the first time since the conflict over slavery, issues of large social significance took center stage in American politics. The most prominent of these were prohibition, women's suffrage, and immigration restriction. Each had been discussed for decades, but primarily by interested groups: evangelical drys, dedicated suffragists, labor unions, genteel racists fearful of immigrant hordes. Now, in the more expansive political environment of the Progressive years, these causes engaged a much broader spectrum of public opinion.

Whites (and some blacks) feared the effect of liquor on race relations in the South. And social and public health reformers concerned over drinking's impact on family life and physical well-being joined the traditional anti-immigrant, anti-Catholic evangelical prohibitionist core. Much the same thing happened with women's suffrage. It attracted advocates of social and political reform who saw in votes for women a way of expanding their base of popular support. Scientific racism, concern over the earning power of American workingmen, and (especially during and after World War I) anxiety over threats to the old native American culture gave immigration restriction a similarly large appeal to American public opinion.

Appropriately enough, these social policies were enacted as a direct result of America's participation in the First World War, that ultimate application of the Progressive belief in forceful, active government. The Progressive leitmotif of government taking on powerful, harmful interests (party bosses and machines, plutocrats and trusts) readily transferred to an overbearing kaiser and a hegemonic German war machine. Wilson's rhetoric—"a war to make the world safe for democracy," "a war to end war"—oozed Progressive idealism from every pore. Anti-war Progressives such as Jane Addams and some midwestern senators were in a distinct minority. Even some American socialists (in particular, those of British origin) favored intervention.

The American war effort was infused with the Progressive ideal of an administrative state. The War Industries Board, run by banker-fixer Bernard Baruch and a mix of businessmen, bureaucrats, and labor leaders, directed industrial mobilization. The Food Administration, headed by businessman-engineer Herbert Hoover, did the same with agriculture. The Fuel Administration had a similar authority over the nation's coal, oil, and gas. The Railroad Administration took over and ran the railroads. Finally, the Committee on Public Information, led by Colorado Progressive journalist George Creel, was charged to educate Americans in the reformist goals of the war and the need for unity transcending the divisions of class, ethnicity, religion, and region. And after victory came Wilson's call for the establishment of the League of Nations, a grand international organization charged to prevent the greatest of all social evils: war.

This was state intervention on a scale beyond the boldest Progressives' imagining. Social control, efficiency, the non-partisan consolidation of diverse interests under beneficent government oversight: that was Progressivism gone to war. Small wonder that Herbert Croly's magazine *The New Republic* welcomed intervention. So did ur-Progressive philosopher John Dewey, who thought the war was not too great a price to pay for the "constructive social engineering" that could come out of it. Journalist Walter Lippmann proclaimed: "We shall turn with fresh interest to our own tyrannies—to our Colorado mines, our autocratic steel industries, our sweatshops and our slums. We shall call that man un-American and no patriot who prates of liberty in Europe and resists it at home." As the war neared its end, Progressives drew up plans for a post-war reconstruction aimed at creating a more efficiently organized economy, a more benignly regulated society.

But these actions and ideas ran into powerful countercurrents. Wheat farmers voted against the Democrats in 1918 to protest price controls. An American population made more diverse by the massive immigration of the pre-war decades split along ethno-cultural lines over American entry into the war. Once the United States declared hostilities, there was an explosion of popular (and official) insistence on undivided loyalty. Wilson condemned "hyphenated Americans": "A man who thinks of himself as belonging to a particular national group in America has not yet become an American. . . . Such creatures of passion, disloyalty, and anarchy must be crushed out."

Anti-German drumbeating, government and popular suppression of anti-war sentiment: that was the nightmarish outcome of the Progressive-wartime ideal of national unity. It was an object lesson in what could happen when public power in America exceeded the limits that ordinarily contained it. And wartime intolerance had a post-war afterlife. Domestic radicalism replaced Prussian militarism as a threat to the nation. Though a Red scare in 1919 quickly petered out, xenophobic forces unleashed by the war helped to pass prohibition and immigration restriction and fed the rise of a reborn Ku Klux Klan.

But the larger pattern of post-war public policy was not the expansion of the active state but its contraction. The war's end led not to wartime supervision and control applied to the post-war economy but rather to dismantling that apparatus as quickly as possible. The railroads, as well as large shippers who wanted a return to rate-cutting competition, saw to it that the lines quickly returned to private ownership after the war ended. Federal expenditure almost halved between 1920 and 1930, and the number of government employees dropped from 655,000 to 600,000. America in the 1920s, observed historian William Leuchtenberg, "had almost no institutional structure to which Europeans would accord the term 'the State.'"

POLITICS

The core Progressive sequence—a sharp increase in the range of what was politically possible, and then an equally sharp reminder of what was *not* politically possible—played out most dramatically in electoral politics. Here could be seen with special clarity the Progressive challenge to the party-democratic regime, and that regime's capacity to co-opt and persist.

For all its new form and content, early-twentieth-century national politics did not lead to regime change comparable to the 1830s or the 1930s. Early-twentieth-century voting patterns did not differ markedly from those of the late nineteenth century. The terms of Democrats Grover Cleveland (1885–89, 1893–97) and Woodrow Wilson (1913–21) had a shared lack of long-term electoral consequence. The more accurate overview of presidential politics is Republican hegemony from 1860 to 1932, interrupted by two Democratic interludes.

One feature of the Progressive impulse was its desire to transcend the ethno-cultural and regional sources of political identity that were so central to the party regime, and substitute for them the appeal of a regulatory-administrative state. This was a theme common to Progressive presidents Roosevelt, Taft, and Wilson. But the politics of ethnicity, religion, and region returned with a rush in the 1920s. The Progressive challenge gave way to what Warren Harding so memorably called the politics of normalcy.

The election of 1912 made clear the temporarily weakened hold of party on national politics wrought by the Progressive impulse. For the first time since 1860, four aspirants with significant voter appeal ran for the presidency. And for the first (and only) time since 1860, the nominee of a new party (Theodore Roosevelt) won more popular and electoral votes than the candidate of one of the two major parties (incumbent President Taft).

The spectrum of candidates in 1912 represented not sectional variety, as in 1860, but differing responses to the core Progressive issue of how to respond to the new American industrial order. This was the first presidential contest to be distinguished by packaged programs, prefixed by the label "new." But 1912 turned out to be something less than a turning point in American national politics. In its wake, most Progressives returned to their Republican base. And the Democrats remained the party of the white South and the Irish North.

William Howard Taft, the 350-pound White House incumbent (geographically described by a foe as "a large land mass entirely surrounded by men who know exactly what they want"), was the choice of the regular Republican organization. He was a staunch exponent of the Constitution and the rule of law, but also a devotee of the Progressive ideals of expertise, economy, and efficiency in government. This was something more than standpattism (the phrase "to stand pat" expanded from poker to politics around 1900). Taft himself insisted, not unreasonably, that his was a variant of Progressivism.

Theodore Roosevelt sought to sidetrack Taft and get the GOP nomination. When that failed, in an act of political apostasy—the primal sin of the party regime—he ran as the candidate of a custom-built Progressive party, the first American political party to adopt that name. He proposed a "New Nationalism" consisting of advanced Progressive proposals for an active state: regulating rather than breaking up trusts, a federal health program, restriction of child labor, workmen's compensation, women's minimum wage laws, and the recall of judicial decisions. Roosevelt's appeal was potent enough to give him 27.4 percent of the popular vote, compared to Taft's 23.1 percent, and eighty-eight electoral votes to Taft's eight: a challenge to two-party hegemony on a scale not seen since 1860.

Woodrow Wilson, the Democratic candidate and ultimate victor, was his party's first southern-born candidate since the Civil War. Along with his Progressive persona of the academic turned politician, Wilson's candidacy was a Democratic variation on the Progressive theme. "The New Freedom," he called his program: a mix of Progressively correct concern for workers, farmers, and small businessmen and traditionally Democratic distaste for the protective tariff. (Wilson: "When I sit down and compare my views with those of a progressive republican, I can't see what the difference is, except that he has a sort of pious feeling about the doctrine of protection which I have never felt.")

Eugene Debs's Socialist party candidacy attracted more than nine hundred thousand popular votes, 6 percent of the total. This was comparable to Populist candidate James Weaver's million-plus votes and 8.5 percent in 1892: another sign of the range of political options unleashed by the loosened grasp of the major parties.

Wisconsin's Robert La Follette also sought to be a candidate. His was yet another Progressive voice, though of the Midwest and of middling farmers and businessman. He claimed to speak for "the New Individualism." In a neat bit of political symbolism, La Follette's campaign imploded when he had a minor nervous breakdown while speaking to the nation's major magazine publishers, shapers of the new mass culture so at odds with La Follette's agrarian and small-town roots.

The entry of the United States into World War I, the conduct of the war, and the peacemaking that followed were arguably the grandest single application of Progressivism to public policy. Yet—or therefore—it wound up stripping away the Progressive claim on the political culture.

The election of 1920 made it clear that Progressivism was an unsettling interlude rather than a regime-changing force. Men prominent in the war effort—Herbert Hoover of the Food Administration, William G. McAdoo, Wilson's son-in-law and head of the Railroad Administration, Attorney General A. Mitchell Palmer of the 1919 Red scare—wanted the Democratic nomination, as indeed did Wilson, incapacitated though he was by a stroke. Instead, the party chose grayish Ohio governor James M. Cox, acceptable chiefly because he was remote from the war and its issues and had managed to get reelected to the governorship in the midst of the Republican sweep of 1918.

Warren G. Harding, the Republican candidate, most vividly embodied the rejection of Progressivism. Profoundly unlearned, a thorough party man and reflexive standpatter, he was the polar opposite of the Progressive presidents. TR's rallying cry at his 1912 Progressive party nomination, "We stand at Armageddon, and we battle for the Lord," may be contrasted with Harding's reaction to his selection in 1920: "Well, we drew to a pair of deuces and filled." Wilson's compelling phrase-making about making the world safe for democracy and fighting a war to end war was replaced now by Harding's most notable contribution to American political rhetoric: "not nostrums but normalcy."

Harding's quotidian persona and pent-up grievances against Wilson's Progressivism-gone-to-war won him sixteen million votes against Cox's nine million and a 404–127 electoral victory, the largest margin until then in post-1820s American politics. The large cities, gradually slipping into the Democratic column during the Progressive years, now swung back to the Republicans, as did the House (by a three-to-one margin).

The Republicans, restored to their customary role as the nation's governing party, had close ties to major financial and industrial interests. They had to face complex domestic economic and social issues, as well as an international economy struggling to right itself after the war. At the same time their core voting base, Protestant and native-born, responded most strongly to a political message that stressed traditional American values and set itself against the people and ideas of a new, urban, industrial society.

This raised a problem of party identity comparable to post–Civil War days. The GOP sloughed off its older support for active government and redefined itself as the party of laissez-faire and the old America. Its economic policies spoke to big business, its social policies to its non-southern native Protestant electoral core. The party thus ensured itself notable political success during the 1920s—and deep political distress during the Great Depression.

The Democrats had a comparably wide ideological gap to bridge. Like the Republicans, they adapted their traditional commitments (to states' rights, limited government, personal freedom, and white supremacy) to post–World War I American life. The major Democratic components—rural southern Protestant whites, urban northern Catholics—never co-existed easily. Prohibition and anti-Catholicism, along with the economic gulf between the industrial North and the agrarian South, widened the gap. This came to a head in the 1924 Democratic convention. A resolution denouncing the anti-Catholic Ku Klux Klan lost by a fraction of a vote. And it took two weeks and 103 ballots before West Virginia–born corporation lawyer John W. Davis was chosen as the compromise alternative to New York Catholic governor Al Smith. The emollient grand bargain: northern Democratic acceptance of white supremacy and the

Jeffersonian small-government, states'-rights ideal, southern acceptance of liberal hostility to big business and northern party leadership.

The most substantial challenges to the hegemony of the major parties during the 1920s came from Robert La Follette's third-party campaign in 1924 and a reborn Ku Klux Klan. The Progressive party of 1924 resembled the Populists of the 1890s more than the Progressives of 1912. It too was the product of an overarching grievance, not agrarian depression but World War I and its aftermath. Its major components were liberals, radicals, and ethnic groups such as German Americans disillusioned by the wartime repression of dissent and the Versailles Treaty; railroad workers unhappy over the return of the lines to private ownership after the war; and northern Plains farmers angry over wartime controls and the post-war collapse of wheat prices. It was quite appropriate that its leader was Robert La Follette, the senator most conspicuously identified with opposition to the war.

La Follette won a substantial five million votes, compared to Democrat John W. Davis's eight million, even though he was kept off the ballot in several states. But the fading memory of the war, the rise of newer issues, and the ability of the major parties to co-opt them doomed La Follette's Progressives to the one-election marginality that is the fate of most third parties.

The twentieth-century Klan adopted the name, trappings, and ideology of its post-Reconstruction prototype, updated to the new century. It was national, not southern, as strong in Indiana and Oregon as in Georgia. While it retained the anti-black racism of its prototype, the new Klan added—indeed, gave pride of place to—other hatreds: of Jews and especially Catholics, of modern, secular, urban culture. The Klan peaked in the early 1920s, with somewhere between three million and six million members (a quarter or more of adult white Protestant males).

The new Klan was not a separate party but an infiltrator: of the Democrats in the South and Far West, of the Republicans in the Midwest. At its peak it attained considerable local and state power. It was more of an urban movement than a rural one, with particular appeal to lower-middle-class white newcomers from farms and small towns to the cities, arriving before and during the First World War and existing in a state of tension with their black, Jewish, and Catholic neighbors.

The Klan fell as rapidly as it rose. Internal scandals added to the aura of the disreputable that was part of its persona. Most of all, the major parties drew off the discontents—and the discontented—to whom the Klan appealed. Southern Democratic racism was strong enough to satisfy all but the most discriminating taste. Republican nativism and xenophobia played a comparable role in other regions. Once again the regnant party regime, a century old, met and mastered challenges to its hegemony.

The restoration of the pre-Progressive party culture reached its apogee in the election of 1928. Both Republican candidate Herbert Hoover and his Democratic opponent Al Smith in fact had strong Progressive bona fides. Each had a reputation as an efficient administrator: Smith as a reformist governor of New York, Hoover as the engineer-turned-humanitarian head of Belgian and Russian relief programs, the wartime food administrator, and a modern-minded secretary of commerce in the 1920s.

But the political dynamic of the time compelled them to embody the conflict between old and new America: native versus immigrant, rural and small town versus city, Protestant versus Catholic. Smith's Lower East Side accent, many thought, became more pronounced in the course of the campaign, to the extent that much of his heartland audience could not understand him when he spoke on what he called the "raddio." He made "East Side, West Side" his less than universally appealing campaign song. He was supposed to have said that he would rather be a lamppost on Park Avenue than governor of California, and when asked for his views on the problems of the states west of the Mississippi, he was reputed to have replied: "What *are* the states west of the Mississippi?"

Hoover underwent a comparable but polar transformation. This Stanford graduate, international businessman-engineer, and advocate of a more "associational" relationship between big business and big government morphed into the down-home voice of rural Protestant America. He dwelt on his Iowa orphan childhood, his belief in rugged individualism, his commitment to prohibition.

McKinley and Bryan in 1896 took the major economic concerns of their day and converted them into a dialogue that ensured the dominance of the major parties over national policymaking. So did Hoover and Smith co-opt the ethno-cultural tensions of the 1920s. Less than 50 percent of those eligible voted in 1924. In 1928, 67.5 percent turned out. As had McKinley in 1896, Hoover won a decisive, sweeping victory. Smith's Catholicism and his opposition to prohibition enabled the GOP to make previously unparalleled gains in the South. North Carolina, Georgia, Texas, and Florida went Republican for the first time since Reconstruction, with almost no blacks voting to speak of.

At the same time Smith went far to restore the urban Democratic majority of most of the nineteenth century. The ten largest cities, whose margin for Coolidge in 1924 was 1.3 million votes, went narrowly for Smith. Immigrants and their children (in particular, Catholic women), previously underrepresented in the electorate, now became a substantial voting presence. Massachusetts and Rhode Island were the only northeastern states Smith carried; but they went Democratic for the first time since the Civil War.

The onset of the Great Depression in 1930–32 was notable at first not for political or governmental change but for the degree to which the parties and public policy stayed on familiar, traditional paths. Political leaders and public opinion at large were slow to see that the nation faced an economic disaster of unprecedented scope. More than a century of recurrent downswings and depressions had deeply embedded the view that the rise and fall of the economy was much like the weather: inevitable, but not predictable, not controllable, and certain to change.

In polls during the early 1930s, a thousand leading Americans ranked crime and the administration of justice, prohibition, and economy and efficiency in government well ahead of unemployment or the distribution of wealth as the most pressing American issues. President Hoover continued to rely on the rhetoric of individualism, self-help, and laissez-faire. "The sole function of government," he declared, "is to bring about a condition of affairs favorable to the beneficial development of private enterprise."

When steadily worsening conditions became impossible to ignore, Hoover responded in ways that drew on his, and the nation's, immediate past: World War I, the 1920s. He indulged in wartime-like appeals for national unity in the face of a national emergency. He urged employers to maintain existing levels of employment and wages, and tried through conferences to stimulate agricultural leaders, public utilities executives, railroad presidents, industrialists and bankers to hire more people and do more business.

Hoover sought especially to revive the investment deemed necessary to reverse the deflationary spiral. He relied on tax cuts, lower rediscount rates by the Federal Reserve Board, and a new agency, the Reconstruction Finance Corporation, charged to lend to banks on easy terms. Finally he resorted to grants to the states to bolster unemployment compensation and (limited) public works. He asked Congress to spend more money on river and harbor improvements, new public buildings, aid to the states for road construction, and the completion of Boulder (soon to be Hoover) Dam.

One difficulty: nothing seemed to have much effect. There are as many complex economic explanations of this as there are complex economists doing the explaining. But the insufficiencies of the policy response, the intractability of what was in fact a worldwide crisis, and the ever-widening gap between the controlling assumptions of the political regime and the realities of a changing society were prime contributors to what became the greatest challenge to the American polity since the Civil War.

Hoover declared himself "willing to pledge myself that if the time should ever come that the voluntary agencies of the country together with the local and state governments are unable to fund resources with which to prevent hunger and suffering in my country, I will ask the aid of every resource of the federal government." But when *would* that time arrive? His principled opposition to direct government aid to individuals—the dreaded "dole"—was deeply grounded in his (and his party's) social, moral, even psychological underpinnings. He had a near-pathological lack of interest in statistics detailing the human cost of the Depression. When the lower Mississippi valley was ravaged by drought in 1930, Hoover expanded highway construction in the area, got railroads to cut their freight rates, and encouraged the Red Cross to raise and spend more money for relief of the victims. But when Congress considered a $25 million federal contribution to this relief effort, he (and the Red Cross) opposed it as a threat to voluntarism.

In fact, neither party and no branch of government had much to offer that was markedly different. House Speaker John Garner (soon to be Franklin D. Roosevelt's 1932 running mate) attacked Hoover for too much spending, and the House Democratic leadership favored a federal sales tax to balance the budget. The Revenue Act of 1932 passed by a Democratic-controlled Congress was notable for its regressive taxes. Franklin Delano Roosevelt, the Democrats' 1932 candidate, paid homage to his party's oldest tradition by making Hoover's expanding bureaucracy and irresponsible spending conspicuous targets: "I accuse the present administration of being the greatest spending administration in peace times in all our history. It is an administration that has piled bureau on bureau, commission on commission. . . . I regard the reduction in Federal spending as one of the most important issues of this campaign. In my opinion, it is the most direct and effective contribution that Government can make to business." The repeal of Prohibition was by far the most popular and compelling political issue during the early Depression years. Philosopher John Dewey wonderingly observed: "Here we are in the midst of the greatest crisis since the Civil War, and the only thing the two national parties want to debate is booze."

Dissenters from the prevailing policy mind-set—urban and agrarian Progressives, socialists—were beginning to make their mark, and intimations of the New Deal were part of FDR's message. But old party commitments were slow to change. In 1930 the Republicans increased their share of the vote in many cities. Philadelphia was as hard hit by unemployment as any large industrial city, yet the GOP candidate for mayor in 1931 won by a vote of 180,000 to 30,000.

FDR's 57 percent of the popular vote and forty-two of the forty-eight states in 1932 gave him the biggest victory margin of any Democrat since before the Civil War. But the scale and sweep of the victory—he won 2,721 of the nation's 3,100 counties—suggests that this was an across-the-board protest vote of the sort that had happened before, in 1894 and 1920. The Socialists and Communists, who offered the strongest alternative programs, won respectively 885,000 (less than 1912 or 1920) and 102,000 votes, out of some 39 million cast.

Over the course of a century, from the 1820s to the 1930s, the major-party system, limited and decentralized government, and a judicial system that favored property rights made for a notably durable regime. It persisted in the face of massive industrialization, urbanization, immigration, internal migration, and culture change. It weathered the greatest of American crises, the Civil War. It contained (and absorbed) the agrarian unrest of the 1890s and the challenge of the Progressive impulse.

Would this continue to be the case in the face of the changes that swept over America, and the world, during the rest of the twentieth century? Or would the Great Depression, the New Deal, World War II, the Cold War, post-war affluence, and the cultural upheaval of the 1960s and after lead to regime change comparable to the Republic's early years?

PART FOUR

THE POPULIST-BUREAUCRATIC REGIME

Since the 1930s the American polity has been under the sway of a new regime, populist and bureaucratic. Today, after three-quarters of a century, this regime is in its full maturity: as distinctive, and as pervasive, as its party-democratic predecessor. Political scientist Theodore Lowi observed in 1985: "What we now have is an entirely new regime, which deserves to be called the Second Republic of the United States."

The new regime is *populist* in the sense that public affairs are defined increasingly by voices outside of the party-political apparatus—the media, advocacy groups, experts, bureaucrats, judges—who claim to speak for particular social interests or for the people at large. The term *populist* used to be confined to specific political movements, most notably the American

Populist party and the Russian Populists of the late nineteenth century. But in modern times it has taken on a more generic political meaning. *Time* observed in 1972: "Populism is a label that covers disparate policies and passions: among many others, New Deal reforms, consumer rage against business, ethnic belligerence. Often it is merely a catch phrase. Yet it describes something real: the politics of the little guy against the big guy—the classic struggle of the haves [or, one might add, the recent-gots] against the have-nots or the have-not-enoughs." Modern populist politics is "as much a matter of style as substance."

Before the 1930s the American polity's primary concern was with the degree to which government power in general, and the power of the federal government in particular, could be *constrained*. Modern populist politics focuses on how that power can be *used*: primarily to enforce and enhance the rights of individuals and groups. Thus in the party regime, voting was viewed primarily as a way to safeguard citizens' liberty from government coercion. Today it is regarded as an instrument to induce government to respond to the popular will as that will is expressed through public opinion polls, the media, and advocacy groups, as well as through the more traditional medium of the parties.

The new regime is also *bureaucratic*, relying on government agencies and the courts to define and enforce public policy. The American administrative state, whose coming has been proclaimed since the Civil War, is now finally, undeniably here. It got its first firm footing in the New Deal and more deeply entrenched itself in the course of World War II. It steadily grew on the sustenance of the Cold War, the Great Society, and the rights revolution of the late twentieth century.

More, and more powerful, administrative agencies are a major part of the new bureaucratic regime. So is a bureaucratic mind-set fed by military, corporate, and professional-expert thought. Joining in are the courts, which evolved during the second half of the twentieth century from an institution whose primary function was to tell the government and corporations what they could *not* do to one that tells them what they *must* do. And just as the populist impulse sought to displace parties as the primary definers of public policy, so have bureaucrats and judges sought to displace politicians as the primary dispensers of public power.

A series of shocks comparable to those of the late eighteenth and early nineteenth centuries spurred the evolution of the party-democratic regime into the populist-bureaucratic one. A new way of doing politics, government, and law emerged from the Great Depression, the New Deal, World War II, and the Cold War. The new regime was further entrenched by the economic, social, and cultural changes that have swept over the country since the 1940s, as broad as their early-nineteenth-century counterparts.

Some benchmarks of change:

- The century-long dominance of party politics has given way to a new political culture, as different from the party regime of the nineteenth and early twentieth centuries as that was from the deferential-republican regime of the Colonial-Revolutionary era. Large-scale shifts in voter identity led to the displacement of the Republicans as the "normal majority" party during the 1930s and then to the slower, more hesitant erosion of the Democratic majority since the 1960s. In the course of these tectonic shifts in voter preference, many of the ethno-cultural, regional, and class differences that defined political identity through the course of the party regime were upended. So were the parties themselves, as other institutions—most notably the media, advocacy groups, and the courts—laid claim to be the definers of public policy.
- At the same time the emergence of a regulatory-welfare state created a flock of new interactions between government and the people, the parties, and the courts. A new constitutional and civil law came into being, with transforming consequences for federal power, civil liberties, civil rights, and the law of contracts and torts.
- Finally, a century-long American foreign policy of non-engagement, punctuated by occasional wars (the Mexican War of 1846–48, the Spanish-American War of 1898, World War I in 1917–18), has been replaced by its mirror image: normal engagement, often military, always worldwide, punctuated by brief interludes of withdrawal.

As before, the lingua franca of public affairs changed with the polity. The populist and bureaucratic regime brought with it a new vocabulary of American public life.

The erosion of party as the norm of political identity led to a rise in references to *nonpartisan, bipartisan, independent, centrist, moderate,* and *mainstream* positions: the language of a more fluid politics. But ideology—what columnist Westbrook Pegler in the 1930s called "galloping ismatism"—also claims a more prominent place when politics is populist. Labels—*liberal* and *progressive, fascist* and *communist, conservative* and *neo-conservative, radical* and *progressive, left* and *right, New Left* and *Radical Right*—come as trippingly to political tongues as *Democrat* or *Republican* once did. *Activists, militants,* and *advocates* are thick on the ground. Talk of *red* and *blue* America has a two-nations tone that echoes the North and the South of the Civil War era. Modern *movement politics* has its own vocabulary: of *black power* and *civil disobedience*, the *civil rights coalition* and the *gun lobby*, *pro-choice* and *pro-life*, *feminists* and *gays*, the *Moral Majority* and the *religious right*, the *angry left*.

Worker-capitalist and Protestant-Catholic-Jewish divisions have receded. But foreign policy is a fruitful source of sharp-edged confrontation. *Isolationists* and *interventionists*, *hawks* and *doves*, *warmongers* and *peaceniks* have been conspicuous occupants of the modern American political bestiary.

The left, says the right, is populated by *bleeding hearts*, *parlor pinks* who morphed into *limousine liberals* and *Park Avenue populists*. If not *card-carrying Communists*, they are *soft on Communism* and subscribe to a *party line* that is *politically correct* (terms, as it happens, of Stalinist and Maoist origin). The right, responds the left, includes a *lunatic fringe* of *hard-line*, *hard-core*, *right-wing kooks* and *hidebound reactionaries*.

Liberals, in the eyes of liberals, are advocates of the *public interest*, the *common man* (or, more recently, the *middle class*). They like to call government spending *investments*, subsidized housing *affordable*, and tariff protection *fair trade*. They prefer *affirmative action* to quotas, a *single-payer system* to government-run health care, and *public-protection attorneys* to trial lawyers. They are *pro-choice* when it comes to procreation but not when it comes to education.

Conservatives, in the eyes of conservatives, are *apostles* of *freedom* and *individualism*, *law and order*, and *Middle America*. They prefer to call school vouchers *opportunity scholarships*, the inheritance tax the *death tax*, tax cuts *tax relief*, opposition to abortion *pro-life*, government-run health care *socialized medicine*. Other favored euphemisms: *the Free World* (America's Cold War allies), *right to work* (anti-closed-shop laws), and *choice* (in education, not procreation).

The *media* (a term that came into frequent use in the 1970s) feeds the language of modern politics. *Press secretaries* and *press agents* (or *flacks*) *manage the news* and set up *photo opportunities* and *off-the-record backgrounders*. Speechwriters—*phrasemakers*, *wordsmiths*—*spin doctors*, and *handlers* help the candidate *stay on message* through *sound bites* and *TV spots*. *Networking* goes far beyond TV and radio and appearances: politicians *sign on* to *scenarios* and worry about *equal time* on the *tube*, *leaks* in their offices, and above all their *image* with *pundits* and the public. *Pollsters*, ever alert to premature *peaking*, advise on the *demographics* of a campaign.

The bureaucratic regime relies on the vocabulary of a managerial society as the party regime did on the language of agrarian and then industrial America. Evocative names—*Foggy Bottom, the Pentagon, the*

Beltway, the Oval Office, the West Wing—identify the vital organs of the new American state. Some of the language of bureaucracy is custom-built: *boondoggle* and *gobbledegook* are invented words. But most of it comes from the corporate and military worlds. It includes relatively technical, value-free terms—*red tape, feedback, input* and *throughput, glitches* and *quick fixes, gridlock, fallback position, technocrats* and *bean counters, cost-efficient, state-of-the-art, position papers* and *game plans, in-house, decision-making process, time frame, infrastructure, options, zero in, task force, power curve, expertise, phase in* (and *out*). And it embraces as well the more Hobbesian language of bureaucratic conflict: *clout, crunch time, flak, backlash, power broker, influence peddler.* Acronyms, the mother's milk of bureaucracy, are commonplace in the new regime. The New Deal's *alphabet agencies* (the *AAA, NRA, SEC, CCC, TVA,* and *WPA*) set the standard; the Great Society's *NASA, OEO, EEOC,* and *EPA* continued the tradition.

Foreign policy discourse has been laden with the technical language of the Cold War: *deterrents, containment, fail-safe, escalation, open skies, MAD, fallout, missile gap, missile systems, hot line.* The domestic welfare-regulatory state, like the (cold) warfare state, draws verbal sustenance from the managerial-bureaucratic well. The *interests* and *lobbyists* of earlier days are supplemented by more sophisticated constructs: the *power elite,* the *military-industrial* and *welfare-educational* complexes, *Iron Triangles* of interconnected congressional committees, bureaucrats, and interest groups. FDR's *Brain Trust* is closer in spirit to Robert McNamara's *Whiz Kids* than to Andrew Jackson's *Kitchen Cabinet.* The idea of checks and balances may seem antediluvian in the age of the *imperial Congress* or the *imperial presidency* or the *imperial judiciary.*

CHAPTER TEN

THE RISE OF THE POPULIST-BUREAUCRATIC REGIME

From the 1930s to the 1960s, American politics, government, and law went through a forcing house of change. The Great Depression, World War II, the Cold War, and the post-1945 transformation of American material and cultural life saw to that. Politics evolved from its boss- and machine-dominated past into a more populist mode, defined increasingly by advocacy groups and the media. Public policy, redefined by the New Deal and World War II, persisted in its new course, sustained by the Cold War and the new social demands of modern America. A massive new federal state, going beyond the exigencies of wartime, became a permanent fact of American public life. And the judiciary began to carve out a new place for itself as the polity's third force.

THE NEW DEAL: POLITICS

Half a century ago most historians saw the New Deal as the culmination of a reform tradition rooted in Jacksonian democracy, Populism, and Progressivism. That changed in the 1960s and 1970s, when the prevailing leftist perspective reduced the New Deal to another faux reform in the long history of predatory American capitalism. Now, in the twenty-first century, the New Deal has taken on another meaning: as historian Barry Karl puts it, "the central event in the creation of America as a national society."

In a literal sense, the New Deal was a cluster of policies and programs. It also brought a new framework to American public life: changing vote alignments, innovative instruments of government. But it did not become the social-democratic party that its strongest proponents wanted it to be. The New Deal dramatically demonstrated the possibilities of political change when conditions were sufficiently unsettling. But it also showed how persistent deep-seated values, institutions, and interests could be, even in a time of national crisis.

The 1932 election was a traditional one, in the sense that popular anger with incumbent Herbert Hoover and his party was more decisive than the ideas of his challenger, Franklin Delano Roosevelt. Then things changed. For the first time ever, in the off-year election of 1934 the incumbent party increased its already hefty congressional majority. The election of 1936 produced a Congress more than 75 percent Democratic, and the party's candidates for governor won twenty-six of thirty-three state elections: a sweep unparalleled since the Era of Good Feelings more than a century before.

Many traditionally Republican midwestern rural counties, which in protest against the Depression voted for FDR in 1932, returned to their core GOP identity in 1936. (In this they resembled rock-ribbed Federalist enclaves after 1815.) But that visceral Republicanism was overwhelmed by an urban, working-class, immigrant, and ethnic minority outpouring for FDR and the Democrats. An estimated 95 percent of potential new voters in the big cities turned out in 1936, and 90 percent of them voted for Roosevelt. Although this is a matter for debate, the mobilization of new voters more than the conversion of existing ones appears to have been the primary source of the FDR–New Deal majority.

Much has been made of the spectacular 1936 misjudgment of the nation's major presidential election poll, conducted by the *Literary Digest*. It predicted that FDR would get 41 percent of the vote, a tad short of the 61 percent he in fact received. Yet four years before, when the poll concluded that FDR would win 56 percent of the vote, it was almost spot-on to his actual 57 percent. What changed was not the *Literary Digest's* technique but the new, poorer urban voters missed by its telephone- and mail-based polling.

The relative marginality of third parties was a surprising feature of political life in the Great Depression. Consequential protest parties figured importantly in the elections of 1892, 1912, and 1924, and there was good reason to expect that the Depression-ridden 1930s would be a fecund time for them.

Extra-party protest did increase, but in forms that hardly evoked comparison with the parties of the left and right so conspicuous in other

Western countries. Most significant was a trio of movements that sprang up in the mid-thirties. Much ink has been spent trying to decide whether Huey Long's Share Our Wealth movement, Father Charles Coughlin's National Union for Social Justice, and Dr. Francis Townsend's plan for $100-a-month pensions to be spent immediately were proto-socialist or proto-fascist. What *is* clear is that they were in the American grain of special-purpose political protest, where shared grievances and commonalities of region, religion, or ethnicity weighed more heavily than class.

Long's lower Mississippi valley farmers, Coughlin's northern urban Catholics, and Townsend's midwestern Protestants displaced to California had little in common beyond Depression-fed economic misfortune. This became evident in 1936, when leaders of the three movements came together into a Union Party alternative to FDR and the New Deal. Their candidate, North Dakota Non-Partisan Leaguer William Lemke, won 800,000 of 44.5 million voter, less than 2 percent of the total. Soon after, the coalition broke apart under the strain of its members' religious, ethnic, regional, and programmatic differences, to become a footnote in the long history of third-party failure to crack the major parties.

The real political transformation occurred within the Democratic party. FDR's four elections to the presidency, the majorities that elected him, and the changes in government that he oversaw added up to a sea change in American public life. Its only historical counterpart was the early nineteenth century, when the deferential political culture of the Early Republic gave way to mass democratic politics.

FDR was as close as could be to an American aristocrat, in sharp contrast to Jackson and Lincoln. His highly developed political sensitivity enabled him to take on the seemingly contradictory role of what historian Richard Hofstadter called "the patrician as opportunist" (and could have been called the patrician as populist). FDR came into office exuding the forceful, take-charge persona that a Depression-battered nation wanted. (His first inaugural address had sixteen references to *nation* or *national*, five to *leadership*.) Four years later, he wooed his New Deal constituency with sharp-edged class rhetoric. Four years after that, as war took over the American scene, he smoothly reverted to the role of the nation's leader.

For millions of lower-income Americans, FDR was the benevolent prince, a stock figure in peasant cultures. His New Deal swung open the gates of participation in national affairs to previously excluded groups. It redefined American nationality, reversing the exclusionary trend of previous decades. One major beneficiary was organized labor, previously scattered in its political identity. The pro-labor legislation of the New Deal welded an alliance between labor unions and the Democratic party that would be solidly in place seventy years later (despite substantial rank-and-file defections).

FDR and the New Deal had the same leveling impact on the politics of ethnicity that Andrew Jackson and Jacksonian democracy had on the politics of social status. Irish Catholics were always Democratic but traditionally subordinate to the southern wing of the party. Now they came into their own. One in four of FDR's appointments to the federal judiciary was Catholic, in sum six times the number appointed previously. The Harvard-educated but marginally respectable entrepreneur Joseph P. Kennedy was the first head of the Securities and Exchange Commission, and then (previously unimaginable for an Irish Catholic) ambassador to the Court of St. James. It is not surprising that Kennedy put his name on a 1936 campaign book called *I'm for Roosevelt* (in which he assured his readers: "I have no political ambitions for myself or my five children").

Jewish lawyers and economists, led by FDR adviser and then Supreme Court justice Felix Frankfurter, also were thick on the New Deal ground. Roosevelt made his Hudson Valley neighbor Henry Morgenthau secretary of the Treasury, the first Jewish holder of a top-rank cabinet post. Before the 1930s, most Jewish voters were Republican or Socialist. From then on, they were overwhelmingly Democratic.

African Americans most dramatically reversed their political identity. There were no black delegates at the Democrats' 1928 convention in Houston, and the few alternates were seated in a separate area, surrounded by a wire mesh fence. Not surprisingly, black voters' ties to the party of Lincoln were durable. Even in 1932, 80 percent of Chicago's black electorate who cast ballots voted Republican. FDR showed no particular sensitivity to black needs and desires, though his wife, Eleanor, did. But New Deal programs were the first public policies since Reconstruction to have a measurably beneficial impact on blacks. By the mid-1930s an estimated 40 percent of African Americans were getting some federal aid. And by the late 1930s, 75 percent of blacks voted Democratic.

These accretions lifted the Democratic party to a political domination comparable to the Jeffersonian Republicans after the War of 1812. In the wake of the 1936 election, there was talk of a Republican future as bleak as the Federalists'. But that election turned out to be the high point of the New Deal–Democratic coalition. From then on the fissiparous forces of American life that erode every political alliance came into play.

FDR's attempt to wrench his party from its Jeffersonian-Jacksonian small-government base and redefine it as the voice of social democracy and an active state alienated traditional Democrats. Advised by an "elimination commission" of New Dealers operating outside the regular party organization, Roosevelt tried in 1938 to get rid of influential anti–New Deal congressmen by supporting their primary opponents. This "purge" (a word then in common use to describe Stalin's removal of opposition real or imagined) failed in all but one instance. And much of the machinery of Congress remained in the hands of southern party traditionalists.

With varying degrees of enthusiasm, northern urban machine bosses supported the New Deal, especially the programs that brought federal funds and jobs. The Chicago, St. Louis, and Pittsburgh Democratic machines superseded their Republican counterparts and developed a mutually beneficial relationship with the New Deal. More than 90 percent of Pittsburgh's Democratic ward committeemen were WPA foremen.

But party mastodons such as Frank Hague of Jersey City, who opposed social security on the ground that it took the romance out of old age, were much like their southern counterparts in their hostility to the New Deal's social democratic impulses. New York's Tammany, cool to the national party, was at war with Mayor Fiorello LaGuardia, a strong New Dealer despite his Republican party roots.

Still, the marriage between the post-FDR Democratic party and the big-city machines proved to be a durable one. In ensuing decades, skillful politicos such as mayors Robert Wagner Jr. of New York, Richard Daley of Chicago, and Richard Lee of New Haven let New Deal liberals have a large voice in education, urban renewal, and social welfare, while they maintained organization control over fire and police patronage. Not until the rise of the race-and-culture wars of the 1960s did this Democratic urban arrangement begin to come apart.

A comparable blend of resistance and adaptation was evident in the Republican party. The GOP was as badly damaged by its failure to respond to the Great Depression as the mid-nineteenth-century Democrats had been by their failure to respond to slavery and secession. And like the Democrats after the Civil War, the party quickly regained its footing.

The Republican presidential candidates of the 1930s, 1940s, and 1950s were moderate by party standards. Kansas governor Alfred M. Landon, the 1936 nominee, had been a pro-TR Bull Moose Progressive and was the only GOP governor to win reelection in the Depression year of 1934. In 1940 the party rejected Robert Taft, the epitome of GOP conservatism, for utilities lawyer Wendell Willkie, who came from a left-wing Democratic family and had been a Democrat as late as 1938. Media magnate Henry Luce of *Time* and *Life* and the admen of Madison Avenue—harbingers of a new politics—played a key role in Willkie's nomination. In 1944 and

1948 the GOP candidate was Thomas E. Dewey, enough of a moderate to be elected and then twice reelected governor of New York. The 1944 Republican platform explicitly "accept[ed] the purposes" of the New Deal's labor and welfare programs.

True, the Republicans never figured out how to defeat FDR, and even managed to lose in 1948 to Harry Truman. But they recovered enough congressional, state, and local political muscle to remain a viable player in the two-party game. In 1938 they regained six Senate and seventy-two House seats, seventeen of thirty-one governorships, and four hundred counties and 150,000 state and local patronage jobs.

The GOP retained its traditional sources of strength: lower-middle-class and white-collar Protestants outside the South, managerial and professional voters across the nation. With the coming of World War II the party gained new support, notably urban Irish Catholics hostile to FDR's support for Britain and Russia in the war against Hitler.

So the major parties responded to, and in a sense mastered, the challenges posed by the Great Depression. But in the course of doing so, each in its own way became more "populist," more ready to reach out to groups and issues beyond their traditional political domains. The political consequences of this transformation would unfold over the course of the mid- and late twentieth century.

THE NEW DEAL: POLICY AND INSTITUTIONS

Since the two major parties continued to dominate American politics, what becomes of the regime-change hypothesis? The answer is that a flood of new policy and practice filled the old institutional bottles. The formal structure of the American polity—parties and elections, the presidency, Congress, the bureaucracy, the courts—persisted. The Constitution and the realities of American life made alternatives all but impossible. But the content and character of that structure decisively changed.

As was the case with its party-democratic predecessor, the ascendancy of the populist-bureaucratic regime took time. The frustrations of a Depression-ravaged people and widespread demands that the government do something about the situation generated enormous political force. But of necessity the new impulses played out along lines dictated by existing ideas, interests, and institutions.

The words in FDR's first inaugural address that evoked the strongest response were not his famous declaration that the only thing we had to fear was fear itself but his request for the powers granted a chief executive in time of war. The World War I experience was the obvious model to turn to in a time of crisis, especially since FDR himself and many other early New Dealers cut their policy-making teeth in that conflict. Historian William Leuchtenberg concludes: "The New Dealers resorted to the analogue of war, because in America the source of community is weak, the distrust of the state strong."

But the sheer scale of the Depression, and the new voting groups and policy ideas that gained power after 1932, opened the sluice gates of government. New Deal policy rapidly evolved from analogue-of-war responses linked to major interest groups (industry, agriculture, labor) to innovative policies aimed at previously unrecognized social groups: a profoundly populist development.

Agricultural policy went in a few years from the Agricultural Adjustment Act of 1933, with marketing agreements and subsidies aimed at substantial market farmers, to the Resettlement and Farm Security Administrations, designed to aid sharecroppers and migrant farm workers. The Rural Electrification Administration brought low-cost electricity to farm homes.

Industrial policy morphed from the production controls of the 1933 National Industrial Recovery Act (NIRA) to higher corporate taxes and a crackdown on public utilities holding companies in 1935. Unions got a groundbreaking endorsement of their right to organize in NIRA's Section 7A. They got much more with the Wagner Act of 1935, which set up the National Labor Relations Board to oversee elections and certify unions for collective bargaining. The Fair Labor Standards Act of 1938 set minimum wage and maximum hours standards and opened the way to child labor regulation. In 1940, only seven years after Section 7A, came the Fair Employment Practices Committee (FEPC), the first tentative federal entry into the hitherto forbidden territory of racial equality in the workforce: a breathtaking evolution of labor policy.

Relief, welfare, and housing policy underwent similar sea changes. The Public Works Administration, headed by former Bull Moose Progressive Harold Ickes, focused on bread-and-butter construction projects such as dams and bridges. The Works Progress Administration under New Dealer Harry Hopkins put people before projects, addressing the needs of unskilled workers, actors, academics, and writers. Welfare entered a new era with the Social Security Act of 1935, which brought the government into the business of providing large-scale old-age, unemployment, and child-care benefits. Housing policy went from a guarantee of existing mortgages through the Home Owners' Loan Corporation to subsidizing new home ownership through the Federal Housing Administration and on to public housing (on a small scale) with the United States Housing Authority of 1937.

The FDR–New Deal coalition that emerged in the 1934 and 1936 elections was a political spur to this explosion of new directions in public policy: regime change at work. But the shift in emphasis from the economic infrastructure to the human costs of the Depression had intellectual sources as well. Law professors, social scientists, civil servants, and social workers—"service intellectuals"—fed ideas to New Deal agencies and New Dealish legislators. Some seventy-eight hundred social scientists, including twenty-eight hundred economists, worked for the federal government by 1938.

Early New Deal mover and shaker Raymond Moley was a political scientist, the more radical Rexford Tugwell an economist, Harry Hopkins a professional social worker. The New Deal's most conspicuous bill drafters were the Irish Catholic Thomas Corcoran and the Jew Ben Cohen. Felix Frankfurter was the most prominent talent recruiter. These men did not share the traditional American suspicion of the state. They were more responsive to the collectivist impulses so attractive in the Western world of the 1930s.

But the "social Keynesianism" of more advanced New Dealers did not prevail. Instead, a "commercial Keynesianism" took center stage. Subsidized investment capital, cheap and abundant electric power, and the spur of World War II made the government a major player in the economic rise of the South and the West. This "public capitalism" had little to do with social democratic ideals. Even the Great Depression could not override the political interests, regional variations, and social complexities that worked against class politics.

That did not preclude major institutional aftershocks from following the electoral earthquake of the New Deal. FDR developed a style of governance, transcending his party and its congressional leadership, that has been the presidential standard since. The executive office of the president became a not-so-mini bureaucracy. The West Wing, with its Oval Office, was added to the White House in 1934, expanding that building from 15,000 to 40,000 square feet. And FDR ended the presidency's hoariest tradition by running for and getting elected to a third and then a fourth term. (This went too far. Bipartisan support enacted the Twenty-Second Amendment in 1951, embedding the two-term limit in the Constitution: a measure of how profoundly FDR shook up the office.)

In the wake of his 1936 triumph, FDR embarked on a series of institutional changes designed to ensure the success of a more social-democratic New Deal. His effort to remodel American government had three high points: the attempted purge of leading conservative Democratic congressmen in the 1938 primaries, his 1937 Supreme Court "packing" plan, and the Executive Reorganization Act of 1938–39. Each, in its way, failed. The institutions challenged—Congress, the Supreme Court, the bureaucracy—were able to retain their traditional identities despite the tsunami-like forces for change unleashed by the Great Depression.

It seemed at first that the New Deal had put paid to the congressional government of the party-democratic regime. Congress shouted through FDR's early proposals. But as the New Deal turned left, foot-dragging by more conservative members of the party became more prevalent. In response, FDR sought to remove the leading conservative congressional Democrats by campaigning in the 1938 primaries for their more pro–New Deal challengers.

This effort failed in all but one case. Instead, a sharp increase in the number of Republican congressmen opened the door to something new in American political life: a conservative coalition of southern Democrats and midwestern Republicans. These two political bodies, at odds over the past century, came together to oppose attempts to extend the New Deal. Through seniority-enforced chairmanships in key committees and parliamentary tools such as the filibuster, the coalition would be a powerful force in Congress for decades to come.

Congress did more than preserve its perks. The Hatch Act of 1939 was a congressional reaction to the rise of the New Deal bureaucracy. The bill severely restricted the political participation of lower-level federal employees, most of whom were not under the classified civil service and hence not subject to existing restrictions on political activity. Carl Hatch of New Mexico, the bill's sponsor, was a Democratic senator, and a heavily Democratic Congress overwhelmingly supported it.

The judiciary, too, showed its capacity for institutional self-preservation. Initially it was the branch of government least responsive to the New Deal. More than three hundred cases challenging aspects of New Deal programs came before federal and state courts. The Supreme Court was a particularly irritating obstacle. In 1935 it voided the National Recovery Administration and the Agricultural Adjustment Act, the centerpieces of the early New Deal.

FDR was the first president since James Monroe in the 1820s to have no Court vacancy to fill in his first term. After his 1936 reelection he proposed a Supreme Court reorganization plan that gave him the power to appoint additional justices to balance those over seventy years of age who stayed on the bench. This led to his first major legislative defeat.

Democratic senators fearful of this threat to the constitutional balance of power joined with the Republicans to defeat the plan. Packing the Court, like purging congressmen, did not sit well in the age of dictators.

The strategic switch of Justice Owen Roberts from opposing to accepting major New Deal laws ended the crisis. And then the life cycle kicked in. By the end of 1939, Roosevelt had appointed three pro–New Deal judges, Hugo Black, Felix Frankfurter, and William O. Douglas. Not coincidentally, the Court from 1937 on adopted a broad view of federal power. It approved almost anything that the government chose to do, from late New Deal labor and agriculture laws to constraints on civil liberties such as the anti-subversives Smith Act of 1940, enforced flag saluting during World War II, relocation camps for Japanese Americans, and the loyalty-security programs of the Cold War.

By dropping its opposition to the New Deal, the Court retained its institutional autonomy. It also laid the groundwork for what would become the most important source of judicial power in the late twentieth century: the incorporation of the Bill of Rights into the Fourteenth Amendment. Justice Benjamin Cardozo held in 1937 that the amendment might apply to state laws affecting civil rights "implicit in the concept of ordered liberty." A year later Harlan Fiske Stone more explicitly applied the amendment to all state laws touching on the Bill of Rights, thus opening the door to judicial oversight.

Sixty of the sixty-five new government agencies created in Roosevelt's first two years were exempt from the classified civil service. This eased the entry into government jobs of the wet-behind-the-ears lawyers, economists, and lesser bureaucrats who were part of the mythos of the early New Deal: "a kind of Phi Beta Kappa version of Tammany Hall," said one observer. By the mid-1930s, some 40 percent of federal officeholders were non-civil-service appointees, the highest proportion since the beginning of the century. With a critical mass of pro–New Deal bureaucrats in place, civil service protection was extended to most of the add-ons. The Ramspeck Act of 1940 locked in two hundred thousand of them, and a 1941 executive order extended coverage to 95 percent of the federal workforce.

The Executive Reorganization Act of 1937 sought to strengthen the burgeoning New Deal bureaucracy through what was fondly thought to be the science of public administration. "The President needs help," declared the Brownlow Commission, responsible for the substance of the act. Its prescription: "salvation by staff." The bill called for new Departments of Public Welfare and Public Works, the absorption of the Interstate Commerce Commission and the Civil Service Commission into cabinet departments under the president's control, a beefed-up core of administrative assistants to the president, and a Budget Bureau reporting directly to the White House.

This sweeping expansion of presidential power over the bureaucracy ran into large-scale resistance. The conservative National Committee to Uphold Constitutional Government warned of executive dictatorship, a resonant theme in the age of Hitler, Mussolini, and Stalin. More surprising, perhaps, was the range of opposition from other, often pro–New Deal sources.

Democratic congressional committee chairmen bridled at a bill that threatened to upset their established relationships with client agencies in the federal bureaucracy. Civil service reformers worried about the patronage and political control that would flow to the White House. Veterans' organizations feared that their constituents' preferential status in civil service appointments would be endangered. State medical societies opposed the transfer of the Public Health Service to a new Department of Welfare. Catholics worried about the anti-parochial-school possibilities of a strengthened Office of Education. The railroad unions did not want the Interstate Commerce Commission to lose its independent status and be absorbed into the business-dominated Commerce Department. Senator Robert F. Wagner, the doyen of New Deal labor legislation, opposed the Executive Reorganization Act as a threat to the independence of the National Labor Relations Board. The National Association for the Advancement of Colored People objected on the ground that a single civil service commissioner ended the prospect that the existing commission might one day have a black member.

Roosevelt had enough political clout to secure a revised reorganization bill in 1939 that put the Bureau of the Budget into the White House and gave him more executive assistants. But the new Departments of Welfare and Public Works fell by the wayside. The bureaucracy, like Congress and the Court, bent but did not break before the winds of change.

The same was true of state and local government. Public administration expert Luther Gulick announced in 1933: "The American state is finished." But state, local, and (in the case of the South) regional interests continued to flourish in Congress. Important parts of the New Deal such as social security welfare payments were state-administered.

Northern city machines battened on New Deal job programs and public works spending. Business, labor, and other interests saw to it that national policy remained subject to parochial concerns. Federalism was alive and well, despite Depression–New Deal pressure for a more centralized American state.

WAR, POSTWAR, AND COLD WAR

Conventional historical wisdom has it that the Great Depression and the New Deal were one thing, World War II another. As FDR put it, Dr. New Deal gave way to Dr. Win the War. Certainly the prospect for New Deal social democracy, never very high, got no leverage from the war. But in other ways World War II sustained the regime change that began in the 1930s. It reinforced some of the major features of the New Deal: a more active state and unprecedented levels of spending, a more inclusive cultural nationalism. Nor did the post-war decades see a reversion to the pre-Depression political past, in sharp contrast with the 1920s. A strong presidency, an interventionist foreign policy, and an active, high-spending welfare-warfare state would continue to characterize American public life.

The sequence of World War II and the Cold War made foreign affairs a prominent, permanent part of politics and policy—a state of affairs not seen since the late eighteenth and early nineteenth centuries. As in that earlier time, foreign policy contributed to regime change. The isolationist-interventionist debate of 1939–40 cut across class, ethnic, ideological, and regional lines. But it was resolved much more decisively than the similar dispute prior to American entry into World War I. The Japanese attack on Pearl Harbor and the subsequent German and Italian declarations of war meant that Roosevelt, unlike Wilson, faced almost no political and popular dissent at home. Like the widespread national demand in 1933 that something be done about the Depression, the all-but-unanimous wish for victory over the Axis led to policies with long-term consequences.

World War II cleared the way for FDR's election to third and fourth terms and helped sustain Democratic control of Congress (except for a one-shot Republican win in 1946). Exploding wartime public expenditure (from $8.8 billion in 1939 to $98 billion in 1945) entrenched popular acceptance of a vastly expanded American state. A dramatic reversal of economic and social conditions made the war years the mirror image of the Great Depression: heady expansion instead of headlong contraction.

The unemployment that disfigured the 1930s vanished. The eleven million men inducted into the armed services, the tide of migrants both black (five million from 1940 to 1945) and white from farms to industrial jobs, and an exploding female industrial workforce underwent life-transforming, society-altering experiences. Farm income quadrupled. Federal income taxpayers (tax withholding from salaries began in 1942) skyrocketed from 3.9 million in 1939 to 43 million in 1945. By 1945, 90 percent of the workforce was filing tax returns.

Even more than the Depression, the war opened the door to the expansion of the American state. The buildup of the military and its weapons, culminating in the Manhattan Project for the atomic bomb, required federal direction, oversight, and spending on a scale that outstripped anything attempted in the New Deal. A burgeoning federal bureaucracy was much more acceptable when its purpose was national defense. The Pentagon, the world's largest office building when it was completed in 1943 (as had been the post–Civil War State, War, and Navy Building and the Pension Office of the 1890s before it), embodied not big government, New Deal–social democratic style, but the nation's wartime military mission.

Like the New Deal, World War II schooled a generation of movers and shakers—in politics, government, law, business, academia, science—in the possibilities of government planning. Agencies such as the Office of Scientific Research and Development, the State Department's Policy Planning Staff, the War Production Board, the Office of Price Administration, and the Office of Strategic Services (soon remade into the Central Intelligence Agency) echoed the government's response to the Depression with a grander and less contentious effort to win the war. The high New Deal lasted for five years, from 1933 to 1938. The preparedness and war efforts, from 1940 to 1945, matched that time precisely.

The war taught a compelling lesson in the pump-priming possibilities of large-scale government taxation and spending. It showed what was possible when higher rather than lower agricultural and industrial production was the policy goal. It revealed that high wages and induced savings could lead to previously unimagined levels of investment capital and consumer spending. And it reminded Americans that opportunity still lay in mobility and migration.

The beefed-up wartime state also had a more repressive side. The forced relocation of Japanese Americans into detention centers generated little protest, aside from some civil libertarians and principled anti-statists such as conservative Republican Robert Taft. The maintenance of a racially segregated military met with approval or indifference. And reservations about the use of the atomic bomb came very much after the fact.

The 1933–45 expansion of the American state was unprecedented in its scale and scope. Never before had there been so long and sustained a period of government growth. Wartime discussion of post-war policy spoke not of *reconstruction*, as after the Civil War and World War I, but of *reconversion*: retaining and adapting rather than replacing the New Deal–wartime state.

There were left and right readings of what the post-war polity should look like. Liberals were for dismantling what would later be called the military-industrial complex and the loyalty-security state. But they supported the extension of other forms of active government: redistributive tax and welfare policies, wage and price controls, large-scale economic planning. Conservatives had different but no less picky expectations. They hoped to strip away the apparatus of government regulation, intervention, taxation, and redistribution that had grown up over the course of the Depression and the war. They were less inclined to support the removal of the agricultural subsidies, military expenditures, and loyalty-security measures that also were part of the New Deal–World War II legacy.

At first it appeared that the traditional American distaste for a strong state would reassert itself after the war. Helter-skelter military demobilization followed the conflict's end in 1945, as after the Civil War and World War I. Popular pressure to get the boys home overwhelmed geopolitical planning in Defense and State. Wartime production and price controls were dismantled with similar haste. The pull of the past appeared as well in the election of 1946, when the Republicans regained control of Congress for the first time since 1930. The new Congress's Taft-Hartley Act of 1947 sought to contain the political clout of organized labor, an important component of the New Deal.

But Taft-Hartley had little effect on the post-war expansion of unionized labor, which peaked at about a third of the industrial workforce in the late 1950s. In general the post–World War I "normalcy" scenario was not replayed. There was no return to the pre–New Deal party culture. One sign of the changed political ambience was the Servicemen's Readjustment Act of 1944, the GI Bill. It abandoned the traditional bonus/pension approach to veterans in favor of educational, home mortgage, and other forms of economic assistance on a scale previously unimaginable. The prime movers behind this bold venture in social assistance were the American Legion and racist Mississippi congressman John Rankin, neither an advance agent of socialism.

The Administrative Procedure Act of 1946, a "bill of rights for all who deal with government," in effect announced that large-scale interaction between private parties and federal agencies was a settled fact of American public life. It assumed that organized interest groups would deal directly with government agencies and not necessarily rely on the intercession of parties and politicians.

The agency-creating that had begun during the New Deal and war years went on. The National Security Acts of 1947 and 1949 set up the key institutions of the post-1945 American military establishment: the Secretary and then the Department of Defense, the National Security Council, the Central Intelligence Agency. New domestic agencies continued to appear, responding to the needs of post-war America: the Council of Economic Advisors and the Atomic Energy Commission (1946), the National Institutes of Health (1947), the National Science Foundation (1950).

Harry Truman successfully ran for reelection as president in 1948 against the "do-nothing Eightieth Congress." The core New Deal coalition of union members, minorities, and affluent liberals still had political muscle. Truman proposed an ambitious "Fair Deal" program that called for expanded Social Security benefits, a higher minimum wage, a full employment law, a permanent Fair Employment Practices Committee, public housing and slum clearance programs, national health insurance, federal aid to education, and the nationalization of atomic energy.

His bolder initiatives—public housing, health insurance, central economic planning—got nowhere, in good part because of the conservative coalition between Republicans and southern Democrats in Congress. But it was clear that the post-war American polity would not return to pre–New Deal norms. Social Security benefits were increased by 75 percent and extended to an additional ten million people. The minimum wage rose from 40 to 75 cents an hour. Most notably, the military (by executive order, not by act of Congress) began racial integration in 1948.

The election of Dwight Eisenhower and a Republican Congress in 1952 revived the prospect for a rollback of the New Deal. In his campaign Ike relegated the Tennessee Valley Authority to the realm of "creeping socialism" and opposed large-scale public works, government support for farm prices, and an active federal role in civil rights. He even had his doubts about social security.

Eisenhower's 1952 and 1956 electoral victories were comparable to FDR's triumphs. But except for 1953–54, he had to live with Democratic Congresses. And his political appeal rested on far more than conservative Republicans: about 30 percent of those who voted for him supported Democratic congressional candidates. His core constituency was a greatly expanded middle class, many of them FDR supporters, created by the war and the post-war boom. Small wonder that when his brother Edgar chided him for abandoning GOP conservatism, Ike testily replied: "[S]hould any political party attempt to abolish social security and eliminate labor laws and farm programs, you should not hear of that party again in political history."

In fact, social and geographical mobility and the changing popular culture embodied by the automobile, television, and the suburbs was eroding the party basis of voters' political identity. FDR once defined himself as a Christian and a Democrat; Eisenhower had tenuous ties to the GOP. His was a "plebiscitory presidency" of the sort that would recur in the 1980s with Ronald Reagan, the only other president to serve two full terms between 1945 and 1992.

Eisenhower retained and in some cases expanded the active state. FDR's Federal Security Agency of 1939 became a full-blown Department of Health, Education, and Welfare in 1953. Ike went along when a Democratic Congress substantially increased social security payouts and unemployment compensation. He (reluctantly) committed federal troops to enforce school integration in Little Rock in 1957, and in that year signed a (weak) Civil Rights Act. He backed the Federal Highway Act of 1956, which committed the federal government to an interstate highway system that became the largest public works project in American history. And he accepted an end to the Korean War based on compromise, not victory.

Some historians argue that the Cold War defined domestic as well as foreign policy in post-war America. They hold that it bred McCarthyism and the Red scare, fed the case for the civil rights movement as an international public relations prop, and encouraged consumerism as a social sedative to sustain a tranquilized public. It is not necessary to adopt so conspiratorial a sequence of cause and effect to see the Cold War as a major force in American public life. Like the New Deal and World War II, the confrontation with communism was in many respects a unifying force. It reinforced popular cultural nationalism and further eroded the traditional political battle lines of class, religion, and ethnicity.

Polls showed strong popular support for the broad lines of the American response to communism. Hitler, Munich, and Pearl Harbor schooled a generation in the lessons of military preparedness at home and a strong stand against dictators and expansionist regimes abroad. Foreign policy underwent a transformation during World War II and the Cold War comparable to domestic policy during the Great Depression. The new immigrants and their children had come of age politically. Cold War policies such as the Marshall Plan (which benefited Italy and Germany as well as Great Britain and Ireland), aid to Greece and Turkey, and the recognition of Israel accorded with the sentiments of these new constituencies. The strongly Anglophilic Department of State now shared its responsibilities with new, more socially and ideologically diverse players in the Pentagon, the FBI, the CIA, and think tanks such as RAND.

Dissenters—those who thought the United States was doing too little to oppose communism, and those who thought it was doing too much—came from the right and left fringes of the political spectrum. But disquieting events such as the Soviets' hegemony in Eastern Europe and their development of a nuclear capability, the Chinese communist triumph, and the outbreak of the Korean War in 1950 fed broader popular anxieties already stirred by a rapidly changing society.

In the hoary American tradition, that unease found an outlet in the politics of foreign policy. The Federalists and the Jeffersonians built their political power in the 1790s by tarring their opponents as un-American supporters of revolutionary France or monarchist-aristocratic Britain. So now did many Republicans seek to blame Cold War setbacks on the near-treasonous culpability of those in office.

McCarthyism, the most potent political exploitation of popular anticommunism, had a populist base that went beyond its anti–New Deal Republican core. Many Catholic Democrats (including John F. Kennedy and his brother Robert) were supportive. Important too was McCarthy's attraction to nouveaux riches—suburbanites, Texas oil men, media celebrities—not part of the traditional GOP base.

McCarthy's appeal was national, multi-class, multi-ethnic: in a word, populist. His primary target was the Protestant American elite—the people, he said, born with silver spoons in their mouths—and their institutions: Alger Hiss, Owen Lattimore, Averell Harriman, Dean Acheson, Adlai Stevenson, George Marshall, Harvard, the State Department, the army. Those who brought him down—attorney Joseph Welch, Maine Republican senator Margaret Chase Smith, broadcaster Edward R. Murrow—spoke for the Anglo-Saxon Protestant American culture that McCarthy challenged.

Unlike its Anti-Masonic, Know-Nothing, Populist, and Long-Coughlin-Townsend predecessors, McCarthyism never became a third party. It rose and fell between 1950 and 1954 on the back of poll-measured public opinion and on the rise and decline of the Korean War. Its populist style of media-focused revelations and extra-party protest would reappear (in very different garb) in the pro- and anti-civil-rights and anti-Vietnam movements a decade later.

Politically and thematically, the Kennedy-Johnson administrations of 1961–69 were the last hurrah of the New Deal. An assertive foreign policy; a domestic agenda responsive to organized labor, cities, minorities, and the poor; and heavy reliance on social science expertise were characteristics of the Kennedy-Johnson years, as they had been of FDR's New Deal and Truman's Fair Deal before.

But the 1960s were not merely the 1930s and 1940s *revivitus*. Kennedy, the Harvard-educated scion of an elite Irish Catholic family, adapted FDR's upper-class noblesse oblige to a post–World War II American society in which industrial-immigrant Americans had moved to a higher socio-economic level. Lyndon Johnson, in his youth a faithful supporter of FDR and committed now to civil rights and a war on poverty, engaged in a no less conspicuous updating of southern liberalism, one that took account of the civil rights revolution and a rapidly modernizing regional economy.

The Democratic party co-existed awkwardly with these new political realities. Kennedy tapped his party's machinery as a Massachusetts congressman and senator and as an aspirant for national office. But in no real sense was he a product of Democratic machine politics. Like his personal appeal, his campaign relied on resources (his father's, not least) that stood apart from the party. His was a family-led more than party-led campaign organization.

Old-time party machines (Mayor Richard Daley's in Chicago, LBJ's Texas Democratic organization) may have secured (or stolen) Kennedy's 1960 election. But his celebrity charisma and war-hero record, his ability to reach out to Catholics and some of the new middle class who had been attracted to Ike in the 1950s, and his performance against Nixon in their TV debates outweighed his pallid standing as a senator and a Democrat. His opponent, Richard Nixon, also appealed beyond the traditional Republican base, to new suburbanites and anti-communist ethnics. Indeed, during the campaign Nixon was more highly regarded than Kennedy for his experience, his presidential persona, and even his personal qualities.

Lyndon Johnson's 1964 landslide owed more to Kennedy's assassination a year before and to the eccentric candidacy of the ultra-conservative Barry Goldwater than to his Democratic party identity or his links to the FDR–New Deal tradition. LBJ made larger gains among managerial-professional voters put off by Goldwater than had any of his Democratic predecessors—a portent of politics to come.

On its face, Johnson's characteristically outsized Great Society program could claim direct ideological descent from the New Deal. But a closer look at its highlights reveals significant changes in content and objectives:

> 1964: *Civil Rights Act, Anti-Poll Tax Amendment, Tax Reduction Act, Economic Opportunity Act, Urban Mass Transit Act, Wilderness Preservation Act*
>
> 1965: *Elementary and Secondary Education Act, Medicare, Voting Rights Act, Omnibus Housing Act, National Endowments for the Humanities and the Arts, Water and Air Quality Acts, Immigration Reform Act, Higher Education Act*
>
> 1966: *National Traffic and Highway Safety Acts, minimum wage increase, Department of Transportation, Model Cities Act*
>
> 1967: *food stamps, Corporation for Public Broadcasting*

The Great Society was as representative of late-twentieth-century America and the populist-bureaucratic regime as the New Deal was of Depression America. It was fed not by depression or war but by a growing demand for rights by spokesmen of previously deprived groups and by a heightened concern for the quality of life in a mature industrial society: products of the affluent, booming post-war years. And its content was defined as much outside party discourse as through it.

As early as the mid-1950s, historian Arthur Schlesinger Jr. distinguished the "quantitative liberalism" of the 1930s from the "qualitative liberalism" of the future. The most commanding political interests of the past—manufacturing, banking, organized agriculture, union labor—continued to be powerful players in American politics and government. But now new causes and new interests made themselves heard: the civil rights and environmental establishments, advocates for teachers, women, gays, the handicapped, the urban (and especially the black) poor. Advocacy groups claiming to speak for "the people," legislative entrepreneurs, and "experts" in bureaucracy, think tanks, universities, and the media were the major policy makers of the Great Society. Johnson summed up their message in his May 1964 speech at the University of Michigan, which went beyond material and economic needs to speak of the people's desire for beauty and their hunger for community.

Belief in the ability of programs, experts, and judges to solve society's ills superseded belief in the ability of parties, presidents, and Congress to do so. The prevailing style was to expect more but trust less—a mix of aspiration and alienation. Traditional American political humor, ironic in tone but without much programmatic content (Mark Twain,

Mr. Dooley, Will Rogers), now gave way to the more ideological satire of Mort Sahl and Lenny Bruce. Social theory rose in esteem, displacing the try-anything pragmatism of the New Deal.

Just as Eisenhower did not repudiate the New Deal, Richard Nixon hardly shut down the Great Society. His (failed) Family Assistance Plan came closer to providing a guaranteed income to the poor than anything in Johnson's War on Poverty. Nixon-supported legislation such as the Occupational Safety and Health Act and Clean Air Act of 1970, the Clean Water and Water Pollution Control Acts of 1972, and the Comprehensive Employment and Training Act of 1973 extended the Great Society impulse to more middle-class concerns.

This new American state of mandates, programs, regulations, and large-scale cash distributions required a complex bureaucracy. During the 1970s the Code of Federal Regulations grew from 54,000 to 100,000 pages. That wallow in specificity was designed to eliminate the discretion, ambiguity, and lassitude of governance past. And the bureaucracy expanded in pace. The Washington workforce grew from about 2.2 million civilian employees in 1960 to just under 3 million in 1980. There were twenty-eight federal regulatory agencies in 1960, fifty-six in 1980. Four hundred domestic programs were in place in 1969, ten times the 1961 number. Non-defense spending rose from 50 percent of federal outlays in 1960 to 60 percent in 1970 despite the burden of the Vietnam War, and to 74 percent in 1975.

As a more populist politics and a growing bureaucratic-regulatory state took form, the nation's capital changed accordingly. Megalithic new House and Senate office buildings rose, not to serve a larger membership—the House had been fixed at 435 seats since the mid-1920s, the Senate had grown only from 96 to 100 since 1914—but to accommodate burgeoning congressional staffs. They were there to provide ever more elaborate constituency services and to keep members of Congress plugged into an ever more massive and complex government.

The federal bureaucracy of the party-democratic regime had been concentrated in the Federal Triangle, a jumble of departments and agencies tucked between its political masters in the Capitol and the White House. The new populist-bureaucratic regime had a more capacious setting: inside the Beltway, the interstate ring road around Washington. Geographically and figuratively, the Beltway embraced the new federal agencies, think tanks, foundations, media outlets, and social and economic interest groups that challenged the primacy of Congress and the parties.

Washington's high-pressure social style under Kennedy and its physical expansion under Johnson sent the same message. This was an imperial capital, ready to take on the great challenges of communism, racial inequality, poverty, space exploration, the environment. The key nodes of influence in this bureaucracy were "iron triangles": coalitions of interest and advocacy groups, bureaucrats, and the congressmen who dealt most directly with them. Conspicuously absent from this matrix of power were the political parties.

THE COURTS' DOMINION

The primacy of Congress and the parties was challenged not only by a more populist politics and a more autonomous bureaucracy but also by a more assertive judiciary. The courts adopted policy positions that can be described as populist and took actions that can be described as bureaucratic.

Adversarial legalism, as one critic labeled it, was as distinctive a judicial style as the instrumentalism of the young Republic or the formalism of the Gilded Age. Using the law to change public policy was hardly unprecedented: Aaron Burr's dictum "Law is anything which is boldly asserted and plausibly maintained" would be repeatedly implemented over the course of American history. What distinguishes the interventionist judiciary of the late twentieth century is the degree to which it shifted emphasis from individual rights to group rights and treated precedent as more an encumbrance than a guidepost.

For a third of a century, under chief justices Earl Warren (1953–69) and Warren Burger (1969–86), the traditionally least powerful branch of government set new standards of freedom of speech and press, racial policy, criminal justice, abortion, privacy, and welfare. It did so not only by traditional case-by-case resolution and rule setting but also by new forms of interpretation and intervention. The federal courts added to the procedural and substantive due process of the past a "structural due process" that enabled them to greatly expand their role as bureaucrat-like overseers and regulators. The importance of legal precedent declined—but not the heavy citation of legal and other sources. In the new regime, judicial decisions, like law review articles, were gravid with footnotes. This was not because their authors were in thrall to the formalist norms of the legal-constitutional past but because to demonstrate sensitivity to complex social forces it was necessary that the evidentiary net be widely cast.

Late-twentieth-century courts fed as well on the steadily expanding social importance of the law. The same growth in wealth, education, and mobility that eroded the old party politics encouraged recourse to the courts. By the mid-1980s an American population of 240 million filed 13.2 million lawsuits, an 11:1 ratio. (The comparable ratio in Japan was 390:1.) America had 279 lawyers per 100,000 population; Britain had 114, West Germany 77, France 29, Japan 11.

The judicial populism of modern courts, like the legislative populism of the Great Society, had its roots in the 1930s. Legal realism, the juridical philosophy of the New Dealers, held that law was not a science but a social science, an instrument of public policy as well as an arbiter between contesting parties. Since judges were as subject to the ideas, issues, and interests of their time as everyone else in public life, they were not bound to venerable legal principles but were free to create rules ("only a mnemonic device") appropriate to their policy purposes.

The legal realist perspective lay behind the green light the Supreme Court gave to federal authority from the late 1930s to the early 1950s. By accepting the constitutionality of New Deal legislation after 1937, the Court appeared to yield much of its authority to the executive branch. But acceptance did not necessarily mean impotence. The rise of First Amendment issues during World War II and the McCarthy years, along with the civil rights movement in the 1950s and 1960s, gave the Court opportunities to assert itself on a grand scale. The intensely constitutional nature of the issues raised, and the disinclination (or inability) of the political system to deal with them, opened the way for judges to fill large voids in public policy.

After he became chief justice in 1953, Earl Warren and his co-adjutors William O. Douglas and (after 1955) William Brennan engineered a "progressive constitutional revolution" that was the judicial equivalent of the New Deal and the Great Society. They did to judicial restraint what FDR did to limited government. Supreme Court decisions striking down state and local laws on constitutional grounds went from 181 between 1937 and 1962 to 422 between 1963 and 1986.

A populist commitment to democracy and social justice gave form to the Court's constitutional revolution. The first assumption of that role came in the realm of civil liberties. In 1943 the Court reversed itself and concluded that not saluting the American flag was "a form of utterance" that deserved constitutional protection. A year later, while upholding the evacuation order that sent Japanese Americans to wartime relocation camps, it warned that restricting a single racial group was suspect behavior calling for "the most rigid scrutiny." (Justice Frank Murphy's more forward-looking dissent declared that the government's policy "falls into the ugly abyss of racism.") While the Court did little to limit the government's loyalty-security program during the height of the Cold War, from the late 1950s on it substantially broadened the First Amendment guarantee of freedom of speech and press.

The most conspicuous instance of the Court's more assertive role was in the realm of civil rights. The need to do something about race and racism in American life only gradually entered American political consciousness. The FEPC in 1940 and desegregation of the armed forces in 1948 came through executive orders, not acts of Congress. The Court moved at a similarly measured pace, nibbling away at segregation in professional education and racially restrictive housing covenants. But in the 1950s it adopted a more cutting-edge stance on civil rights. The judiciary was more responsive than politicians to elite opinion, where belief in the wrong of segregation had made its greatest headway.

In *Brown v. Board of Education* (1954) the Court sought to set public policy as consciously as Taney had in *Dred Scott* a century before. Like *Dred Scott*, the case was carefully crafted. Five segregated school districts were challenged for posing what Warren called "a common legal question." But unlike Taney in *Dred Scott*, Warren so managed the *Brown* decision as to secure a unanimous Court. He used social science research (as, in its way, did the *Plessy* Court of 1896, which legitimated segregation) to buttress the judgment that segregated education was "inherently unequal" and thus violated the Fourteenth Amendment's equal protection clause.

The *Brown* decision was widely seen as a judicial expression of public policy—as was its intention—and not merely a legal response to individual grievances. Inevitably the question of implementation rose, and in *Brown II* (1955) the Court shifted to a more administrative mode. It assigned federal district courts to oversee desegregation, and with fine bureaucratic vagueness it enjoined the parties to act with "all deliberate speed."

The built-in limits on the Court's capacity to implement as well as make policy, a fact of American public life learned by Marshall, Taney, and the anti–New Deal justices of the 1930s, soon became evident. Southern resistance, public and private, stymied school desegregation for a decade. Not until racist violence, the civil rights movement, and the Civil Rights Act of 1964 and Voting Rights Act of 1965 did public opinion and the political system respond in the spirit of the Court's mandate. And not until 1968 did the Court change its policy prescription from "all deliberate speed" to a "root and branch" end to discrimination.

The Court handed down comparably attention-getting decisions extending the rights of accused criminals, striking down restrictions on voting, and affirming one-man-one-vote legislative reapportionment. It more controversially extended constitutional protection to the sale of birth control devices and to abortion. Civil liberties and civil rights were merging into a larger, more expansive definition of human rights. Large principles broadly stated, backed up by administrative devices that made the courts not only arbiters but implementers of public policy, proclaimed the emergence of an important new player in the populist-bureaucratic regime.

Like the political and governmental branches of the polity, the Court took on ever more sensitive issues and adopted ever more contentious remedies. But its bold, creative agenda encroached on the prerogatives and self-esteem of the legislative and executive branches, state and local government, and the beliefs of large segments of the population. The consequence of the populist-bureaucratic impulse in law, as in politics and government, was backlash.

CHAPTER ELEVEN

BUREAUCRACY AND DEMOCRACY

I T WAS DURING the New Deal–World War II years that the American government began the long march from its small-scale, low-tax, federalism-bound past to the regulatory-welfare-warfare state of today. Not until the 1960s did large-scale spending become a permanent part of peacetime American government. Non-defense spending sharply climbed between 1960 and 1975 from half to three-quarters of all federal outlays and stayed in the 75–80 percent range for the rest of the century. Federal spending rose from 17 percent of gross domestic product in 1961 to over 23 percent by the early 1980s. That was hardly outsized among developed countries: it was about half the rate of most other Western nations. But in the American context, the change was a true watershed.

Political scientist Theodore Lowi warned in 1969 that "a deep and permanent change in the American Constitution" was under way. A decade later he concluded that the First Republic—the Republic of the Founding Fathers—was gone. A Second Republic had taken its place, in which a strong national state was seen not as an unavoidable evil but as a positive good, raising serious issues of democratic accountability.

The new American state had major achievements to its credit, stretching from the welfare state and civil rights to the defeat of fascism and communism. Yet as the American state grew, popular trust in government declined: by one poll measure, from 76 percent in 1960 to 24 percent in 1966. By the end of the 1970s, some thought that the nation was becoming "ungovernable." The problem, according to political scientist James Q. Wilson, was that in the 1960s there emerged "a true national state within the confines of a constitutional system designed to ensure that no such state would be created."

One problem: the self-protective mechanisms of bureaucracy. Dismissal for incompetence is virtually unknown: an evaluation of federal employees gave 99.6 percent of them a "fully satisfactory" rating. Almost no teachers or other state or local workers are fired for incompetence. But this hardly strengthens public confidence.

Another source of unease was whether the ambitious objectives and higher spending levels of the new regime were worth the candle in terms of competence in execution or desirability of outcome. Large government projects expeditiously done, such as the Erie Canal and the transcontinental railroad of the nineteenth century, or the Tennessee Valley Authority and the atomic bomb of the twentieth, had, it seemed, become history. New York City's George Washington Bridge was built in thirty-nine months during the early 1930s; the more recent reconstruction of the city's West Side Highway took thirty-five years. And there was an ever-growing awareness of what Leo Tolstoy called the unintended consequences of human events, restated by sociologist Robert Merton as "the unanticipated consequences of purposeful social action."

These concerns had profound effects on the major institutions of American government: the presidency, Congress, the courts. From the 1970s to the end of the century, a recurring issue would be their capacity to deal with the tension between an active, bureaucratic state and popular, representative government.

AN EMBATTLED PRESIDENCY

Three chief executives held office in the course of the seven presidential terms from 1933 to 1961; seven did so in the eight terms from 1961 to 1993. One reason for shorter incumbencies was the decline of a party-driven politics. As a populist political culture took hold, presidents became more autonomous public figures, and hence more vulnerable to the winds of public approval or disapproval.

Changes in the candidate selection process contributed to a less party-defined presidency. Nominating conventions, once the supreme gatherings of the party regime, turned into little more than media entertainments. The last Republican convention to go beyond a first-ballot nomination was in 1948, the last Democratic one in 1952. Favorite sons and uncommitted delegates were gone by the 1960s. Primary-selected delegates went from about 15 percent of the total in 1952 to 74 percent in 1980. Choice by party leaders gave way to choice by "the people"—or at least those fractions of fractions who voted in the primaries or participated in uprisings against the party leaders (the Goldwater coup in 1964, the McGovern coup in 1972). References to their party all but disappeared from candidates' convention acceptance speeches and TV debates.

Modern presidential politics is heavily dependent on the media and public opinion. It was different in the party regime. Taft was renominated by his party in 1912 despite the far greater popularity of Theodore Roosevelt. And even the Great Depression did not prevent the GOP from turning again to Hoover in 1932. But Truman, though eligible to run for reelection in 1952, chose not to buck his abysmal poll standings, the appeal of Ike, and the albatross of the Korean War.

Lyndon Johnson succumbed to even greater pressure to pull out in 1968, despite his landslide victory four years before. In 1974, less than two years after retaining the presidency by one of the largest popular margins in American political history, Richard Nixon resigned to avoid impeachment. Vice President Gerald Ford, who replaced him, finished out Nixon's term, but no more than that. His successor, Jimmy Carter, and later George H. W. Bush, also had one-term presidencies. All three ran for reelection (or, in Ford's case, election); all were defeated.

Lyndon Johnson's withdrawal, the near-impeachment and resignation of Nixon, and the impeachment (but not conviction) of Bill Clinton constituted, thought Daniel Patrick Moynihan, "a crisis in the regime." These episodes had much in common. In each case a chief executive fresh from a successful reelection was enmeshed in a calamitous event: Vietnam, Watergate, the Monica Lewinsky affair. Each ran afoul of the culture of populist politics, in which media exposure (except in Clinton's more personal than policy case) trumped party protection.

Political scientists took note of the rise of a "separated" or "personal" presidency. They spoke also of an "administrative presidency." The concept of a "presidential branch of government" embodied in the Executive Reorganization Act of 1939 has come to pass, but without the New Deal–social democratic ideological tone envisioned by its advocates. The executive office of the president has come to be like the home office of a large corporation. The president's staff and bodies such as the Council of Economic Advisers, the National Security Council, and more than a hundred interagency task forces, commissions, and working groups allowed presidential policy making to go on (or get bogged down) around and about, rather than through, the cabinet.

Powerful aides beholden only to the president, conspicuous in the New Deal, strengthened the detachment of the executive office from the parties, Congress, and the government at large. Nixon's national security adviser, Henry Kissinger, his chief of staff, H. R. Haldeman, and his domestic affairs adviser, John Ehrlichman, had no strong party ties. Of the thirty-five Nixon staffers most involved in Watergate, almost none had been active in pre-1972 GOP politics. Jimmy Carter's press secretary Jody Powell, chief of staff Hamilton Jordan, and budget director Bert Lance, all fellow Georgians, played comparable roles in his presidency. So (for a while) did David Stockman and his Office of Policy Development under Ronald Reagan.

But this more autonomous presidency had to make its way in a system full of constraints on its power. The scale and complexity of late-twentieth-century government defeated efforts by Nixon and Reagan to reduce it, and by Clinton to make it more efficient. A civil-service-protected bureaucracy could raise potent obstacles to disfavored chief executives such as Nixon and Reagan (or, more recently, George W. Bush). A more imperial presidency was not necessarily a more effective one.

AN AUTONOMOUS CONGRESS

The populist-bureaucratic regime had a similarly transforming effect on Congress. The electoral basis of the old mixed congressional parties of northern liberal and southern conservative Democrats and midwestern conservative and eastern liberal Republicans eroded. The solid Democratic South of the party regime became an ever more solid Republican South. Many congressional districts in the old core Republican tier of upper New England, the upper Midwest, and the Northwest turned Democratic.

Congressional redistricting contributed to this ideological sorting out. The Supreme Court kicked off a "reapportionment revolution" with its *Baker v. Carr* decision of 1962 setting a one-man-one-vote standard, with reinforcing follow-up cases. These set off a wave of state redistricting. Of 329 non-southern districts, 301 were redrawn between 1964 and 1970. Since most state legislatures were Democratic, that party was the principal beneficiary. Democratic-dominated state supreme courts in Michigan, Ohio, New Jersey, and New York—states with the largest Republican congressional majorities—played an active role in the redistricting process.

Redistricting hardly put an end to the venerable American tradition of gerrymandering, the creation of grotesquely shaped districts designed to serve one party's interests. California Democratic mover and shaker Phillip Burton called his 1981 redistricting plan for that state a work of modern art. (Given the configuration of some of the districts, he appears to have had Jackson Pollock rather than Piet Mondrian in mind.) Similar partisan configuring in years to come, such as the 2004 recrafting of the Texas delegation by Republican congressman Tom DeLay, kept adding to the number of safe—and ideologically distinct—seats.

Incumbency protection went on inside Congress as well. In 1971 the House Committee on Administration, chaired by Wayne Hays, expanded allowances for mail, travel home, and the costs of constituency service ("casework," as the revealing jargon called it). Incumbency and insulation became more than ever the hallmarks of Congress. From the 1980s on, almost every congressman running for reelection won, most by margins of 60 percent or more. (Of the six defeated incumbents in 1990, four were under indictment.) The first riposte to this development, a term limits movement, had some success. But it soon ran aground on the shoals of politicians' self-interest and the argument that voters had the right to choose the representatives they wanted.

Cosseted incumbency helped the Democrats control the House from 1931 to 1994 (except for 1947–48 and 1953–54). Aside from 1947–48 and 1981–86, they ran the Senate as well. This was a stretch of one-party control unique in congressional history. But it did not necessarily mean that party identity mattered most. Incumbency mattered more. Congressmen depended for their seats on primaries and elections in which name recognition and money—perks of incumbency—were the prime determinants. So entrenched, they were difficult indeed to dislodge.

Incumbents further embedded themselves through constituency relations that had little or nothing to do with party. They provided services comparable to those of old-time political bosses. Categorical grants embedded in general appropriations acts smoothed the flow of constituency benefits while avoiding committee conflict and floor fights over scarce goodies. Congressional staffs underwent "stafflation," increasing from an average of 3.5 staffers for each member in 1947 to 17.5 in 1987; in the Senate, the average rose from 6.1 to 40.8. The new staffers manned a growing structure of constituency services that supplanted the old party machines and supplemented the federal bureaucracy.

Being a congressman became less of a stepping-stone to higher office or the private sector and more of a career in itself. Fewer left to become judges or take on other government positions, in part because patronage dispensed by bosses and machines was on its way out. At the same time more congressmen tried to get on presidential tickets, and more made it. Senators Harding (1920) and La Follette (1924) were the only congressional nominees for president in the early twentieth century. The list since 1944 includes Truman, Kennedy, Goldwater, Johnson, Nixon, Humphrey, McGovern, Ford, Mondale, Dole, Gore, and Kerry.

But while congressmen became more entrenched in office and more autonomous as politicians, their institution became weaker. "The new Congress," concludes political scientist William Lunch, "is less than the sum of its parts." It evolved from a leader-dominated body, where members got along by going along, to a collection of independent political entrepreneurs, the legislative equivalent of tenured college faculty. (Other resemblances: low institutional loyalty, an inability to work together.)

The seniority system, and the power of the barons who chaired the major committees, came under assault. Liberal Democratic uprisings in the 1960s changed the makeup of the Appropriations and Ways and Means committees and reduced the power of Rules chairman Howard Smith. In 1974, after the Watergate scandal, the Democrats gained fifty-two seats, bringing in a new generation of anti-establishment members, not unlike the War Hawks of 1810. Speaker Tip O'Neill said of them: "They don't think about party loyalty. They [are] interested in spreading the power." The newcomers forced out three long-serving committee chairmen: Edward Hebert in Armed Services, Robert Poage in Agriculture, and Wright Patman in Banking.

Congressional subcommittees (at their height, 175 of them, each with its own chair and staff) spread like kudzu. Huey Long's every-man-a-king populism was alive and well in the halls of Congress. By 1990, 61 percent of House Democrats either were on major committees such as Appropriations, Ways and Means, and Budget or chaired subcommittees. Caucuses multiplied: of freshman and sophomore congressmen, of black, Jewish, female, Hispanic, and northeastern members. Textile, Frost Belt, steel, arts, and mushroom coalitions contributed to an atomized congressional landscape. So too did registered lobbyists, those intermediaries between interests and congressmen. There were 365 of them in 1961, 23,031 in 1987. Senate filibusters—the ultimate art form of the autonomous legislator—multiplied: more of them occurred between 1968 and 1975 than during the previous 170 years.

The new Congress, like the new presidency, had its problems. It became more difficult for a hobbled party leadership to work out compromises, easier for militant members to assert themselves. Ongoing working relationships of the type that Democratic House Speaker Sam Rayburn and Senate majority leader Lyndon Johnson had with Eisenhower were relics of a bygone era. Speaker O'Neill recalled of a

Ronald Reagan budget resolution in the 1980s: "I had all my ultraliberal friends saying, 'Jesus, you shouldn't let the son of a bitch get it on the floor.' But he'd just had an election that he'd won, and that isn't the way democracy works. You give him his opportunity to get his stuff out for a vote." But his was the voice of Congress past.

Vietnam and Watergate led to unprecedented (at least since Reconstruction) congressional attempts to rein in presidential power and more forcefully assert legislative prerogatives. A series of commissions from 1965 to 1980 looked for ways to increase the oversight role of Congress. The very meaning of "oversight," defined in the Legislative Reorganization Act of 1946 as "continual watchfulness," was changed in 1970 to the more hands-on "legislative review."

The War Powers Resolution of 1973 sought to assert Congress's war-deciding authority. The Budget and Impoundment Control Act of 1974 established the Congressional Budget Office to enhance the legislature's role in budget making. The Office of Technology Assessment (1972) staked a claim to a congressional hand in the burgeoning technological revolution. And the Ethics in Government Act of 1978 created the (court-appointed) position of independent counsel, vested with an all but unlimited authority to investigate the executive branch.

To put it mildly, these laws did not fulfill their objectives. Presidents reported their military actions to Congress, but waging war without a formal declaration of hostilities by the legislature continued to be the norm, as it had been since 1945. The expansion (and hence the diffusion) of the congressional budget-making role made it more difficult to limit expenditures; continuing resolutions and supplemental budgets became more common. The toothless Office of Technology Assessment was closed down in 1994. The role of independent counsels Lawrence Walsh (on Iran-contra) and Kenneth Starr (on Monicagate) generated intense partisan controversy, and by general agreement the office was allowed to lapse in 1999. A would-be imperial Congress, no less than a would-be imperial presidency, found it difficult to assert itself in the new regime.

THE MOST DANGEROUS BRANCH?

Ambitious judges, like ambitious presidents and congressmen, ran into obstacles that the American political culture imposed on the exercise of power. From the 1960s on, the courts flexed their muscles procedurally as well as substantively. They expanded the legal capacity of individuals and advocacy groups to bring suits against the government. A concrete "legal interest" was no longer necessary to be a party to these cases. This encouraged special interest groups to turn to litigation as a policy instrument.

Congress expanded the scope of judicial authority by calling on the courts to ensure compliance with its legislative demands on state and local government. Judges willingly took on the essentially bureaucratic roles of overseeing performance and imposing administrative requirements—"democracy by decree."

The new judicial activism had its benefits. It made the legal process more meaningful for previously neglected social groups—blacks, the poor, the handicapped, women, gays. But it had costs as well. The separation of powers was blurred: "When a bureaucrat becomes a judge he acts like one, and when a judge becomes a bureaucrat he acts like one." The relationship of unelected, unaccountable judges to a democratic polity, a matter of concern in the early New Deal, again became an issue. Federal district judge Charles Wyzanski warned: "Choosing among values is much too important a business for judges to do the choosing. That is something the citizens must keep for themselves."

A case in point: special education in New York. Congress imposed new special ed requirements on states and localities in the mid-1970s. In 1979 a federal judge, responding to a class-action suit, found that New York City's Board of Education violated those standards, even though the number of special ed students in the system had doubled since 1971. That population continued to grow, from 59,000 in 1979 to 168,000 in 2001. New York's special ed budget rose from $433 million in 1980 to $2.7 billion in 2000. Nevertheless. a "controlling group" consisting of a federal judge, the judge-appointed master in equity, and special ed advocacy organizations continued to find the city out of compliance. Other affected groups—regular students and their parents, the elected officials accountable to the population at large—had little or no voice.

The growth of judicial outreach and a consequent political backlash was most evident in the case of the Supreme Court. As in the New Deal years, the more interventionist the Court became, the more political contention it stirred. In the past the Court's strained readings of due process, the contract clause, and the Sherman Act roused liberals. Now it stirred up social conservatives.

When the Court in *Roe v. Wade* (1973) established a constitutional right to abortion, a storm of controversy rose, surpassing the fuss over its anti–New Deal decisions in the 1930s. Contention grew as well when the federal courts moved from dismantling discrimination in education and voting—actions widely supported in Congress and public opinion—to more divisive remedies such as busing and "affirmative action" (initially based on "goals," then sometimes converted into "quotas"). The *Bakke* case (1978) gave qualified Supreme Court approval to letting race be a consideration in medical school admissions. This set off a debate, like the one over abortion, that would persist for decades.

The same sequence—a declaration of constitutional principle, then growing controversy over its application and enforcement—occurred when the courts spoke out on other social policies: welfare, education, environmentalism, criminal justice. Typical flash points: *Shapiro v. Thompson* (1969) and *Goldberg v. Kelley* (1970) found that welfare recipients had a "property interest" in their benefits. *Goss v. Lopez* (1975) subjected the disciplining of unruly elementary and high school students to the constraints of due process.

The moral clarity of *Brown v. Board of Education* clouded up when the Court moved into more socially controversial areas and turned to more invasive remedies. Supporters welcomed these decisions as admirable extensions of constitutional rights to previously unexplored policy terrain. Critics attacked them as the work of a legal-judicial elite whose values were at odds with much of the electorate.

The mode of judicial argument, as well as the substance of its decisions, became more controversial. The near abandonment of precedent, reliance on (often ambiguous) social science research, and a strong policy undertone heightened by a heavy flow of amicus briefs from interested parties added to the swirl of controversy.

The Court, like Congress, became more encapsulated in a professional cocoon. From FDR to LBJ, Supreme Court appointees often had political as well as juridical experience. FDR adviser Felix Frankfurter, Michigan governor and attorney general Frank Murphy, Senator Hugo Black, congressmen and Cabinet members Jimmy Byrnes and Fred Vinson, attorney general Tom Clark, SEC chairman William Douglas, and California governor Earl Warren are notable examples. But from the Nixon presidency on, the field of selection narrowed. The appointment of relatively obscure appellate judges came to be the norm. Justices whose careers were almost exclusively in the courts were likely to have a vested interest in advancing the power of their institution. Judicial restraint and deference to the legislature withered.

The impulse to strike out on new paths of public policy appeared in state courts as well. New Jersey's supreme court made a notable effort to open suburban housing to the black poor. Racial discrimination in education, employment, and public facilities could, at least in theory, be ended by federal law. But housing was another story. There was little machinery, and less will, to do anything about white flight from the cities or to regulate a suburbia whose whiteness derived as much from the economics of home ownership as overt racial bias.

The New Jersey court tried to fill the void. Its *Mount Laurel* decision of 1975 dealt with a Philadelphia suburb whose population exploded in the 1960s. A 1964 zoning ordinance prescribed half-acre-minimum housing lots. The court responded with what came to be known as the Mount Laurel doctrine: since zoning rested on the state's police power to provide for the general welfare, and cultural diversity was a proper public policy goal, it was incumbent on the state's communities to make all types of housing available.

This was an attempt to adapt the spirit and substance of the *Brown* decision to housing. And like the federal courts, the New Jersey tribunal sought to enforce its writ with bureaucratic specificity. Mount Laurel was instructed to come up with a "plan of affirmative public action." Lower courts were directed to use remedial orders to enforce progress and call on independent experts for guidance. In short, they were to act as the administrators of the high court's policy directive.

As in the case of southern school desegregation, progress was glacial. *Mount Laurel II* (1983) sought to light a fire under recalcitrant local authorities. "We may not build houses," the court angrily declared, "but we do enforce the [state] Constitution." It warned that "[t]he State controls the use of land, all of the land," and ordered New Jersey's townships to reserve 20 percent of their new housing for low- and moderately priced units. It divided the state into three judicial areas, with trial judges serving as special masters to enforce the court's mandate. A carrot came along with these sticks: developers who included low-cost units would be allowed to put up more housing than local zoning ordinances allowed.

Governor Thomas Kean called this decision "communist." The legislature quickly passed a fair housing act, establishing a Council on Affordable Housing to substitute for the court-designated masters. It also provided for regional contribution agreements, in which communities satisfied up to half of their court-mandated housing obligations by paying for the construction of low-income units in urban areas.

Minority-owned construction firms and the NAACP supported this spur to home building in the big cities. Environmentalists were torn between their commitment to social justice and their desire to ease population pressure on the countryside. Bowing to political necessity, the court accepted the legislature's proposals. By 1995 it certified almost half of the state's 567 local units as meeting their *Mount Laurel* obligation.

But only 15,400 of the estimated 830,000 low-cost units required had been built, and many of these were rental units for the elderly. Other states failed to follow even this modest example. Housing markets were too complex, and the social values embedded in the suburban-home setting too deeply entrenched, to be readily altered by "courthouse engineering."

The activist constitutional law of the populist-bureaucratic regime developed hand in hand with a transformation of product liability law. Here too the courts sought to convert individual grievances into public policy. Roger Traynor, who was on the California supreme court from 1940 to 1970, did much to free tort law from the strict fault standard of the past. A New Torts movement in progressive legal circles sought to turn manufacturers' liability into a tool of wealth redistribution.

Sometimes the consequences were large indeed. By 2004, juries had awarded some $70 billion in compensation for asbestos-related illness, often on shaky evidentiary grounds. Large awards in liability suits became a cottage industry. Ripe pickings were to be found in a few jurisdictions noted for sympathetic juries, acquiescent trial judges, and aggressive personal injury attorneys. Juries were asked not only to respond to the case at issue but to make public policy—to "send a message." (One magistrate said, when declining to review an outsized jury award, "Who am I to judge?")

The harm inflicted by the liability explosion can be exaggerated. Of the eighty-four thousand or so product liability cases each year during the early 1980s, manufacturers won three out of four that went to a jury. The average award in those they lost was under $4,000: not an outsized imposition on the economy. In any event, corporations usually passed on the cost of their penalties to the public at large. But erratic, gargantuan individual awards (much of the money scooped up by the attending attorneys) did not build public confidence in the process.

In private as in public law, unanticipated consequences abounded. No-fault auto insurance, it turned out, encouraged reckless driving. High medical malpractice awards appeared to foster more defensive (and less effective) medical practice. As insurance premiums for doctors rose, there was some evidence that doctors avoided high-cost states such as Pennsylvania and high-risk branches of medicine such as obstetrics. Critics claimed that regulation by litigation was costly, inefficient, and imbalanced: precisely the argument leveled against governance by judicial decree in public law.

FLOURISHING STATES, FLOUNDERING CITIES,
SUBURBS IN FLUX

The United States has an enormous infrastructure of local government. By the end of the twentieth century there were some eighty-five thousand local units, including more than three thousand counties and tens of thousands of townships, municipalities, special districts, and school districts.

An exponential growth in fund transfers from Washington, along with rising state and local revenues, sustained this web of governance. Federal aid to state and local government increased from $24 billion in 1970 to $91 billion in 1980. Federal funding programs expanded from about 30 in 1940 to 160 in 1963; 227 were added between 1963 and 1968. By the mid-1980s there were more than 500 main-line categorical grant-in-aid programs.

That largesse slowed during the 1980s, as federal budget deficits escalated. Nevertheless, state government rose, Lazarus-like, from the irrelevance to which the New Deal and the growth of the federal government supposedly had consigned it. State agencies and their federal patrons developed close relationships. State government became more professional. State attorneys general—not, before this, conspicuous political players—now directed their regulatory (and money-extracting) powers against toothsome targets such as big auto, big tobacco, and big finance. And state politics became more populist. Long-underused Progressive-era instruments of direct democracy—the initiative, the referendum, the recall—flourished as never before, becoming favored instruments in popular uprisings against taxes, regulation, and other instruments of big government.

While the states became more potent units of government, the opposite happened to the big cities. From the New Deal through the Great Society, the size of urban Democratic votes secured the cities an important place in national politics and a steady flow of federal money. A direct line of descent connected WPA and other urban-oriented New Deal programs to the War on Poverty and the Model Cities Act of Lyndon Johnson's Great Society.

But all the while, population inexorably flowed out of the cities and into the suburbs and exurbs. *The Last Hurrah*, Edwin O'Connor's 1957 eulogy to Mayor James Michael Curley of Boston, marked the passing not only of the old-fashioned city boss and his machine but of urban versus rural and Protestant versus Catholic as the primary American political divides.

The urban saga of grand expectations from the 1930s to the 1960s, and growing reservations thereafter, most dramatically played out in New York, America's premier city. Here as elsewhere, the out-migration of working- and middle-class whites and their replacement by blacks and Hispanics was the most important demographic fact of urban life. A new political alliance, of the black and Hispanic poor, professional and academic reformers, advocacy groups, and young single whites, posed a major challenge to the old ethnic and working-class Democratic city organizations.

The consequences appeared most vividly during John V. Lindsay's New York mayoralty in the late 1960s and early 1970s. A populist politics of race and ideology came to the fore, as did a government culture in which bureaucracy and expertise were supposed to replace politicians and patronage. As in the case of national politics and the courts, a backlash ensued, with corrosive consequences for the city.

Lindsay, formerly a Republican congressman, had few ties to New York's traditional political culture. In this he resembled Progressive-era mayor John Purroy Mitchel, who had a similar belief in social engineering and distaste for the messiness of ethnic machine politics. Lindsay relied heavily not on the existing municipal bureaucracy, unions, and politicians but on a new generation of activists, products of the counterculture and the new left of the 1960s. This had a dramatic impact on major areas of city governance: crime and public order, education, welfare, and race relations. A more populist, race-and-class-based politics and a supposedly more responsive bureaucracy came into their own. For a while, New York was the poster child of the populist-bureaucratic regime.

But the can-do optimism of the 1960s played out with sad consequences on the mean streets of New York, as it did in the rice paddies of Vietnam. The core of this experiment in urban governance was a network of poverty programs headed by "community leaders," with the support of activist advocacy groups, sympathetic academic policy wonks, and radicals with bigger fish to fry. The city's welfare population had risen by a modest 47,000 between 1945 and 1960. Despite a major economic boom during the 1960s, it almost quintupled, to 1.65 million, by 1971. Four percent of New York's population was on welfare in 1960, 16 percent in 1972.

The new style of urban governance came to a crisis point in a struggle over "community control" of the schools. Black militants sought to force out white, predominantly Jewish teachers from schools under their control. They were supported by the large foundations (Ford,

Rockefeller), the American Civil Liberties Union, the *New York Times*, and the Lindsay administration: a prototype for liberal-left politics in the decades to come. Ideology and self-interest conjoined: the poor and the professionals were the chief beneficiaries.

The new political alignment did allow Lindsay to exert a tempering influence on urban riots. And his policies gave more of a voice to the new minorities (or at least to some of their leaders). But there were heavy costs. One was the erosion of the city's tax and employment base. Journalist Ken Auletta observed that New York's "experiment in local socialism and income distribution redistribut[ed] much of its tax base and jobs to other parts of the country." Large corporations found the worsening quality of city life (and, for some CEOs, the metropolitan area's lack of good golf courses) a disincentive to stay. Of the Fortune 500 companies, 140 were headquartered in New York in 1956, 98 in 1975. Clothing and other light manufacturing—staples of the city's economy—slid away. The only job growth came in the public sector's social services.

Lower-middle-class and white ethnics—overlapping constituencies—were alienated by these policies. Lindsay's proposal for a civilian review board to look into charges of police brutality was defeated by a two-to-one margin in a city referendum. Crime went up; the quality of city life went down. And in 1975 the city had a fiscal crisis that brought it close to bankruptcy: what Vincent Cannato called "the Left's Vietnam." In the wake of these troubles, a rising law-and-order politics culminated in the election of Republican Rudolph Giuliani in 1993.

Variations of New York's story occurred in other major American cities. Crime and drugs, riots, decaying schools, and racial tension afflicted Los Angeles, Washington, Chicago, and Detroit. By the early 1990s, 60 percent of New Yorkers said they wanted to leave their city, as did 48 percent of Los Angelenos and 43 percent of Bostonians. In the late nineteenth century, the cities were called America's greatest failure in government. The prevailing judgment was the same a hundred years later.

Suburbs, exurbs, edge cities, gated communities: these labels described the new ambience, neither urban nor rural nor small-town, in which most Americans lived by the end of the twentieth century. Seventy percent of white families owned their own homes by 2000. Affluence, the interstate system, and then the Internet eroded the economies of scale and density of interchange that made large cities such vibrant places in the past.

Suburbia became a substantial political force, vigorously fought over in presidential elections. But its place in the structure of American government was ambiguous. In 1989, 130,000 community associations governed planned and gated communities, co-ops, and condos, with 30 million residents. By 2005 the number of these quasi-governmental entities had climbed to 274,000, with 22.1 million units housing 54.6 million people. The relationship of these bodies to the townships, municipal corporations, counties, and states with which they overlapped was unclear. Late-twentieth-century American government may have attained an unprecedented level of uniformity and centralized direction on the national level. But federalism, localism, and voluntarism saw to it that suburban Americans had a high degree of autonomy when it came to the everyday agenda of local government.

NEW PUBLIC POLICY

Public policy in the party era responded primarily to the strongest economic, regional, and local interests: business, agriculture, and labor; South, North, and West; farms, small towns, and cities. Its primary purpose was to foster the well-being of those interests, and American economic growth at large, by the distribution of natural resources.

That changed in the populist-bureaucratic regime. Modern public policy came to serve an ever-growing variety of ideological, generational, and cultural as well as economic interests. And it embraced new goals: ensuring equal access to civil rights, education, welfare, and medical care; reducing risk in the workplace, on highways, in public health, in the environment.

New players—the courts, the media, advocacy groups—took center stage in policy making. What law professor Peter Schuck has called "disappointed entitlement seekers" and their advocacy group and media allies turned to the legal process and the bureaucracy for redress. Congressional acts laid down goals and timetables, imposed detailed requirements on state and local government, and empowered the courts to supervise enforcement.

Grand programs—the New Deal, the Great Frontier, the Great Society—fell out of favor after the 1960s. (Lyndon Johnson referred to the Great Society only once in his State of the Union address in 1967, and not at all in 1968.) "Rights talk" serving the aspirations of particular groups—African Americans, Native Americans, women, gays, the disabled—came into vogue. Old reservations about the balance of powers gave way to a readiness to use whatever instruments of power lay at hand.

The result was a massive social (as distinct from economic) redistribution: a leveling and broadening of civil rights that was the most notable achievement of the new regime. Yet often the voices of newly empowered groups turned out to be not vox populi but activists whose claims as spokesmen lacked verification by elections and opinion polls. This development cut across the ideological spectrum, from feminists, environmentalists, and welfare advocates on the left to evangelicals and right-to-lifers on the right. The policy agenda came to be defined less by the parties, with the tempering effect that that usually brought, and more by leading voices of the new regime: the media, advocacy groups, judges, lawyers and law professors, academic experts and foundations, bureaucrats, presidential and congressional staffers. Labels—*issue networks, policy intellectuals, policy entrepreneurs*—came into use to describe the new public policy milieu.

As the populist-bureaucratic regime evolved from its New Deal beginnings to its apotheosis in the Great Society, the policy emphasis shifted from equality of opportunity to equality of results. But often the primary beneficiaries of this approach were the dispensers rather than the recipients of the new policies. The Vietnam War may or may not have strengthened national security, but indisputably it fattened the military-industrial complex. Medicare raised doctors' fees along with the level of health care of millions of Americans. Federal support for education benefited the burgeoning college professoriate, public school bureaucracies, and (less so) grade and high school teachers. As welfare spending spiraled, so did jobs for ancillary service providers. The War on Poverty and its "maximum feasible participation" standard of community involvement (what LBJ aide John Roche called participatory bureaucracy) turned out to be a boon for activists: feeding the sparrows by feeding the horses, as Daniel Patrick Moynihan put it.

K Street, home to many lobbyists, and "Gucci Gulch," the halls of Congress where, suitably shod, they hung out, spoke to the persistence of the old ways. The District of Columbia bar grew from 11,000 in 1972 to 45,000 in 1987. Nor did the established iron triangles of vested interests, bureaucrats, and congressmen fade away with the rise of the new policy agenda. But now the triangles often turned into quadrilaterals, including advocacy groups and supporters in the media.

Squabbles over federal funding, familiar in the heyday of the Cold War military-industrial complex, flourished as well in the new welfare, education, and environmentalism complexes. So did another standby of the old regulatory system, the "capture" of government agencies by interested outside parties: the Council on Environmental Quality by environmentalists, the Office for Civil Rights by civil rights advocates, the National Science Foundation by scientists. These advocates sought not only the money, contracts, and authorizations that government could provide but also to shape policy in a regime defined as much by the attainment of social and ideological goals as by the allocation of scarce goods.

Ever greater attention to detail characterized the new public policy, as it did judicial decisions. The Heritage Foundation's 1981 policy recommendations for the incoming Reagan administration went on for 3,000 pages and included 1,270 specific proposals. Dense congressional hearings on tax policy and the Clintons' 1,300-page 1993 health plan reflected this highly technical—and bureaucratic—policy milieu. The Program-Planning-Budgeting System (PPBS) of the 1960s, management by objectives under Nixon, the Carter administration's zero-based budgeting, and the Clinton administration's National Partnership for Reinventing Government contributed to the new lingua franca of complex, technical, bureaucratic governance.

The looming presence of adversarial legalism put great pressure on bill drafters to ensure that every t was crossed, every i dotted. The Federal-Highway Aid Act of 1956, authorizing the interstate system, consisted of twenty-nine pages. The follow-up Intermodal Surface Transportation Efficiency Act of 1991 was more than ten times as long. This was a product not only of the need for legal certitude but also of an ever more complex and diverse agenda: encouraging public transportation, metropolitan area planning, preserving historical sites, fighting erosion, requiring the use of seat belts, reducing drunken driving, using recycled rubber to make asphalt, specifying that iron and steel be bought from American suppliers, limiting the use of calcium acetate in seismic refits of bridges, and ensuring that 10 percent of construction funds went to firms owned by women or other "disadvantaged" individuals.

VIETNAM

The Vietnam War is the great modern (pre–Iraq War) example of American public policy gone off the rails, the most notable instance of leaders and experts in the grip of a limitless belief in the power of the American state. The war epitomized the tension between public policy and democracy in the populist-bureaucratic regime. It relied on decisions secretly arrived at, clashes with the North Vietnamese in the Tonkin Gulf that may or may not have happened, and an American civil and military leadership frequently acting on unjustified assumptions.

The breakdown of the World War II–Cold War consensus on American foreign policy went hand in hand with the breakdown of the New Deal–Great Society consensus on domestic policy. Of course, polarities of ideology and social makeup distinguish the anti-Vietnam movement from the reaction against the civil rights movement and the War on Poverty. Nevertheless, they had certain common qualities: a populist style of political expression, distaste for government by experts, a chiliastic belief in the rightness of their cause.

SOCIAL JUSTICE: CIVIL RIGHTS, POVERTY, AND WELFARE

The domestic policies of the Great Society are said to have evolved "from opportunity to entitlement." This is evident in the realms of civil rights, the War on Poverty, and welfare.

The black civil rights movement was the first great policy success of the mature populist-bureaucratic regime. The fortitude of its participants and the televised brutality of the white southern opposition made it a broadly appealing cause. The Civil Rights Act of 1964 and the Voting Rights Act of 1965 transcended party lines: indeed, both passed with more support from Republicans than from Democrats. What followed was one of the great successes in the history of American democracy: an increase in black voting and the dismantling of the century-old structure of racial segregation.

But enforcing school desegregation in the face of local intransigence in the North as well as the South required ever greater use of government power, with adverse political consequences. Urban riots—Watts exploded days after Congress passed the Voting Rights Act—suggested that the situation of the black underclass in the central cities was hardly changed by the civil rights revolution. Partly from its own momentum, partly in response to the opposition it engendered, the movement came to include a militant black nationalism that deepened the schism. The Kerner Commission report after the 1967 riots ignored the Civil Rights and Voting Rights Acts, called for a massively funded new war on poverty, and adopted the we-are-two-nations rhetoric of the black nationalists. A broad consensus of popular support gave way to a divisive, populist politics of southern white and northern ethnic and working-class hostility on one side and a coalition of white liberals and blacks on the other.

The original appeal of the civil rights movement lay in its emphasis on equality: of opportunity, of access to the basic rights of citizenship.

But the bureaucratic culture of the new regime allowed other meanings to be written into public policy. The Equal Employment Opportunity Commission (EEOC), established to enforce the Civil Rights Act, adopted a "creative interpretation" of the act's Title VII on employment. It held hiring practices illegal unless a demonstrable increase in black hiring occurred. EEOC and the Office of Federal Contract Compliance came to rely on statistical oversight and on the readiness of many firms to accept racial quotas as an acceptable way of meeting goals. A unanimous Supreme Court in *Griggs v. Duke Power* (1971) upheld the EEOC definition of discrimination; *Weber v. Kaiser Aluminum* (1979) upheld race-conscious affirmative action plans.

The backlash to this bureaucratic-judicial policy making stemmed in part from residual white racism but also from a broader distaste for racial favoritism. A populist politics of protest rose against bureaucrats and courts perceived as undemocratic and unresponsive. One unanticipated by-product was the failure of the Equal Rights Amendment, an effort to secure constitutional protection for women's rights. It easily passed in both Houses of Congress in the early 1970s, and President Nixon endorsed it. But ERA failed to be ratified by a sufficient number of state legislatures: a victim of the backlash against affirmative action, as well as of concern over ERA's effect on existing laws protecting women's rights.

Lyndon Johnson's suggestively named Economic Opportunity Act of 1964, the signature law in his War on Poverty, closely resembled the Civil Rights and Voting Rights Act in tone, purpose, and enforcement mechanism. The Office of Economic Opportunity (OEO) was supposed to do in the War on Poverty what the Office of Civil Rights and the EEOC were supposed to do in the war on racial discrimination. Head Start, Upward Bound, the Job Corps, legal services, and health centers were OEO ventures steeped in the level-the-playing-field, equal-opportunity spirit of the civil rights movement.

Like affirmative action in civil rights, the OEO bureaucracy came up with a seemingly innocuous concept: "community action." And just as affirmative action morphed into the more contentious policy of quotas, so did community action open the door to activists taking over some War on Poverty programs, to the distress of local politicians, established bureaucracies such as the Department of Labor, and mainstream public opinion.

Something very similar happened in welfare. Although unemployment halved during the 1960s, Aid to Families with Dependent Children (AFDC) beneficiaries rose from 4.4 million in 1965 to 11.4 million in

1975. Once again a widely supported federal program came under the influence of more radical advocates. Academic social workers, poverty lawyers, and the National Welfare Rights Organization sought to make income an entitlement, with a $6,500 a year guaranteed income scheme (taken up by George McGovern in his 1972 campaign). A New York welfare official declared: "Our agency doesn't provide social services. Its function is management of entitlements."

Public hostility grew as welfare outlays exploded. The Nixon-Moynihan Family Assistance Plan (which was sent to HEW secretary Robert Finch with the facetiously voter-pleasing title of "the Christian Working Man's Anti-Communist National Defense Rivers and Harbors Act of 1969") did not survive the hostility of it's-not-enough liberals and it's-too-much conservatives. Welfare reform came to be defined not as expanding the system but as tightening it up against those who abused it and encouraging recipients to get off the rolls and into jobs. These goals shaped Ronald Reagan's welfare law of 1988, which swept through Congress, and Clinton's legislation of 1996.

THE QUALITY OF LIFE: THE ENVIRONMENT AND PUBLIC HEALTH

The Vietnam War and the War on Poverty lost public support in the late 1960s for similar reasons: lack of political accountability, unwanted results. In their wake, public policy making turned to less contentious subjects: in particular, the environment and public health.

Environmentalism was the quality-of-life issue that most strongly appealed to affluent Americans. The pantheism and nature-is-in-danger threnody of the sixties counterculture melded with the appeal of clean water and air to an urban-suburban population. And environmentalism fit readily into the new doxology of rights. The head of the National Wildlife Federation declared: "The right to a healthy environment is as inalienable as the right to free speech and freedom of worship."

To use an appropriately aquatic analogy, the tributaries of environmental concern ultimately joined to become a policy mainstream. This led to a cluster of laws: the Water Quality Act of 1965, the Clean Air Act, the Endangered Species Act, and the Environmental Protection Agency (EPA) in 1970, and the Clean Water Act of 1972.

The new environmentalism came up with significant and appealing responses to real problems. Like its civil rights and anti-Vietnam counterparts, it attained a conspicuous place in public policy, thanks in good part to the media. But—or perhaps consequently—it also had its share of questionable results. Some environmentalists, like their early-twentieth-century counterparts, had a trees-are-better-than-people distaste for immigration, cities, and economic growth. And unsubstantiated doomsday scenarios of vanishing resources and mass starvation, or cancer-causing apples and cranberries, incurred costs in credibility.

Like civil rights and welfare, the new environmentalism had expanding court- and agency-enforced goals. Believing that rigidly maintained objectives avoided the danger of capture by the interests regulated, EPA set strict guidelines designed to eliminate harmful auto emissions, acid rain, pesticides, and polluted industrial sites. The 1970 Clean Air Act appeared to require that strict new air standards be satisfied by the end of the decade, despite astronomical costs and well-nigh impossible prospects of implementation. Congress in 1972 told EPA to review all pesticides and in three years decide which ones should be taken off the market. After a thousand agency employees worked on the project for more than twenty years, only thirty pesticides had been checked out: a pace that, if sustained, meant that the EPA would meet its remit sometime around the year 15,000.

The Endangered Species Act was a well-meaning attempt to safeguard the nation's rich variety of fauna. But it kept entangling itself in economically harmful, readily parodied attempts to preserve esoterica such as the northern spotted owl and the snail darter. Troubled too was EPA's Superfund, created to clean up the nation's most badly polluted industrial sites. Litigation and transaction costs accounted for nearly half the money spent, and expenditure had little grounding in reasonable cost-benefit analysis.

The inherently subjective goal of a clean environment was difficult for the populist-bureaucratic regime to handle. The emotional quotient of the issue lured politicians. But a regulatory style of strict guidelines and close court supervision led to what a leading authority called "a self-contradictory attempt at 'central planning through litigation.'" More than 80 percent of EPA regulations faced legal challenges. Still, for all its inefficiency, rigidity, and waste, the new environmentalism could point to significant improvements in the nation's air and water and to heightened public concern over the nation's natural legacy.

Medicare and Medicaid were to the Great Society what social security was to the New Deal. Enacted in 1965 as a set of amendments to the Social Security Act, Medicare was a universal entitlement for the elderly, like the old-age pensions of social security. Medicaid was an entitlement for the poor comparable to social security's unemployment insurance and Aid to Families with Dependent Children.

Medicare supplemented rather than replaced the existing American system of health care. Its enabling statute declared: "Nothing in this title shall be construed to authorize any federal official or employee to exercise any supervision or control over the practice of medicine." Private insurance companies processed payments, hospitals selected their fiscal intermediaries.

But over time the role of the bureaucracy expanded, in particular through the Health Care Finance Administration (HCFA) Act of 1975. Doctors, hospitals, and health insurers came under HCFA supervision. And health care politics became more populist in spirit. The Health Planning and Resources Development Act of 1974 called for the "broad participation" of representatives of social, economic, linguistic, and racial groups in the formulation and conduct of health care. Coverage expanded to include midwives, osteopaths, and acupuncturists. What began as a classic example of interest-group liberalism became a poster child of governance in the populist regime.

In this benign policy environment, the expansion (and escalating cost) of Medicare and Medicaid flourished. Blue Cross and other health insurance companies, corporate financial officers, and union leaders—major purchasers of health care—came to be included among the providers entitled to a Medicare policy voice. So were organizations such as the National League of Cities and the National Association of Regional Councils. The public and political appeal of the programs was irresistible, and so, consequently, was their growth. Federal public health expenditures, primarily for Medicare and Medicaid, went from $18 billion in 1970 to $193 billion in 1990 and $415 billion in 2000.

Widely read exposés spurring public support for new causes were a recurrent feature of the populist regime: Michael Harrington's *The Other Americans* (1962) for poverty, Rachel Carson's *Silent Spring* (1962) for environmentalism, Betty Friedan's *The Feminine Mystique* (1963) for the feminist movement, Ralph Nader's *Unsafe at Any Speed* (1965) for auto safety. Popular movies—*The Snake Pit* (1948), *One Flew Over the Cuckoo's Nest* (1975)—similarly dramatized the dehumanizing conditions of large state hospitals for the insane.

Mental health experts called for closing down big mental institutions and moving their inmates to community-based shelters. But once again the iron law of unintended consequences came into play. While the number of hospitalized mental patients declined by 57 percent during the 1970s, the community health centers supposed to take over their care failed to materialize. New York City was due to have seventy-three such centers by 1980; in fact it had three. The move from state hospital snake pits to the mean streets of the cities produced homelessness, cheap welfare hotels, street people, more drugs and crime—and no evident decline in social misery. Nevertheless, civil libertarians and public interest lawyers urged the homeless to protect, as one critic put it, their right to die with their rights on.

A populist politics encouraged congressmen, bureaucrats, advocacy groups, and the courts to seek the perfect in public health. But that could easily turn into the enemy of the good. In prosperous postwar America, concern over the quality of food replaced Depression-era concern over its quantity. Congress in the 1950s required the Food and Drug Administration to reject any food as unsafe if it contained an additive (however minute) that appeared to cause cancer in laboratory animals (however massive the dose). Surely it was desirable to do something about potentially carcinogenic auto emissions, possibly cancer-causing food additives, or the dangers of nuclear power. But how completely? And at what cost?

Political bidding between the parties led a near-unanimous Congress to create the Occupational Safety and Health Administration (OSHA) in 1970. OSHA's mandate extended to some four million enterprises, down to mom-and-pop stores. But the values and concerns of the bureaucrats who ran OSHA, rather than those of labor unions or business groups, shaped its agenda. Unrealistic goals, skyrocketing compliance costs, constant litigation, and the sheer impossibility of tight supervision of millions of workplaces led to the by-now-familiar regulatory frustrations of the populist-bureaucratic regime.

A case in point: a 1968 law required that new or remodeled buildings be wheelchair-accessible. The Rehabilitation Act of 1973 included a provision, inserted by the Office of Civil Rights, extending that obligation to every school, hospital, library, and transit system. The national cost estimate was $100 billion, $4 billion for New York's subways alone. No congressional funding came with the mandate. Yet the Americans with Disabilities Act of 1990 gave the disabled broad power to sue almost any establishment, public or private, for discrimination. A federal court ordered Philadelphia to make 320,000 curb cuts at 80,000 intersections at a cost of $180 million, when the city's capital budget was $125 million. Needless to say, compliance fell short. Once again a worthwhile cause was encased in a system of mandates that relied on enforcement through litigation not subject to cost-effectiveness or public opinion.

UNINTENDED CONSEQUENCES:
CAMPAIGN FINANCE REFORM

The Watergate scandal of 1972–74 reawakened old concerns over the intimate connection between big money and elections. Nixon's Committee to Re-Elect the President (whose evocative acronym was CREEP) raised more than $10 million from oil and defense companies, some of which went to pay for the Watergate break-in and cover-up. It was by no means clear that Watergate reflected the wishes of corporate contributors. But Common Cause and other advocacy groups successfully defined the scandal as an abuse of campaign financing.

What to do about money in politics was a difficult problem. Common Cause wanted public financing of elections. But distrust of government as a political paymaster, along with incumbents' understandable lack of enthusiasm for a more level financial playing field, made this a non-starter. And the major television networks did not warm to the proposal that they provide free airtime to candidates.

The Campaign Finance Act of 1973 created a Federal Election Commission (FEC) to oversee campaign fund-raising. That statute put some limits on contributions and enabled candidates to qualify for public funds. A coalition of liberal and conservative advocacy groups challenged the law as a violation of the First Amendment. The Supreme Court in *Buckley v. Valeo* (1976) held that a government-imposed limit on candidates' spending did in fact violate free speech. But it also decided that caps on contributions accorded with a proper government concern over "corruption or the appearance of corruption," finessing the fact that old-style political corruption had become an endangered species of misbehavior.

Quite understandably, the flow of money into politics continued to expand. Politicians in the populist regime had to deal with issues (social and cultural as well as economic) that were important to substantial numbers of people. But they could not rely on the traditional, relatively inexpensive tools of party loyalty and organization to bring voters to the polls. Meanwhile, television and modern marketing techniques steadily raised campaign costs. The major parties spent $225 million in the presidential election of 1968, $693 million in 2000. The politics of the new regime was not politics on the cheap.

Unexpected consequences followed hard on the heels of the 1973 campaign finance law. The political action committee (PAC)—a fund-raising and campaign-spending instrument pioneered by organized labor in the 1940s and exempt from campaign-finance limits—became a favored device of business and "cause" interests. By 1990 there were more than 4,100 PACs, primarily benefiting incumbents.

In the venerable American tradition of regulatory impotence, the FEC did little to stanch the flow of money into politics. And the rise of the PACs weakened the role of the parties. Seventeen percent of campaign spending in the House elections of 1972 came from party organizations, but only 4.5 percent did so in 1978. How, and if, this was a good thing remained unclear.

In response to complaints over the erosion of grassroots party strength, the FEC in 1978 allowed the parties to receive unlimited sums from PACs and use the money to help federal candidates. Funding thus exempt from the hard limits of the federal law was known as soft money— which became the next target for reformers determined to keep their fingers in the sieve-like dike of campaign finance reform.

By 1996, thirty-five states limited the size of individual campaign contributions, many prohibited contributions from corporations, unions, or PACs, and twenty-two of them had some form of public financing. Candidate Bill Clinton pledged abstinence from soft money in 1992. But soon he was blazing new trails of fund-raising: arm-twisting "coffees," pocket-emptying nights in the Lincoln Bedroom of the White House (the only hotel in America, it was said, where the *guest* left a mint on the pillow).

The Supreme Court thickened the fog of the campaign finance war by holding that a party could spend unlimited amounts of soft money on a candidate so long as there was no coordination or communication between them. Thus a soft money ad could speak well of an office seeker but not suggest voting for him. This exercise in casuistry allowed the parties to raise $261 million ($200 million over the federal campaign limit) in 1996.

But the open sesame to soft money did not revitalize state and local parties, as it was intended to do. The national parties co-opted most of the money and spent it on issue ads rather than grassroots organization and voter participation. The political realities of the populist regime trumped the pieties of campaign finance reform. One observer thought that "[p]robably no American public policy is a more comprehensive failure."

What to do? Well, there was public financing, but only about 12 percent of poll respondents favored that. So up came McCain-Feingold, a complex bill that outlawed soft money contributions to the parties and cut back donations to PACs. It was enacted on the eve of the 2004 election, to much acclaim as a definitive answer to the campaign finance problem. The result: more fund-raising and campaign spending, and a more visible role for well-heeled donors, than ever before.

UNINTENDED CONSEQUENCES:
THE ANTI-SMOKING CRUSADE

The pitfalls of policy making in the populist-bureaucratic regime emerged with special clarity in the crusade against smoking, especially so when it is compared to the not dissimilar movement for liquor prohibition in the early twentieth century.

Mounting data made it clear that tobacco, like alcohol, was a major danger to public health. Once again, an unsettling exposé—in this case the 1964 surgeon general's report—led to congressional action. The Cigarette Labeling and Advertising Act of 1965 required the tobacco companies to put a health warning on cigarette packages. That law was buttressed by hefty hikes in the federal cigarette tax—negated, alas, by commensurate increases in federal price support for tobacco growers.

State regulation marched in pace with federal policy. Cigarette taxes rose and advertising was restricted. So were sales to the young and legal smoking locales. Consumption declined, from 624 billion cigarettes in 1963 to 596 billion in 1983. Per capita intake shrank from 4,287 in 1966 to 2,493 in 1994.

But further restricting smoking turned out to be as difficult as prohibiting the sale of liquor or eliminating big money from politics. The anti-cigarette forces turned to the courts. Litigation at first ran into serious problems. Of 813 lung cancer cases brought from the 1950s to the early 1990s, the companies won all but two. Traditional product liability doctrine held that if a manufacturer conformed to reasonable standards (in this case, putting the government-directed warning label on cigarette packages), it was not liable, even if its product was intrinsically harmful. And juries were reluctant to find for smokers, who they thought had a responsibility to pay heed to the warning.

The legal environment changed in the mid-1980s. Courts began to apply a stricter liability standard to inherently dangerous products. And cancer deaths were on the rise, as were medical studies demonstrating a link between cancer and smoking. Tort lawyers and state attorneys general came together and in 1998 produced a Master Settlement Agreement (MSA) between forty-six states and the major tobacco companies. The firms agreed to pay $246 billion to the states over a twenty-five-year period. The money was to be used to educate people on the dangers of smoking and help meet the medical costs incurred by diseased smokers. Tobacco advertising was severely limited. And the companies were prohibited from lobbying against or challenging the constitutionality of the MSA, or seeking to escape their obligations through bankruptcy.

The new cigarette regulation sharply differed from the banning of alcohol in the early twentieth century. Prohibition was the product of popular referenda, election campaigns, congressional legislation, and a constitutional amendment. It relied on an elaborate infrastructure of national, state, and local law enforcement. In contrast, the tobacco agreement had no political, legislative, or regulatory base. Polls revealed no popular support for the MSA. It was the product of a large-scale media assault on cigarette smoking and the lure of big bucks for the states and big publicity for state attorneys general.

Enforcement lay in the hands of the courts. Chairman David Kessler of the Food and Drug Administration (FDA) wanted his agency to regulate and ultimately suppress cigarette smoking, and he criticized the MSA as too soft on the industry. But the Supreme Court held that FDA lacked the requisite statutory authority.

Spectacular unintended consequences followed on the implementation of the MSA. Its cost, primarily in the form of attorneys' fees, turned out to be substantial. Massachusetts arbitrators awarded $775 million in fees to the lawyers who had worked on the settlement with the state attorney general; they (unsuccessfully) asked the state supreme court to raise that to a cool $1 billion. The five attorneys who assisted Texas attorney general Dan Morales in that state's tobacco settlement shared $3.3 billion in fees. (When Morales ran in the Democratic gubernatorial primary, he not unreasonably solicited large contributions from the beneficiaries. For his pains, he was indicted on corruption charges.) These outsized awards led one law professor to observe: "To pay this kind of public money to private entrepreneurs for what is basically a public function is extraordinary, unprecedented, and deeply unprincipled."

If the ostensible purpose of the MSA was to put a stop to cigarette smoking, how could the states ensure that the cigarette revenue stream kept flowing? One answer was heavy increases in state excise taxes. Cigarettes that cost $1.90 a pack in 1997 cost $4.00 in 2001. Given the socioeconomic profile of heavy smokers, this was one of the most regressive tax hikes in American history.

Most states passed laws allowing only the companies who were party to the MSA to sell cigarettes in their jurisdiction. Authorities closed their eyes to the companies' successful efforts to sell more cigarettes in foreign markets and to American teenagers. Virginia's supreme court blocked the incorporation of a small company that proposed to develop a nicotine-free cigarette. Satirist Dave Barry observed: "[T]he sale of cigarettes is the heart and soul of the War on Smoking."

And then there was what the states did with their windfalls, as opposed to what they were supposed to do. A Senate bill in Congress that obligated them to spend their money on anti-smoking and other health programs was overwhelmingly defeated. Instead, states diverted the annual MSA intake to property tax relief, flood control, and other purposes. By 2001, Massachusetts was using all of its MSA revenue for its general budget. Virginia devoted much of its windfall to subsidies to its tobacco growers. A number of states sold general expenditure bonds backed by future MSA payments. More than $19 billion had been raised in this way by 2003. Meanwhile, health-care programs for tobacco sufferers and anti-smoking educational campaigns lost funding.

Governance in the populist-bureaucratic regime responded in a large way to the demands of the new social order of late-twentieth-century America. It took on issues of social welfare, race, gender, sexual behavior, the environment, and public health that the former party-democratic regime had ignored. The regime relied not so much on the major parties as on new instruments of opinion formation: the media, advocacy groups, the techniques of populist politics. And it adopted new instruments of command and control: litigation and the courts, powerful regulatory agencies.

But by the century's end it was by no means clear that the new regime had overcome deeply embedded counter-forces in American public life: federalism, pluralism, hostility to active government. In many respects the populist-bureaucratic regime, like its party regime predecessor, expanded the reach of American democracy. But in others, it restoked old American fears of a lack of representation and the abuse of government power.

CHAPTER TWELVE

POPULISM AND PARTY

A S OF 1960, the polity appeared to be adapting reasonably well to the demands of modern America. The dark cloud of McCarthyism had lifted. Eisenhower's emollient presidency won widespread public approval. Spurred by the Supreme Court and changing public opinion, the assault on racial segregation was gathering force.

The 1960 election did not alter this sense of well-being. The near dead heat in the popular vote, the fact that John F. Kennedy's Catholicism turned out to be not an ethno-cultural flash point but a damp squib, and Kennedy's essentially me-too-but-I'll-be-tougher foreign policy stance implied that the consensualism of the late Eisenhower years was alive and well. Strong media approval of the photogenic First Couple and a ministry-of-all-the-talents administration added to the feel-good tone of the time.

Then came the sixties: an across-the-board upheaval in American politics and culture. The bill of particulars:

- The civil rights movement and the heating up of the Cold War, this time in Vietnam, had the most unsettling political consequences since the Great Depression. The violent response of many southern whites to black civil rights evoked a northern counterreaction that deepened the gulf between the two regional wings of the Democratic party. The quixotic Republican nomination of Barry Goldwater in 1964 fed the rise of a white southern Republicanism unmatched since the southern Whigs of the 1840s.
- The civil rights movement came increasingly under the sway of militant black nationalists, and the black ghettos of the major

American cities were swept by riots of unprecedented scale. These developments, along with growing concern over crime, induced large numbers of urban ethnic voters in the North to abandon their traditional New Deal–Democratic identification. Among the political consequences were the George Wallace candidacy of 1968 (the first urban populist challenge to the Democratic party since Father Coughlin in the mid-1930s) and the election of Richard Nixon, who was not a politically neuter war hero like Eisenhower but a polarizing figure identified with McCarthyite Republicanism.

- The excesses and failures—for many, the very existence—of the Vietnam War stoked an anti-war reaction unique in its scale and passion. The American Cold War consensus, tested in the Korean War and severely tried by McCarthyism, now buckled. One political consequence was LBJ's decision not to seek renomination in 1968, four years after he had won the largest victory in modern American history. Another was the disastrous 1972 candidacy of George McGovern, with electoral consequences for the Democrats comparable to those suffered by the Republicans in the Goldwater campaign eight years before.

- At the same time a massive generational shift in cultural style and social attitudes swept through American society. Confidence in the American political system slid precipitously. An adversarial relationship between the academic-literary world and the media, on one hand, and the larger society, on the other, replaced the widely shared democratic nationalism of the New Deal and World War II. Three decades of relative cultural homogeneity gave way to cultural, social, and generational divisions as deep as any in American history.

The intense clashes over civil rights, Vietnam, and the counterculture began to subside in the early 1970s. But other disruptive events—the oil crisis of 1973, stagflation (a word coined to describe the strange hybrid of a stagnant economy and inflation), a continuing upsurge of crime, social disorder, and fiscal chaos in America's cities—sustained the widespread sense of malaise. So did such unprecedented events as the 1973 resignation of Vice President Spiro Agnew after exposure of his ethics violations while governor of Maryland, and the Watergate scandal and Nixon's abrupt departure from the presidency in 1974. The one-term presidencies of Gerald Ford and Jimmy Carter, and later the nearly successful impeachment of Bill Clinton in the 1990s, reinforced the view that the American presidency was in a serious state of institutional disarray. And the contested election of 2000 was hardly confidence-restoring.

For thirty of the thirty-five years from 1965 to 2000, polls showed that a majority of Americans thought their country was on the wrong track. An upsurge in political assassinations reinforced the sense that this was a time of troubles. True, three American presidents had been killed and two attacked between the 1830s and the 1930s. But the general view was that the perpetrators—demented loners—and not their times were out of joint. Not so with Lee Harvey Oswald, Kennedy's killer. Despite abundant evidence that he fit the *déraciné* mold of his predecessors, his act was variously ascribed to the Castroite left, the extreme right, the Mafia, and indeed the government itself: Johnson, the FBI, the CIA. That last theme was pursued on the stage, in Hollywood, and in respectable intellectual and academic journals. To this day, despite the overwhelming weight of evidence to the contrary, a majority of Americans believe that Kennedy was the victim of a conspiracy.

The Kennedy assassination was not an isolated event. Two other major public figures, JFK's brother Robert and civil rights leader Martin Luther King Jr., were killed by ideologically motivated gunmen in 1968. Attempts were made on the lives of President Gerald Ford in 1975 (twice, in September, in California, by women) and Ronald Reagan in 1981. Fringe political figures also were targets: black nationalist Malcolm X in 1965, Nazi party head George Lincoln Rockwell in 1967, segregationist George Wallace (badly wounded) in 1972, Jewish Defense League leader Meir Kahane in 1990. Like a Shakespeare play, the American political stage was littered with dead bodies.

POLITICS, PARTIES, AND ELECTIONS

The impact of the 1960s on the Democrats was strikingly similar to that of the 1930s on the Republicans.

Percentage of Popular Vote	
Republicans	Democrats
1928–58.2	1964–61.1
1932–39.6 (−18.6)	1968–42.7 (−18.4)*
1936–36.5 (−3.1)	1972–37.5 (−5.2)

14 percent of the vote went to third-party candidate George Wallace.

Except for Carter's 50.1 percent in 1976, no Democratic candidate for president would win half or more of the popular vote in the forty years after 1964. The great cultural upheaval of the 1960s had an impact on American politics comparable to the great economic depression of the 1930s.

But this political turmoil did not lead to a change in the culture of the populist political regime. It continued to be composed of weakened parties and political agendas defined and driven by the media and advocacy groups. In this sense the sixties resembled the Civil War–Reconstruction years: more transformative of American society than of the polity. Politicians, bureaucrats, judges, and activists had a large stake in the prevailing forms of public life. Powerful pressures for persistence and continuity in the American polity had sustained the party-democratic regime through the challenges of the Civil War, industrialization, and Progressivism. There was a comparable continuity to the populist-bureaucratic regime stretching from the 1930s into the early twenty-first century.

The major parties continued to be the primary units in American political life, despite the rise of alternative modes of political expression and identity and the erosion of their traditional ethnocultural, regional, ideological, and organizational bases of support. Even in 1971, at the height of popular disillusionment with the country's public institutions, 61 percent of those polled retained a strong party identity, and another 22 percent had partisan leanings.

At the same time the fluidity in party loyalty that began with the Great Depression and the New Deal continued to the end of the century, and beyond. Many younger voters were more influenced by the prevailing events of their time than by the ties of family, region, and political tradition. Eisenhower in 1952 and 1956 made substantial inroads among traditionally Democratic white southerners and ethnic northerners. In 1964 Lyndon Johnson (with the considerable help of Barry Goldwater) scored comparably large gains among traditionally Republican business, professional, and white-collar voters. George McGovern made a similar contribution to Nixon's 1972 margin among blue-collar industrial voters. Jimmy Carter in 1976 temporarily lured back southern whites drifting to Republicanism. Ronald Reagan reversed that flow.

Groups with especially strong internal cohesion and historical memories—most notably, blacks and Jews—remained true to their New Deal–Democratic faith. The Democratic commitment of blacks (many newly enfranchised in the South) stayed at 90 percent or more of those voting. There was a substantial reactive shift of southern white voters: from 78 percent Democratic even in the Eisenhower year of 1952 to 37 percent in Reagan's 1984 reelection.

When a 1968 Harris Poll asked if liberals had been running the country too long, 64 percent of working-class whites said yes. This group was two-thirds Democratic in 1968, one-third in 1972. At the same time Republicans in the northern tier from New England to the Pacific Northwest and non-southern professional and managerial whites were drawn to Democratic candidates. Middle-class whites were 25 percent Democratic in 1948, 40 percent in 1986. A 1970 poll found that 35 percent of professional-managerial whites identified themselves as liberal, compared to 18 percent of unskilled laborers.

Between 1972 and 2000, self-identified liberals were 16 to 20 percent of the electorate, self-identified conservatives 25 to 35 percent. The rest were moderates or don't-knows. This was a splintered but not polarized voting public. Region, ethnicity, and class, the core definers of party identity in the party regime, dissolved in the solvent of a more populist political culture. Out of this came no clear, permanent realignment of voters, but rather a *dealignment* (a term that gained currency in 1972) that eroded the idea of a normal majority party.

For a long time the dominant view of American politics was that party systems succeeded one another through the deus ex machina of "critical" or "realigning" elections. The primary benchmarks were 1828, 1860, 1896, and 1932. Attempts have been made to apply this party systems approach to post–New Deal American politics. A new Republican majority was thought to be taking form in the 1950s. Then in the 1960s it looked as if the New Deal coalition had returned. The GOP again seemed to be on the cusp of majority status in the early 1970s and the Reaganite 1980s. There was talk of a Democratic resurgence in the Clintonian 1990s.

Critical elections guru Walter Dean Burnham has tried to lift realignment out of its traditional party context by calling the modern situation "a critical realignment to end all critical realignments . . . a reality whose essence is the end of two-party politics." But the growing ideological and electoral division between the major parties, the edgy two-party politics of Congress, the intensity of the elections of 2000 and 2004, and the lack of major third parties suggest otherwise.

Political scientist John Aldrich has another way of interpreting American party history. He argues that the balance between the parties is a "punctuated equilibrium" constantly upset by demographic, cultural, economic, and policy change. From this perspective, the 1950s and early 1960s were a "steady-state" period between the profound disequilibria of the Depression–New Deal era and the tumultuous 1960s and 1970s.

But the modern political culture in which this drama of change has taken place is quite different from the past. One feature of the new regime was a decline in straight-ticket voting. Republicans Eisenhower in 1956 and Nixon in 1968 won the presidency but lost both houses of Congress, something that had last happened in 1848. From 1899 to 1952, twenty-six Congresses were under one-party control, and only five were divided. Between 1952 and 2005, nine were run by one party, seventeen were divided. One-party states, a common feature of the pre–World War II political landscape, were as dead as the dodo by the 1960s.

The parties' weakness showed up in opinion polling as well. In 1960 about 45 percent of a sample of the electorate identified themselves as strong or weak Democrats, 30 percent as Republicans, 23 percent as varying degrees of independent. By 1980 Democrats had dropped to 41 percent and Republicans to 23 percent, while independents rose to 33 percent. By 2000 the distribution was Democrats 34 percent, Republicans 27 percent, independents 40 percent. And each succeeding cohort of young voters seemed ready to pursue their own political identity.

These were years of substantial progress in removing obstacles to voting. The Twenty-third Amendment to the Constitution (1961) gave presidential electors to the District of Columbia. The Supreme Court in *Baker v. Carr* (1962) struck down state apportionments that violated the one-man-one-vote principle. The Twenty-fourth Amendment (1964) outlawed poll taxes. Literacy tests and other racial barriers were eliminated by the 1965 Voting Rights Act. The Twenty-sixth Amendment (1971) lowered the voting age to eighteen. In 1972 the Court limited state residency requirements for voting to thirty days. The 1995 National Voter Registration Act (the "motor voter" law) was supposed to add as many as nine million additional voters to the lists. And the voting population was ever more educated and affluent: in theory, spurs to participation.

Yet the portion of eligibles voting remained well below nineteenth-century levels. Sixty-three percent voted in the presidential election of 1960, 52 percent in 1980, the lowest of twenty democracies, including India. If anything, the rise in education may have kept the drop in voting from being substantially larger than it was. (Pollster: "What do you think is most responsible for low voter turnouts: ignorance or indifference?" Respondent: "I don't know, and I don't care.")

To explain the anomaly between access and engagement, the left points to that old standby, alienation, along with surviving rules that make registration and voting difficult for the poor. But in the early 1970s, when political disillusionment was at its peak, only 10 percent of the electorate described itself as alienated. A less ideological explanation is that when the suffrage is expanded, the percentage of eligibles voting will (at least initially) drop, as was the case when women got the ballot in the 1920s. Weakened party identity and the decay of the traditional get-out-the-vote party machinery depress turnout. And in an age noted for other pleasures of the senses and for a bureaucratized government detached from the political process, participation in elections is not as compelling a form of entertainment (or identification) as it once was.

The parties might reasonably be expected to compete vigorously for an electorate whose attitude on most issues takes the form of a bell curve: clustered in the moderate middle, with radical tails at each end. Yet modern political appeals appear to be based on a different market model: that voters are ideologically polarized. The Goldwater Republican candidacy of 1964 and its doppelgänger the McGovern Democratic candidacy of 1972 were sharp-edged ideological efforts. And for a time the electorate too appeared to be more polarized. Voters who defined themselves as centrists declined from 41 percent in 1956 to 27 percent in 1973, while those who identified with the liberal left or the conservative right increased from 28 to 44 percent.

But this was a deviation from a more centrist norm, a product of the crisis years of the late 1960s and early 1970s. From 1976 to the century's end, between 45 and 50 percent of the electorate clustered in the range from slightly liberal to slightly conservative. It was as though an inverted bell curve of the parties' ideological character—depressed in the middle, high at the tails—was superimposed on the normal bell curve of public opinion: high in the middle, low at the tails.

Why? Many political scientists see modern parties as highly inner-directed institutions, defined by the political officeholders, hired professionals, and constituents or interest groups with strong economic or ideological commitments, who are the parties' primary benefit seekers. From this perspective, the average voter today is not a party member in the sense of being affiliated with a voluntary association, as was the case in the nineteenth and early twentieth centuries. Instead he or she is more like a modern consumer, responding (or not responding) to the blandishments of political entrepreneurs who hawk their products in the political market.

A new political culture forged a new relationship between parties and their consumer-voters. The voting public in the party regime had a "private-regarding" relationship to the parties. What bound them was machine- and policy-nurtured loyalty and the fruits of patronage and constituency services. Coincident with the decline of the boss-machine politics of the party regime, there rose a new "public-regarding" party ethos, where support relied more on public policy than private payoffs.

But reliance on issues, extra-party advocacy groups, and the media put a premium on sharply focused appeals, directed at those predisposed to respond favorably. These voters were likely to be located at the tail of the public opinion curve most ideologically congenial to the party, rather than in the majoritarian center.

As the character of politics changed, so did the relationship of the parties to government. During the party-democratic regime, patronage was the means by which the parties rewarded their workers and (through kickbacks) nourished themselves financially. But legislative restrictions and judicial decisions turned patronage into a diminished, marginal practice. Justice William Brennan dismissively declared in 1976: "The democratic process functions as well without the practice of patronage, perhaps even better."

At the same time, primaries (which Harry Truman called "eyewash") became the chief means of choosing presidential candidates. Sixteen states had them in 1968, twenty-eight in 1972, thirty-two in 1980. Less than half of the delegates at the 1968 conventions were chosen by primaries. By 1980, 75 percent of the Democratic and 54 percent of the Republican delegates were so selected. In theory, primaries were a populist way of choosing candidates. But in practice their minuscule turnouts made them ideal instruments for moneyed and/or ideologically committed elements.

The parties responded to these forces of change by more sharply defining their ideological orientations: liberal, conservative. Anti–New Deal Democrats who turned Republican were the first of a stream of ideological refugees fleeing from particular turns in Democratic foreign and domestic policy, as blacks did from the Republicans. Another sign of the new political culture was the increasing importance of "amateur Democrats," for whom politics was more an avocation than a profession. They differed from their genteel reformer ancestors in being strong party men. As the old Democratic machines and politicos faded away, new kinds of leaders rose: the Henry Waxman–Howard Berman organization in West Los Angeles, or the West Side and Greenwich Village Democrats of New York, endlessly at odds with Tammany, with corruption, with each other. (Political operative Frank Mankiewicz summed up a visit to a West Side Democratic club by inverting the text of an old burlesque song: "every little meaning has a movement of its own.") For all their ethnic, locational, and ideological differences, Goldwater and other issue-driven Republicans had similar characteristics.

Politics of the sort that fueled McCarthyism in the 1950s became a recurring feature of American political life. In the past, such efforts—the Coughlin-Townsend Union party of 1936, the Strom Thurmond and Henry Wallace campaigns of 1948—were consigned to the below-stairs politics of third parties. Alabama segregationist governor George Wallace captured 14 percent of the popular vote in 1968, the best showing by a third-party candidate since Robert La Follette in 1924. Even more notable was the nearly 20 percent of the vote garnered by eccentric businessman-turned-politician Ross Perot in 1992. He campaigned primarily through television commercials and talk show appearances, and launched his candidacy not at a nominating convention but on the *Larry King Live* talk show. While Perot dwelt on the job-destroying potential of the North American Free Trade Agreement (NAFTA), the core of his candidacy echoed the contentless populism of the movie *Network* (1976): "I'm as mad as hell, and I'm not gonna take it anymore!"

But in a populist political culture, these impulses gained entry to the grand ballroom of the major parties as well. That was evident in the "eerily similar" candidacies of Barry Goldwater in 1964 and George McGovern in 1972. Almost certainly they would have run as third-party candidates in the previous party regime. And unlike their one prototype, William Jennings Bryan in 1896, they left substantial legacies to their respective parties despite their resounding defeats.

Goldwater and McGovern drew on the anxieties stirred by the major issues of the time: the civil rights movement and the Vietnam War. Each spoke to important groups in post-1945 America who could lay claim to the sobriquet of "new": Goldwater to the new suburbia that Joseph McCarthy had tapped before him, McGovern to the new left of the college young and the new class of urban professionals.

Their candidacies cut across the political class lines drawn by the Great Depression and the New Deal. Goldwater tried to appeal not only to Republican conservatives but also to Democratic, lower-middle-class white voters distrustful of the civil rights movement. McGovern attracted many members of the traditionally Republican, educated upper middle class. Both nominations were the work of a core of ideologues: "purists" operating within a more vulnerable, less boss- and machine-dominated party system. Many Goldwater and McGovern activists were "amateurs," previously not engaged in regular party politics. The Goldwaterites shouting down Nelson Rockefeller at the 1964 GOP convention were echoed by the McGovernite verbal assault on Chicago's mayor Richard Daley in 1972.

A contemporary discussion of the Goldwater campaign called it "the great mystery of American politics," in that it violated the traditional politic norm of seeking as broad a coalition as possible. There was no real expectation of winning, no readiness to compromise. It was populist passion injected into major party politics. Political scientist Aaron Wildavsky called it "the beginnings of ideology in the United States."

Old-time political shibboleths fell like leaves in autumn in the Goldwater campaign. The candidate was the first national party nominee of Jewish ancestry; his running mate, William Miller, was the first Catholic GOP national candidate. For the first time the Democratic candidate, incumbent president Lyndon Johnson, was the preferred choice of America's business elites and the upper middle class. The result was predictably lopsided: Johnson won the largest margin of the popular vote in American party history. He captured every county in New England, New York, and the Midwest, something that even FDR in 1936 had not been able to do.

The Goldwater campaign was stirred in part by the civil rights movement and the revival of the New Deal approach to governance under Kennedy and Johnson. George McGovern, the 1972 Democratic counterpart to Goldwater, emerged from the bitterness stirred by the Vietnam War. He co-headed the McGovern-Fraser Commission, established in the wake of the disastrous Chicago Democratic convention of 1968 and Hubert Humphrey's subsequent loss to Nixon. Its purpose was to reform the party's delegate selection procedure. Fred Harris, the chair of the Democratic National Committee (who would write a book called *The New Populism*), later boasted: "I made up the membership of the commission in such a way as to ensure that they would come up with what they came up with."

And what was that? In theory, broader citizen participation in delegate selection—populist politics at work—joined to the European model of a centrally run party. The commission called for ideology-tuning party conventions midway between the presidential election years. The intent, said co-chair Donald Fraser, was "the creation of a truly national party."

The McGovern-Fraser Commission banned delegates chosen in party caucuses or in "open" primaries where non-Democratic voters participated. Wisconsin's state party challenged this rule. But the Supreme Court later upheld the right of a national convention to seat or unseat delegates as it chose. And the District of Columbia Court of Appeals sustained a McGovernite challenge to California's primary law, which allocated delegates according to the percentage of the vote each candidate received. As a result, McGovern got a unanimous California delegation with 44 percent of the primary vote.

The assault on the existing party system led to a very different Democratic convention indeed in 1972. Only 20 percent of the seats were reserved for "super-delegates," severely reducing both the number and influence of the party's elected leaders. (In 1968, 68 percent of Democratic senators and 39 percent of the party's congressmen were delegates; by 1980 the percentages had dropped to 14 and 15.) Delegate slots reserved for women, African Americans, and the young were in practice occupied by feminists, black activists, and new-left types. Almost 40 percent of the 1972 delegates had postgraduate degrees, compared to 4 percent of the population; more than two hundred belonged to the National Education Association. The elderly, the poor, white ethnics, and union members were substantially underrepresented.

McGovern won only 27 percent of the popular vote in the party's primaries and was favored by no more than 30 percent of Democrats in pre-convention polling. But he got the support of 57 percent of the delegates on the first ballot. The consequences were as disastrous for the Democrats as the Goldwater candidacy had been for the Republicans. Nixon, an even less attractive candidate than Johnson, won 60.7 percent of the popular vote, a shade under Johnson's 1964 total. Only one in five white male adults voted for McGovern.

By the early 1970s it seemed to many observers that, as a book of the time put it, "the party's over." Over the course of the century from 1830 to 1930, except for the 1850s and the 1860s and the Progressive years, the parties set the terms of political debate. Now it appeared that that primacy was gone, perhaps irretrievably.

True, the dictates of the constitutional order made third parties unviable: two-party politics remained the rule. But the appeal of the major parties substantially declined from its pre-1930s level. More and more people defined themselves politically not by their party label but by issues (abortion, environmentalism, gun control, foreign policy, race). Dissent once expressed through third parties now found its voice in movements, causes, coalitions such as the McCarthyism of the 1950s, the civil rights (and anti-civil-rights) and anti-Vietnam movements of the 1960s, the anti-abortion movement of the 1980s.

By the end of the century, references to "populist" or "populism" in the press were fifteen times as common as in the Eisenhower years. But while politics had become more populist, whether or not it had become more democratic remained a matter for debate.

THE MEDIA, ADVOCACY GROUPS, AND THINK TANKS

The decline of the party regime was abetted by the rise of extra-party voices in American public affairs: the media, advocacy groups, policy-manufacturing think tanks. In some respects they strengthened the democratic character of politics. They engaged more people in more issues, and added to the store of information and attitudes that fueled public controversy. But they also reinforced elitist-bureaucratic influence in American public life. Plutocratic newspaper publishers, New York– and Washington-based journalists and television anchors ("presenters," in England's more call-a-spade-a-spade language style), inside-the-Beltway think tanks and institutes, and the hermetic worlds of the big foundations and academic policy wonks were not necessarily more plugged in to the larger society than the bosses, machines, and lobbyists of the party regime; arguably, they were less so. The claim of the media and advocacy groups to speak for "the people" could be taken with the same dose of salt as the similar rhetoric of the party bosses they displaced.

Almost all American newspapers were affiliated with one party or the other in the nineteenth century. They faithfully disseminated their party's ideology and often depended on its financial largesse. Larger circulations and the growth of advertising gradually generated sources of income independent of party ties. But it was not easy for politically ambitious publishers to wield influence outside of the party system, as Horace Greeley and William Randolph Hearst learned to their regret.

From the 1930s on, publishers with political attitude such as Robert R. McCormick of the *Chicago Tribune,* Joseph Patterson of the New York *Daily News,* and Henry Luce of *Time* and *Life* marched to their own, often idiosyncratically ideological drummers. But it was never easy for the media to sway an electorate whose political responses were so deeply encased in culture, economics, even psychology. New Dealer Harold Ickes thought that in 1936 "the very bitterness of the assault upon the President by the newspapers reacted in his favor."

During the first half of the twentieth century the press was much more Republican than Democratic. Adlai Stevenson worried in 1952 about "a one-party press in a two-party country." By the end of the century, the major metropolitan newspapers had become comparably Democratic-leaning, reflecting a larger shift in *bien-pensant* political attitudes.

In an age of weakened parties and a media-driven popular culture, newspapers and television were voices to be reckoned with. Carl Bernstein and Bob Woodward of the *Washington Post,* who broke the Watergate story, became celebrities: the journalists who brought down a president. And with its nightly news, presidential debates, and unique platform for political advertising, television emerged as the most conspicuous influence in American public life. (From Boss Tweed to Boss Tube, the saying went.) The Kennedy-Nixon confrontation of 1960 was the first presidential debate broadcast on television. Its emphasis on appearance rather than substance (most of those who listened to the debate on radio thought Nixon had won) made it a far cry indeed from the Lincoln-Douglas debates a century before. After resuming in 1976, the televised candidate debate became the focal point of each presidential election. By its very nature it strengthened the popular perception of the campaign as a contest between candidates rather than between parties.

As the parties' ethno-cultural, regional, and class claims on voters lessened, the influence of the media grew. The televised Army-McCarthy hearings and a critical documentary by CBS newsman Edward R. Murrow did more to bring McCarthy's careening career to an end than did the parties or Congress. The vivid tele-reporting of southern anti-black violence during the civil rights movement had a comparable impact. The Big Three networks' evening news programs—lengthened from fifteen to thirty minutes in the 1960s—had more than seventy million viewers at their 1969 peak. Avuncular news presenters such as Walter Cronkite, Chet Huntley, and David Brinkley came to wield great influence. LBJ said that when Cronkite turned against America's Vietnam effort, the game was over.

Hollywood's self-protective maxim in the 1930s was "If you have a message, send it by Western Union." Now big media and big entertainment began a long march into political engagement. Oliver Stone's movie *JFK* portrayed Chief Justice Earl Warren as covering up the real culprits behind the Kennedy assassination: the CIA, the FBI, LBJ. Not since the anti-black, anti-Reconstruction *Birth of a Nation* (1915) had a major film conveyed so strong a political message.

Like the party press, advocacy groups were part of American politics from its earliest days. The democratic culture of the party regime opened the door to groups with special causes. Most weightily in the case of opposition to slavery, and later with free silver, prohibition, and women's suffrage, movements with strong appeal took on a political life of their own. But the parties usually managed to contain or use them.

During the early twentieth century a few large organizations dominated political lobbying: the American Farm Bureau Federation, the National Association of Manufacturers and the United States Chamber of Commerce, the American Federation of Labor, the American Legion.

A secondary level of advocacy groups grew out of the fecund soil of modern American society during the Progressive period: the National Association for the Advancement of Colored People (NAACP) for blacks, the Sierra Club for environmentalists, the American Civil Liberties Union (ACLU) for defenders of free speech. They sought to be influential political voices, linked to but independent of the parties: not unlike the major press barons of the time.

The New Deal, World War II, and the high-spending American state of the prosperous postwar decades created a golden age of "interest-group liberalism." Thousands of trade associations, law firms, and lobbyists, seeking what they regarded as their due share of appropriations and sympathetic regulation, engaged in elaborate ballets of understandings with congressmen and bureaucrats. In return for support, they provided money and other help to politicians increasingly needful of these benefits as the traditional party structure faded away.

What distinguished the advocacy groups of the late twentieth century from this world of influence? For one thing, the number and variety of their causes grew exponentially. Organizations committed to social and cultural issues gained political clout on a par with the traditional spokesmen for economic interests. And they became major incubators of public policy. In true populist fashion, the new advocacy groups identified themselves as spokesmen for "the public interest," a phrase that now gained widespread currency. (The first magazine so named appeared in the fall of 1965. It ceased publication in 2005.)

The first political action committee (PAC) was created by the AFL-CIO to work for the reelection of FDR in 1944. Americans for Democratic Action (ADA) appeared in 1947 as a liberal anti-Communist organization similarly tied to the Democratic party. As the century wore on, the most prominent advocacy groups became more identified with particular causes than with parties or campaigns. The Association for the Advancement of Retired Persons (AARP)—whose name paid homage to the NAACP—was founded in 1958, primarily to sell term insurance to retirees. The rapidly rising number of older voters, higher social security payments, Medicare, and the benefits bestowed by the Older Americans Act of 1965 gave the AARP a vastly expanded market and a growing role as a political voice for the elderly.

In an "explosion of organized advocacy," the number of trade associations, professional societies, lobbyists, law firms, and public relations specialists in Washington tripled between 1960 and 1991. Pressure groups representing economic or professional interests continued to outnumber advocates of social causes by four to one. But the latter became more important as civil rights, the Vietnam War, women's rights, abortion, environmentalism, and a host of lesser issues came into political prominence.

The first wave of social advocacy groups, in the 1950s and 1960s, was left-liberal. The conservative backlash of the 1970s and 1980s saw the rise of conservative counterparts. Together they made social issues the most prominent part of the agenda of late-twentieth-century American public life. More than the parties, they attracted media attention, and through their access to Congress and the courts they assumed a leading role in public policy making. The Magnuson-Moss Act of 1975 established an "intervenor funding program" that gave grants to pro-consumer groups participating in Federal Trade Commission proceedings. The courts allowed these organizations to join lawsuits related to their causes and to share in the ensuing financial awards.

Many of these advocacy groups became household names (at least in political households): the John Birch Society, the Southern Christian Leadership Council, Common Cause, the National Organization for Women, Planned Parenthood, the Moral Majority, the National Right to Life Committee. Students for a Democratic Society (SDS) on the left and Young Americans for Freedom (whose membership soon outnumbered that of SDS) on the right championed ideological approaches with strong links to, but an identity separate from, the major parties. Policy entrepreneurs such as Martin Luther King Jr. and Ralph Nader mobilized supporters, and public opinion at large, to their causes of civil rights and anti-corporatism. Jerry Falwell and Pat Robertson sought something similar with their brand of fundamentalist conservatism, as did their black counterparts Jesse Jackson and Al Sharpton. They were the antitheses of professional party politicians: not party nor office but their causes defined them. Theirs were quintessentially populist American political voices.

Issue organizations, linked with like-thinking counterparts in issue networks, brought concerns such as civil rights, abortion, gun control, environmentalism, feminism, gay rights, and evangelicalism into mainstream public discourse. They were mightily helped by the media, for whom the new advocacy politics was refreshingly free of the ambiguities that obscured the story line of more traditional issues such as labor policy or economic regulation. The same qualities often led the social-agenda makers to the courts, which could cut through the frustrating processes of politics and legislation.

There are parallels here to the grassroots party building of the 1820s and 1830s and the interest-group liberalism of the early and mid-twentieth century. Of necessity, and because it was advantageous, the parties responded to these new voices. Interest groups once sought party support; now the opposite was the norm. But the parties wooed the groups at a price: the danger of a more sharply ideological politics, with advocacy-group tails wagging party dogs. The shift left its mark on everything from congressional roll call votes and hearings on Supreme Court appointments to the character of presidential campaigns.

This new political force fostered new kinds of political dirty tricks. The Kennedy administration recognized the importance of advocacy groups when its Internal Revenue Service undertook an "Ideological Organization Project": reviewing fifteen advocacy groups, of which fourteen were right-wing, and recommending the revocation of the tax-exempt status of seven of them. Nixon's better-known "enemies list" of the early 1970s focused more on media and advocacy opponents than on Democratic party leaders.

Advocacy groups had financial resources, access to the media, and a popular appeal that expanded the public agenda. But advocacy politics, like the media and the courts, posed a challenge to the parties as the primary instruments of American democracy. What one critic called "hyper-pluralism" eroded the ability of political leaders to act with a sense of obligation to the public at large. On leaving office, Jimmy Carter warned: "The national interest is not always the sum of all our simple or special interests."

There developed as well a new infrastructure of policy analysis, made up of foundations, university centers and institutes, and that distinctive adornment of the populist polity, the think tank. (The term derived from World War II military jargon for a secure room where plans and strategies could be discussed.) By 1991 there were more than a thousand such organizations, a tenth of them clustered in the Washington area.

Like advocacy groups, some think tanks dated from the early years of the twentieth century. The Russell Sage Foundation (1907), the Brookings Institution (1916), the Twentieth Century Fund (1919), and the National Bureau of Economic Research (1920) came out of the fact-based government instrumentalism of the Progressive and World War I years.

But think tanks did not take a commanding place in policy making until after World War II, when social-science-based policy analysis came into its own. Defense-driven outfits such as RAND and the Hudson Institute took on the chilling task of advising on military policy in the atomic age. The big foundations—Ford, Rockefeller, Carnegie—financed and publicized public policy agendas.

More specialized and overtly ideological think tanks multiplied to meet the growing demand for policy wonkery. Conservative ones—the American Enterprise Institute (which began in 1953 with the help—ironically, in retrospect—of the Ford Foundation), the Heritage Foundation (1973), the Cato Institute (1978), New York's Manhattan Institute (1980)—were ideological counterweights to moderate-to-liberal Brookings and the increasingly left-leaning big foundations. The Institute for Policy Studies, started in 1943 with money from liberal Jewish donors, moved leftward in the 1950s and 1960s. The Ethics and Public Policy Center of the Rockford Institute (1976) espoused a heartland, religion-infused social and economic conservatism. The Progressive Policy Institute (1985) was the think tank arm of the middle-of-the-road Democratic Leadership Council.

The new cottage industry of policy production found a ready market in the populist, bureaucratized political regime. It drew sustenance from a wide belief in the efficacy of policy analysis: part of the obeisance that social science paid to real science. Government contracts enabled Brookings, RAND, and other think tanks to crank out policy prescriptions, often taken up by politicians and the parties. The major foundations spread largesse as their increasingly left-liberal officers desired (while the original conservative donors spun steadily in their graves). The foundations and think tanks, said *The Economist*, were becoming "America's shadow government," replacing the parties and the old business, labor, agricultural, and veterans' pressure groups as major sources of political issues and ideas.

THE PARTY EMPIRE STRIKES BACK

By the end of the 1970s, a disastrous war, unsafe cities, failed presidencies, and a fraught economy fed the widespread sense that the nation's best days were behind it. Upbeat passing events—the lunar landing in 1969, the celebration of the nation's bicentennial in 1976—lightened but did not lift the prevailing dispirit.

The next quarter of a century, from 1980 to 2005, hardly saw a 180-degree turnaround. Recurring economic uncertainty, bitter party politics, concern over a popular culture seemingly hell-bent on defining deviancy downward, more blemishes on the presidency (Iran-contra, the Clinton impeachment, the 2000 election), capped by the trauma of 9/11, made it clear that the anxieties of the late twentieth century would persist as the calendar moved from 19— to 20—.

But those years saw something else as well. Far from fading into irrelevance, the parties recovered much of their political authority. What occurred was not one majority party replacing the other, the sequence typical of the party-democratic regime, but a less bipolar process: both parties adapting to new cultural and political realities, as happened in the 1830s and 1840s and then again in the 1880s.

Among the signs of a returning equilibrium was the emergence of a more stable political configuration from the 1980s on. It bore a mirror-image resemblance to the high noon of the nineteenth-century party regime. The old line between the Democratic South and the Republican North was replaced by a strongly Republican South and Democratic coastal states east and west. And the ethno-cultural fault line of the party regime between pietistic Republicans and ritualistic Democrats re-appeared in the form of a political division between those who were more religious and those who were less so.

The new Republican Sunbelt majority rose as the party's old Mid-west-Northeast core declined. Democratic gains occurred not in the white ethnic working class (which if anything became more Republican), but among managers and professionals attracted to Democratic social liberalism or repelled by Republican social conservatism. Abortion and the environment came to matter more than unionization or the minimum wage.

This reshuffling had stabilizing electoral consequences. None of the five presidents who were in office between 1961 and 1981 served two full terms. Since 1981, all but one (George H. W. Bush) has (or bids fair to have) done so. Ronald Reagan and Bill Clinton are the representative chief executives of this new era of party resurgence, much as LBJ and Nixon embodied the time of troubles before.

Clinton thought it was in 1968, when Nixon won the presidency, "that conservative populism replaced progressive populism as the dominant political force in our nation." He was twelve years ahead of himself. It was Reagan who came up with a formula that transcended the ideological narrowness of Goldwater and the unforgiving partisanship of Nixon.

Reagan's political background was letter-perfect for the new populism. He had been a New Deal Democrat, and he packaged his free-market, "Morning in America" message in rhetoric that echoed the all-inclusive popular nationalism of the New Deal. This was political leagues away from the more dour messages of Goldwater and Nixon. Reagan's was the new politics of populism in its purest form: what John Micklethwait and Adrian Wooldridge termed "the conservatism not of country clubs and boardrooms, but of talk radio, precinct meetings and tax revolts." As late as 1980, the Democrats ran 16 percent ahead of the Republicans in party preference. By 1988, 46 percent of white voters identified themselves as Republicans, compared to 40 percent as Democrats. So did 53 percent of those eighteen to twenty-five years old. Jerry Falwell's Moral Majority, created in 1979 as an independent political voice, disbanded in 1989, made superfluous by Reagan Republicanism.

Yet like Eisenhower, Reagan did not preside over a realignment of American politics. Although his 1984 election sweep rivaled that of FDR in 1936, it had no perceptible impact on Congress: the GOP lost two seats in the Senate and made only modest gains in the House. About a third of the congressional districts carried by Reagan elected Democratic representatives, and a third of the electorate in 1984 had no strong sense of identity with either party. Although his successor, George H. W. Bush, easily won in 1988, the Democrats carried both houses of Congress and a majority of governorships and state legislatures.

A similar tale may be told about Clinton. He worked Reagan-like alchemy on the FDR-Truman-Kennedy-Johnson tradition, associating himself with it but updating its message to late-twentieth-century American life. He came to his 1992 campaign as the voice of moderate Democrats in the JFK tradition (including a vapid label: the New Covenant). Perot's candidacy led Clinton to identify more closely with the Democratic left, to which the party's voters of the sixties-McGovern generation (and the younger Clinton himself) had belonged. And at first he inclined to govern that way, as Reagan initially sought to govern according to conservative principles. A member of the moderate Democratic Leadership Council (which Clinton had headed when he was governor of Arkansas) observed: "Clinton ran like Jack Kennedy and governed like Ted Kennedy."

Clinton's romp in the liberal hay came to an abrupt halt with the defeat of his wife Hillary's grandiose health care plan and the big GOP congressional win of 1994. Reagan ran against big government and then oversaw its growth as a percentage of GNP. Clinton now announced: "The era of big government is over." (It wasn't.) And with NAFTA and then welfare reform, he challenged two core Democratic constituencies: organized labor and social liberals. Like Reagan, Clinton won easy re-election. And his two terms as president no more led to a normal Democratic majority than Reagan's two terms led to a normal Republican majority.

It can be argued that the candidacy of Ross Perot in 1992, like TR's run in 1912, produced an accidental Democratic president, who then capitalized on his incumbency and a weak Republican opponent to win a second term in 1996: the only Democrat to do so since FDR. (Similarly, Wilson's 1912 back-door win and 1916 reelection was the one Democratic exception between Grover Cleveland and FDR.) The case for a new normal Republican majority found further support in the Newt Gingrich–led GOP congressional landslide of 1994. But the 30 percent increase in Republican seats in that year was no more indicative of a long-term political realignment than George H. W. Bush's 16 percent vote drop between 1988 and 1992 (which compared with Herbert Hoover's 18 percent falloff between 1928 and 1932). Nor did the 1998 Democratic congressional gains—the first to follow the same party's presidential win since 1934—presage the return of a normal Democratic congressional majority. The swings revealed the inherent instability of a populist political culture rather than tectonic shifts in political allegiance.

Politicians and parties were helped by the ideological polarization that came with a more populist politics. Congressmen may have become more autonomous in their fund-raising and constituency service. But they were also more tightly tied to their parties by shared ideology, as the growing cohesiveness of party roll call votes showed. The end of the conservative coalition between midwestern Republicans and southern Democrats strengthened that trend. By the late 1980s, southern Democrats were as loyal to their party as were their northern counterparts, and liberal Republicans were an endangered species. Incumbency became a virtual guarantee of reelection. In part this was a consequence of the growing ideological—and party—cohesiveness of congressional districts, fostered by redistricting and demography.

The party-destabilizing influence of third parties—something to be expected in a populist regime—did not occur. The substantial George Wallace vote in 1968 and the 20 percent that were attracted in 1992 by what Jacob Weisberg called Perot's "post-modern faux populism" were expressions of popular discontent with no evident long-term political consequences. Party identification, which fell from the 1950s to the 1970s, leveled off or even rose thereafter. More than 80 percent of the electorate consistently claimed to lean toward one or the other of the major parties.

Seeking to woo and hold their constituencies, the parties regained strength as political organizations, money-gatherers, and generators of public policy. The new campaign finance laws of the 1970s allowed government funding of third parties only after an election, and the Supreme Court's *Buckley* decision of 1976 opened the door to large individual donations to the major parties. In 1981–82 the GOP raised more money—

about 85 percent of it in small contributions that came in by mail—than the thousands of corporate, labor, and independent PACs combined.

Both parties engaged in institutional restoration. The Republican political style relied more on individual than group appeals, and on political ideology more than programs and benefits. In the 1980s, GOP national chairman William Brock strengthened the ties between the national and state parties and made a great success of direct mail and other modern fund-raising devices. A decade later former congressman Tony Coelho secured similar, though smaller-scale, results in getting business PACs to contribute to the regnant congressional Democrats. The GOP's Lee Atwater in the 1980s and the Democrats' James Carville in the 1990s were a new breed of take-no-prisoners campaign manager. They were well attuned to the political style of the populist regime, pushing a consumer model of targeted issue marketing rather than generic party appeal.

Bright-line partisan divisions over issues such as foreign policy or the budget deficit were slow to develop. Instead the parties sharply divided over the social and cultural issues that mattered to their constituents. Anti-abortion Democrats and secularist Republicans became *rarae aves* in the political aviary. The red-blue electoral divide of the 2000s emerged in the 1980s and 1990s. One sign was the increase in the level of same-party state presidential and senatorial voting. In 1984, 55 percent of the senators in the forty-four states that went for Reagan were Republican. In 1992 the presidential-senatorial accord in states that voted for Clinton was 60 percent. (More recently the ratio has been over 75 percent.)

This story of party adaptation to a new political culture was echoed across the Atlantic. Just as British politics in the nineteenth century bore some (pale) resemblance to its American counterpart, so was this the case in the late twentieth century. British quangos (quasi-autonomous nongovernmental organizations), comparable to America's advocacy groups, were a "ripening hotbed of influence." Party politics in Britain, as in America, became more ideological, the electorate more volatile.

Britain's Labor party, like the Democrats, turned left in the 1960s and 1970s, with similarly doleful consequences. Among Labor's accoutrements was a new reselection process for incumbent MPs that, like the McGovern-Fraser reforms, opened the door to the left. Michael Foot's defeat of Denis Healey for the party chairmanship in 1980 led to the spin-off of the Social Democrats in 1981, leaving Labor as weak as the Democrats were in the time of McGovern.

But the Social Democratic challenge to Labor-Tory hegemony was no more successful than the sporadic third-party efforts of Wallace, John

Anderson, or Perot. And the prime ministerships of the Tories' Margaret Thatcher and Labor's Tony Blair resembled the presidencies of Reagan and Clinton. Thatcher, like Reagan, appealed beyond her Conservative party base. Her massive 1983 victory was bracketed by Reagan's 1980 and 1984 triumphs. Thatcherite policy resembled Reaganism in its dedication to market economics, slash-and-burn anti-government rhetoric, and far less forceful implementation. And like Reagan, her impact on British politics was not limited to her own party.

Blair, who had as close a political affinity with Clinton as Thatcher had with Reagan, sought to move Labor to the center as Clinton tried to do with the Democrats. But the degree to which strong personal leadership could override the weight of national political cultures remained unclear. The underlying structural differences between the two great Atlantic democracies—over the separation of government powers, over the level of federalism—persisted despite the pressure for cultural similarity that modernity so famously brings.

By the end of the twentieth century, tension between the dictates of the politics of populism and the politics of party characterized American politics, much as the tension between the dictates of bureaucracy and democracy pervaded American government and law. Would the new century see an ever more intense politics of polarization and confrontation? Or would the traditional forces of compromise, equilibrium, and the vital center prevail, as most (but not all) American political history suggested?

EPILOGUE

Today and Tomorrow

I N THE HURLY-BURLY of American politics, it is difficult indeed to sort out the inconsequential and transient from the substantial and long-lasting. So it is proper to end this book with an overview of the state of the American polity today, set in the perspective of two centuries and more of public history, and indulge in some speculation as to its likely course in the near future.

Some hold that fundamental change is in the offing. Journalist Michael Lind foresees a "Fourth American Republic," hostile to affirmative action and immigration but egalitarian in its economics. Political scientist Walter Dean Burnham thought that Ross Perot's strong third-party vote in 1992 and the Republican congressional victory of 1994 (the largest turnover since the Whig collapse in 1854) presaged "a wholly unprecedented breakdown of traditional political order." He too expected a (vaguely defined) Fourth Republic to emerge from the rubble, succeeding those established by the Founding, the Civil War and Reconstruction, and the New Deal.

The Clinton impeachment trial of 1998, the contested election of 2000, the divisive war in Iraq, and the virulence of the 2004 campaign reinforced the prevailing belief that the American polity was in a state of near crisis. So did polls showing historically high levels of public distrust of the nation's major governing institutions.

The sense of malaise stretches across the political spectrum. Conservatives fear that freedom and social morality are endangered by an out-of-control bureaucracy, judiciary, media, advocacy groups, and popular culture. Liberals believe that American democracy is imperiled by a political marriage of evangelical religion and secular neoconservatism. The literary-academic left has a boundless sense of foreboding. Writer Jonathan Schell thinks that "the American Republic is in the deepest crisis of my lifetime," as do a number of constitutional law experts. Academic Benjamin Barber fears that under the Bush administration "an American Eichmann is not altogether impossible." Other leading political scientists turn to hoary panaceas: "responsible" (i.e., programmatic and ideological) parties, multiple parties, proportional instead of first-past-the-post representation, a British-style parliamentary system, the abolition of the electoral college.

Two observations are in order. The first is that after three-quarters of a century, the American populist-bureaucratic regime in fact has notable accomplishments to its credit. For all its inadequacies, the welfare state crafted since the 1930s benefits a substantial portion of the needy (and, it may be conceded, many of the less- or non-needy). The economy remains prone to ups and downs, and there is understandable concern over the size of the federal deficit. But there has been no recurrence of anything like the Great Depression. Indeed, the growth (however unevenly distributed) of the wealth and health of Americans since the 1930s are major accomplishments, in part due to public policy.

No less notable were the American triumphs over fascism in World War II and over Soviet communism in the Cold War. The Cold War end game was more peaceful and more successful than almost anyone expected. (A political scientist said of the Soviet Union's collapse: "None of us predicted it, and all of us can tell you why it was inevitable.")

Finally, there has been an unparalleled expansion of civil liberties and civil rights. Freedom of speech, press, religion, and sexual behavior faces fewer constraints in American law and custom than ever before. The same can be said for traditionally discriminated-against or marginalized social groups: African Americans and women most notably, but Native Americans, Hispanics, gays, the disabled, and eighteen-year-olds as well.

So any fair summing up of the recent American past may reasonably conclude that in important respects the record of the populist-bureaucratic regime is at least as good as—indeed, in many respects superior to—those of its predecessors.

The second point to make is that the current regime has considerable institutional coherence. For all their inadequacies, America's public institutions have been engaged in a process of adaptation (very stressful, and by no means ended) to the demands of explosively changing domestic and international settings. From this perspective, the polity is not careening out of control but is in the midst of an ongoing quest for equilibrium. How successful that quest will be—whether or not it may experience an 1850s-level crackup—is the larger question still up for grabs.

POLITICS

The institutional continuity of American politics is one of its defining features. There is no reason to think that a multi-party politics will replace the two-party system. The lack of a significant, ongoing third party in recent years is testimony to the major parties' capacity to control the political culture of modern America. In the course of this adaptation, the parties have abandoned or reversed much of what defined them in the past. The traditional ethno-cultural, regional, and ideological measures of party identity have been upended.

Nineteenth-century Republicans supported the (anti-Catholic-tinted) separation of church and state, social reform, a protective tariff, and hostility to states' rights. The party attracted businessmen and professionals, academics, and the solid middle class, members of the more pietistic sects, and those of no religion at all. (Robert Ingersoll, the most conspicuous atheist in late-nineteenth-century America, was a prominent GOP figure.) In the early twentieth century the GOP became more socially conservative, echoing its native-born Protestant core. It opposed the welfare state, was hostile to immigration, and leaned toward an isolationist foreign policy.

Today the GOP stands in opposition to most of what defined it from the 1850s to the 1930s. Its regional core has shifted from its traditional base in the North and the Midwest to the South and the Southwest, from main-line to evangelical Protestantism, from managers and professionals to blue-collar Catholics and the white lower middle class. It has become more free trade than protectionist, more receptive than hostile to Catholics, more international- and intervention-minded than isolationist.

The Democrats were once the party of states' rights, small government, white supremacy, and free trade. By the mid-twentieth century much of the party was committed to a New Deal/post–New Deal liberalism that included belief in a color-blind Constitution, support for nuclear power, hostility to judicial activism, and a readiness to see the United States wield its military force as a world power. Since then, the Democrats have undergone as thorough a transformation as the GOP. The core constituency has changed from white southerners, urban Irish Catholics, and adherents of the more ritualistic faiths to blacks north and south, the professional and chattering classes, and the non-religious. The silk-stocking districts in the nation's large cities trend Democratic, while Appalachia, the nation's poorest region, trends Republican.

If the traditional party identifiers of region, class, and ethnic identity have become less important, what has replaced them? Culture—"the most elusive and mysterious influence on our lives and times," according to the *Wall Street Journal*—is the favored term of art in discussions of party preference. Family status (married or unmarried), age (to which generation you belong), education and lifestyle (whether you do or do not identify with the urban-elite media culture), and most of all religion (not which one you belong to but how religious you are) appear to be the most significant determinants of political choice.

Religious conservatives and churchgoing families, Catholic or Protestant, trend Republican; secular liberals trend Democratic. Without regard to class or ethnicity, married women with children lean Republican, younger single people lean Democratic. African Americans, Jews, and academics are Democrats with little regard to their income or location but with much regard to the degree of their religiosity: the more religious, the less Democratic. The cultural hearts of technocrats, lawyers, and high-tech entrepreneurs beat Democratic, even if their wallets speak Republican.

These alignments reflect contemporary social issues and attitudes. But their larger form is hardly new in American politics. Party divisions along ethno-cultural lines were evident in the Federalist-Jeffersonian 1790s, the Jacksonian-Whig 1840s, the pietist Republican–ritualist Democratic 1880s. Today the defining issues are not slavery, states' rights, white supremacy, the tariff, prohibition, or Protestantism versus Catholicism, but abortion, affirmative action, same-sex marriage, and (most recently) foreign policy.

The distinction between red and blue states has been the fashionable way of describing the cultural basis of modern party identity. The clustering of the Democratic electoral vote in the Northeast, in the upper Midwest, and on the West Coast and of the Republican vote everywhere else is visually arresting. White southerners are more solidly drawn to the Republicans, Democrats are more solidly ensconced in the ethnic-minority, rich-and-poor big cities. (But the traditional linkage between cities and the Democratic vote has diminished as the character of American urban life has changed. Kerry's 2004 vote averaged 72 percent in the five blue-state big cities of New York, Chicago, Los Angeles, Philadelphia, and Detroit. It averaged 45 percent in the five red-state big cities of Houston, Phoenix, San Diego, San Antonio, and Dallas.)

Red-blue in fact is something of an ecological fallacy. Varying shades of purple are a more accurate coloring of the American political map. The losing party's candidates invariably attract 40 percent or more of the votes in their opponents' safest states. There has been a crazy-quilt pattern of Republican governors in blue states such as New York, California, and Massachusetts, and Democratic governors in red states such as Montana, Wyoming, and Oklahoma. Mixed or against-the-grain state legislatures are thick on the ground.

The Great Depression, World War II, the Cold War, and the economic, demographic, and social changes of the late twentieth century fueled these alterations in the parties' identity. But neither of them has secured the normal-majority status that the Republicans had in the late nineteenth and early twentieth centuries or the Democrats had from the 1930s through the 1960s. A new generation of voters may be drawn to an appealing candidate (FDR in 1936, Eisenhower in 1952, Reagan in 1980) or be affected by a major event (the Vietnam War, the 9/11 terrorist attacks, the Iraq War). While most voters lean to one party or the other, new voter cohorts not so firmly committed are appearing all the time. This appears to be inherent in the political culture of the populist regime and is likely to continue.

Nevertheless, the "party's over" hypothesis is unpersuasive. Ideology enables the parties to make up for the loss of the patronage-fed organizations that helped them thrive in the former regime. If traditional regional, ethnic, and class identities are no longer enough to keep the faithful in line, more purposeful, culturally keyed party positions compensate.

The parties are engaged in an ongoing struggle for success in a new political environment. In the Progressive era, political "reform" focused on efforts to cleanse (i.e., reduce) the electorate. Now the stress is on expanding it (at least among predictably supportive voters): something that helps the parties. Mail registration and balloting can lead to increased turnouts (though they may also foster fraudulent voting). The pervasive primaries reinforce the predominance of the parties (though they can constrain popular choice: primary turnouts of 25 percent or less of the potential electorate give likely-to-vote activists an outsized say in who gets nominated).

For some time now the media has made a strong claim to set the tone of American politics. The mainstream media, commercial and public television, and Hollywood are increasingly ready to broadcast their left-liberal take on public matters. A similarly confrontational conservative counter-media—widely listened-to radio talk shows, the Fox News network—has emerged as an opposing voice.

This extra-party media presence has been substantially augmented by the spread of the Internet. Bloggers, clustered at the ideological tails of the political bell curve, are a loud new addition to political discourse. Direct fund-raising on the Web, pioneered by Howard Dean in 2004, markedly expanded the ability of candidates to secure money outside the regular party infrastructure.

But while these new political voices have raised the decibel level of political discourse, they have not displaced the parties as the ultimate arbiters of public power. The anti-Bush assault of CBS, the *New York Times*, and other media voices in 2004 served the interests of the Kerry campaign. Countering anti-Kerry blogs such as Swift Boat Veterans for Truth and the unmasking of the probable forgery of evidence in CBS's exposé of Bush's Texas National Guard record served GOP party purposes. And the parties retain the power that comes with being major spenders of campaign money. When the Republicans realized that most watchers of big-network TV were Democrats, they shifted advertising money to cable and niche radio. Movie theaters also were hostile territory, and GOP ads there were infrequent. Health clubs were friendlier terrain, so the GOP advertised in them.

The McCain-Feingold law of 2002 allowed soft money to flow without restriction to organizations with no formal link to the parties: 527s, in tax-code jargon. This appeared to add to the power of ideological loose cannons. Almost 80 percent of the $553 million contributed to 527s during the 2004 federal election cycle went to cause-minded advocacy groups. Americans Coming Together (ACT) and MoveOn.org were the chief Democratic 527s. ACT got $64 million from three anti-Bush donors: currency speculator George Soros, Hollywood executive Stephen Bing, and insurance magnate Peter Lewis. At its peak, ACT had seventy-eight field offices and six thousand employees. The Democrats' 2004 campaign in the decisive state of Ohio was run not by party regulars but by ACT operatives.

Republican 527s got into the game later. Their largest individual 527 contribution was $5 million; their total was $113 million. Overall the Democratic presidential campaign raised $128 million more than the Republicans: a first in modern American history. But this was a relatively small difference in a presidential campaign whose cost approached a billion dollars.

The danger of the media, advocacy groups, and ideologically driven constituencies wagging the party dog is as real as the threat that corporations and other special interest groups posed in the party regime. One critic has likened the Democrats to a shell corporation, whose policy making is in the hands of dozens of largely independent groups. The same could be said of the Republican relationship to corporate backers and the religious right.

But the capacity of politicians to use rather than be used by their supporters should not be underestimated. Ideology-driven money seeks compatible candidates as much as the reverse. The parties may be expected to continue to find ways to benefit from Internet fund-raising and 527s, as they did with corporate and labor contributions and PACs in the past. And they continue to contain their more impassioned elements, as the failure of Howard Dean's 2004 campaign demonstrated. When they don't do so, as with Goldwater in 1964 and McGovern in 1972, the results are disastrous.

Despite their high profile in the 2004 election, the 527s and other ideologically driven political organizations are not necessarily the next big thing in American politics. George Soros in effect closed down ACT in the summer of 2005, an echo of Jerry Falwell's dissolution of the Moral Majority in 1989. True, the money-gathering potential of 527s is likely to lead to their reemergence in future election cycles (barring the unlikely event that they are brought within the confines of McCain-Feingold). But while 527s "seem to favor millionaires over workers, and ideologues over pragmatists," there are built-in limits to their influence.

The national and state parties remain what *The Economist* calls "the enabling machines through which men rise to power." The major success story of the 2004 election turned out to be not the 527s but Republican party strategist Karl Rove, who effectively used volunteers to bring out the party's evangelical base. However modern his tactics, Rove's strategy drew heavily on lessons taught by ur–professional party builder Mark Hanna of the 1890s. Rove and Bush, like Hanna and McKinley, crafted a political identity that embraced but also transcended the agenda of the GOP's more ideological components.

Senator Charles Schumer and Congressman Rahm Emanuel, who led the Democrats' 2006 congressional effort, showed comparable skill in fostering candidacies that appealed to the popular desire for change while reflecting the widespread centrism of the electorate. Rove, meanwhile, misjudged and mismanaged the Republican 2006 campaign. There is a notably short half-life to political prescience in the populist regime.

Instances abound of party adaptation. Take, for instance, the evolution of the presidential nominating convention. It was once the place where party barons struck deals and chose the candidate. Now it is three days of commercial programming, with free airtime, in which the nominee anointed by the primaries is introduced to the nation (most of which, alas, is not watching). This is not the media manipulating the pols but the reverse. And it is conceivable that the front-loaded, big-state primaries scheduled for early 2008 could leave several major, well-funded candidates in each party, thereby resurrecting that long-gone artifact of party potency, national conventions selecting the candidates.

Tensions over agendas and campaigns persist in each party. The uneasy relationship between the country-club, business-oriented, white-collar GOP and the religious right is a decades-old story, its end not in sight. A similar drama goes on in the Democratic party. In the past, moderate New Deal Democrats, white southerners, and the left fought for control. Now civil rights, environmentalist, pro-abortion, and anti–Iraq War advocacy groups are the Democrats' equivalent of the Republicans' Moral Majority–Christian Coalition evangelical wing, in uneasy alliance with the party's less clearly defined elements clustered in the South and the West.

As they have done since the 1790s, the parties seek to maximize the number of voters and the amount of money that their political stances can attract. It is incontestable that today they have more sharply defined, ideologically cohesive cores than in the past. A vituperative politics emerges naturally from that polarization. The prevailing view is that the current political scene is unusually bitter.

But in fact the linkage of populist politics and ideological confrontation dates from the 1930s. Republicans in the New Deal years engaged in unrestrained Roosevelt-bashing (which did them no great electoral good). The excesses of the McCarthy era and of some of the wilder tribes of Republicanland—most notably evangelical right-to-lifers and no-gun-control advocates—continued in that tradition. The Newt Gingrich and Tom DeLay slash-and-burn congressional leadership and the ill-fated congressional Republican venture that was the Clinton impeachment were high (or low) points in this politics *à outrance*.

Democrats (the assertion by supporters that they are the kinder, gentler party to the contrary notwithstanding) have been comparably drawn to a politics of defamation. The Robert Bork and Clarence Thomas Supreme Court nomination hearings had a tone reminiscent of the palmy days of McCarthy. George W. Bush has been the object of an assault by the media, advocacy groups, and celebrity and academic critics—subcultures no more given to moderation and nuance than their Republican counterparts—comparable to the GOP war against FDR.

While the volume of political vitriol has been turned way up, the disparity in size between the parties has been turned way down. Roughly speaking, the early-twenty-first-century electorate is a little more than a third Democratic, a quarter or so Republican, and 40 percent independent. In its ideological leanings, the electorate is a third or so conservative, a fifth or so liberal, and over 40 percent in between.

In recent decades the Republicans had a slight edge in the presidential, congressional, and state sweepstakes. But as the 2006 election showed, there was no reason to think that the Republican majorities were set in concrete. The popularity of candidates, party promises and performance, the evolution of issues, and social and economic change are as likely to matter at least as much as the inherent potency of each party's appeal. In 2006 both parties held on to their core support. The Democrats did markedly better with the moderate/independent cohort. And that was the ball game.

The largest challenge facing the parties today and tomorrow is not money, advocacy groups, or the media but the decline of intergenerational political loyalty. GOP consultant Roger Stone has observed: "[T]here really is no mass-based party anymore.... Each election cycle presents a new series of party alignments. Most voters [more accurately, most new or independent voters] align temporarily with one party or the other." In 1984, under-thirty voters were the most Republican age group. In 2004 they were the most Democratic.

At the same time the substantial increase in and equalization of party spending between 2000 and 2004 and the (not unrelated) rise in voting from 51 percent to 61 percent of those eligible has strengthened the parties' hold on the political process. Divided government, that ultimate measure of weak parties, appears to be declining. One-party states are on the rise. Voters preferred the presidential candidate of one party and the congressional candidate of the other in one hundred districts in 1996, eighty-six in 2000, and fifty-nine in 2004.

Attempts—often at cross-purposes—have been made to find a pattern in this contemporary electoral carpet. Some observers predict "a diverse but stable Republican coalition gradually eclipsing a diverse and stable Democratic coalition," or a major realignment in favor of the Republicans. Others foresee an "emerging Democratic majority." Both are conceivable. But so too is the view that neither party is likely to attain long-term dominance.

What does the current state of affairs portend for the American political future? Is it on the path to a deeply polarized, class- and culture-based politics, a European-style division between a party of order and a party of change? (To understate, neither party quite fits that bill today.) Does it pose a threat to democracy by putting a premium on sharp-edged and divisive issues, media and advocacy groups with a stake in ideological confrontation, and consequent polarization of the body politic?

Barring a major depression, a deepening quagmire in Iraq, or other comparable regime-changing events, the present configuration of party politics is likely to persist. In style and substance it well reflects the populist regime of which it is a part. The persisting closeness of the national divide (neither party has gotten more than 53 percent of the popular vote in a presidential election since 1984) is a strong incentive for party leaders to go with the present flow.

There are some signs that the major demographic trends in contemporary American life favor the Republicans over the Democrats. Measured by counties or states, the flow of population is into Republicanland (though how many of these are Democrats bringing their party affiliation with them is difficult to say). Between 1988 and 2004, twenty-seven electoral votes shifted from northern blue states to southern and western red states. Bush won ninety-seven of the nation's hundred fastest-growing counties in 2004. Conservatives solidly outstrip liberals when people are asked about their ideological leanings. And while non-church-going Americans have doubled in the past decade to about twenty-nine million people, evangelicals are twice as numerous, making up about a quarter of the electorate.

But the tendency of a plurality of voters to be in the ideological center—that eight-hundred-pound gorilla in the American electoral room—goes against the grain of a normal majority party. And over time it should temper the impulse of politicos to play to their ideological bases. As political scientist Morris Fiorina has observed, Americans are closely but not deeply divided. Substantial evidence suggests that most Americans have middle-of-the-road views on hot-button issues. The concept of a culture war was popularized by right-wing third-partyite Pat Buchanan in 1992: "There is a religious war going on in this country, a cultural war as critical to the kind of nation we shall be as the Cold War itself, for this war is for the soul of America." That may excite true believers on the right and left; it discomfits most everyone else.

When the balance between the parties is so close and a populist political culture puts a premium on heated rhetoric, playing with ideological fire will continue to have strong appeal in American electoral politics. But the long-term political utility of a take-no-prisoners politics is questionable. The larger history of American public life suggests that electoral failure is the inevitable consequence of a too-narrow ideological appeal.

The Republicans (like the Democrats until the 1960s) found electoral profit by putting on what a *Wall Street Journal* writer called "the new face of moderate, mixed-bag, political-mutt America." But Bush and his political guru Karl Rove chose to govern from the partisan right, presumably on the assumption that a normal Republican majority was in the offing. This turned out to be as premature as the recurring discovery by left-liberal pundits that a normal Democratic majority is about to emerge.

It is unlikely that this lesson will be indefinitely ignored by party regulars, Democratic as well as Republican, who have a larger stake in winning than in ideological purity. Stylistic borrowing went on between the Whigs and the Jacksonian Democrats in the 1830s and 1840s. It continued with the post–Civil War subsidence of the sectional schism (at the cost of black civil rights) and the post–Great Depression accord on much of the New Deal (at the cost of its social-democratic ambitions). The bottom line of American politics, that normal conditions push the parties toward a (never attained) equilibrium, remains valid, whatever the inclinations of the chattering classes. The most likely scenario is of strong and persistent ideological supporters at the core of each party but a larger independent or weakly partisan middling group acting as the decisive electoral element.

Both parties are well positioned to appeal to likely changes in the public agenda. The growth of imported products and outsourced jobs, along with a high-tech work world with increasing numbers of "free agent" workers, buttresses Democratic advocacy of higher tariffs, job protection, retraining, and government-run health care. Greater affluence feeds environmentalism, another Democratic standby. And if Iraq comes more to resemble Vietnam, that party is better situated than the Republicans to tap into a resurgent isolationism.

But the spread of stock and home ownership and the concerns of the young regarding social security play into the nascent Republican theme of an "ownership society" with personal health care and social security investment accounts. And it is likely that the GOP will remain the party best able to confront Islamic terrorism. A politics not of a normal majority but of substantial groups of voters (in particular, new ones) always in play appears to be the most likely scenario for the foreseeable future.

At various times over the past three-quarters of a century, one or another branch of government has threatened to upset the constitutional balance of power. But then equilibrium of a sort returned. The modern American state is like a balloon: ever expanding in size, but in its shape—the relation of the component parts to the whole—remaining the same.

Historian Arthur Schlesinger Jr. warned in 1973 against the "imperial presidency." But that office, in the wake of Vietnam and Watergate, had already lost much of the luster it acquired under FDR, Truman, Eisenhower, Kennedy, and Johnson. Its descent is caught in memorable presidential declarations: "The only thing we have to fear is fear itself" (FDR); "Ask not what your country can do for you, but what you can do for your country" (John F. Kennedy); "I am not a crook" (Richard Nixon); "I did not have sex with that woman" (Bill Clinton).

While Truman, Kennedy, and Johnson turned to (temporarily) effective reformulations of the New Deal–Democratic political tradition, Eisenhower and Reagan had considerable success in crafting presidential personae that went well beyond party identification. And the truncated presidencies of Johnson, Nixon, Carter, and George H. W. Bush demonstrated how vulnerable the presidency could be in a populist political regime.

But Clinton and George W. Bush showed that party-oriented presidencies are not necessarily a relic of the political past. "Bush," said one observer, "has reinvented the party machine for the world of far-flung suburbs and exurbs." At the same time they cavalierly dealt with venerable party traditions. Clinton challenged the Democrats' New Deal–Great Society domestic liberalism. After 9/11, Bush adopted a foreign policy stance that echoed the Wilson-FDR-Truman-Kennedy-Johnson mantra of active engagement in the cause of freedom. The presidency of the populist regime, like party politics, is an institution very much in flux.

The Imperial Congress (1988) focused on the branch of government that seemed to have adapted most successfully to the populist regime. Its members were ensconced in all-but-invulnerable seats: the old solid South gone national. A grand total of four incumbents lost in 2002, seven in 2004. Of the 435 2004 winners, only 37 got 55 percent or less of the vote.

But in 2006 six incumbent senators and twenty members of the House lost their seats, suggesting that invulnerability is not cast in stone. Nor have secure seats strengthened the capacity of Congress to do its legislative job. The relative autonomy of the members encourages corruption (a major issue in 2006) and an autarkic each-for-his-own approach to legislation. One measure: earmarks—the spending priorities of individual members attached to annual appropriations bills—increased from just over four thousand in 1994 to some fourteen thousand in 2004.

Another distinctive attribute of the modern Congress is the intensity of party polarization. In part this was a consequence of the decline of the old-time southern Democrats. And in part it was because the Republicans, so long out of power, had their knives out when they got back in. (Nor did the Democrats, so long *in* power, go gently into that good night of minority status.)

One consequence of a Congress defined more by ideology than by institutional identity is that effective leaders are an endangered species. The last member to try to assert himself in a large way was Newt Gingrich, whose rise and fall spectacularly demonstrated how difficult it was to try to turn the House Speakership into a policy-making alternative to the presidency. And there is always the danger that ideologically driven donors or advocacy groups will turn on an incumbent who takes a wrong policy turn.

Autonomy and polarization have made an imperial Congress as uncertain a prospect as an imperial presidency. But just as recent presidents have sought to flex the powers of their office by taking highly personal policy stances, so Congress has tried to buttress its place in the American scheme of government by asserting its prerogatives as against the White House. And the active political ambitions of the members (representatives who want to be senators, senators who want to be president) spurs them to be something more than autonomous political rent seekers.

The bureaucracy, like the presidency and Congress, grew in size and ambition during the 1960s and 1970s. (There is as yet no book titled *The Imperial Bureaucracy*. There should be.)

The Great Society added to the muscle of government through civil rights legislation, the War on Poverty, and new environmental laws. But the plethora of interests—Congress, the courts, the media, advocacy groups—that swirl around the new bureaucracy can make, and often has made, for administrative chaos. (The 16,342 lobbyists in Washington in 2000 fruitfully multiplied to more than 35,000 by 2005.) And a more ideological, populist politics ensured that a bureaucrat's lot was not a happy one.

The odd couple of the American suspicion of strong, unrepresentative government and the American desire for the goodies that government can provide are alive and well and living together. But there is reason to think that the regulatory state and aggrieved interests are tending toward the uneasy equilibrium characteristic of a mature regime. Neither a groundswell for deregulation nor a strong demand for tighter government control is in the offing.

And checks on bureaucratic autonomy are not necessarily bad. After all, government by administrative decree, like government by legal decree, raises profound issues of representation and democracy. The tong wars between the Department of State, CIA, and the Bush administration suggest that these tensions are an unavoidable aspect of the populist-bureaucratic regime.

An Imperial Judiciary: Fact or Myth? (1979) reflected growing concern over the place of the courts in the American polity. For half a century they have taken an active part in the formulation, implementation, and oversight of the most sensitive public policy issues: race, abortion, crime, education, marriage, life and death. Just as entrenched incumbency fostered the autonomy of congressmen, so has the life tenure of the judiciary fed its readiness to assert itself. The sense that judges are important players in the public policy game cuts across party or ideological lines.

The policy-making impulse of the Warren and Burger Courts continued in the Rehnquist Court, where federalism had a new (though underweight) birth of constitutional life. Some conservative legal theorists have been accused of wanting to restore the pre-1937, pre–New Deal Constitution. And some of their liberal-left counterparts propose that the Court create a new, more social democratic Constitution, recognizing every American's right to a job, an education, and a minimum income. Liberal judges favor, and conservative ones disfavor, the idea that American constitutional law should be more responsive to precedents from the European Union and other foreign legal entities.

It is a measure of the modern judiciary's importance that it, rather than the parties (as had been the case in 1876–77), resolved the 2000 presidential election dispute. Democratic contender Al Gore thought that public opinion "didn't matter..., because it's a legal question." Eight major judicial decisions and a number of minor ones, rather than inter-party negotiation, dominated the crisis and its resolution. The Florida Supreme Court rode roughshod over the secretary of state and the canvassing boards, relying in good populist fashion on the "people power" provision of the state constitution. And when the United States Supreme Court finally brought the crisis to a conclusion, it was governed more by a take-charge desire to end the agony (and for the Republican majority and the Democratic minority the desire to see their man chosen) than by closely reasoned constitutional law.

The combination of legal autonomy and ideological engagement continues to make for decisions that read like public policy papers: the spirit of *Brown v. Board of Education* applied to less elevated social ends. This may be seen in *Grutter v. Bollinger* (2003), which endorsed affirmative action by setting aside the strict scrutiny test for racial discrimination, and found sanction, inter alia, in the UN Convention on the Elimination of All Forms of Racial Discrimination. *Roper v. Simmons* (2005) voided the death penalty on grounds of age for a seventeen-year-old murderer with the psychobabbleish declaration that "the State cannot extinguish his life potential to attain a mature understanding of his own humanity." *Kelo v. New London* (2005) took eminent domain to a realm where no court had gone before.

So long as the courts are conspicuous players in the public policy arena, appointments will be a contentious feature of party politics. This is to the good: the issues at stake are, after all, matters of broad public concern. Courts that have become more populist, and more bureaucratic, inevitably and properly enter into the public life of the regime.

But the appointments of Chief Justice John Roberts and Associate Justice Samuel Alito, both publicly committed to constraining judicial activism, may mark a turning point. If the Court comes to be a less contentious public body, it is likely that judicial nominations, like presidential elections and the conduct of Congress, will get to be less deeply mired in ideological confrontation. Here as elsewhere, there is a built-in stake in more tempered conflict—especially if public opinion appears to favor judicial restraint.

Private law, like public law, has become deeply entrenched in the political process. Accident liability cases, once dismissed as disreputable legal bottom-fishing, have become a potent device for class-action suits against big business. By the beginning of the twenty-first century, yearly liability settlements added up to about $200 billion, 2 percent of GNP. Trial lawyers got about 20 percent of that total and began to invest in promising new litigation markets: those obesity generators, fast-food restaurants; that insidious ear damager, the mobile telephone; that prolific burn producer, hot water from the tap. As Finley Peter Dunne's

Mr. Dooley observed, what looks like a stone wall to the ordinary man is a triumphal arch to the lawyer.

Liability lawyers have become an important source of Democratic campaign funds, and reached a milestone of sorts when Senator John Edwards, one of their own, ran in 2004 as the party's vice presidential candidate. Republicans in response made tort liability "reform"—that is, its containment—an important cause. The Class Action Fairness Act of 2005 sought to reduce lawyers' ability to shop for complaisant county judges by shifting litigation to the federal courts. Strong bipartisan support for the bill reflected both its popularity with the public and the concern among Democrats that trial lawyers could prove to be bulls in the party china shop.

BACK TO THE FUTURE

Let us end this book where we began: with the relationship of the American polity to the world outside. And why not? This polyglot, ever-changing nation has had to define itself in terms of its place in an ever more intrusive international setting. Indeed, one of the things that distinguishes the now seventy-five-year-old populist-bureaucratic regime from its century-long party-democratic predecessor is the elevated place of foreign affairs within it, reminiscent of the early Republic.

There is a notable continuity to the American response to the challenges of fascism in the 1930s and 1940s, communism from the 1940s to the 1980s, and Islamic terrorism in our own time. There also has been recurring conflict, often labeled isolationist versus interventionist, over the character and degree of that response. The rapidity with which the Cold War followed on World War II temporarily repressed that division, so conspicuous in the years before Pearl Harbor. But Vietnam and the dissolution of the Soviet Union revitalized the conflict over whether to engage or disengage. It was evident in the reluctance of the Clinton administration to get involved in Bosnia and Kosovo. It resurfaced in the considerable Democratic opposition to the U.S.-led coalition that drove Saddam Hussein out of Kuwait, a UN-sanctioned reprise of the Korean "police action." And it lay behind the muted, sporadic reaction of the Reagan, George H. W. Bush, Clinton, and pre-9/11 George W. Bush administrations to the rise of Islamic terrorism.

Then came 9/11 and the Afghanistan and Iraq ventures. The American response to militant Islam has ignited the most contentious foreign policy dispute since Vietnam. It raises large questions regarding the conduct of foreign policy in the mature populist-bureaucratic regime, engaging Congress, the courts, and party politics. Will left-liberal hostility to American engagement, echoing the Vietnam period, escalate into a new isolationism? Will American setbacks in the war on terrorism generate a McCarthyite backlash from the right? Or will something like the general Cold War consensus prevail?

In the wake of 9/11, as in the wake of Pearl Harbor, there was an across-the-board upsurge of national unity. Dissent was initially limited to the overlapping enclaves of the left, the academy, and the literary world, as well as the isolationist right. But the costs and frustrations of the American response to Islamic terrorism turned Iraq into a touchstone issue, reminiscent of the division over the French Revolution and the England-France conflict in the 1790s and over the isolationist-interventionist clashes preceding American entry into World Wars I and II. As in the past, the gulf between the parties on social and cultural issues feeds into, and draws nourishment from, foreign policy differences. Thus Iraq, the globalization of manufacturing and the outsourcing of jobs, the phoenix-like rebirth of protectionism, and the rise of concern over immigration (primarily of illegals, but beyond that as well) interact with one another as cognate parts of a changing American relationship to the world outside. Its political consequences are still very much in flux.

When the Korean and Vietnam wars turned sour, disruptive political movements rose: the McCarthyite right in the 1950s, the anti-Vietnam left in the 1960s. Those overseas ventures had substantial political costs for the responsible party. In the 1950 congressional elections, the Democrats lost twenty-nine House and six Senate seats, and Eisenhower swept into the White House in 1952. In 1966, the Republicans gained forty-seven House and four Senate seats, and Nixon won the presidency in 1968. There are signs of a similar reaction to the Iraq War: in 2006, the Republicans lost thirty House and six Senate seats.

Will the Bush Doctrine's mixed political lineage of security through democracy ("[a] conservative Republican administration responded by embracing a liberal Democratic ideal—making the world safe for democracy—as a national security imperative") allow a Cold War–like consensus to hold? Political analyst Peter Beinart calls for a resurgent Cold War liberalism to take the lead in resisting militant Islam. But that appears to be a long-ago-and-far-away prospect. The populist regime appears to be highly receptive to a polarized rather than consensual politics of foreign policy. If Iraq turns into a Vietnam-scale catastrophe, there could be profound political consequences. The tendency to see the Republicans as the "power party" and the Democrats as the "peace party" could come to be the most compelling distinction between them, displacing the red-blue cultural division of the recent past.

But the tempering forces in American public life must not be ruled out. Predictions that there would be a reactionary turn in the wake of the Vietnam defeat were not fulfilled, unless (by a stretch) the rise of Ronald Reagan a decade later is proposed as evidence. And the war on terror has not brought any suppression of civil liberties comparable to the incarceration of Japanese Americans during World War II or the scapegoat hunting of McCarthyism. Americans' distaste for intrusive government is deeply embedded, and the political culture of the populist regime strengthens that attitude.

Still, the core question remains: Are we consigned to a polarized politics, resting on cultural, demographic, and ideological differences, that erodes the capacity of our public institutions to govern effectively? Or will less visible but more deeply embedded forces for compromise and equilibrium shape our political future, as they have shaped most (but not all) of our political past?

Substantial cultural, institutional, and financial resources feed polarization. But comparably powerful forces work to temper it. The bias in favor of coalition building that is built into the ground rules of the Constitution weighs against a deeply ideological politics. Most Americans cluster not in polarized camps but in attitudinal realms full of reservations and inconsistencies. Mainstream opinion on issues such as abortion, gun control, gay marriage, immigration, affirmative action, and foreign policy tends to be nuanced, conflicted, or indifferent.

Take, for example, the legality of gay marriage. Advocates of a constitutional amendment banning the practice have to deal with a large number of otherwise sympathetic Americans with strong reservations about using the Constitution to outlaw social behavior. Similarly, gay marriage advocates have many supporters who are uncomfortable with the notion that the issue should be decided by courts rather than legislatures. Comparable complexities swirl around other hot-button issues: abortion, affirmative action, immigration, terrorism. And as times change, public opinion on major issues keeps shifting. This ceaseless evolution ceaselessly erodes the settled policy positions of politicians, bureaucrats, policy wonks, and judges.

We are in the eighth decade of the populist-bureaucratic regime, not just somewhere between the election of 2004 and the election of 2008. This longer perspective suggests that we live in a regime endlessly engaged in conflict between the social force of cultural and economic change and the polity's need for institutional and political stability. Here the perspective of the historian comes into play: what, after all, is so new about this? We have seen that over the course of the history of American public life, powerful currents of continuity flow beneath the tempests of change. Large tensions—between democracy and power, union and liberty, security and individuality, community and independence—are as old as the Republic. They show no sign of being soon, or finally, resolved.

New wine—the wine of changing times and changing regimes— keeps pouring forth. But it flows into old bottles: a society in which abundance, space, openness, and mobility remain powerful realities; a Constitution that after a quarter of a millennium continues to set the rules of public life; venerable party and legal systems that respond to pressures for substantive change within the confines of a tough, dense carapace of institutional continuity; a state that for all its scope and power remains notably subject to popular, political, and media oversight. This is still a Republic worth keeping, with a polity capable of doing the job.

NOTES

The character of this book led me to an overview of the readings that I found particularly useful, rather than detailed footnotes. I have used the following journal abbreviations:

AJPS   *American Journal of Political Science*
APSR   *American Political Science Review*
CSSH   *Comparative Studies in Society and History*
JAH: *Journal of American History*
JER   *Journal of the Early Republic*
JEH   *Journal of Economic History*
JIH   *Journal of Interdisciplinary History*
JP   *Journal of Politics*
JPH   *Journal of Policy History*
JSH   *Journal of Southern History*
NEQ   *New England Quarterly*
NR   *New Republic*
NYT   *New York Times*
POQ   *Public Opinion Quarterly*
PSQ   *Political Science Quarterly*
SAPD   *Studies in American Political Development*
WMQ   *William and Mary Quarterly*
WSJ   *Wall Street Journal*

Introduction: The American Polity and Its Regimes

Other attempts to set American political development in a broader perspective than that of party systems include Joel Silbey, "Foundation Stones of Present Discontents: The American Political Nation, 1776–1945," in Byron E. Shafer et al., *Present Discontents:*

American Politics in the Very Late Twentieth Century (1997), 1–29, and Calvin Jillson, "Patterns and Personality in American National Politics," in Lawrence C. Dodd and Calvin Jillson, *The Dynamics of American Politics* (1994), 24–58.

On regimes, see Mark Tushnet, "The Supreme Court 1998 Term: Forward, " *Harvard Law Review*, 113 (1999), 31, and Bruce A. Ackerman, *We the People* (2 vols., 1991, 1998).

Chapter One: Old Ways and New

On deference, J. R. Pole, "Historians and the Problem of Early American Democracy," *AHR*, 67 (1962), 626–46, and John B. Kirby, "Early American Politics—The Search for Ideology: A Historiographical Analysis and Critique of the Concept of 'Deference,' " *JP*, 32 (1970), 808–38.

On early American politics, David D. Hall, *Saints and Revolutionaries: Essays on Early American History* (1984), Samuel P. Huntington, "Political Modernization: America vs. Europe," in his *Political Order in Changing Societies* (1968), Timothy H. Breen, *The Character of the Good Ruler: A Study of Puritan Political Ideas in New England, 1630–1730* (1970), Darrett E. Rutman, *Winthrop's Boston* (1972), Stephen Sanders Webb, *1676: The End of American Independence* (1984), Bernard Bailyn, "Politics and Social Structure in Virginia," in James Morton Smith, ed., *Seventeenth-Century America* (1959), Edmund S. Morgan, *American Slavery American Freedom: The Ordeal of Colonial Virginia* (1975), Charles S. Sydnor, *Gentleman Freeholders: Political Practices in Washington's Virginia* (1952).

On Bacon, Wilcomb E. Washburn, *The Governor and the Rebel: A History of Bacon's Rebellion* (1957); on Leisler, Jerome R. Reich, *Leisler's Rebellion* (1953), Charles H. McCormick, *Leisler's Rebellion* (1971), David W. Voorhees, "The 'Fervent Zeale' of Jacob Leisler," *WMQ*, 51 (1994), 447–72; on Salem, Peter C. Hoffer, *The Salem Witchcraft Trials: A Legal History* (1997); on Zenger, Stanley N. Katz, ed., *A Brief Narrative of the Case and Trial of John Peter Zenger* (1963), William Z. Putnam, *John Peter Zenger and the Fundamental Freedom* (1997).

On law, "Symposium on Law and Society in Early America," *William and Mary Quarterly*, 3d ser., 50 (1993), John Murrin, "The Legal Transformation: The Bench and Bar of Eighteenth-Century Massachusetts," in Stanley Katz, ed., *Colonial America* (1971), 415–49, John P. Reid, "Lawless Law and Lawful Mobs," *NYU Law Review*, 23 (1977), 32–40, Pauline Maier, "Popular Uprisings and Civil Authority in Eighteenth-Century America," *WMQ*, 27 (1970), 3–35.

On the empire, David Underdown, *A Freeborn People: Politics and the Nation in Seventeenth Century England* (1996), John Brewer, *The Sinews of Power: War, Money, and the English State 1688–1783* (1989), Kathleen Wilson, *The Sense of the People: Politics, Culture, and Imperialism in England, 1715–1815* (1995).

On British politics, J. H. Plumb, *The Origins of Political Stability, England, 1675–1725* (1967), John Brewer, *Party Ideology and Popular Politics at the Accession of George III* (1976), J. C. D. Clark, *English Society 1688–1832: Ideology, Social Structure, and Political Practice During the Ancien Regime* (1985).

On eighteenth-century American politics, Patricia U. Bonomi, *A Factious People: Politics and Society in Colonial New York* (1971), Gary B. Nash, *Quakers and Politics in Pennsylvania, 1681–1726* (1968), Robert J. Dinkin, *Voting in Provincial America* (1977) and *Voting in Revolutionary America* (1982), Alan Tully, *Forming American Politics: Ideas, Interests, and Institutions in Colonial New York and Pennsylvania* (1994), Jon Butler, *Becoming America: The Revolution Before 1776* (2000), Gordon S. Wood, "Conspiracy and the Paranoid Style: Causality and Deceit in the Eighteenth Century," *WMQ*, 39 (1982), 401–41.

Chapter Two: The Republican Revolution

On counterfactuals, J. C. D. Clark, *Our Shadowed Present* (2004), ch. 5. On comparisons, Crane Brinton, *The Anatomy of Revolution* (1952), Susan Dunn, *Sister Revolutions* (1999), J. G. A. Pocock, ed., *Three British Revolutions: 1641, 1688, 1776* (1980), Edmund S. Morgan, *Inventing the People: The Rise of Popular Sovereignty in England and America* (1988).

On the English revolution and Cromwell, Sean Kelsey, *Inventing a Republic: The Political Culture of the English Commonwealth 1649–53* (1997), Maurice Ashley, *The Greatness of Oliver Cromwell* (1957), Barry Coward, *Oliver Cromwell* (1991), Christopher Hill, *God's Englishman: Oliver Cromwell and the English Revolution* (1970).

On the French revolution and Napoleon, Robert B. Holtman, *The Napoleonic Revolution* (1967), John Thompson, *Napoleon Bonaparte: His Rise and Fall* (1952), Mona Onouf, *Festivals and the French Revolution* (1988), Isser Woloch, *Napoleon and His Collaborators: The Making of a Dictatorship* (2001). More favorably disposed is Steven Englund, *Napoleon: A Political Life* (2004).

On the American revolution and Washington, Richard Ellis, *His Excellency: George Washington* (2005), Richard Brookhiser, *Founding Father: Rediscovering George Washington* (1996), Barry Schwartz, *George Washington: The Making of an American Symbol* (1987), Paul K. Longmore, *The Invention of George Washington* (1988), Paul A. Varg, "The Advent of Nationalism, 1758–1776," *American Quarterly*, 16 (1964), 169–81.

On the Declaration, Pauline Maier, *American Scripture* (1997). See also Bernard Bailyn, *The Ideological Origins of the American Revolution* (1966) and *The Origins of American Politics* (1968), Gordon Wood, *The Radicalism of the American Revolution* (1992). Gary Nash, *The Unknown American Revolution* (2005), is a class-based interpretation, dismantled by Gordon Wood in *NR*, June 6 and 13, 2005), 34–42.

On the political consequences of the Revolution, Jack N. Rakove, *The Beginnings of National Politics: An Interpretive History of the Continental Congress* (1979), James H. Henderson, "Constitutionalists and Republicans in the Continental Congress, 1778–1786," *PH*, 36 (1969), 119–44, Oscar and Mary Handlin, " 'Radicals' and 'Conservatives' in Massachusetts After Independence," *NEQ*, 17 (1944), 343–55.

On religion, Catherine L. Albanese, *Sons of the Fathers: The Civil Religion of the American Revolution* (1976), Ruth H. Bloch, *Visionary Republic: Millennial Themes in American Thought, 1756–1800* (1985), J. C. D. Clark, *The Language of Liberty 1660–1832* (1994).

On the Constitution, Gordon Wood, *The Creation of the American Republic 1776–1787* (1969), Jack N. Rakove, *Original Meanings: Politics and Ideas in the Making of the Constitution* (1996), Richard Beeman et al, eds., *Beyond Confederation: Origins of the Constitution and American National Identity* (1987). On slavery, Don E. Fehrenbacher, *The Slaveholding Republic* (2001). See also John P. Roche, "The Founding Fathers: A Reform Caucus in Action," *APSR*, 55 (1961), 799–816, William E. Nelson, "Reason and Compromise in the Establishment of the Federal Constitution, 1787–1801," *WMQ*, 44 (1987), Robert A. McGuire and Robert L. Ohsfeldt, "Economic Interests and the American Constitution: A Quantitative Rehabilitation of Charles A. Beard," *JEH*, 44 (1984), 508–29.

On the cosmopolitan-local distinction, Christopher Wolfe, "On Understanding the Constitutional Convention of 1787," *JP*, 39 (1977), 97–118, William A. Benton, "Pennsylvania Revolutionary Officers and the Federal Constitution," *PH*, 31 (1964), 419–35. On the generational gulf, Stanley Elkins and Eric McKitrick, "The Founding Fathers: Young Men of the Revolution," *PSQ*, 76 (1961), 181–216. See also James H. Hutson, "Country, Court, and Constitution: Antifederalism and the Historians," *WMQ*, 38 (1981), 337–68.

Chapter Three: From Factions to Parties

On Republicanism, Daniel T. Rodgers, "Republicanism: The Career of a Concept," *JAH*, 79 (1992), 11–38. On the contrast with England, Charles Tilly, *Popular Contention: Great Britain, 1758–1834* (1995). On the early Republic, Stanley Elkins and Eric McKitrick, *The Age of Federalism* (1993), Joseph Charles, *The Origins of the American Party System* (1956), William N. Chambers, *Political Parties in a New Nation* (1963), Seymour M. Lipset, *The First New Nation* (1963), John F. Hoadley, *Origins of American Political Parties 1789–1803* (1986).

See also Ralph Ketchum, *Presidents Above Party: The First American Presidency, 1789–1829* (1984), Carl F. Prince, *The Federalists and the Origins of the U.S. Civil Service* (1977), Rudolph M. Bell, *Party and Faction in American Politics: The House of Representatives, 1789–1801* (1974), Mary P. Ryan, "Party Formation in the United States Congress, 1789 to 1796: A Quantitative Analysis," *WMQ*, 28 (1971), 523–92, H. James Henderson, "Quantitative Approaches to Party Formation in the United States Congress: A Comment," *WMQ*, 30 (1973), 307–23, John H. Aldrich and Ruth W. Grant, "The Antifederalists, the First Congress, and the First Parties," *JP*, 55 (1993), 295–326, John H. Aldrich, Calvin C. Jillson, and Richard K. Wilson, "Why Congress? What the Failure of the Confederation Congress and the Survival of the Federal Congress Tell Us About the New Institutionalism," in David Brady and Matthew McCubbins, eds., *Party, Process, and Political Change* (2002), Sarah A. Binder, "Partisanship and Procedural Choice: Institutional Change in the Early Congress, 1789–1823," *JP*, 57 (1995), 1093–118, Norman K. Risjord, "Partisanship and Power: House Committees and the Powers of the Speaker, 1789–1801," *WMQ*, 49 (1992), 628–51.

On foreign affairs, Felix Gilbert, *To the Farewell Address* (1961); Matthew Schoenbachler, "Republicanism in the Age of Democratic Revolution: The Democratic-Republican Societies of the 1790s," *JER*, 18 (1998), 237–61, Michael Durey, *Transatlantic*

Radicals and the Early American Republic (1997), Robert Kagan, *Dangerous Nation* (2006). On rebellions, Jacob E. Cooke, "The Whiskey Rebellion: A Re-Evaluation," *PH*, 30 (1963), 316–46, Peter Levine, "The Fries Rebellion: Social Violence and the Politics of the New Nation," *PH*, 40 (1973), 241–58.

On political culture, Robert L. Kelley, *The Cultural Pattern in American Politics: The First Century* (1979), Joanne Freeman, *Affairs of Honor: National Politics in the New Republic* (2001), Ralph Formisano, "Deferential-Participant Politics: The Early Republic's Political Culture, 1789–1840," *APSR*, 68 (1974), 473–87, David Waldstreicher, *In the Midst of Perpetual Fetes: The Making of American Nationalism, 1776–1820* (1997), Simon P. Newman, *Parades and the Politics of the Street: Festive Culture in the Early American Republic* (1997), Peter S. Onuf, *Jefferson's Empire: The Language of American Nationhood* (2000), Martin S. Pernick, "Politics, Parties, and Pestilence: Epidemic Yellow Fever in Philadelphia and the Rise of the First Party System," *WMQ*, 29 (1972), 559–86, Richard John, *Spreading the News: The American Postal System from Franklin to Morse* (1995), Jeffrey L. Pasley et al., eds., *Beyond the Founders: New Approaches to the Political History of the Early American Republic* (2004).

On the Jeffersonian era, Noble E. Cunningham, *The Jeffersonian Republicans in Power* (1963) and *The Process of Government Under Jefferson* (1978), Lance Banning, *The Jeffersonian Persuasion: Evolution of a Party Ideology* (1978), Carl E. Prince, "The Passing of the Aristocracy: Jefferson's Removal of the Federalists, 1801–1805," *JAH*, 57 (1970), 563–75.

On the War of 1812 and after, Roger H. Brown, *The Republic in Peril: 1812* (1964), Steven Watts, *The Republic Reborn: War and the Making of Liberal America, 1790–1820* (1987), Rudolph M. Bell, "Mr. Madison's War and Long-Term Congressional Voting Behavior," *WMQ*, 36 (1979), 373–95, Ronald L. Hatzenbuehler, "Party Unity and the Decision for War in the House of Representatives, 1812," *WMQ*, 29 (1972), 367–90, Jeffrey A. Jenkins and Charles H. Stewart III, "Order from Chaos: The Transformation of the Committee System in the House, 1816–1822," in Brady and McCubbins, eds., *Parties, Process, and Political Change*.

On the decline of the Federalists, David H. Fischer, *The Revolution of American Conservatism* (1965), Doron Ben-Atar and Barbara B. Oberg, eds., *Federalists Reconsidered* (1998), Donald J. Ratcliffe, *Party Spirit in a Frontier Republic: Democratic Politics in Ohio, 1793–1821* (1998).

Part II: The Party-Democratic Regime: The Democratic Polity

Joel Silbey, *The American Political Nation, 1838–1893* (1991), Charles Sellers, *The Market Revolution: Jacksonian America 1815–1846* (1991) (challenged by William Gienapp, "The Myth of Class in Jacksonian America," *JPH*, 6 (1994), 232–59). See also Richard E. Ellis, "The Market Revolution and the Transformation of American Politics, 1801–1837," in Melvyn Stokes and Stephen Conway, eds., *The Market Revolution in America* (1996), 149–76.

On nationalism, Wilbur Zelinsky, *Nation into State: The Shifting Symbolic Foundations of American Nationalism* (1988), Linda Colley, *Britons: Forging the Nation 1707–1837* (1992). David A. Bell, *The Cult of the Nation in France: Inventing Nationalism,*

1680–1800 (2001), Jonathan Clark, *Our Shadowed Present* (2003). On English politics, Michael Bentley, *Politics Without Democracy* (2nd ed., 1996), David C. Moore, *The Politics of Deference: A Study of the Mid-Nineteenth Century English Political System* (1976).

Chapter Four: The Culture of Democratic Party Politics

On scant voting, James H. Broussard, "Party and Partisanship in American Legislatures: The South Atlantic States, 1800–1812," *JSH*, 43 (1977), 39–58. On governmental change, Herman James, *Local Government in the United States* (1926).

On language, H. L. Mencken, *The American Language* (1923), William Safire, *Safire's New Political Dictionary* (1993), Thomas Gustafson, *Representative Words: Politics, Literature, and the American Language, 1776–1865* (1992), David Simpson, *The Politics of American English, 1776–1850* (1986), Andrew W. Robertson, *The Language of Democracy* (1995), Daniel T. Rodgers, *Contested Truths* (1987). On Bingham's paintings, Jean Harvey Baker, "Politics, Paradigms, and Public Culture," *JAH*, 84 (1997), 894–99.

On corruption, Morton Keller, "Corruption in America: Continuity and Change," in Abraham S. Eisenstadt et al., *Before Watergate: Problems of Corruption in American Society* (1978), 9–19.

On Van Buren and Weed, Robert V. Remini, *Martin Van Buren and the Making of the Democratic Party* (1959), Donald B. Cole, *Martin Van Buren and the American Political System* (1984), Glyndon van Deusen, *Thurlow Weed* (1947).

On the Anti-Masons, Mark Voss-Hubbard, "The 'Third Party Tradition' Reconsidered: Third Parties and American Political Life, 1830–1900," *JAH*, 86 (1999), 121–50, William P. Vaughn, *The Antimasonic Party in the United States, 1826–1843* (1983), Kathleen Smith Kutolowski, "Antimasonry Reexamined: Social Bases of the Grass-Roots Party," *JAH*, 71 (1984), 269–93.

On the limits of party appeal, Glenn C. Alschuler and Stuart M. Blumin, *Rude Republic: Americans and Their Politics in the Nineteenth Century* (2000), Richard F. Bensel, *The American Ballot Box in the Mid-Nineteenth Century* (2004).

On post-1815 politics, Joel H. Sibley, "The Incomplete World of American Politics, 1815–1829: Presidents, Parties, and Politics in the 'Era of Good Feelings,'" *Congress and the Presidency*, 11 (1984), 1–17, Daniel P. Jordan, *Political Leadership in Jefferson's Virginia* (1983), Paul C. Nagel, *John Quincy Adams: A Public Life, A Private Life* (1997). Richard Hofstadter, *The Idea of a Party System: The Rise of Legitimate Opposition in the United States, 1780–1840* (1969) and Michael F. Holt, "The Primacy of Party Reasserted," *JAH*, 86 (1999), 151–57, make the case for a new party culture; Ronald P. Formisano, "The 'Party Period' Revisited," *JAH*, 86 (1999), 93–120, demurs.

On electoral politics, M. J. Heale, *The Presidential Quest: Candidates and Images in American Political Culture, 1787–1852* (1982); on 1824 polls, James W. Tankard Jr., "Public Opinion Polling by Newspapers in the Presidential Election Campaign of 1824," *Journalism Quarterly*, 49 (1972), 361–65, and Tom W. Smith, "First Straw? A Study of the Origin of Election Polls," *POQ*, 54 (1990), 21–36.

On Jackson and the Democrats, Robert Remini, *Andrew Jackson and the Course of American Freedom, 1822–1832* (1981) and *Andrew Jackson and the Course of American*

Democracy, 1833–1845 (1984). For interpretations, Arthur M. Schlesinger Jr., *The Age of Jackson* (1945), Marvin Meyers, *The Jacksonian Persuasion* (1957), Harry L. Watson, *Liberty and Power: The Politics of Jacksonian America* (1990), Daniel Feller, *The Jacksonian Promise: America, 1815–1840* (1995). See also David Brown, "Jeffersonian Ideology and the Second Party System," *Historian*, 62 (19999), 17–30, Norma Basch, "Marriage, Morals, and Politics in the Election of 1828," *JAH*, 80 (1993), 890–918, Major L. Wilson, "The 'Country' Versus the 'Court': A Republican Consensus and Party Debate in the Bank War," *JER*, 15 (1995), 619–47, David F. Ericson, "The Nullification Crisis, American Republicanism, and the Force Bill Debate," *JSH*, 61 (1995), 249–70, Merrill Peterson, *The Great Triumvirate* (1987), Lawrence F. Kohl, *The Politics of Individualism: Parties and the American Character in the Jacksonian Era* (1989).

On the Whigs, Lynn L. Marshall, "The Strange Stillbirth of the Whig Party," *AHR*, 72 (1967), 445–68, Daniel W. Howe, *The Political Culture of the American Whigs* (1979), Thomas Brown, *Politics and Statesmanship: Essays on the American Whig Party* (1985), Michael F. Holt, *The Rise and Fall of the American Whig Party* (1999). See also Herbert Eshkowitz and William G. Shade, "Consensus or Conflict? Political Behavior in the State Legislatures During the Jacksonian Era," *JAH*, 58 (1971), 592–621, Ronald P. Formisano, "The New Political History and the Election of 1840," *JIH*, 23 (1993), 661–82.

Chapter Five: Governing a Democratic Polity

Quotation from William E. Nelson, *The Roots of American Bureaucracy, 1830–1900* (1982); Richard B. Latner, "The Kitchen Cabinet and Andrew Jackson's Advisory System," *JAH*, 65 (1978), 367–88; Leonard White, *The Jacksonians: A Study in Administrative History, 1829–1861* (1954); Richard R. John, "Governmental Institutions as Agents of Change: Rethinking American Political Development in the Early Republic, 1787–1835," *SAPD*, 11 (1997), 347–80, John, ed., *Ruling Passions: Political Economy in Nineteenth-Century America* (2007).

On Congress, David Mayhew, *The Electoral Connection* (1974) elevates career ambitions over party dictates. Elaine K. Swift, "The Electoral Connection Meets the Past: Lessons from Congressional History, 1789–1899," *PSQ*, 102 (1987), 625–45, differs. See also William T. Bianco et al., "The Electoral Connection in the Salary Grab: The Case of the Compensation Act of 1816," *AJPS*, 40 (1996), 145–71.

On government, James S. Young, *The Washington Community, 1800–1828* (1966), Matthew A. Crenson, *The Federal Machine: Beginnings of Bureaucracy in Jacksonian America* (1975), Richard R. John, *Spreading the News: The American Postal System from Franklin to Morse* (1995), Lois Craig et al., *The Federal Presence: Architecture, Politics, and Symbols in United States Government Building* (1977).

On law, James Willard Hurst, *Law and the Conditions of Freedom in Nineteenth-Century America* (1956); William E. Nelson, *The Americanization of the Common Law* (1994), G. Edward White, *The Marshall Court and Cultural Change, 1815–35* (1988). Morton J. Horwitz, *The Transformation of American Law, 1780–1860* (1977) argues that judges sought to preserve vested interests.

On constitutional law, William E. Nelson, "Changing Conceptions of Judicial Review: The Evolution of Constitutional Theory in the States, 1790–1860," *University* of *Pennsylvania Law Review*, 120 (1972), 1166–85, R. Kent Newmyer, *John Marshall and the Heroic Age of the Supreme Court* (2001), William E. Nelson, *Marbury v. Madison: The Origins and Legacy of Judicial Review* (2000), Bruce A. Ackerman, *The Failure of the Founding Fathers* (2005), Stanley Kutler, *Privilege and Creative Destruction: The Charles River Bridge Case* (1971), Leonard Levy, *The Law of the Commonwealth and Chief Justice Shaw* (1957), William J. Novak, *The People's Welfare: Law and Regulation in Nineteenth-Century America* (1996), Stanley Kutler, "John Bannister Gibson: Judicial Restraint and the 'Positive State,'" *Journal of Public Law*, 14 (1965), 181–97.

On common law, Lawrence M. Friedman, *A History of American Law* (1985) and *Contract Law in America* (1965), Grant Gilmore, *The Ages of American Law* (1977).

On public policy, Richard L. McCormick, "The Party Period and Public Policy: An Exploratory Hypothesis," *JAH*, 66 (1979), 279–98; James L. Huston, "Virtue Besieged: Virtue, Equality, and the General Welfare in the Tariff Debates of the 1820s," *JER*, 14 (1994), 523–47.

On banking, Bray Hammond, *Banks and Politics in America, from the Revolution to the Civil War* (1957), William G. Shade, *Banks or No Banks: The Money Issue in Western Politics 1832–1865* (1972), James R. Sharp, *The Jacksonians Versus the Banks* (1970). On internal improvements, John L. Larson, *Internal Improvement: National Public Works and the Promise of Popular Government in the Early United States* (2001), Carter Goodrich, ed., *Canals and American Economic Development* (1961).

On social policy, Alice F. Tyler, *Freedom's Ferment: Phases of American Social History to 1860* (1962), Charles Sellers, *The Market Revolution in America, 1815–1846* (1991) ("Liberalism" quote on p. 275), Melvin Stokes and Stephen Conway, eds., *The Market Revolution in America: Social, Political, and Religious Expressions, 1800–1880* (1996), Ian R. Tyrell, *Sobering Up: From Temperance to Prohibition in Antebellum America, 1800–1860* (1979), Ray Allen Billington, *The Protestant Crusade 1800–1860: A Study of the Origins of American Nativism* (1938), Mary P. Ryan, *Women in Public: Between Banners and Ballots, 1825–1880* (1990).

On the opposition to slavery, David Donald, "Toward a Reconsideration of Abolitionists," in Donald, *Lincoln Reconsidered* (1961), 19–36, Seymour Drescher, *Capitalism and Antislavery: British Mobilization in Comparative Perspective* (1987), Richard S. Newman, *The Transformation of American Abolitionism: Fighting Slavery in the Early Republic* (2002).

Chapter Six: Crisis

David Donald, "An Excess of Democracy: The American Civil War and the Social Process," in his *Lincoln Reconsidered* (1961), William G. Shade, "Revolutions May Go Backwards: The American Civil War and the Problem of Political Development," *Social Science Quarterly*, 55 (1974–75), 753–67, Arthur Bestor, "The American Civil War as a Constitutional Crisis," *AHR*, 69 (1964), 327–52, and Philip S. Paludan, "The American Civil War Considered as a Crisis in Law and Order," *AHR*, 77 (1971), 1013–34. See in general Michael F. Holt, *The Political Crisis of the 1850s* (1978), Allan Nevins, *Ordeal of the Union* (1947).

On the presidency and Congress, M. J. Heale, *The Presidential Quest: Candidates and Images in American Political Culture, 1787–1852* (1982), Raymond A. Mohl, "Presidential Views of National Power, 1837–1861," *Mid-America*, 52 (1970), 177–89, Randall Strahan, "Leadership and Institutional Change in the Nineteenth Century House" and Nolan McCarthy et al., "Congress and the Territorial Expansion of the United States," in David Brady and Matthew McCubbins, eds., *Party, Process, and Political Change in Congress* (2002), Jeffrey R. Hummel and Barry Weingast, "The Fugitive Slave Act of 1850: An Instrumental Interpretation," in David Brady and Matthew McCubbins, eds., *Party, Process, and Political Change in Congress: Further New Perspectives on the History of Congress* (2007).

On the states, L. Ray Gunn, *The Decline of Authority: Public Economic Policy and Political Development in New York, 1800–1860* (1988). On cities, Robert A. McCaughey, "Boston in the 1820s," *PSQ*, 88 (1973), 191–213, Hendrik Hartog, *Public Property and Private Power* (1983), M. J. Heale, "From City Fathers to Social Critics: Humanitarianism and Government in New York, 1790–1860," *JAH*, 63 (1976), 21–41, Amy Bridges, *A City in the Republic: Antebellum New York and the Origins of Machine Politics* (1984), Edward Pessen, "Who Governed the Nation's Cities in the 'Era of the Common Man?'" *PSQ*, 87 (1972), 591–614.

On law and slavery, Robert M. Cover, *Justice Accused: Antislavery and the Judicial Process* (1975), Don Fehrenbacher, *Slavery, Law, and Politics: The Dred Scott Case in Historical Perspective* (1981).

On parties and politics, Joel Silbey, *The Partisan Imperative: The Dynamics of American Politics Before the Civil War* (1985), Michael F. Holt, *Political Parties and American Political Development from the Age of Jackson to the Age of Lincoln* (1992), Mark W. Summers, *The Plundering Generation: Corruption and the Crisis of the Union, 1849–1861* (1987).

On the Democrats, Jean Baker, *Affairs of Party: The Political Culture of the Northern Democrats in the Mid-Nineteenth Century* (1983); on the Whigs, Michael F. Holt, *The Rise and Fall of the American Whig Party* (1999); on the Know-Nothings, Michael F. Holt, "The Politics of Impatience: The Origins of Know-Nothingism," *JAH*, 60 (1973), 209–21, Mark Voss-Hubbard, *Beyond Party: Cultures of Antipartisanship in Northern Politics Before the Civil War* (2002), Tyler G. Anbinder, *Nativism and Slavery: The Northern Know-Nothings and the Politics of the 1850s* (2002).

On the Republicans, William E. Gienapp, *The Origins of the Republican Party 1852–1856* (1987), Eric Foner, *Free Soil, Free Labor, Free Men: The Ideology of the Republican Party Before the Civil War* (1976). The characterization of Lincoln is by David Waldstreicher in Byron E. Shafer and Anthony J. Badger, eds., *Contesting Democracy* (2001), 55.

On the South, Charles S. Sydnor, *The Development of Southern Sectionalism, 1819–1848* (1948), Avery Craven, *The Growth of Southern Nationalism 1848–1861* (1953), David Donald, "The Pro-Slavery Argument Reconsidered," *JSH*, 37 (1971), 3–18. On the North, Susan-Mary Grant, *North over South: Northern Nationalism and American Identity in the Antebellum Era* (2000), Richard Ellis and Aaron Wildavsky, "A Cultural Analysis of the Abolitionists in the Coming of the Civil War," *CSSH*, 32 (1990), 89–116.

On the Civil War, Morton Keller, *Affairs of State* (1977), ch. 1, Philip Paludan, *A People's Contest: The Union and the Civil War 1861–1865* (1989), George Fredrickson, *The Inner Civil War: Northern Intellectuals and the Crisis of the Union* (1965).

On the Confederacy, George C. Rable, *The Confederate Republic* (1994), Emery M. Thomas, *The Confederate Nation 1861–1865* (1979) and *The Confederacy as a Revolutionary Experience* (1971), Jeffrey A. Jenkins, "Examining the Binding Effects of Party: A Comparative Analysis of Roll-Call Voting in the U.S. and Confederate Houses," *AJPS*, 43 (1999), 1144–65, Jenkins, "Why No Parties? Investigating the Disappearance of Democratic-Whig Divisions in the Confederacy," *SAPD*, 13 (1999), 245–62, and Roger D. Hardaway, "The Confederate Constitution: A Legal and Historical Examination," *Alabama Historical Quarterly*, 44 (1982), 18–31.

On Reconstruction, Keller, *Affairs of State*, part one. On constitutional change, Bruce A. Ackerman, *We the People* (1991). See also Richard F. Bensel, *Yankee Leviathan: The Origins of Central State Authority in America, 1859–1877* (1990).

Part III: The Party-Democratic Regime: The Industrial Polity

On Van Buren, Joel Silbey, " 'To One or Another of These Parties Every Man Belongs': The American Political Experience from Andrew Jackson to the Civil War," in Byron E. Shafer and Anthony J. Badger, eds., *Contesting Democracy* (2000), 86. Much of what follows is based on Morton Keller, *Affairs of State: Public Life in Late Nineteenth-Century America* (1977), part two. See also Silbey, *The American Political Nation, 1838–1893* (1991), Martin Shefter, *Political Parties in the State* (1994) and, for a more economic materialist interpretation, Richard Bensel, *The Political Economy of American Industrialization, 1877–1900* (2000).

Chapter Seven: The Age of the Politicos

Bryce on parties in *The American Commonwealth* (3rd ed., 1895), II:28–29. See also Morton Keller, "The Liberal Commonwealthman: James Bryce and *The American Commonwealth*," *Wilson Quarterly* (1985), 86–95. On late-nineteenth-century European politics, see Norman Stone, *Europe Transformed 1878–1919* (1983), Theodore Zeldin, *France, 1848–1945: Politics and Anger* (1984), Richard J. Evans, *German History 1867–1915* (1981). On Britain, Robert Kelley, *The Transatlantic Persuasion: The Liberal-Democratic Mind in the Age of Gladstone* (1969), Michael Bentley, *Politics Without Democracy* (2nd ed., 1996), Gary Cox, *The Efficient Secret: The Cabinet and the Development of Political Parties in Victorian England* (1987), Roy Jenkins, *Gladstone* (1995).

Quotes on American political culture in Keller, *Affairs of State*, ch. 7.See also Keller, *The Art and Politics of Thomas Nast* (1968), Mark W. Summers, *The Press Gang: Newspapers and Politics, 1865–1878* (1994). On the 1877 Compromise, Allan Peskin, "Was There a Compromise of 1877?" *JAH*, 60 (1973), 63–75, Michael Les Benedict, "The Southern Democrats in the Crisis of 1876–1877: A Reconsideration of Reunion and Reaction," *JSH*, 46 (1980), 489–524.

On voting, Paul Kleppner, *The Third Electoral System, 1831–1892* (1979), quotation on 144, Walter Dean Burnham, "Those High Nineteenth-Century American Voting Turnouts: Fact or Fiction?" *JIH*, 16 (1986), 613–44, Keller, *Affairs of State*, ch. 14.

On fraud and corruption, James C. Scott, "Corruption, Machine Politics, and Political Change," *APSR*, 63 (1969), 1142–58, Mark W. Summers, *The Era of Good Stealings* (1993), Peter H. Argersinger, "New Perspectives on Election Fraud: The Gilded Age," *PSQ*, 100 (1985–86), 669–87, John F. Reynolds, "A Symbiotic Relationship: Vote Fraud and Electoral Reform in the Gilded Age," *Social Science History*, 17 (1993), 227–51.

On the Republicans, Charles W. Calhoun, "Political Economy in the Gilded Age: The Republican Party's Industrial Policy," *JPH*, 8 (1996), 291–309, James L. Huston, "A Political Response to Industrialism: The Republican Embrace of Protectionist Labor Doctrines," *JAH*, 70 (1983), 35–57, Robert S. Salisbury, "The Republican Party and Positive Government: 1860–1890," *Mid-America*, 68 (1986), 17–34.

On assassinations, Charles Rosenberg, *The Assassin Guiteau* (1968), James W. Clarke, *American Assassins* (1982).

On the Democrats, Kelley, *Transatlantic Persuasion*, Michael Perman, *The Road to Redemption: Southern Politics, 1869–1879* (1984), Jerome Mushkat, *The Reconstruction of the New York Democracy, 1861–1974* (1981), Horace S. Merrill, *Bourbon Democracy of the Middle West, 1865–1896* (1953), Seymour J. Mandelbaum, *Boss Tweed's New York* (1965), Keller, *Affairs of State*, ch. 14.

Chapter Eight: A State of Parties and Courts

Much of this discussion is based on Morton Keller, *Affairs of State*, part two. See also Stephen Skowronek, *Building a New American State: The Expansion of National Administrative Capacities, 1877–1920* (1982), Matthew G. Hanna, *Governmentality and the Mastery of Territory in Nineteenth-Century America* (2000), Daniel P. Carpenter, *The Forging of Bureaucratic Autonomy: Reputations, Networks, and Policy Innovation in Executive Agencies, 1862–1928* (2001), Robert M. Goldman, "The 'Weakened Spring of Government' and the Executive Branch: The Department of Justice in the Late 19th Century," *Congress and the Presidency*, 11 (1984), 165–78, Robert Harrison, "The 'Weakened Spring of Government' Revisited: The Growth of Federal Power in the Late Nineteenth Century," in Rhondi Jeffrey-Jones and Bruce Collins, eds., *The Growth of Federal Power in American History* (1983), 62–75.

On comparative perspective, Bernard S. Silberman, *Cages of Reason: The Rise of the National State in France, Japan, the United States, and Great Britain* (1993), Keith Thomas, "The United Kingdom," in Raymond Grew, ed., *Crises of Political Development in Europe and the United States* (1978), Michael Bentley, *Politics Without Democracy 1815–1914* (2nd ed., 1996), xiii.

On the president and Congress, Keller, *Affairs of State*, 297–307, Margaret S. Thompson, *The 'Spider Web': Congress and Lobbying in the Age of Grant* (1986), Nelson W. Polsby, "The Institutionalization of the House of Representatives," *APSR*, 62 (1968), 144–68, David J. Rothman, *Politics and Power: The United States Senate, 1869–1901* (1966), William G. Shade et al., "Partisanship in the United States Senate: 1869–1901," *JIH*, 4 (1973), 185–205, David W. Brady, *Critical Elections and Congressional Policymaking* (1988), Eric Schickler, *Disjointed Pluralism: Institutional Innovation and the Development of the United States Congress* (2001).

On the bureaucracy, Keller, *Affairs of State*, 307–18, Peter Argersinger, "The Transformation of American Politics: Political Institutions and Public Policy, 1865–1910," in Byron E. Shafer and Anthony J. Badger, eds., *Contesting Democracy* (2001), Mark W. Summers, *The Era of Good Stealings* (1993). On states and cities, Keller, *Affairs of State*, 319–42, 538–41. On law, Keller, *Affairs of State*, ch. 9. On public policy, Keller, *Affairs of State*, ch. 10–13. See also Morton Keller, "Social Policy in Nineteenth-Century America," in Donald T. Critchlow and Ellis W. Hawley, eds., *Federal Social Policy: The Historical Dimension* (1988), 99–139.

On dissent and 1896, Keller, *Affairs of State*, ch. 14–15, Paul W. Glad, *McKinley, Bryan, and the People* (1964).

Chapter Nine: The Progressive Interlude

Robert Kagan, *Dangerous Nation* (2006), Gerald Linderman, *The Mirror of War: American Society and the Spanish-American War* (1974), David Healy, *U.S. Expansionism: The Imperialist Urge in the 1890s* (1970), Robert L. Beisner, *Twelve Against Empire: The Anti-Imperialists, 1898–1900* (1968).

On voting, Mark L. Kornbluh, *Why America Stopped Voting: The Decline of Participatory Democracy and the Emergence of Modern American Politics* (2000), Paul Kleppner, *Continuity and Change in Electoral Politics: 1893–1928* (1987).

On the nature of Progressivism, Richard Hofstadter, *The Age of Reform: From Bryan to F.D.R.* (1955), Daniel Rodgers, *Atlantic Crossings* (1998), Michael McGerr, *A Fierce Discontent: The Rise and Fall of the Progressive Movement in America, 1870–1920* (2003), Morton Keller, "Anglo-American Politics, 1900–1930, in Anglo-American Perspective: A Case Study in Comparative History," *Comparative Studies in Society and History*, 22 (1980), 458–77, Keith Middlemas, *Politics in Industrial Society: The Experience of the British System Since 1911* (1979).

On cities, Melvin G. Holli, *Reform in Detroit: Hazen S. Pingree and Urban Politics* (1969), Eugene C. Murdoch, *Tom Johnson of Cleveland* (1994), Edwin R. Lewinson, *John Purroy Mitchel, The Boy Mayor of New York* (1965). See also John D. Buenker, *Urban Liberalism and Progressive Reform* (1973), Thomas M. Henderson, *Tammany Hall and the New Immigrants: The Progressive Years* (1976), James J. Connolly, *The Triumph of Ethnic Progressivism: Urban Political Culture in Boston, 1900–1925* (1998), Douglas Bukowski, *Big Bill Thompson, Chicago, and the Politics of Image* (1998), Melvin G. Holli, ed., *Biographical Dictionary of American Mayors* (1981).

For the French map of the states, George E. Mowry, *The Era of Theodore Roosevelt, 1900–1912* (1958), 67; Robert S. Maxwell, *La Follette and the Rise of the Progressive Movement in Wisconsin* (1956), Herbert F. Margulies, *The Decline of the Progressive Movement in Wisconsin, 1890–1920* (1968). See also Richard L. McCormick, *From Realignment to Reform: Political Change in New York State, 1893–1910* (1981).

On the South, C. Vann Woodward, *Origins of the New South, 1877–1913* (1951), Raymond Arsenault, *The Wild Ass of the Ozarks: Jeff Davis and the Social Bases of Southern Politics* (1984).

On Congress, Robert Harrison, *Congress, Progressive Reform, and the New American State* (2004), Joseph Cooper and David W. Brady, "Institutional Context and

Leadership Style: The House from Cannon to Rayburn," *APSR*, 75 (1981), 411–25, Daniel Wirls, "Regionalism, Rotten Boroughs, Race, and Realignment: The Seventeenth Amendment and the Politics of Representation," *SAPD*, 13 (1999), 1–30, Morton Keller, "Progressivism and Normalcy (1900–1933)," in Donald C. Bacon et al., *The Encyclopedia of the United States Congress* (1995), 1012–23.

On courts, Morton Keller, "Constitutional History, 1901–1921," in Leonard W. Levy et al., *American Constitutional History* (1989), 174–83, Michael Willrich, *City of Courts* (2003).

On policy, Morton Keller, *Regulating a New Economy: Public Policy and Economic Change in America, 1900–1933* (1990) and *Regulating a New Society: Public Policy and Social Change in America, 1900–1933* (1994). See also Elisabeth Clemens, *The People's Lobby: Organizational Innovation and the Rise of Interest Group Politics in the United States, 1890–1925* (1997), Elizabeth Sanders, *Roots of Reform: Farmers, Workers, and the American State, 1877–1917* (1999), Scott C. James, *Presidents, Parties, and the State: A Party System Perspective on Democratic Regulatory Choice, 1884–1936* (2000).

On World War I, David Kennedy, *Over Here: The First World War and American Society* (1980), Robert Cuff, *The War Industries Board* (1973), Marc A. Eisner, *From Warfare State to Welfare State: World War I, Compensatory State-Building, and the Limits of the Modern Order* (2000).

On national politics, Mowry, *Era of Theodore Roosevelt*, Arthur S. Link, *Woodrow Wilson and the Progressive Era 1910–1917* (1954), and John D. Hicks, *Republican Ascendancy 1921–1933* (1960). On 1912, James Chace, *1912: Wilson, Roosevelt, Taft & Debs: The Election that Changed the Country* (2004), Norman M. Wilensky, *Conservatism in the Progressive Era: The Taft Republicans of 1912* (1965). On the 1920s, David Burner, *The Politics of Provincialism: The Democratic Party in Transition, 1918–1932* (1968), Douglas B. Craig, *After Wilson: The Struggle for the Democratic Party, 1920–1934* (1992), Francis Russell, *The Shadow of Blooming Grove: Warren G. Harding in His Times* (1968), Robert K. Murray, *The Harding Era* (1969), William Allen White, *A Puritan in Babylon: The Story of Calvin Coolidge* (1938), Robert H. Ferrell, *The Presidency of Calvin Coolidge* (1998), Allan Lichtman, *Prejudice and the Old Politics: The Presidential Election of 1928* (1979).

On the Depression, Harris G. Warren, *Herbert Hoover and the Great Depression* (1959), Albert U. Romasco, *The Poverty of Abundance: Hoover, the Nation, the Depression* (1965), Arthur M. Schlesinger, *The Crisis of the Old Order 1919–1933* (1957).

Part IV: The Populist-Bureaucratic Regime

On language, William Safire, *Safire's New Political Dictionary* (1993), Frank Lutz, "Language of the 21st Century," *NYT*, Apr. 20, 2001, Geoffrey Nunberg, "The Curious Fate of Populism," *NYT*, Aug. 15, 2004.

Chapter Ten: The Rise of the Populist-Bureaucratic Regime

On New Deal, Barry Karl, *The Uneasy State: The United States from 1915 to 1945* (1985), Morton Keller, "The New Deal and Progressivism: A Fresh Look," in Sidney M. Milkis and Jerome M. Mileur, eds., *The New Deal and the Triumph of Liberalism* (2002), 313–22, William E. Leuchtenberg, *Franklin D. Roosevelt and the New Deal, 1932–1940* (1963),

Steve Fraser and Gary Gerstle, eds., *The Rise and Fall of the New Deal Order* (1989), Anthony Badger, *The New Deal: The Depression Years, 1933–1940* (1989), David M. Kennedy, *Freedom from Fear: The American People in Depression and War, 1929–1945* (1999).

On New Deal politics, Anthony Badger, "The Limits of Federal Power and Social Politics, 1910–1955," in Byron E. Shafer et al., *Present Discontents*, Michael S. Lewis-Beck and Peverill Squire, "The Transformation of the American State: The New Era-New Deal Test," *JP*, 53 (1991), 106–21, Colin Gordon, *New Deals: Business, Labor, and Politics in America, 1920–1935* (1934), Ruth O'Brien, *Workers' Paradox: The Republican Origins of New Deal Labor Policy, 1886–1935* (1998). See also Theodore J. Lowi, "The Roosevelt Revolution and the New American State," in Peter J. Katzenstein et al., eds., *Comparative Theory and Political Experience* (1990), 188–211.

On protest movements, David Brinkley, *Voices of Protest: Huey Long, Father Coughlin, and the Great Depression* (1982). On Democrats and the FDR–New Deal coalition, Kristi Anderson, *The Creation of a Democratic Majority 1928–1936* (1979), Norman H. Nie et al., *The Changing American Voter* (1976), Samuel Lubell, *The Future of American Politics* (1952), John M. Allswang, *The New Deal and American Politics* (1978), William E. Leuchtenberg, "The New Deal and the Analogue of War," in John Braeman, ed., *Change and Continuity in Twentieth-Century America* (1964), 81–14.

On FDR's presidency, Sidney M. Milkis, "Franklin D. Roosevelt and the Transcendence of Partisan Politics," *PSQ*, 100 (1985), 479–504, and Milkis, *The President and the Parties* (1993), John P. Burke, *The Institutional Presidency* (1992). On the later New Deal, Jordan A. Schwartz, *The New Dealers: Power Politics in the Age of Roosevelt* (1993), Alan Brinkley, *The End of Reform: New Deal Liberalism in Recession and War* (1995).

On Congress, James T. Patterson, *Congressional Conservatives and the New Deal: The Growth of the Conservative Coalition in Congress* (1967). On the Court, William E. Leuchtenberg, *The Supreme Court Reborn: The Constitutional Revolution in the Age of Roosevelt* (1995).

On executive reorganization, Richard Polenberg, *Reorganizing Roosevelt's Government: The Controversy over Executive Reorganization, 1936–1939* (1966). On states, James T. Patterson, *The New Deal and the States: Federalism in Transition* (1969).

On World War II, Richard Polenberg, *War and Society: The United States, 1941–1945* (1980), John M. Blum, *V Was for Victory: Politics and American Culture During World War II* (1976), Thomas J. Fleming, *The New Dealers' War* (2001), James M. Burns, *Roosevelt: The Soldier of Freedom* (1970).

On the post-war period, James Patterson, *Grand Expectations: The United States, 1945–1974* (1996). On Truman, Alonzo L. Hamby, *Beyond the New Deal: Harry S. Truman and American Liberalism* (1973). On McCarthyism, Thomas C. Reeves, *McCarthyism* (1973), David Oshinsky, *"A Conspiracy So Immense": The World of Joe McCarthy* (1983), M. J. Heale, *McCarthy's Americans: Red Scare Politics in State and Nation, 1935–1965* (1998). On Eisenhower, Samuel Lubell, *The Future of American Politics* (1956) and *The Revolt of the Moderates* (1956), Fred I. Greenstein, *The Hidden-Hand Presidency: Eisenhower as Leader* (1982), Shirley Anne Warshaw, ed., *Reexamining the Eisenhower Presidency* (1993).

On the Great Society, Patterson, *Grand Expectations*, Irwin Unger, *The Best of Intentions* (1996), Allen J. Matusow, *The Unraveling of America: A History of Liberalism in the 1960s* (1984), Alonzo J. Hamby, *Liberalism and Its Challengers: F.D.R. to Bush* (1992), Sidney M. Milkis and Jerome M. Mileur, eds., *The Great Society and the High Tide of Liberalism* (2005).

On courts, Robert A. Kagan, *Adversarial Legalism: The American Way of Law* (2001), Morton J. Horwitz, *The Warren Court and the Pursuit of Justice* (1998), Richard Kluger, *Simple Justice: The History of* Brown v. Board of Education (1976, 2004), Gerald N. Rosenberg, *The Hollow Hope: Can Courts Bring About Social Change?* (1993).

Chapter Eleven: Bureaucracy and Democracy

James Q. Wilson, "New Politics, New Elites, Old Publics," in Marc K. Landy and Martin A. Levin, eds., *The New Politics of Public Policy* (1995), 249, Theodore K. Lowi, *The End of Liberalism: The Second Republic of the United States* (2nd ed., 1979), xi. See also Matthew A. Crenson and Benjamin Ginsberg, *Downsizing Democracy: How America Sidelined Its Citizens and Privatized Its Public* (2002), Louis Galambos, ed., *The New American State: Bureaucracies and Policies Since World War II* (1987). On the George Washington Bridge and the West Side Highway, David Frum, *How We Got Here: The 70s* (2000), 217f. See also "The Withering Away of the State," *The Economist*, Apr. 6, 1966, 82.

On the presidency, Theodore J. Lowi, *The Personal President* (1985), Jeffrey Tulis, *The Rhetorical Presidency* (1987), Stephen Skowronek, *The Politics Presidents Make* (1993), Richard P. Nathan, *The Plot That Failed: Nixon and the Administrative Presidency* (1975). Moynihan quoted in *The Economist*, Sept. 19, 1998, 27.

On Congress, David Mayhew, *The Electoral Connection* (1974), Morris Fiorina, *Congress: Keystone of the Washington Establishment* (2nd ed., 1989), as against Joseph Cooper, "From Congressional to Presidential Preeminence: Power and Politics in Nineteenth-Century America and Today," in Lawrence C. Dodd and Bruce I. Oppenheimer, eds., *Congress Reconsidered* (8th ed., 2005), 363–93. See also William M.Lunch, *The Nationalization of American Politics* (1987), Eric Schickler, *Disjointed Pluralism: Institutional Innovation and the Development of the U.S. Congress* (2001), David H. Rosenbloom, *Building a Legislative-Centered Public Administration: Congress and the Administrative State, 1946–1999* (2000). On redistricting, Gary W. Cox and Jonathan N. Katz, *Elbridge Gerry's Salamander: The Electoral Consequences of the Reapportionment Revolution* (2002). Burton quoted in "Gerrymandering Gets Focus," *WSJ*, Dec. 4, 2003. See also Nelson W. Polsby, *How Congress Evolves: Social Bases of Institutional Change* (2004), David W. Brady and Craig Volden, *Revolving Gridlock: Politics and Policy from Carter to Clinton* (1998), David W. Brady, John F. Cogan, and Morris P. Fiorina, eds, *Continuity and Change in House Elections* (2000).

On the courts, Mark Tushnet, *The New Constitutional Order* (2003), Robert A. Kagan, *Adversarial Legalism* (2001), "The Gavel and the Robe," *The Economist*, Aug. 7, 1999, 43, Karen Orren, "Standing to Sue: Interest Group Conflict in the Federal Courts," *APSR*, 70 (1976), 723–41, Nathan Glazer, "The Imperial Judiciary," *The Public Interest*, 4 (1975), 104–23. On special education, Ross Sandler and David

Schoenbrud, *Democracy by Decree* (2002). On judges' backgrounds, Cass Sunstein, *After the Rights Revolution: Reconceiving the Regulatory State* (1990). On judges and bureaucrats, Richard Neely, *How Courts Govern America* (1981).

On the *Mount Laurel* decision, Charles Haar, *Suburbs Under Siege* (1996), David Kirp et al., *Our Town: Race, Housing and the Soul of Suburbia* (1995). On liability, "Trial Lawyers Inc.," *The Economist*, Sept. 27, 2003, 67, Walter Olson, *The Litigation Explosion* (1991), Jethro K. Lieberman, *The Litigious Society* (1981).

On states and cities, Jon C. Teaford, *The Rise of the States* (2002), Leon D. Epstein, "States," in Anthony King, ed., *The New American Political System* (1978), Kenneth Fox, *Metropolitan America: Urban Life and Urban Policy in the United States, 1940–1980* (1986), Vincent Cannato, *The Ungovernable City: John Lindsay and His Struggle to Save New York* (2001), Fred Siegel, *The Future Once Happened Here* (1997).

On local government, "Government in California," *The Economist*, Feb. 13, 1993, 21–23, "Government by the Nice, for the Nice," *The Economist*, July 25, 1992, 25–26, Joel Garreau, *Edge City: Life on the New Frontier* (1991), Robert J. Bolger, *Neighborhood Politics* (1992); on community associations, *caionline.org*.

On public policy, Landy and Levin, eds., *New Politics of Public Policy*, Hugh Heclo, "Sixties Civics," in Sidney Milkis and Jerry Mileur, eds., *The Great Society: Then and Now* (typescript), Morton Keller and Shep Melnick, eds., *Taking Stock: American Government in the Twentieth Century* (1999). On highway acts, James Q. Wilson, "Mr. Clinton, Meet Mr. Gore," *WSJ*, Oct. 28, 1993. For critiques of government, Derek C. Bok, *The Trouble with Government* (2001), Steven M. Gillon, *"That's Not What We Meant to Do": Reform and Its Unintended Consequences in Twentieth-Century America* (2000), Irwin Unger, *The Best of Intentions: The Triumph and Failure of the Great Society* (1996), Gareth Davies, *From Opportunity to Entitlement: The Transformation and Decline of Great Society Liberalism* (1996), Eugene Bardach and Robert Kagan, *Going by the Book: The Problem of Regulatory Unreasonableness* (1982), James Q. Wilson, ed., *The Politics of Regulation* (1980). See also Daniel P. Moynihan, *The Politics of a Guaranteed Income* (1973), R. Shep Melnick, *Between the Lines: Interpreting Welfare Rights* (1994) and *Regulation and the Courts: The Case of the Clean Air Act* (1983).

On McCain-Feingold, Morton Keller, "Money and Politics: The Long View," *The Forum* (2003) [online]. On tobacco regulation, Martha Derthick, *Up in Smoke: From Legislation to Litigation in Tobacco Politics* (2002), Crenson and Ginsberg, *Downsizing Democracy*, 157f.

Chapter Twelve: Populism and Party

James T. Patterson, *Grand Expectations: The United States, 1945–1974* (1996) and *Restless Giant: The United States from Watergate to Bush v. Gore* (2005), David W. Belin, "Earl Warren's Assassins," *NYT*, Mar. 7, 1992, 25, Gerald L. Posner, *Case Closed: Lee Harvey Oswald and the Assassination of JFK* (1993).

On politics, parties, and elections, Anthony King, ed., *The New American Political System* (1978, 1990), Sidney M. Milkis, *The President and the Parties* (1993), Michael Barone, *Our Country: The Shaping of America from Roosevelt to Reagan* (1990), A. James Reichley, *The Life of the Parties* (1992), Everett C. Ladd Jr., *Transformations of the*

American Party System (2nd ed., 1978), Paul Kleppner, *Who Voted? The Dynamics of Electoral Turnout, 1870–1980* (1982), David Knoke, *Change and Continuity in American Politics* (1976); on Burton and redistricting, "Gerrymandering Gets Focus," *WSJ*, Dec. 4, 2003.

On realignments, James L. Sundquist, *Dynamics of the Party System: Alignment and Realignment of Political Parties in the United States* (1973), challenged by Everett C. Ladd, "Liberalism Upside Down: The Inversion of the New Deal Order," *PSQ*, 91 (1976–77), 577–600, Morris P. Fiorina, *Divided Government* (2nd ed., 1996), James Q. Wilson, *The Amateur Democrats* (1966), Samuel Lubell, *The Hidden Crisis in American Politics* (1970).

Data on party and ideological leanings from American National Election Survey [online]. On education and turnout, Paul R. Abramson et al., *Change and Continuity in the 1996 and 1998 Elections* (1999).

On Goldwater and McGovern, Aaron Wildavsky, "The Goldwater Phenomenon: Purists, Politicians, and the Two-Party System," *Review of Politics*, 27 (1965), 386–413, Paul R. Abramson et al., "Third-Party and Independent Candidates in American Politics: Wallace, Anderson, and Perot," *PSQ*, 110 (1995), 349–67; Arthur H. Miller et al., "A Majority Party in Disarray: Policy Polarization in the 1972 Election," *APSR*, 70 (1976), 753–78. On McGovern Commission, Austin Ranney, *Curing the Mischiefs of Faction: Party Reform in America* (1975). See also Nelson W. Polsby, *The Consequences of Party Reform* (1983), John J. Coleman, *Party Decline in America: Policy, Politics, and the Fiscal State* (1996), David Broder, *The Party's Over* (1972), Martin P. Wattenberg, *The Decline of American Political Parties, 1952–1996* (1998), and *The Rise of Candidate-Centered Politics* (1991).

On media, Benjamin Ginsberg and Martin Shefter, *Politics by Other Means: The Declining Importance of Elections in America* (1990), James R. Barber, *The Pulse of Politics: Electing Presidents in the Media Age* (1980), Morton Keller, "The Media: What They Are Today, and How They Got That Way," *Forum* (2005) [online], Larry Sabato, *Peepshow* (2000), Nelson Polsby, *Political Innovation in America* (1984), James L. Baughman, *The Republic of Mass Culture* (2006).

On advocacy groups, Grant McConnell, *Private Power and American Democracy* (1966), Jack Walker, *Mobilizing Interest Groups* (1991), Jeffrey M. Berry, *The Interest Group Society* (2nd ed., 1989) and *The New Liberalism: The Rising Power of Citizen Groups* (1999), James Q. Wilson, *Political Organizations* (1995), Carter in "Ex Uno, Plures," *The Economist*, Aug. 21, 1999, 344–45.

James Allen Smith, *The Idea Brokers: Think Tanks and the Rise of the New Policy Elite* (1991), "The Charge of the Think-Tanks," *The Economist*, Feb. 15, 2003, 33. On Kennedy and the IRS, John A. Andrew III, *The Other Side of the Sixties: Young Americans for Freedom and the Rise of Conservative Politics* (1997).

On party recovery, L. Sandy Maisel, ed., *The Parties Respond: Changes in American Parties and Campaigns* (4th ed., 2002), Larry J. Sabato, *The Party's Just Begun* (1988), Jo Freeman, "The Political Culture of the Democratic and Republican Parties," *PSQ*, 101 (1986), 327–56, John E. Chubb and Paul E. Peterson, eds., *The New Direction in American Politics* (1985), Keith T. Poole and Howard Rosenthal, "The Polarization of American Politics," *JP*, 46 (1984), 1061–79, Alan Ehrenhalt, *The United States of Ambition: Politics, Power, and the Pursuit of Power* (1991), James Ceasar and Andrew Busch, *Upside Down and Inside Out: The 1992 Elections and American Politics* (1993).

On ideology, David W. Rohde, *Parties and Leaders in the Postreform House* (1991), Martin P. Wattenberg, "The Hollow Realignment: Partisan Change in a Candidate-Centered Era," *POQ*, 51 (1987), 58–74.

On Britain, "A Tale of Two Legacies," *The Economist*, Dec. 31, 2002, 64–66, Vernon Bogdanor, ed., *Parties and Democracy in Britain and America* (1984), Barry Cooper et al., eds., *The Resurgence of Conservatism in Anglo-American Democracies* (1988), Geoffrey Smith, *Reagan and Thatcher* (1990).

Epilogue: Today and Tomorrow

Michael Lind, *The Next American Nation: The New Nationalism and the Fourth American Revolution* (1995), Walter Dean Burnham, "The Fourth American Republic?" *WSJ*, Oct. 16, 1995. On forebodings, Edward Rothstein, "Arendt's Insights Echo Around a Troubled World," *NYT*, Oct. 9, 2006. See also Lawrence C. Dodd, "The New American Politics," in Bryan D. Jones, ed., *The New American Politics: Reflections on Political Change and the Clinton Administration* (1995).

On politics, James Q. Wilson in Marc K. Landy and Martin A. Levin, eds., *The New Politics of Public Policy* (1995), 256, "The Politics of Rage," *The Economist*, Nov. 22, 2003, 34, Matt Bai, "Who Lost Ohio?" *NYT Magazine*, Nov. 21, 2004, 67f., and Bai, "Machine Dreams," *NYT Magazine*, Aug. 21, 2005, 11. See also Peter Beinart, "Battle for the 'Burbs," *NR*, Oct. 19, 1998, 25–40, "Last Chance for the Democrats?" *The Economist*, Oct. 16, 2004, 32, Jeffrey M. Stonebash et al., *Diverging Parties* (2003).

On gentler Democrats, James Traub, "Temperament Wars," *NYT Magazine*, July 6, 2003, Alan Wolfe, "Learning to Love to Hate," *NYT Magazine*, Oct. 26, 2003. But see "The Paranoid Style in American Politics," *The Economist*, Jan. 7, 2006, 32, "The Politics of Rage," *The Economist*, Nov. 22, 2003, 34.

Donald Green et al., *Partisan Hearts and Minds: Political Parties and the Social Identities of Voters* (2002) stresses voter continuities. See also John B. Judis and Ruy Texeira, *The Emerging Democratic Majority* (2002) versus "The Emerging Democratic Minority," *The Economist*, Jan. 8, 2005, 36, and Michael Barone, *The Almanac of American Politics* (2006), introduction.

On adaptation, L. Sandy Maisel, ed., *The Parties Respond: Changes in American Parties and Campaigns* (4th ed., 2002), J. P. Monroe, *The Political Party Matrix: The Persistence of Organization* (2001), Paul R. Abramson et al., *Change and Continuity in the 2000 and 2002 Elections* (2003), Richard M. Skinner, "Do 527's Add Up to a Party?" *Forum* [online], no. 3, art. 5, *The Economist*, May 19, 1996, 23.

On the cultural divide, James D. Hunter, *Culture Wars* (1991), Robert D. Sullivan, "Beyond Red and Blue," *CommonWealth Magazine* (Winter 2003) [online], Morris P. Fiorina, *Culture War? The Myth of a Polarized America* (2005). Gertrude Himmelfarb, *One Nation, Two Cultures* (1999) stresses the depth of division; Alan Wolfe, *One Nation After All* (1998) downplays it. See also "Bush's America," *The Economist*, Jan. 20, 2003, 21–24, Wayne E. Baker, *America's Crisis of Values: Reality and Perception*

(2005), "When American Politics Turned European," *The Economist*, Oct. 25, 2003, 74; Larry Seindentop, *Democracy in Europe* (2000), Susan Pharr and Robert Putnam, *Disaffected Democracies* (2000).

On government, Landy and Levin, eds, *New Politics*; on Bush, "Last Chance for the Democrats?" *The Economist*, Oct. 16, 2004, 32; on Gingrich, John B. Judis, "Historical Error," *NR*, Nov. 30, 1998, 8–12; on Congress, "A Weakened Congress?" *The Economist*, July 15, 2006, 32; on bureaucracy, James Q. Wilson, *Bureaucracy* (1989).

On courts, Mark Tushnet, *The New Constitutional Order* (2003) and *A Court Divided: The Rehnquist Court and the Future of Constitutional Law* (2005), Jeffrey Rosen, "The Unregulated Offensive," *NYT Magazine*, Apr. 17, 2005, 42f., Stuart Taylor, "In Praise of Judicial Modesty," NationalJournal.com, Mar. 20, 2006, "Skewering the Lawyers," *The Economist*, Feb. 19, 2005, 29.

On 2000, James W. Caesar and Andrew E. Busch, *The Perfect Tie: The True Story of the 2000 Presidential Election* (2001), Richard A. Posner, *Breaking the Deadlock: The 2000 Election, the Constitution, and the Courts* (2001).

On Clinton's foreign policy, David Halberstam, *War in a Time of Peace* (2002), on Bush, John W. Gaddis, *Surprise, Security, and the American Experience* (2004), Peter Beinart, *The Good Fight* (2006), Matthew Continetti, "The Peace Party vs. the Power Party," *Weekly Standard*, Jan. 11, 2007.

On polarization, Pietro S. Nivola and David W. Brady, eds., *Red and Blue Nation?* vol. 1 (2006), Stephen Ansolabehere et al., "Purple America," *Journal of Economic Perspectives*, 20 (2006), 97–118.

INDEX